The Idea of America

A collection of essays
selected by
William Bonner
and
Pierre Lemieux

"In the beginning, all the world was America."

John Locke

Jacket Design: Debra Ranson, Buckeye Graphics
Contributing Editors: Rita J. Smith, Ken Danz and Sanford D. Cook

Table of Contents

FOREWORD

"In the beginning, all the world was America."

John Locke

"The Garden of Eden was a perfect place," my friend Manuel explained. "Man had free will. He could live in harmony with nature and God...and everything would be fine. But if he defied God, the stain of original sin would be on his descendants forever."

Eve ate the forbidden fruit. Ever after, men and women have been tarnished; every silver lining has a cloud...and a correction follows every bubble market.

When America was discovered, some people thought it might be a kind of Eden. Explorers recounted their tales of naked savages, snakes, and low-hanging tropical fruit. Maybe it was Eden, but gone to seed.

Whatever it was, many people thought they could make a paradise out of it. Adventurers, entrepreneurs, religious zealots of every stripe – all made their way to the New World intent upon turning it into the Eden of their dreams. Five hundred years later, America is what they made of it – both a paradise...and a complete mess.

But if Americans have a special gift, it is a talent for ignoring irony and ambiguity and going on with their special mission: getting rich. Most Americans look at the country as if it were an Enron financial statement. Sure, many of the assets are fictitious and the liabilities are understated. But, like Merrill Lynch, we are all bullish on America.

"Proud to be an American," says one bumper sticker. "One nation – indivisible," says another. America was, of course, founded on the opposite principle...the idea that people were free to separate themselves from a parent government whenever they felt they had come of age. But no fraud, no matter how stupendous, is so obvious as to be detected by the average American. That is America's great strength...or its most serious weakness.

After Sept. 11, 2001 so many people bought flags that the shops ran short. Old Glory festooned nearly every porch and bridge. Patriotism swelled every heart.

Europeans, coming back to the Old Country, reported that they had never seen anything like it. A Frenchman takes his country for granted. He is born into it, just as he is born into his religion. He may be proud of La Belle France the way he is proud of his cheese. But he is not fool enough to claim credit for either one. He just feels lucky to have them for his own.

America, by contrast, is a nation of people who chose to become Americans. Even the oldest family tree in the New World has immigrants at its root. And where did its government, its courts, its businesses, and its saloons come from? They were all invented by us. Having chosen the country...and made it what it is...Americans feel more responsibility for what it has become than the citizens of most other nations. And they take more pride in it too.

But what is it? What has it become? What makes America different from any other nation? Why should we care more about it than about, say, Lithuania or Chad?

Most Americans, if pressed for an answer, would reply, "Because America is a free country." What else can be said of the place? Its land mass is as varied as the earth itself. Inhabiting the sands of Tucson as well as the steppes of Alaska, Americans could as well be called a desert race as an arctic one. Its religions are equally diverse – from moss-backed Episcopalians of the Virginia tidewater to the Holy Rollers of East Texas and the Muslims of East Harlem. Nor does blood itself give the country any mark of distinction. The individual American has more in common genetically with the people his people come from than with his fellow Americans. In a DNA test, this writer is more likely to be mistaken for an IRA hitman than a Baltimore drug dealer.

America never was a nation in the usual sense of the word. Though there are plenty of exceptions – especially among the made-up nations of former European colonies — nations are usually composed of groups of people who share common blood, a common culture, and a common language.

Americans mostly speak English, but they might just as well speak Spanish.

And at the debut of the republic, the founding fathers narrowly avoided declaring German the official language...at least, that is the legend. A Frenchman has to speak French. A German has to speak the language of the Vaterland. But an American could speak anything. And often does.

Nor is there even a common history. The average immigrant didn't arrive until the early 20th century. By then, America's history was already three centuries old. The average family missed the whole thing.

If Americans weren't united by blood, history, religion, or language – what else is left? Only an idea: that you could come to America and be whatever you wanted to be. You might have been a bog-trotter in Ireland or a baron in Silesia; in America, you were free to become whatever you could make of yourself.

"Give me liberty or give me death," said Patrick Henry, raising the rhetorical stakes and praying no one would call him on it. Yet, the average man at the time lived in near perfect freedom. There were few books and few laws on them. And there were fewer people to enforce them. Henry, if he wanted to do so, could have merely crossed the Blue Ridge west of Charlottesville and never seen another government agent again.

Thomas Jefferson complained, in the Declaration of Independence, that Britain had "erected a multitude of New Offices, and set hither swarms of Officers to harass our people, and eat out their substance." Yet the swarms of officers sent by George III would have barely filled a midsized regional office of the IRS or city zoning department today.

Likewise, the Founding Fathers kvetched about taxation without representation. But history has shown that representation only makes taxation worse. Kings, emperors, and tyrants must keep tax rates low...otherwise, the people rise in rebellion. It is democrats who really eat out the substance of the people: The illusion of self-government lets them get away with it. Tax rates were only an average of 3% under the tyranny of King George III. Among the dubious blessings of democracy are average tax rates that are 10 times as high.

"Americans today," wrote Rose Wilder Lane in 1936, after the Lincoln administration had annihilated the principle of self-government... but before the Roosevelt team had finished its work, "are the most reckless and lawless of peoples... we are also the most imaginative, the most temperamental, the most infinitely varied."

But by the end of the 20th century, Americans were required to wear seat belts and they ate low-fat yogurt without a gun to their heads. By the beginning of the

21st century, they were submitting to strip searches at airport terminals and demanding higher taxes to protect freedom. The recklessness seems to have been bred out of them. And the variety too. North, south, east and west, people all wear the same clothes and cherish the same ideas. Liberty has been hollowed out in modern America, but it is still worshipped as though it were a religious relic.

William Bonner

Introduction

By Pierre Lemieux

What is America? What does it mean to be an American? What is, or what used to be, the idea of America? The documents collected in this anthology try to answer these questions. Some of the pieces are well known, others less conventional. Many interesting documents had to be ignored because of space constraints.[1]

In Part I, we start with two of the main founding documents: the Declaration of Independence, and the Bill of Rights.

Part II looks at some of the ideas behind the American Revolution, through the lenses of two actors, Patrick Henry and Thomas Paine, and of one later student of American history, Lord Acton.

The political system put in place after the Revolution was meant to reflect self-, decentralized, and limited government. To make these points, Part III presents Madison's Federalist No. 41, as well as excerpts from Alexis de Tocqueville's famous *Democracy in America* about decentralization, the dangers of powerful democratic governments, and the usefulness of private associations.

The pieces of Part IV dwell on the central place of religion in the American tradition, with the help of Tocqueville's obervations.

Part V tries to look deeper into the American character, with a classic piece by St. John Crevecoeur and some reflections from H.L. Mencken. Self-reliance, a crucial feature of the American character, is discussed in an extraordinary piece of

---

[1]We benefited from the advice of a few scholars, including Prof. Alan Kors (University of Pennsylvania), Dr. Robert Higgs (The Independent Institute), and Prof. Martine Brownley (Emory University). However, they are not responsible for the decisions about which pieces to include in this short anthology.

advice to would-be immigrants by Benjamin Franklin, as well as by Ralph Waldo Emerson's famous celebration of individual and religious self-reliance.

Part VI pursues the theme of self-reliance and character with the theme of the frontier. A Norwegian immigrant who became a novelist, Ole Rölvaag, narrates the hard life of pioneers in the Dakota Territory. Novelist Mark Twain relates the Mississippi adventures from which he borrowed his pen name.

In a sense, the idea of America works *against* government and politics, and this is part of its attractiveness. Part VII of this anthology features three pieces on American indocility and resistance: the famous Jefferson "tree of liberty" letter ("[W]hat country can preserve it's liberties if their rulers are not warned from time to time that their people preserve the spirit of resistance?"), the no less famous defense of civil disobedience by Henry David Thoreau, and an interesting piece by Voltairine de Cleyre extolling the anarchist elements in American traditions.

A watermark runs through many of the pieces in this anthology. There was a time when anybody who felt like an American could become one. Benjamin Franklin wrote, about a foreigner who would "remove to America": "One or two Years Residence give him the Rights of a Citizen. ... there being no Restraints preventing Strangers from exercising any Art they understand, nor any Permission necessary."

This reflection leads us to Part VIII, devoted to the tradition of an open America, of the type so vividly depicted by Emma Lazarus' poem inscribed on the Statue of Liberty. John Quincy Adams argued that this did not mean meddling in other peoples' affairs.

The idea of America was in large part the idea of individual liberty. In Thoreau's time, less than two centuries ago, there were places in America where "the State was nowhere to be seen." Against the rise of the surveillance state, it is urgent to rediscover the idea of America.

Pierre Lemieux

PART I

FOUNDING DOCUMENTS

The Declaration of Independence

*The unanimous Declaration of the thirteen united States of America,
in Congress, July 4, 1776*

When in the Course of human events, it becomes necessary for one people to dissolve the political bands which have connected them with another, and to assume among the powers of the earth, the separate and equal station to which the Laws of Nature and of Nature's God entitle them, a decent respect to the opinions of mankind requires that they should declare the causes which impel them to the separation.

We hold these truths to be self-evident, that all men are created equal, that they are endowed by their Creator with certain unalienable Rights, that among these are Life, Liberty and the pursuit of Happiness.—That to secure these rights, Governments are instituted among Men, deriving their just powers from the consent of the governed, —That whenever any Form of Government becomes destructive of these ends, it is the Right of the People to alter or to abolish it, and to institute new Government, laying its foundation on such principles and organizing its powers in such form, as to them shall seem most likely to effect their Safety and Happiness. Prudence, indeed, will dictate that Governments long established should not be changed for light and transient causes; and accordingly all experience hath shewn, that mankind are more disposed to suffer, while evils are sufferable, than to right themselves by abolishing the forms to which they are accustomed. But when a long train of abuses and usurpations, pursuing invariably the same Object evinces a design to reduce them under absolute Despotism, it is their right, it is their duty, to throw off such Government, and to provide new Guards for their future security.—Such has been the patient sufferance of these Colonies; and such is now the necessity which constrains them to alter their former Systems of Government. The history of the present King of Great Britain is a history of repeated injuries and usurpations, all having in direct object the establishment of an absolute Tyranny over these States. To prove this, let Facts be submitted to a candid world.

He has refused his Assent to Laws, the most wholesome and necessary for the public good.

He has forbidden his Governors to pass Laws of immediate and pressing importance, unless suspended in their operation till his Assent should be obtained; and when so suspended, he has utterly neglected to attend to them.

He has refused to pass other Laws for the accommodation of large districts of people, unless those people would relinquish the right of Representation in the Legislature, a right inestimable to them and formidable to tyrants only.

He has called together legislative bodies at places unusual, uncomfortable, and distant from the depository of their public Records, for the sole purpose of fatiguing them into compliance with his measures.

He has dissolved Representative Houses repeatedly, for opposing with manly firmness his invasions on the rights of the people.

He has refused for a long time, after such dissolutions, to cause others to be elected; whereby the Legislative powers, incapable of Annihilation, have returned to the People at large for their exercise; the State remaining in the mean time exposed to all the dangers of invasion from without, and convulsions within.

He has endeavoured to prevent the population of these States; for that purpose obstructing the Laws for Naturalization of Foreigners; refusing to pass others to encourage their migrations hither, and raising the conditions of new Appropriations of Lands.

He has obstructed the Administration of Justice, by refusing his Assent to Laws for establishing Judiciary powers.

He has made Judges dependent on his Will alone, for the tenure of their offices, and the amount and payment of their salaries.

He has erected a multitude of New Offices, and sent hither swarms of Officers to harrass our people, and eat out their substance.

He has kept among us, in times of peace, Standing Armies without the Consent of our legislatures.

He has affected to render the Military independent of and superior to the Civil power.

He has combined with others to subject us to a jurisdiction foreign to our constitution, and unacknowledged by our laws; giving his Assent to their Acts of pretended Legislation:

For Quartering large bodies of armed troops among us:

For protecting them, by a mock Trial, from punishment for any Murders which they should commit on the Inhabitants of these States:

For cutting off our Trade with all parts of the world:

For imposing Taxes on us without our Consent:

For depriving us in many cases, of the benefits of Trial by Jury:

For transporting us beyond Seas to be tried for pretended offences:

For abolishing the free System of English Laws in a neighbouring Province, establishing therein an Arbitrary government, and enlarging its Boundaries so as to render it at once an example and fit instrument for introducing the same absolute rule into these Colonies:

For taking away our Charters, abolishing our most valuable Laws, and altering fundamentally the Forms of our Governments:

For suspending our own Legislatures, and declaring themselves invested with power to legislate for us in all cases whatsoever.

He has abdicated Government here, by declaring us out of his Protection and waging War against us.

He has plundered our seas, ravaged our Coasts, burnt our towns, and destroyed the lives of our people.

He is at this time transporting large Armies of foreign Mercenaries to compleat the works of death, desolation and tyranny, already begun with circumstances of Cruelty & perfidy scarcely paralleled in the most barbarous ages, and totally unworthy the Head of a civilized nation.

He has constrained our fellow Citizens taken Captive on the high Seas to bear Arms against their Country, to become the executioners of their friends and Brethren, or to fall themselves by their Hands.

He has excited domestic insurrections amongst us, and has endeavoured to bring on the inhabitants of our frontiers, the merciless Indian Savages, whose known rule of warfare, is an undistinguished destruction of all ages, sexes and conditions.

In every stage of these Oppressions We have Petitioned for Redress in the most humble terms: Our repeated Petitions have been answered only by repeated injury. A Prince whose character is thus marked by every act which may define a Tyrant, is unfit to be the ruler of a free people.

Nor have We been wanting in attentions to our Brittish brethren. We have warned them from time to time of attempts by their legislature to extend an unwarrantable jurisdiction over us. We have reminded them of the circumstances of our emigration and settlement here. We have appealed to their native justice and magnanimity, and we have conjured them by the ties of our common kindred to disavow these usurpations, which, would inevitably interrupt our connections and correspondence. They too have been deaf to the voice of justice and of consanguinity. We must, therefore, acquiesce in the necessity, which denounces our Separation, and hold them, as we hold the rest of mankind, Enemies in War, in Peace Friends.

We, therefore, the Representatives of the united States of America, in General Congress, Assembled, appealing to the Supreme Judge of the world for the rectitude of our intentions, do, in the Name, and by Authority of the good People of these Colonies, solemnly publish and declare, That these United Colonies are, and of Right ought to be Free and Independent States; that they are Absolved from all Allegiance to the British Crown, and that all political connection between them and the State of Great Britain, is and ought to be totally dissolved; and that as Free and Independent States, they have full Power to levy War, conclude Peace, contract Alliances, establish Commerce, and to do all other Acts and Things which Independent States may of right do. And for the support of this Declaration, with a firm reliance on the protection of divine Providence, we mutually pledge to each other our Lives, our Fortunes and our sacred Honor.

The 56 signatures on the Declaration appear in the positions indicated:

[Column 1]
Georgia:
Button Gwinnett
Lyman Hall
George Walton

South Carolina:
Edward Rutledge
Thomas Heyward, Jr.
Thomas Lynch, Jr.
Arthur Middleton

[Column 2]
North Carolina:
William Hooper
Joseph Hewes
John Penn

[Column 3]
Massachusetts:
John Hancock

Maryland:
Samuel Chase
William Paca
Thomas Stone
Charles Carroll of Carrollton

Virginia:
George Wythe
Richard Henry Lee
Thomas Jefferson
Benjamin Harrison
Thomas Nelson, Jr.
Francis Lightfoot Lee
Carter Braxton

[Column 4]
Pennsylvania:
Robert Morris
Benjamin Rush
Benjamin Franklin
John Morton
George Clymer
James Smith
George Taylor
James Wilson
George Ross

Delaware:
Caesar Rodney
George Read
Thomas McKean

[Column 5]
New York:
William Floyd
Philip Livingston
Francis Lewis
Lewis Morris

New Jersey:
Richard Stockton
John Witherspoon
Francis Hopkinson
John Hart
Abraham Clark

[Column 6]
New Hampshire:
Josiah Bartlett
William Whipple
Matthew Thornton

Massachusetts:
Samuel Adams
John Adams
Robert Treat Paine
Elbridge Gerry

Rhode Island:
Stephen Hopkins
William Ellery

Connecticut:
Roger Sherman
Samuel Huntington
William Williams
Oliver Wolcott

The Bill of Rights

The following text is a transcription of the first 10 amendments to the Constitution in their original form. These amendments were ratified December 15, 1791, and form what is known as the "Bill of Rights."

Amendment I

Congress shall make no law respecting an establishment of religion, or prohibiting the free exercise thereof; or abridging the freedom of speech, or of the press; or the right of the people peaceably to assemble, and to petition the Government for a redress of grievances.

Amendment II

A well regulated Militia, being necessary to the security of a free State, the right of the people to keep and bear Arms, shall not be infringed.

Amendment III

No Soldier shall, in time of peace be quartered in any house, without the consent of the Owner, nor in time of war, but in a manner to be prescribed by law.

Amendment IV

The right of the people to be secure in their persons, houses, papers, and effects, against unreasonable searches and seizures, shall not be violated, and no Warrants shall issue, but upon probable cause, supported by Oath or affirmation, and particularly describing the place to be searched, and the persons or things to be seized.

Amendment V

No person shall be held to answer for a capital, or otherwise infamous crime, unless on a presentment or indictment of a Grand Jury, except in cases arising in the land or naval forces, or in the Militia, when in actual service in time of War or public danger; nor shall any person be subject for the same offence to be twice put in jeopardy of life or limb; nor shall be compelled in any criminal case to be a witness against himself, nor be deprived of life, liberty, or property, without due process of law; nor shall private property be taken for public use, without just compensation.

Amendment VI

In all criminal prosecutions, the accused shall enjoy the right to a speedy and public trial, by an impartial jury of the State and district wherein the crime shall have been committed, which district shall have been previously ascertained by law, and to be informed of the nature and cause of the accusation; to be confronted with the witnesses against him; to have compulsory process for obtaining witnesses in his favor, and to have the Assistance of Counsel for his defence.

Amendment VII

In suits at common law, where the value in controversy shall exceed twenty dollars, the right of trial by jury shall be preserved, and no fact tried by a jury, shall be otherwise reexamined in any Court of the United States, than according to the rules of the common law.

Amendment VIII

Excessive bail shall not be required, nor excessive fines imposed, nor cruel and unusual punishments inflicted.

Amendment IX

The enumeration in the Constitution, of certain rights, shall not be construed to deny or disparage others retained by the people.

Amendment X

The powers not delegated to the United States by the Constitution, nor prohibited by it to the States, are reserved to the States respectively, or to the people.

PART II

REVOLUTIONARY IDEALS

Patrick Henry, Give M Liberty or Give Me Death

Speech of March 23, 1775.

Patrick Henry (1736-1799) was a Virginia lawyer and later became Governor of Virginia.

No man thinks more highly than I do of the patriotism, as well as abilities, of the very worthy gentlemen who have just addressed the house. But different men often see the same subject in different lights; and, therefore, I hope it will not be thought disrespectful to those gentlemen if, entertaining as I do opinions of a character very opposite to theirs, I shall speak forth my sentiments freely and without reserve. This is no time for ceremony. The question before the house is one of awful moment to this country. For my own part, I consider it as nothing less than a question of freedom or slavery; and in proportion to the magnitude of the subject ought to be the freedom of the debate. It is only in this way that we can hope to arrive at the truth, and fulfill the great responsibility which we hold to God and our country. Should I keep back my opinions at such a time, through fear of giving offense, I should consider myself as guilty of treason towards my country, and of an act of disloyalty toward the Majesty of Heaven, which I revere above all earthly kings.

Mr. President, it is natural to man to indulge in the illusions of hope. We are apt to shut our eyes against a painful truth, and listen to the song of that siren till she transforms us into beasts. Is this the part of wise men, engaged in a great and arduous struggle for liberty? Are we disposed to be of the numbers of those who, having eyes, see not, and, having ears, hear not, the things which so nearly concern their temporal salvation? For my part, whatever anguish of spirit it may cost, I am willing to know the whole truth, to know the worst, and to provide for it.

I have but one lamp by which my feet are guided, and that is the lamp of experience. I know of no way of judging of the future but by the past. And judging by the past, I wish to know what there has been in the conduct of the British ministry for the last ten years to justify those hopes with which gentlemen have been pleased to solace themselves and the House. Is it that insidious smile with which our petition has been lately received?

Trust it not, sir; it will prove a snare to your feet. Suffer not yourselves to be betrayed with a kiss. Ask yourselves how this gracious reception of our petition comports with those warlike preparations which cover our waters and darken our land. Are fleets and armies necessary to a work of love and reconciliation? Have we shown ourselves so unwilling to be reconciled that force must be called in to win back our love? Let us not deceive ourselves, sir. These are the implements of war and subjugation; the last arguments to which kings resort. I ask gentlemen, sir, what means this martial array, if its purpose be not to force us to submission? Can gentlement assign any other possible motive for it? Has Great Britain any enemy, in this quarter of the world, to call for all this accumulation of navies and armies? No, sir, she has none. They are meant for us: they can be meant for no other. They are sent over to bind and rivet upon us those chains which the British ministry have been so long forging. And what have we to oppose to them? Shall we try argument? Sir, we have been trying that for the last ten years. Have we anything new to offer upon the subject? Nothing. We have held the subject up in every light of which it is capable; but it has been all in vain. Shall we resort to entreaty and humble supplication? What terms shall we find which have not been already exhausted? Let us not, I beseech you, sir, deceive ourselves. Sir, we have done everything that could be done to avert the storm which is now coming on. We have petitioned; we have remonstrated; we have supplicated; we have prostrated ourselves before the throne, and have implored its interposition to arrest the tyrannical hands of the ministry and Parliament. Our petitions have been slighted; our remonstrances have produced additional violence and insult; our supplications have been disregarded; and we have been spurned, with contempt, from the foot of the throne! In vain, after these things, may we indulge the fond hope of peace and reconciliation.

There is no longer any room for hope. If we wish to be free—if we mean to preserve inviolate those inestimable privileges for which we have been so long contending—if we mean not basely to abandon the noble struggle in which we have been so long engaged, and which we have pledged ourselves never to abandon until the glorious object of our contest shall be obtained—we must fight! I repeat it, sir, we must fight! An appeal to arms and to the God of hosts is all that is left us! They tell us, sir, that we are weak; unable to cope with so formidable an adversary. But when shall we be stronger? Will it be the next week, or the next year? Will it be when we are totally disarmed, and when a British guard shall be stationed in every house? Shall we gather strength but irresolution and inaction? Shall we acquire the means of effectual resistance by lying supinely on our backs and hugging the delusive phantom of hope, until our enemies shall have bound us hand and foot? Sir, we are not weak if we make a proper use of those means which the God of nature hath placed in our power. The millions of people, armed in the holy cause of liberty, and in such a country as that which we possess, are invincible by any force which our enemy can send against us. Besides, sir, we shall not fight our battles alone. There is a just God who presides over the destinies of nations, and who will raise up friends to fight our battles for us. The battle, sir, is not to the strong alone; it is to the vigilant, the active, the brave. Besides, sir, we have no election. If we were base enough to desire it, it is now too late to retire from the contest. There is no retreat but in submission and slavery! Our chains are forged! Their clanking may be heard on the plains of Boston! The war is inevitable—and let it come! I repeat it, sir, let it come.

It is in vain, sir, to extentuate the matter. Gentlemen may cry, Peace, Peace—but there is no peace. The war is actually begun! The next gale that sweeps from the north will bring to our ears the clash of resounding arms! Our brethren are already in the field! Why stand we here idle? What is it that gentlemen wish? What would they have? Is life so dear, or peace so sweet, as to be purchased at the price of chains and slavery? Forbid it, Almighty God! I know not what course others may take; but as for me, give me liberty or give me death!

Thomas Paine, Common Sense

Excerpted from Thomas Paine, Common Sense, 1776.

*Thomas Paine (1737-1809) arrived in America when he was 37
and soon became an influential writer and publicist,
as well as an anti-slavery advocate.*

Of the origin and design of government in general.
With concise remarks on the English constitution.

Some writers have so confounded society with government, as to leave little or no distinction between them; whereas they are not only different, but have different origins. Society is produced by our wants, and government by our wickedness; the former promotes our happiness positively by uniting our affections, the latter negatively by restraining our vices. The one encourages intercourse, the other creates distinctions. The first is a patron, the last a punisher.

Society in every state is a blessing, but government even in its best state is but a necessary evil in its worst state an intolerable one; for when we suffer, or are exposed to the same miseries by a government, which we might expect in a country without government, our calamities is heightened by reflecting that we furnish the means by which we suffer! Government, like dress, is the badge of lost innocence; the palaces of kings are built on the ruins of the bowers of paradise. For were the impulses of conscience clear, uniform, and irresistibly obeyed, man would need no other lawgiver; but that not being the case, he finds it necessary to surrender up a part of his property to furnish means for the protection of the rest; and this he is induced to do by the same prudence which in every other case advises him out of two evils to choose the least. Wherefore, security being the true design and end of government, it unanswerably follows that whatever form thereof appears most likely to ensure it to us, with the least expense and greatest benefit, is preferable to all others.

In order to gain a clear and just idea of the design and end of government, let us suppose a small number of persons settled in some sequestered part of the earth, unconnected with the rest, they will then represent the first peopling of any country, or of the world. In this state of natural liberty, society will be their first thought. A thousand motives will excite them thereto, the strength of one man is so unequal to his wants, and his mind so unfitted for perpetual solitude, that he is soon obliged to seek assistance and relief of another, who in his turn requires the same. Four or five united would be able to raise a tolerable dwelling in the midst of a wilderness, but one man might labor out the common period of life without accomplishing any thing; when he had felled his timber he could not remove it, nor erect it after it was removed; hunger in the mean time would urge him from his work, and every different want call him a different way. Disease, nay even misfortune would be death, for though neither might be mortal, yet either would disable him from living, and reduce him to a state in which he might rather be said to perish than to die.

Thus necessity, like a gravitating power, would soon form our newly arrived emigrants into society, the reciprocal blessings of which, would supersede, and render the obligations of law and government unnecessary while they remained perfectly just to each other; but as nothing but heaven is impregnable to vice, it will unavoidably happen, that in proportion as they surmount the first difficulties of emigration, which bound them together in a common cause, they will begin to relax in their duty and attachment to each other; and this remissness, will point out the necessity, of establishing some form of government to supply the defect of moral virtue.

Some convenient tree will afford them a State-House, under the branches of which, the whole colony may assemble to deliberate on public matters. It is more than probable that their first laws will have the title only of Regulations, and be enforced by no other penalty than public disesteem. In this first parliament every man, by natural right will have a seat.

But as the colony increases, the public concerns will increase likewise, and the distance at which the members may be separated, will render it too inconvenient for all of them to meet on every occasion as at first, when their number was small, their habitations near, and the public concerns few and trifling. This will point out the convenience of their consenting to leave the legislative part to be managed by a select number chosen from the whole body, who are supposed to have the same concerns at stake which those have who appointed them, and who will act in the same manner as the whole body would act were they present. If the colony continue increasing, it will become necessary to augment the number of the representatives, and that the interest of every part of the colony may be attended to, it will be found best to divide the whole into convenient parts, each part sending its proper number; and that the elected might never form to themselves an interest separate from the electors, prudence will point out the propriety of having elections often; because as the elected might by that means return and mix again with the general body of the electors in a few months, their fidelity to the public will be secured by the prudent reflection of not making a rod for themselves. And as this frequent interchange will establish a common interest with every part of the community, they will mutually and naturally support each other, and on this (not on the unmeaning name of king) depends the strength of government, and the happiness of the governed.

Here then is the origin and rise of government; namely, a mode rendered necessary by the inability of moral virtue to govern the world; here too is the design and end of government, viz., freedom and security. And however our eyes may be dazzled with snow, or our ears deceived by sound; however prejudice may warp our wills, or interest darken our understanding, the simple voice of nature and of reason will say, it is right.

I draw my idea of the form of government from a principle in nature, which no art can overturn, viz., that the more simple any thing is, the less liable it is to be disordered, and the easier repaired when disordered; and with this maxim in view, I offer a few remarks on the so much boasted constitution of England. That it was noble for the dark and slavish times in which it was erected is granted. When the world was overrun with tyranny the least therefrom was a glorious rescue. But that it is imperfect, subject to convulsions, and incapable of producing what it seems to promise, is easily demonstrated.

Absolute governments (though the disgrace of human nature) have this advantage with them, that they are simple; if the people suffer, they know the head from which their suffering springs, know likewise the remedy, and are not bewildered by a variety of causes and cures. But the constitution of England is so exceedingly complex, that the nation may suffer for years together without being able to discover in which part the fault lies, some will say in one and some in another, and every political physician will advise a different medicine.

I know it is difficult to get over local or long standing prejudices, yet if we will suffer ourselves to examine the component parts of the English constitution, we shall find them to be the base remains of two ancient tyrannies, compounded with some new republican materials.

First. The remains of monarchical tyranny in the person of the king.

Secondly. The remains of aristocratical tyranny in the persons of the peers.

Thirdly. The new republican materials, in the persons of the commons, on whose virtue depends the freedom of England.

The two first, by being hereditary, are independent of the people; wherefore in a constitutional sense they contribute nothing towards the freedom of the state.

To say that the constitution of England is a union of three powers reciprocally checking each other, is farcical, either the words have no meaning, or they are flat contradictions.

To say that the commons is a check upon the king, presupposes two things:

First. That the king is not to be trusted without being looked after, or in other words, that a thirst for absolute power is the natural disease of monarchy.

Secondly. That the commons, by being appointed for that purpose, are either wiser or more worthy of confidence than the crown.

But as the same constitution which gives the commons a power to check the king by withholding the supplies, gives afterwards the king a power to check the commons, by empowering him to reject their other bills; it again supposes that the king is wiser than those whom it has already supposed to be wiser than him. A mere absurdity!

There is something exceedingly ridiculous in the composition of monarchy; it first excludes a man from the means of information, yet empowers him to act in cases where the highest judgment is required. The state of a king shuts him from the world, yet the business of a king requires him to know it thoroughly; wherefore the different parts, unnaturally opposing and destroying each other, prove the whole character to be absurd and useless.

Some writers have explained the English constitution thus; the king, say they, is one, the people another; the peers are an house in behalf of the king; the commons in behalf of the people; but this hath all the distinctions of an house divided against itself; and though the expressions be pleasantly arranged, yet when examined they appear idle and ambiguous; and it will always happen, that the nicest construction that words are capable of, when applied to the description of something which either cannot exist, or is too incomprehensible to be within the compass of description, will be words of sound only, and though they may amuse the ear, they cannot inform the mind, for this explanation includes a previous question, viz. How came the king by a power which the people are afraid to trust, and always obliged to check? Such a power could not be the gift of a wise people, neither can any power, which needs checking, be from God; yet the provision, which the constitution makes, supposes such a power to exist.

But the provision is unequal to the task; the means either cannot or will not accomplish the end, and the whole affair is a felo de se; for as the greater weight will always carry up the less, and as all the wheels of a machine are put in motion by one, it only remains to know which power in the constitution has the most weight, for that will govern; and though the others, or a part of them, may clog, or, as the phrase is, check the rapidity of its motion, yet so long as they cannot stop it, their endeavors will be ineffectual; the first moving power will at last have its way, and what it wants in speed is supplied by time.

That the crown is this overbearing part in the English constitution needs not be mentioned, and that it derives its whole consequence merely from being the giver of places pensions is self evident, wherefore, though we have and wise enough to shut and lock a door against absolute monarchy, we at the same time have been foolish enough to put the crown in possession of the key.

The prejudice of Englishmen, in favor of their own government by king, lords, and commons, arises as much or more from national pride than reason. Individuals are undoubtedly safer in England than in some other countries, but the will of the king is as much the law of the land in Britain as in France, with this difference, that instead of proceeding directly from his mouth, it is handed to the people under the most formidable shape of an act of parliament. For the fate of Charles the First, hath only made kings more subtle not- more just.

Wherefore, laying aside all national pride and prejudice in favor of modes and forms, the plain truth is, that it is wholly owing to the constitution of the people, and not to the constitution of the government that the crown is not as oppressive in England as in Turkey.

An inquiry into the constitutional errors in the English form of government is at this time highly necessary; for as we are never in a proper condition of doing justice to others, while we continue under the influence of some leading partiality, so neither are we capable of doing it to ourselves while we remain fettered by any obstinate prejudice. And as a man, who is attached to a prostitute, is unfitted to choose or judge of a wife, so any prepossession in favor of a rotten constitution of government will disable us from discerning a good one.

Of monarchy and hereditary succession

Mankind being originally equals in the order of creation, the equality could only be destroyed by some subsequent circumstance; the distinctions of rich, and poor, may in a great measure be accounted for, and that without having recourse to the harsh, ill-sounding names of oppression and avarice. Oppression is often the consequence, but seldom or never the means of riches; and though avarice will preserve a man from being necessitously poor, it generally makes him too timorous to be wealthy. But there is another and greater distinction for which no truly natural or religious reason can be assigned, and that is, the distinction of men into KINGS and SUBJECTS. Male and female are the distinctions of nature, good and bad the distinctions of heaven; but how a race of men came into the world so exalted above the rest, and distinguished like some new species, is worth enquiring into, and whether they are the means of happiness or of misery to mankind. In the early ages of the world, according to the scripture chronology, there were no kings; the consequence of which was there were no wars; it is the pride of kings which throw mankind into confusion. Holland without a king hath enjoyed more peace for this last century than any of the monarchial governments in Europe. Antiquity favors the same remark; for the quiet and rural lives of the first patriarchs hath a happy something in them, which vanishes away when we come to the history of Jewish royalty.

Government by kings was first introduced into the world by the Heathens, from whom the children of Israel copied the custom. It was the most prosperous invention the Devil ever set on foot for the promotion of idolatry. The Heathens paid divine honors to their deceased kings, and the Christian world hath improved on the plan by doing the same to their living ones. How impious is the title of sacred majesty applied to a worm, who in the midst of his splendor is crumbling into dust!

As the exalting one man so greatly above the rest cannot be justified on the equal rights of nature, so neither can it be defended on the authority of scripture; for the will of the Almighty, as declared by Gideon and the prophet Samuel, expressly disapproves of government by kings. All anti-monarchial parts of scripture have been very smoothly glossed over in monarchial governments, but they undoubtedly merit the attention of countries which have their governments yet to form. Render unto Caesar the things which are Caesar's is the scriptural doctrine of courts, yet it is no support of monarchial government, for the Jews at that time were without a king, and in a state of vassalage to the Romans.

Near three thousand years passed away from the Mosaic account of the creation, till the Jews under a national delusion requested a king. Till then their form of government (except in extraordinary cases, where the Almighty interposed) was a kind of republic administered by a judge and the elders of the tribes. Kings they had none, and it was held sinful to acknowledge any being under that title but the Lords of Hosts. And when a man seriously reflects on the idolatrous homage which is paid to the persons of kings he need not wonder, that the Almighty, ever jealous of his honor, should disapprove of a form of government which so impiously invades the prerogative of heaven.

Monarchy is ranked in scripture as one of the sins of the Jews, for which a curse in reserve is denounced against them. The history of that transaction is worth attending to.

The children of Israel being oppressed by the Midianites, Gideon marched against them with a small army, and victory, through the divine interposition, decided in his favor. The Jews elate with success, and attributing it to the generalship of Gideon, proposed making him a king, saying, Rule thou over us, thou and thy son and thy son's son. Here was temptation in its fullest extent; not a kingdom only, but an hereditary one, but Gideon in the piety of his soul replied, I will not rule over you, neither shall my son rule over you, THE LORD SHALL RULE OVER YOU. Words need not be more explicit; Gideon doth not decline the honor but denieth their right to give it; neither doth be compliment them with invented declarations of his thanks, but in the positive stile of a prophet charges them with disaffection to their proper sovereign, the King of Heaven.

About one hundred and thirty years after this, they fell again into the same error. The hankering which the Jews had for the idolatrous customs of the Heathens, is something exceedingly unaccountable; but so it was, that laying hold of the misconduct of Samuel's two sons, who were entrusted with some secular concerns, they came in an abrupt and clamorous manner to Samuel, saying, Behold thou art old and thy sons walk not in thy ways, now make us a king to judge us like all the other nations. And here we cannot but observe that their motives were bad, viz., that they might be like unto other nations, i.e., the Heathen, whereas their true glory laid in being as much unlike them as possible. But the thing displeased Samuel when they said, give us a king to judge us; and Samuel prayed unto the Lord, and the Lord said unto Samuel, Hearken unto the voice of the people in all that they say unto thee, for they have not rejected thee, but they have rejected me, THEN I SHOULD NOT REIGN OVER THEM.

According to all the works which have done since the day; wherewith they brought them up out of Egypt, even unto this day; wherewith they have forsaken me and served other Gods; so do they also unto thee. Now therefore hearken unto their voice, howbeit, protest solemnly unto them and show them the manner of the king that shall reign over them, i.e., not of any particular king, but the general manner of the kings of the earth, whom Israel was so eagerly copying after. And notwithstanding the great distance of time and difference of manners, the character is still in fashion. And Samuel told all the words of the Lord unto the people, that asked of him a king. And he said, This shall be the manner of the king that shall reign over you; he will take your sons and appoint them for himself for his chariots, and to be his horsemen, and some shall run before his chariots (this description agrees with the present mode of impressing men) and he will appoint him captains over thousands and captains over fifties, and will set them to ear his ground and to reap his harvest, and to make his instruments of war, and instruments of his chariots; and he will take your daughters to be confectionaries and to be cooks and to be bakers (this describes the expense and luxury as well as the oppression of kings) and he will take your fields and your olive yards, even the best of them, and give them to his servants; and he will take the tenth of your seed, and of your vineyards, and give them to his officers and to his servants (by which we see that bribery, corruption, and favoritism are the standing vices of kings) and he will take the tenth of your men servants, and your maid servants, and your goodliest young men and your asses, and put them to his work; and he will take the tenth of your sheep, and ye shall be his servants, and ye shall cry out in that day because of your king which ye shall have chosen, AND THE LORD WILL NOT HEAR YOU IN THAT DAY. This accounts for the continuation of monarchy; neither do the characters of the few good kings which have lived since, either sanctify the title, or blot out the sinfulness of the origin; the high encomium given of David takes no notice of him officially as a king, but only as a man after God's own heart. Nevertheless the People refused to obey the voice of Samuel, and they said, Nay, but we will have a king over us, that we may be like all the nations, and that our king may judge us, and go out before us and fight our battles. Samuel continued to reason with them, but to no purpose; he set before them their ingratitude, but all would not avail; and seeing them fully bent on their folly, he cried out, I will call unto the Lord, and he shall sent thunder and rain (which then was a punishment, being the time of wheat harvest) that ye may perceive and see that your wickedness is great which ye have done in the sight of the Lord, IN ASKING YOU A KING. So Samuel called unto the Lord, and the Lord sent thunder and rain that day, and all the people greatly feared the Lord and Samuel And all the people said unto Samuel, Pray for thy servants unto the Lord thy God that we die not, for WE HAVE ADDED UNTO OUR SINS THIS EVIL, TO ASK A KING. These portions of scripture are direct and positive. They admit of no equivocal construction. That the Almighty hath here entered his protest against monarchial government is true, or the scripture is false. And a man hath good reason to believe that there is as much of kingcraft, as priestcraft in withholding the scripture from the public in Popish countries. For monarchy in every instance is the Popery of government.

To the evil of monarchy we have added that of hereditary succession; and as the first is a degradation and lessening of ourselves, so the second, claimed as a matter of right, is an insult and an imposition on posterity. For all men being originally equals, no one by birth could have a right to set up his own family in perpetual preference to all others for ever, and though himself might deserve some decent degree of honors of his contemporaries, yet his descendants might be far too unworthy to inherit them. One of the strongest natural proofs of the folly of hereditary right in kings, is, that nature disapproves it, otherwise she would not so frequently turn it into ridicule by giving mankind an ass for a lion.

Secondly, as no man at first could possess any other public honors than were bestowed upon him, so the givers of those honors could have no power to give away the right of posterity, and though they might say, "We choose you for our head," they could not, without manifest injustice to their children, say, "that your children and your children's children shall reign over ours for ever." Because such an unwise, unjust, unnatural compact might (perhaps) in the next succession put them under the government of a rogue or a fool. Most wise men, in their private sentiments, have ever treated hereditary right with contempt; yet it is one of those evils, which when once established is not easily removed; many submit from fear, others from superstition, and the more powerful part shares with the king the plunder of the rest.

This is supposing the present race of kings in the world to have had an honorable origin; whereas it is more than probable, that could we take off the dark covering of antiquity, and trace them to their first rise, that we should find the first of them nothing better than the principal ruffian of some restless gang, whose savage manners of preeminence in subtlety obtained him the title of chief among plunderers; and who by increasing in power, and extending his depredations, overawed the quiet and defenseless to purchase their safety by frequent contributions. Yet his electors could have no idea of giving hereditary right to his descendants, because such a perpetual exclusion of themselves was incompatible with the free and unrestrained principles they professed to live by. Wherefore, hereditary succession in the early ages of monarchy could not take place as a matter of claim, but as something casual or complemental; but as few or no records were extant in those days, and traditionary history stuffed with fables, it was very easy, after the lapse of a few generations, to trump up some superstitious tale, conveniently timed, Mahomet like, to cram hereditary right down the throats of the vulgar. Perhaps the disorders which threatened, or seemed to threaten on the decease of a leader and the choice of a new one (for elections among ruffians could not be very orderly) induced many at first to favor hereditary pretensions; by which means it happened, as it hath happened since, that what at first was submitted to as a convenience, was afterwards claimed as a right.

England, since the conquest, hath known some few good monarchs, but groaned beneath a much larger number of bad ones, yet no man in his senses can say that their claim under William the Conqueror is a very honorable one. A French bastard landing with an armed banditti, and establishing himself king of England against the consent of the natives, is in plain terms a very paltry rascally original. It certainly hath no divinity in it. However, it is needless to spend much time in exposing the folly of hereditary right, if there are any so weak as to believe it, let them promiscuously worship the ass and lion, and welcome. I shall neither copy their humility, nor disturb their devotion.

Yet I should be glad to ask how they suppose kings came at first? The question admits but of three answers, viz., either by lot, by election, or by usurpation. If the first king was taken by lot, it establishes a precedent for the next, which excludes hereditary succession. Saul was by lot, yet the succession was not hereditary, neither does it appear from that transaction there was any intention it ever should. If the first king of any country was by election, that likewise establishes a precedent for the next; for to say, that the right of all future generations is taken away, by the act of the first electors, in their choice not only of a king, but of a family of kings for ever, hath no parallel in or out of scripture but the doctrine of original sin, which supposes the free will of all men lost in Adam; and from such comparison, and it will admit of no other, hereditary succession can derive no glory. For as in Adam all sinned, and as in the first electors all men obeyed; as in the one all mankind were subjected to Satan, and in the other to Sovereignty; as our innocence was lost in the first, and our authority in the last; and as both disable us from reassuming some former state and privilege, it unanswerably follows that original sin and hereditary succession are parallels. Dishonorable rank! Inglorious connection! Yet the most subtle sophist cannot produce a juster simile.

As to usurpation, no man will be so hardy as to defend it; and that William the Conqueror was an usurper is a fact not to be contradicted. The plain truth is, that the antiquity of English monarchy will not bear looking into.

But it is not so much the absurdity as the evil of hereditary succession which concerns mankind. Did it ensure a race of good and wise men it would have the seal of divine authority, but as it opens a door to the foolish, the wicked; and the improper, it hath in it the nature of oppression. Men who look upon themselves born to reign, and others to obey, soon grow insolent; selected from the rest of mankind their minds are early poisoned by importance; and the world they act in differs so materially from the world at large, that they have but little opportunity of knowing its true interests, and when they succeed to the government are frequently the most ignorant and unfit of any throughout the dominions.

Another evil which attends hereditary succession is, that the throne is subject to be possessed by a minor at any age; all which time the regency, acting under the cover of a king, have every opportunity and inducement to betray their trust. The same national misfortune happens, when a king worn out with age and infirmity, enters the last stage of human weakness. In both these cases the public becomes a prey to every miscreant, who can tamper successfully with the follies either of age or infancy.

The most plausible plea, which hath ever been offered in favor of hereditary succession, is, that it preserves a nation from civil wars; and were this true, it would be weighty; whereas, it is the most barefaced falsity ever imposed upon mankind. The whole history of England disowns the fact. Thirty kings and two minors have reigned in that distracted kingdom since the conquest, in which time there have been (including the Revolution) no less than eight civil wars and nineteen rebellions. Wherefore instead of making for peace, it makes against it, and destroys the very foundation it seems to stand on.

The contest for monarchy and succession, between the houses of York and Lancaster, laid England in a scene of blood for many years. Twelve pitched battles, besides skirmishes and sieges, were fought between Henry and Edward. Twice was Henry prisoner to Edward, who in his turn was prisoner to Henry. And so uncertain is the fate of war and the temper of a nation, when nothing but personal matters are the ground of a quarrel, that Henry was taken in triumph from a prison to a palace, and Edward obliged to fly from a palace to a foreign land; yet, as sudden transitions of temper are seldom lasting, Henry in his turn was driven from the throne, and Edward recalled to succeed him. The parliament always following the strongest side.

This contest began in the reign of Henry the Sixth, and was not entirely extinguished till Henry the Seventh, in whom the families were united. Including a period of 67 years, viz., from 1422 to 1489.

In short, monarchy and succession have laid (not this or that kingdom only) but the world in blood and ashes. 'Tis a form of government which the word of God bears testimony against, and blood will attend it.

If we inquire into the business of a king, we shall find that (in some countries they have none) and after sauntering away their lives without pleasure to themselves or advantage to the nation, withdraw from the scene, and leave their successors to tread the same idle round. In absolute monarchies the whole weight of business civil and military, lies on the king; the children of Israel in their request for a king, urged this plea "that he may judge us, and go out before us and fight our battles." But in countries where he is neither a judge nor a general, as in England, a man would be puzzled to know what is his business.

The nearer any government approaches to a republic, the less business there is for a king. It is somewhat difficult to find a proper name for the government of England. Sir William Meredith calls it a republic; but in its present state it is unworthy of the name, because the corrupt influence of the crown, by having all the places in its disposal, hath so effectually swallowed up the power, and eaten out the virtue of the house of commons (the republican part in the constitution) that the government of England is nearly as monarchical as that of France or Spain. Men fall out with names without understanding them. For it is the republican and not the monarchical part of the constitution of England which Englishmen glory in, viz., the liberty of choosing a house of commons from out of their own body- and it is easy to see that when the republican virtue fails, slavery ensues. Why is the constitution of England sickly, but because monarchy hath poisoned the republic, the crown hath engrossed the commons?

In England a king hath little more to do than to make war and give away places; which in plain terms, is to impoverish the nation and set it together by the ears. A pretty business indeed for a man to be allowed eight hundred thousand sterling a year for, and worshipped into the bargain! Of more worth is one honest man to society, and in the sight of God, than all the crowned ruffians that ever lived.

Thoughts of the present state of American affairs

In the following pages I offer nothing more than simple facts, plain arguments, and common sense; and have no other preliminaries to settle with the reader, than that he will divest himself of prejudice and prepossession, and suffer his reason and his feelings to determine for themselves; that he will put on, or rather that he will not put off the true character of a man, and generously enlarge his views beyond the present day.

Volumes have been written on the subject of the struggle between England and America. Men of all ranks have embarked in the controversy, from different motives, and with various designs; but all have been ineffectual, and the period of debate is closed. Arms, as the last resource, decide the contest; the appeal was the choice of the king, and the continent hath accepted the challenge.

It hath been reported of the late Mr. Pelham (who tho' an able minister was not without his faults) that on his being attacked in the house of commons, on the score, that his measures were only of a temporary kind, replied, "they will last my time." Should a thought so fatal and unmanly possess the colonies in the present contest, the name of ancestors will be remembered by future generations with detestation.

The sun never shined on a cause of greater worth. 'Tis not the affair of a city, a country, a province, or a kingdom, but of a continent- of at least one eighth part of the habitable globe. 'Tis not the concern of a day, a year, or an age; posterity are virtually involved in the contest, and will be more or less affected, even to the end of time, by the proceedings now. Now is the seed time of continental union, faith and honor. The least fracture now will be like a name engraved with the point of a pin on the tender rind of a young oak; The wound will enlarge with the tree, and posterity read it in full grown characters.

By referring the matter from argument to arms, a new area for politics is struck; a new method of thinking hath arisen. All plans, proposals, &c. prior to the nineteenth of April, i.e., to the commencement of hostilities, are like the almanacs of the last year; which, though proper then, are superseded and useless now. Whatever was advanced by the advocates on either side of the question then, terminated in one and the same point, viz., a union with Great Britain; the only difference between the parties was the method of effecting it; the one proposing force, the other friendship; but it hath so far happened that the first hath failed, and the second hath withdrawn her influence.

As much hath been said of the advantages of reconciliation, which, like an agreeable dream, hath passed away and left us as we were, it is but right, that we should examine the contrary side of the argument, and inquire into some of the many material injuries which these colonies sustain, and always will sustain, by being connected with, and dependant on Great Britain. To examine that connection and dependance, on the principles of nature and common sense, to see what we have to trust to, if separated, and what we are to expect, if dependant.

I have heard it asserted by some, that as America hath flourished under her former connection with Great Britain, that the same connection is necessary towards her future happiness, and will always have the same effect. Nothing can be more fallacious than this kind of argument. We may as well assert, that because a child has thrived upon milk, that it is never to have meat; or that the first twenty years of our lives is to become a precedent for the next twenty. But even this is admitting more than is true, for I answer roundly, that America would have flourished as much, and probably much more, had no European power had any thing to do with her. The commerce by which she hath enriched herself, are the necessaries of life, and will always have a market while eating is the custom of Europe.

But she has protected us, say some. That she hath engrossed us is true, and defended the continent at our expense as well as her own is admitted, and she would have defended Turkey from the same motive, viz., the sake of trade and dominion.

Alas! we have been long led away by ancient prejudices and made large sacrifices to superstition. We have boasted the protection of Great Britain, without considering, that her motive was interest not attachment; that she did not protect us from our enemies on our account, but from her enemies on her own account, from those who had no quarrel with us on any other account, and who will always be our enemies on the same account. Let Britain wave her pretensions to the continent, or the continent throw off the dependance, and we should be at peace with France and

Spain were they at war with Britain. The miseries of Hanover last war, ought to warn us against connections.

It hath lately been asserted in parliament, that the colonies have no relation to each other but through the parent country, i.e., that Pennsylvania and the Jerseys, and so on for the rest, are sister colonies by the way of England; this is certainly a very roundabout way of proving relationship, but it is the nearest and only true way of proving enemyship, if I may so call it. France and Spain never were, nor perhaps ever will be our enemies as Americans, but as our being the subjects of Great Britain.

But Britain is the parent country, say some. Then the more shame upon her conduct. Even brutes do not devour their young; nor savages make war upon their families; wherefore the assertion, if true, turns to her reproach; but it happens not to be true, or only partly so, and the phrase parent or mother country hath been jesuitically adopted by the king and his parasites, with a low papistical design of gaining an unfair bias on the credulous weakness of our minds. Europe, and not England, is the parent country of America. This new world hath been the asylum for the persecuted lovers of civil and religious liberty from every Part of Europe. Hither have they fled, not from the tender embraces of the mother, but from the cruelty of the monster; and it is so far true of England, that the same tyranny which drove the first emigrants from home pursues their descendants still.

In this extensive quarter of the globe, we forget the narrow limits of three hundred and sixty miles (the extent of England) and carry our friendship on a larger scale; we claim brotherhood with every European Christian, and triumph in the generosity of the sentiment.

It is pleasant to observe by what regular gradations we surmount the force of local prejudice, as we enlarge our acquaintance with the world. A man born in any town in England divided into parishes, will naturally associate most with his fellow parishioners (because their interests in many cases will be common) and distinguish him by the name of neighbor; if he meet him but a few miles from home, he drops the narrow idea of a street, and salutes him by the name of townsman; if he travels out of the county, and meet him in any other, he forgets the minor divisions of street and town, and calls him countryman; i.e., countyman; but if in their foreign excursions they should associate in France or any other part of Europe, their local remembrance would be enlarged into that of Englishmen. And by a just parity of reasoning, all Europeans meeting in America, or any other quarter of the globe, are countrymen; for England, Holland, Germany, or Sweden, when compared with the whole, stand in the same places on the larger scale, which the divisions of street, town, and county do on the smaller ones; distinctions too limited for continental minds. Not one third of the inhabitants, even of this province, are of English descent. Wherefore, I reprobate the phrase of parent or mother country applied to England only, as being false, selfish, narrow and ungenerous.

But admitting that we were all of English descent, what does it amount to? Nothing. Britain, being now an open enemy, extinguishes every other name and title: And to say that reconciliation is our duty, is truly farcical. The first king of England, of the present line (William the Conqueror) was a Frenchman, and half the peers of England are descendants from the same country; wherefore by the same method of reasoning, England ought to be governed by France.

Much hath been said of the united strength of Britain and the colonies, that in conjunction they might bid defiance to the world. But this is mere presumption; the fate of war is uncertain, neither do the expressions mean anything; for this continent would never suffer itself to be drained of inhabitants to support the British arms in either Asia, Africa, or Europe.

Besides, what have we to do with setting the world at defiance? Our plan is commerce, and that, well attended to,will secure us the peace and friendship of all Europe; because it is the interest of all Europe to have America a free port. Her trade will always be a protection, and her barrenness of gold and silver secure her from invaders.

I challenge the warmest advocate for reconciliation, to show, a single advantage that this continent can reap, by being connected with Great Britain. I repeat the challenge, not a single advantage is derived. Our corn will fetch its price in any market in Europe, and our imported goods must be paid for buy them where we will.

But the injuries and disadvantages we sustain by that connection, are without number; and our duty to mankind at large, as well as to ourselves, instruct us to renounce the alliance: Because, any submission to, or dependance on Great Britain, tends directly to involve this continent in European wars and quarrels; and sets us at variance with nations, who would otherwise seek our friendship, and against whom, we have neither anger nor complaint. As Europe is our market for trade, we ought to form no partial connection with any part of it. It is the true interest of America to steer clear of European contentions, which she never can do, while by her dependance on Britain, she is made the make-weight in the scale of British politics.

Europe is too thickly planted with kingdoms to be long at peace, and whenever a war breaks out between England and any foreign power, the trade of America goes to ruin, because of her connection with Britain. The next war may not turn out like the Past, and should it not, the advocates for reconciliation now will be wishing for separation then, because, neutrality in that case, would be a safer convoy than a man of war. Every thing that is right or natural pleads for separation. The blood of the slain, the weeping voice of nature cries, 'tis time to part. Even the distance at which the Almighty hath placed England and America, is a strong and natural proof, that the authority of the one, over the other, was never the design of Heaven. The time likewise at which the continent was discovered, adds weight to the argument, and the manner in which it was peopled increases the force of it. The reformation was preceded by the discovery of America, as if the Almighty graciously meant to open a sanctuary to the persecuted in future years, when home should afford neither friendship nor safety.

The authority of Great Britain over this continent, is a form of government, which sooner or later must have an end: And a serious mind can draw no true pleasure by looking forward, under the painful and positive conviction, that what he calls "the present constitution" is merely temporary. As parents, we can have no joy, knowing that this government is not sufficiently lasting to ensure any thing which we may bequeath to posterity: And by a plain method of argument, as we are running the next generation into debt, we ought to do the work of it, otherwise we use them meanly and pitifully. In order to discover the line of our duty rightly, we should take our children in our hand, and fix our station a few years farther into life; that eminence will present a prospect, which a few present fears and prejudices conceal from our sight. Though I would carefully avoid giving unnecessary offence, yet I am inclined to believe, that all those who espouse the doctrine of reconciliation, may be included within the following descriptions:

Interested men, who are not to be trusted; weak men who cannot see; prejudiced men who will not see; and a certain set of moderate men, who think better of the European world than it deserves; and this last class by an ill-judged deliberation, will be the cause of more calamities to this continent than all the other three.

It is the good fortune of many to live distant from the scene of sorrow; the evil is not sufficiently brought to their doors to make them feel the precariousness with which all American property is possessed. But let our imaginations transport us for a few moments to Boston, that seat of wretchedness will teach us wisdom, and instruct us for ever to renounce a power in whom we can have no trust. The inhabitants of that unfortunate city, who but a few months ago were in ease and affluence, have now no other alternative than to stay and starve, or turn out to beg. Endangered by the fire of their friends if they continue within the city, and plundered by the soldiery if they leave it. In their present condition they are prisoners without the hope of redemption, and in a general attack for their relief, they would be exposed to the fury of both armies.

Men of passive tempers look somewhat lightly over the offenses of Britain, and, still hoping for the best, are apt to call out, Come we shall be friends again for all this. But examine the passions and feelings of mankind. Bring the doctrine of reconciliation to the touchstone of nature, and then tell me, whether you can hereafter love, honor, and faithfully serve the power that hath carried fire and sword into your land? If you cannot do all these, then are you only deceiving yourselves, and by your delay bringing ruin upon posterity. Your future connection with Britain, whom you can neither love nor honor, will be forced and unnatural, and being formed only on the plan of present convenience, will in a little time fall into a relapse more wretched than the first. But if you say, you can still pass the violations over, then I ask, Hath your house been burnt? Hath your property been destroyed before your face? Are your wife and children destitute of a bed to lie on, or bread to live on? Have you lost a parent or a child by their hands, and yourself the ruined and wretched survivor? If you have not, then are you not a judge of those who have. But if you have, and can still shake hands with the murderers, then are you unworthy the name of husband, father, friend, or lover, and whatever may be your rank or title in life, you have the heart of a coward, and the spirit of a sycophant.

This is not inflaming or exaggerating matters, but trying them by those feelings and affections which nature justifies, and without which, we should be incapable of discharging the social duties of life, or enjoying the felicities of it. I mean not to exhibit horror for the purpose of provoking revenge, but to awaken us from fatal and unmanly slumbers, that we may pursue determinately some fixed object. It is not in the power of Britain or of Europe to conquer America, if she do not conquer herself by delay and timidity. The present winter is worth an age if rightly employed, but if lost or neglected, the whole continent will partake of the misfortune; and there is no punishment which that man will not deserve, be he who, or what, or where he will, that may be the means of sacrificing a season so precious and useful.

It is repugnant to reason, to the universal order of things, to all examples from the former ages, to suppose, that this continent can longer remain subject to any external power. The most sanguine in Britain does not think so. The utmost stretch of human wisdom cannot, at this time compass a plan short of separation, which can promise the continent even a year's security. Reconciliation is *now* a fallacious dream. Nature hath deserted the connection, and Art cannot supply her place. For, as Milton wisely expresses, "never can true reconcilement grow where wounds of deadly hate have pierced so deep."

Every quiet method for peace hath been ineffectual. Our prayers have been rejected with disdain; and only tended to convince us, that nothing flatters vanity, or confirms obstinacy in kings more than repeated petitioning- and nothing hath contributed more than that very measure to make the kings of Europe absolute: Witness Denmark and Sweden. Wherefore since nothing but blows will do, for God's sake, let us come to a final separation, and not leave the next generation to be cutting throats, under the violated unmeaning names of parent and child.

To say, they will never attempt it again is idle and visionary, we thought so at the repeal of the stamp act, yet a year or two undeceived us; as well may we suppose that nations, which have been once defeated, will never renew the quarrel.

As to government matters, it is not in the powers of Britain to do this continent justice: The business of it will soon be too weighty, and intricate, to be managed with any tolerable degree of convenience, by a power, so distant from us, and so very ignorant of us; for if they cannot conquer us, they cannot govern us. To be always running three or four thousand miles with a tale or a petition, waiting four or five months for an answer, which when obtained requires five or six more to explain it in, will in a few years be looked upon as folly and childishness- there was a time when it was proper, and there is a proper time for it to cease.

Small islands not capable of protecting themselves, are the proper objects for kingdoms to take under their care; but there is something very absurd, in supposing a continent to be perpetually governed by an island. In no instance hath nature made the satellite larger than its primary planet, and as England and America, with respect to each Other, reverses the common order of nature, it is evident they belong to different systems: England to Europe- America to itself.

I am not induced by motives of pride, party, or resentment to espouse the doctrine of separation and independence; I am clearly, positively, and conscientiously persuaded that it is the true interest of this continent to be so; that every thing short of that is mere patchwork, that it can afford no lasting felicity,- that it is leaving the sword to our children, and shrinking back at a time, when, a little more, a little farther, would have rendered this continent the glory of the earth.

As Britain hath not manifested the least inclination towards a compromise, we may be assured that no terms can be obtained worthy the acceptance of the continent, or any ways equal to the expense of blood and treasure we have been already put to. The object contended for, ought always to bear some just proportion to the expense. The removal of the North, or the whole detestable junto, is a matter unworthy the millions we have expended. A temporary stoppage of trade, was an inconvenience, which would have sufficiently balanced the repeal of all the acts complained of, had such repeals been obtained; but if the whole continent must take up arms, if every man must be a soldier, it is scarcely worth our while to fight against a contemptible ministry only. Dearly, dearly, do we pay for the repeal of the acts, if that is all we fight for; for in a just estimation, it is as great a folly to pay a Bunker Hill price for law, as for land. As I have always considered the independency of this continent, as an event, which sooner or later must arrive, so from the late rapid progress of the continent to maturity, the event could not be far off. Wherefore, on the breaking out of hostilities, it was not worth the while to have disputed a matter, which time would have finally redressed, unless we meant to be in earnest; otherwise, it is like wasting an estate of a suit at law, to regulate the trespasses of a tenant, whose lease is just expiring. No man was a warmer wisher for reconciliation than myself, before the fatal nineteenth of April, 1775 (Massacre at Lexington), but the moment the event of that day was made known, I rejected the hardened, sullen tempered Pharaoh of England for ever; and disdain the wretch, that with the pretended title of Father of his people, can unfeelingly hear of their slaughter, and composedly sleep with their blood upon his soul.

But admitting that matters were now made up, what would be the event? I answer, the ruin of the continent. And that for several reasons:

First. The powers of governing still remaining in the hands of the king, he will have a negative over the whole legislation of this continent. And as he hath shown himself such an inveterate enemy to liberty, and discovered such a thirst for arbitrary power, is he, or is he not, a proper man to say to these colonies, "You shall make no laws but what I please?" And is there any inhabitant in America so ignorant, as not to know, that according to what is called the present constitution, that this continent can make no laws but what the king gives leave to; and is there any man so unwise, as not to see, that (considering what has happened) he will suffer no Law to be made here, but such as suit his purpose? We may be as effectually enslaved by the want of laws in America, as by submitting to laws made for us in England. After matters are made up (as it is called) can there be any doubt but the whole power of the crown will be exerted, to keep this continent as low and humble as possible? Instead of going forward we shall go backward, or be perpetually quarrelling or ridiculously petitioning. We are already greater than the king wishes us to be, and will he not hereafter endeavor to make us less? To bring the matter to one point. Is the power who is jealous of our prosperity, a proper power to govern us? Whoever says No to this question is an independent, for independency means no more, than, whether we shall make our own laws, or whether the king, the greatest enemy this continent hath, or can have, shall tell us, "there shall be no laws but such as I like."

But the king you will say has a negative in England; the people there can make no laws without his consent. In point of right and good order, there is something very ridiculous, that a youth of twenty-one (which hath often happened) shall say to several millions of people, older and wiser than himself, I forbid this or that act of yours to be law. But in this place I decline this sort of reply, though I will never cease to expose the absurdity of it, and only answer, that England being the king's residence, and America not so, make quite another case. The king's negative here is ten times more dangerous and fatal than it can be in England, for there he will scarcely refuse his consent to a bill for putting England into as strong a state of defence as possible, and in America he would never suffer such a bill to be passed.

America is only a secondary object in the system of British politics-England consults the good of this country, no farther than it answers her own purpose. Wherefore, her own interest leads her to suppress the growth of ours in every case which doth not promote her advantage, or in the least interfere with it. A pretty state we should soon be in under such a second-hand government, considering what has happened! Men do not change from enemies to friends by the alteration of a name; and in order to show that reconciliation now is a dangerous doctrine, I affirm, that it would be policy in the kingdom at this time, to repeal the acts for the sake of reinstating himself in the government of the provinces; in order, that he may accomplish by craft and subtlety, in the long run, what he cannot do by force and violence in the short one. Reconciliation and ruin are nearly related.

Secondly. That as even the best terms, which we can expect to obtain, can amount to no more than a temporary expedient, or a kind of government by guardianship, which can last no longer than till the colonies come of age, so the general face and state of things, in the interim, will be unsettled and unpromising. Emigrants of property will not choose to come to a country whose form of government hangs but by a thread, and who is every day tottering on the brink of commotion and disturbance; and numbers of the present inhabitants would lay hold of the interval, to dispose of their effects, and quit the continent.

But the most powerful of all arguments, is, that nothing but independence, i.e., a continental form of government, can keep the peace of the continent and preserve it inviolate from civil wars. I dread the event of a reconciliation with Britain now, as it is more than probable, that it will be followed by a revolt somewhere or other, the consequences of which may be far more fatal than all the malice of Britain.

Thousands are already ruined by British barbarity; (thousands more will probably suffer the same fate.) Those men have other feelings than us who have nothing suffered. All they now possess is liberty, what they before enjoyed is sacrificed to its service, and having nothing more to lose, they disdain submission. Besides, the general temper of the colonies, towards a British government, will be like that of a youth, who is nearly out of his time; they will care very little about her. And a government which cannot preserve the peace, is no government at all, and in that case we pay our money for nothing; and pray what is it that Britain can do, whose power will be wholly on paper, should a civil tumult break out the very day after reconciliation? I have heard some men say, many of whom I believe spoke without thinking, that they dreaded independence, fearing that it would produce civil wars. It is but seldom that our first thoughts are truly correct, and that is the case here; for there are ten times more to dread from a patched up connection than from independence. I make the sufferers case my own, and I protest, that were I driven from house and home, my property destroyed, and my circumstances ruined, that as man, sensible of injuries, I could never relish the doctrine of reconciliation, or consider myself bound thereby.

The colonies have manifested such a spirit of good order and obedience to continental government, as is sufficient to make every reasonable person easy and happy on that head. No man can assign the least pretence for his fears, on any other grounds, than such as are truly childish and ridiculous, viz., that one colony will be striving for superiority over another.

Where there are no distinctions there can be no superiority, perfect equality affords no temptation. The republics of Europe are all (and we may say always) in peace. Holland and Switzerland are without wars, foreign or domestic; monarchical governments, it is true, are never long at rest: the crown itself is a temptation to enterprising ruffians at home; and that degree of pride and insolence ever attendant on regal authority swells into a rupture with foreign powers, in instances where a republican government, by being formed on more natural principles, would negotiate the mistake.

Ye that tell us of harmony and reconciliation, can ye restore to us the time that is past? Can ye give to prostitution its former innocence? Neither can ye reconcile Britain and America. The last cord now is broken, the people of England are presenting addresses against us. There are injuries which nature cannot forgive; she would cease to be nature if she did. As well can the lover forgive the ravisher of his mistress, as the continent forgive the murders of Britain. The Almighty hath implanted in us these inextinguishable feelings for good and wise purposes. They are the guardians of his image in our hearts. They distinguish us from the herd of common animals. The social compact would dissolve, and justice be extirpated the earth, or have only a casual existence were we callous to the touches of affection. The robber and the murderer, would often escape unpunished, did not the injuries which our tempers sustain, provoke us into justice.

O ye that love mankind! Ye that dare oppose, not only the tyranny, but the tyrant, stand forth! Every spot of the old world is overrun with oppression. Freedom hath been hunted round the globe. Asia, and Africa, have long expelled her. Europe regards her like a stranger, and England hath given her warning to depart. O! receive the fugitive, and prepare in time an asylum for mankind.

Lord Acton on The American Revolution

The two parts of this chapter are respectively from Lord Acton's Lectures on Modern History *(London: 1906) and his* Lectures on the French Revolution *(London: 1910).*

Lord Acton (1834-1902) was a British historian.

The rational and humanitarian enlightenment of the eighteenth century did much for the welfare of mankind, but little to promote the securities of freedom. Power was better employed than formerly, but it did not abdicate.

In England, politically the most advanced country, the impetus which the Revolution gave to progress was exhausted, and people began to say, now that the Jacobite peril was over, that no issue remained between parties which made it worth while for men to cut each others' throats. The development of the Whig philosophy was checked by the practical tendency to compromise. Compromise distinguished the Whig from the Roundhead, the man who succeeded from the man who failed, the man who was the teacher of politics to the civilised world from the man who left his head on Temple Bar.

The Seven Years' War renewed the interrupted march by involving America in the concerns of Europe, and causing the colonies to react on the parent state. That was a consequence which followed the Conquest of Canada and the accession of George III. The two events, occurring in quick succession, raised the American question. A traveller who visited America some years earlier reports that there was much discontent, and that separation was expected before very long. That discontent was inoperative whilst a great military power held Canada. Two considerations reconciled the colonists to the disadvantages attending the connection with England. The English fleet guarded the sea against pirates; the English army guarded the land against the French. The former was desirable; the latter was essential to their existence. When the danger on the French side disappeared, it might become very uncertain whether the patrol of the Atlantic was worth the price that America had to pay for it. Therefore Montcalm foretold that the English, if they conquered the French colonies, would lose their own. Many Frenchmen saw this, with satisfaction; and the probability was so manifest that Englishmen saw it too. It was their interest to strengthen their position with new securities, in the place of that one supreme security which they had lost by their victory at Quebec. That victory, with the vast acquisition of territory that followed, would be no increase of imperial power if it loosened the hold on Atlantic colonies. Therefore, the policy of the hour was to enforce the existing claims and to obtain unequivocal recognition of English sovereignty. The most profitable method of doing it was in the shape of heavier taxation; but taxes were a small matter in comparison with the establishment of undisputed authority and unquestioning submission. The tax might be nominal, if the principle was safe. Ways and means would not be wanting in an empire which extended from Hudson's Bay to the Gulf of Mexico. For the moment the need was not money but allegiance. The problem was new, for the age of expansion had come suddenly, in East and West, by the action of Pitt; and Pitt was no longer in office, to find the solution.

Among the Whigs, who were a failing and discredited party, there were men who already knew the policy by which since then the empire has been reared—Adam Smith, Dean Tucker, Edmund Burke. But the great mass went with the times, and held that the object of politics is power, and that the more dominion is extended, the more it must be retained by force. The reason why free trade is better than dominion was a secret obscurely buried in the breast of economists.

Whilst the expulsion of the French from their Transatlantic empire; governed the situation, the immediate difficulty was brought on by the new reign. The right of searching houses and ships for contraband was conveyed by certain warrants called Writs of Assistance, which required no specified designation, no oath or evidence, and enabled , the surprise visit to be paid by day or night. They were introduced under Charles II, and had to be renewed within six months of the demise of the crown. The last renewal had been at the death of George II; and it was now intended that they should be efficacious, and should protect the revenue from smugglers. Between 1717 and 1761 many things had changed, and the colonies had grown to be richer, more confident, more self-respecting. They claimed to extend to the Mississippi, and had no French or Spaniards on their borders. Practically, there was no neighbour but England, and they had a patrimony such as no Englishman had dreamt of. The letter of the law, the practice of the last generation, were no argument with the heirs of unbounded wealth and power, and did not convince them that they ought to lose by the aid which they had given against France. The American jurists argued that this was good by English law, but could not justly be applied to America, where the same constitutional safeguards did not exist—where the cases would be tried by judges without a jury, by judges who could be dismissed at pleasure, by judges who were paid by fees which increased with the amount of the property confiscated, and were interested in deciding against the American importer, and in favour of the revenue. That was a technical and pedestrian argument which every lawyer could understand, without passing the limits of accustomed thought.

Then James Otis spoke, and lifted the question to a different level, in one of the memorable speeches in political history. Assuming, but not admitting, that the Boston custom-house officers were acting legally, and within the statute, then, he said, the statute was wrong. Their action might he authorized by parliament; but if so, parliament had exceeded its authority, like Charles with his ship-money, and James with the dispensing power. There are principles which override precedents. The laws of England may be a very good timing, but there is such a thing as a higher law.

The court decided in favor of the validity of the writs; and John Adams, who heard the judgment, wrote long after that in that hour the child Independence was born. The English view triumphed for the time, and the governor wrote home that the mourners soon ceased. The States, and ultimately the United States, rejected general warrants; and since 1811 they are in agreement with the law of England. On that point, therefore, the colonies were in the right.

Then came the larger question of taxation. Regulation of external traffic was admitted. England patrolled the sea and protected America from the smuggler and the pirate. Some remuneration might be reasonably claimed; but it ought to be obtained in such a way as not to hamper and prohibit the increase of wealth. The restrictions on industry and trade were, however, contrived for the benefit of England and to the injury of her colonies. They demanded that the arrangement should be made for their mutual advantage. They did not go so far as to affirm that it ought to be to their advantage only, irrespective of ours, which is our policy with our colonies at the present time. The claim was not originally excessive. It is the basis of the imputation that the dispute, on both sides, was an affair of sordid interest. We shall find it more just to say that the motive was empire on one side and self-government on the other. It was a question between liberty and authority, government by consent and government by force, the control of the subject by the State, and the control of the State by the subject. The issue had never been so definitely raised. In England it had long been settled. It had been settled that the legislature could, without breach of any ethical or constitutional law, without forfeiting its authority or exposing itself to just revolt, make laws injurious to the subject for the benefit of English religion or English trade. If that principle was abandoned in America it could not well be maintained in Ireland, and the green flag might fly on Dublin Castle.

This was no survival of the dark ages. Both the oppression of Ireland and the oppression of America was the work of the modern school, of men who executed one King and expelled another. It was the work of parliament, of the parliaments of Cromwell and of William III. And the parliament would not consent to renounce its own specific policy, its right of imposing taxes. The crown, the clergy, the aristocrat, were hostile to the Americans; but the real enemy was the House of Commons. The old European securities for good government were found insufficient protection against parliamentary oppression. The nation itself, acting by its representatives, had to be subjected to control. The political problem raised by the New World was more complicated than the simple issues dealt with hitherto in the Old. It had become necessary to turn back the current of the development of politics, to bind and limit and confine the State, which it was the pride of the moderns to exalt. It was a new phase of political history. The American Revolution innovated upon the English Revolution, as the English Revolution innovated on the politics of Bacon or of Hobbes. There was no tyranny to be resented. The colonists were in many ways more completely their own masters than Englishmen at home. They were not roused by the sense of intolerable wrong. The point at issue was a very subtle and refined one, and it required a great deal of mismanagement to make the quarrel irreconcilable.

Successive English governments shifted their ground. They tried the Stamp Act; then the duty on tea and several other articles; then the tea duty alone; and at last something even less than the tea duty. In one thing they were consistent: they never abandoned the right of raising taxes. When the colonists, instigated by Patrick Henry, resisted the use of stamps, and Pitt rejoiced that they had resisted, parliament gave way on that particular measure, declaring that it retained the disputed right. Townshend carried a series of taxes on imports, which produced about three hundred pounds, and were dropped by Lord North. Then an ingenious plan was devised, which would enforce the right of taxation, but which would not be felt by American pockets, and would, indeed, put money into them, in the shape of a bribe. East Indiamen were allowed to carry tea to American ports without paying toll in England. The Navigation Laws were suspended, that people in New England might drink cheap tea, without smuggling. The duty in (England was a shilling a pound. The duty in America was threepence a pound. The shilling was remitted, so that the colonies had only a duty of threepence to pay instead of a duty of fifteenpence. The tea-drinker at Boston got his tea cheaper than the tea-drinker at Bristol. The revenue made a sacrifice, it incurred a loss, in order to gratify the discontented colonials. If it was a grievance to pay more for a commodity, how could it be a grievance to pay less for the same commodity? To gild the pill still further, it was proposed that the threepence should be levied at the British ports, so that the Americans should perceive nothing but the gift, nothing but the welcome fact that their tea was cheaper, and should be spared entirely the taste of the bitterness within. That would have upset the entire scheme. The government would not hear of it. America was to have cheap tea, but was to admit the tax. The sordid purpose was surrendered on our side, and only the constitutional motive was retained, in the belief that the sordid element alone prevailed in the colonies.

That threepence broke up the British empire. Twelve years of renewed contention, ever coming up in altered shape under different ministers, made it clear that the mind of the great parent State was made up, and that all variations of party were illusory. The Americans grew more and more obstinate as they purged the sordid question of interest with which they had begun. At first they had consented to the restrictions imposed under the Navigation Laws. They now rejected them. One of the tea ships in Boston harbour was boarded at night, and the tea chests were flung into the Atlantic. That was the mild beginning of the greatest Revolution that had ever broken out among civilised men. The dispute had been reduced to its simplest expression, and had become a mere question of principle. The argument from the Charters, the argument from the Constitution, was discarded. The case was fought out on the ground of the Law of Nature, more properly speaking, of Divine Right. On that evening of 16th December 1773, it became, for the first time, the reigning force in History. By the rules of right, which had been obeyed till then, England had the better cause. By the principle which was then inaugurated, England was in the wrong, and the future belonged to the colonies.

The revolutionary spirit had been handed down from the seventeenth century sects, through the colonial charters. As early as 1638 a Connecticut preacher said: "The choice of public magistrates belongs unto the people, by God's own allowance. They who have the power to appoint officers and magistrates, it is in their power, also, to set the bounds and limitations of the power and place unto which they call them." In Rhode Island, where the Royal Charter was so liberal that it lasted until 1842, all power reverted annually to the people, and the authorities had to undergo re-election. Connecticut possessed so finished a system of self-government in the towns, that it served as a model for the federal Constitution. The Quakers of Pennsylvania managed their affairs without privilege, or intolerance, or slavery, or oppression. It was not to imitate England that they went into the desert. Several colonies were in various ways far ahead of the mother country; and the most advanced statesman of the Commonwealth, Vane, had his training in New England.

After the outrage on board the Dartmouth in Boston harbour the government resolved to coerce Massachusetts, and a continental Congress met to devise means for its protection. The king's troops were sent to destroy military stores that had been collected at Concord; and at Lexington, on the outward march, as well as all the way back, they were assailed by militia. The affair at Lexington, 19th April 1775, was the beginning of the War of Independence, which opened with the siege of Boston. Two months later the first action was fought at Bried's Hill, or Bunker Hill, which are low heights overlooking the town, and the colonials were repulsed with very little loss.

The war that followed, and lasted six years, is not illustrious in military annals, and interests us chiefly by the result. After the first battle the colonies declared themselves independent. Virginia, acting for herself only, led the way. Then the great revolutionist, who was the Virginian leader, Jefferson, drew up the Declaration of Independence, which was adopted by the remaining states. It was too rhetorical to be scientific; but it recited the series of ideas which the controversy had carried to the front.

Thirty thousand German soldiers, most of them from Hesse Cassel, were sent out, and were at first partially successful; for they were supported by the fleet, which the estuaries carried far inland. Where the European army had not that advantage things went badly. The Americans attacked Canada, expecting to be welcomed by the French inhabitants who had been so recently turned into British subjects. The attack failed dramatically by the death of General Montgomery, under the walls of Quebec, and the French colonists remained loyal. But an expedition sent from Canada against New York, under Burgoyne, miscarried. Burgoyne had scarcely reached the Hudson when he was forced to surrender at Saratoga. The Congress of the States, which feebly directed operations, wished that the terms of surrender should not be observed, and that the 5000 English and German prisoners, instead of being sent home, should be detained until they could be exchanged. Washington and his officers made known that if this was done they would resign.

The British defeat at Saratoga is the event which determined the issue of the conflict. It put an end to the vacillation of France. The French government had to recover the position it had lost in the last war, and watched the course of events for evidence that American resistance was not about to collapse. At the end of 1777 the victory of Saratoga supplied the requisite proof. Volunteers had been allowed to go over, and much war material was furnished through the agency of a comic poet. Now a treaty of alliance was concluded, a small army was sent to sea, and in March 1778 England was informed that France was at war with her. France was followed by Spain, afterwards by Holland.

It was evident from the first that the combination was more than England could hope to meet. Lord North at once gave way. He offered to satisfy the American demands, and he asked that Chatham should take office. From the moment that his old enemy, France, appeared on the scene, Chatham was passionately warlike. The king agreed that he should be asked to join the ministry, but refused to see him. America declined the English overtures, in fulfillment of her treaty with France. The negotiation with Chatham became impossible. That was no misfortune, for he died a few weeks later, denouncing the government and the opposition.

Then came that phase of war during which the navy of France, under d'Orvilliers in the Channel, under Suffren in the east, under d'Estaing and De Grasse in the west, proved itself equal to the navy of England. It is by the fleet, not by the land forces, that American independence was gained. But it is by the army officers that American ideas, sufficient to subvert every European state, were transplanted into France. When De Grasse drove the English fleet away from Virginian waters, Cornwallis surrendered the army of the south at Yorktown, as Burgoyne had surrendered with the northern army at Saratoga. The Whigs came in and recognized the independence of the colonies, as North would have done four years earlier, when France intervened. Terms of peace with European Powers were made more favourable by the final success of Rodney at Dominica and of Elliot at Gibraltar; but the warlike repute of England fell lower than at any time since the Revolution.

The Americans proceeded to give themselves a Constitution which should hold them together more effectively than the Congress which carried them through the war, and they held a Convention for the purpose at Philadelphia during the summer of 1787. The difficulty was to find terms of union between the three great states—Virginia, Pennsylvania, Massachusetts—and the smaller ones, which included New York. The great states would not allow equal power to the others; the small ones would not allow themselves to be swamped by mere numbers. Therefore one chamber was given to population, and the other, the Senate, to the states on equal terms. Every citizen was made subject to the federal government as well as to that of his own state. The powers of the states were limited. The powers of the federal government were actually enumerated, and thus the states and the union were a check on each other. That principle of division was the most efficacious restraint on democracy that has been devised; for the temper of the Constitutional Convention was as conservative as the Declaration of Independence was revolutionary.

The Federal Constitution did not deal with the question of religious liberty. The rules for the election of the president and for that of the vice-president proved a failure. Slavery was deplored, was denounced, and was retained. The absence of a definition of State Rights led to the most sanguinary civil war of modern times. Weighed in the scales of Liberalism the instrument, as it stood, was a monstrous fraud. And yet, by the development of the principle of Federalism, it has produced a community more powerful, more prosperous, more intelligent, and more free than any other which the world has seen.

The several structures of political thought that arose in France, and clashed in the process of revolution, were not directly responsible for the outbreak. The doctrines hung like a cloud upon the heights, and at critical moments in the reign of Lewis XV men felt that a catastrophe was impending. It befell when there was less provocation, under his successor; and the spark that changed thought into action was supplied by the Declaration of American Independence. It was the system of an international extra-territorial universal Whig, far transcending the English model by its simplicity and rigour. It surpassed in force all the speculations of Paris and Geneva, for it had undergone the test of experiment, and its triumph was the most memorable thing that had been seen by men.

The expectation that the American colonies would separate was an old one. A century before, Harrington had written: "They are yet babes, that cannot live without sucking the breasts of their mother cities; but such as I mistake if, when they come of age, they do not wean themselves; which causes me to wonder at princes that like to be exhausted in that way." When, in 1759, the elder Mirabeau announced it, he meant that the conquest of Canada involved the loss of America, as the colonists would cling to England as long as the French were behind them, and no longer. He came very near to the truth, for the war in Canada gave the signal. The English colonies had meditated the annexation of the French, and they resented that the king's government undertook the expedition, to deprive them of the opportunity for united action. Fifty years later President Adams said that the treatment of American officers by the British made his blood boil.

The agitation began in 1761, and by the innovating ideas which it flung abroad it is as important as the Declaration itself, or the great constitutional debate. The colonies were more advanced than Great Britain in the way of free institutions, and existed only that they might escape the vices of the mother country. They had no remnants of feudalism to cherish or resist. They possessed written constitutions, some of them remarkably original, fit roots of an immense development. George III thought it strange that he should be the sovereign of a democracy like Rhode Island, where all power reverted annually to the people, and the authorities had to be elected anew. Connecticut received from the Stuarts so liberal a charter, and worked out so finished a scheme of local self-government, that it served as a basis for the federal constitution. The Quakers had a plan founded on equality of power, without oppression, or privilege, or intolerance, or slavery. They declared that their holy experiment would not have been worth attempting if it did not offer some very real advantage over England. It was to enjoy freedom, liberty of conscience, and the right to tax themselves, that they went into the desert. There were points on which these men anticipated the doctrines of a more unrestrained democracy, for they established their government not on conventions, but on divine right, and they claimed to be infallible. A Connecticut preacher said in 1638: "The choice of public magistrates belongs unto the people, by God's own allowance. They who have the power to appoint officers and magistrates, it is in their power, also, to set the bounds and limitations of the power and place unto which they call them." The following words, written in 1736, appear in the works of Franklin: "The judgment of a whole people, especially of a free people, is looked upon to be infallible. And this is universally true, while they remain in their proper sphere, unbiassed by faction, undeluded by the tricks of designing men. A body of people thus circumstanced cannot be supposed to judge amiss on any essential points; for if they decide in favour of themselves, which is extremely natural, their decision is just, inasmuch as whatever contributes to their benefit is a general benefit, and advances the real public good." A commentator adds that this notion of the infallible perception by the people of their true interest, and their unerring pursuit of it, was very prevalent in the provinces, and for a time in the States after the establishment of American independence.

In spite of their democratic spirit, these communities consented to have their trade regulated and restricted, to their own detriment and the advantage of English merchants. They had protested, but they had ended by yielding. Now Adam Smith says that to prohibit a great people from making all they can of every part of their own produce, or from employing their stock and industry in the way that they judge most advantageous for themselves, is a manifest violation of the most sacred rights of mankind. There was a latent sense of injury which broke out when, in addition to interference with the freedom of trade, England exercised the right of taxation. An American lately wrote: " The real foundation of the discontent which led to the Revolution was the effort of Great Britain, beginning in 1750, to prevent diversity of occupation, to attack the growth of manufactures and the mechanic arts, and the final cause before the attempt to tax without representation was the effort to enforce the navigation laws." When England argued that the hardship of regulation might be greater than the hardship of taxation, and that those who submitted to the one submitted, in principle, to the other, Franklin replied that the Americans had not taken that view, but that, when it was put before them, they would be willing to reject both one and the other. He knew, however, that the ground taken up by his countrymen was too narrow. He wrote to the French economist, Morellet: "Nothing can be better expressed than your sentiments are on this point, where you prefer liberty of trading, cultivating, manufacturing, etc., even to civil liberty, this being affected but rarely, the other every hour."

These early authors of American independence were generally enthusiasts for the British Constitution, and preceded Burke in the tendency to canonise it, and to magnify it as an ideal exemplar for nations. John Adams said, in 1766: "Here lies the difference between the British Constitution and other forms of government, namely, that liberty is its end, its use, its designation, drift and scope, as much as grinding corn is the use of a mill." Another celebrated Bostonian identified the Constitution with the law of Nature, as Montesquieu called the Civil Law, written Reason. He said: "It is the glory of the British prince and the happiness of all his subjects, that their constitution hath its foundation in the immutable laws of Nature; and as the supreme legislative, as well as the supreme executive, derives its authority from that constitution, it should seem that no laws can be made or executed that are repugnant to any essential law in Nature." The writer of these words, James Otis, is the founder of the revolutionary doctrine. Describing one of his pamphlets, the second President says:

"Look over the declaration of rights and wrongs issued by Congress in 1774; look into the declaration of independence in 1776; look into the writings of Dr. Price and Dr. Priestley; look into all the French constitutions of government; and, to cap the climax, look into Mr. Thomas Paine's Common Sense, Crisis, and Rights of Man. What can you find that is not to be found in solid substance in this 'Vindication of the House of Representatives'?" When these men found that the appeal to the law and the constitution did not avail them, that the king, by bribing the people's representatives with the people's money, was able to enforce his will, they sought a higher tribunal, and turned from the law of England to the law of Nature, and from the king of England to the King of kings. Otis, in 1762, 1764 and 1765, says: "Most governments are, in fact, arbitrary, and consequently the curse and scandal of human nature; yet none are of right arbitrary. By the laws of God and nature, government must not raise taxes on the property of the people without the consent of the people or their deputies. There can be no prescription old enough to supersede the law of Nature and the grant of God Almighty, who has given all men a right to be free. If a man has but little property to protect and defend, yet his life and liberty are things of some importance." About the same time Gadsden wrote: "A confirmation of our essential and common rights as Englishmen may be pleaded from charters clearly enough; but any further dependence on them may be fatal. We should stand upon broad common ground of those natural rights that we all feel and know as men and as descendants of Englishmen."

The primitive fathers of the United States began by preferring abstract moral principle to the letter of the law and the spirit of the Constitution. But they went farther. Not only was their grievance difficult to substantiate at law, but it was trivial in extent. The claim of England was not evidently disproved, and even if it was unjust, the injustice practically was not hard to bear. The suffering that would be caused by submission was immeasurably less than the suffering that must follow resistance, and it was more uncertain and remote. The utilitarian argument was loud in favour of obedience and loyalty. But if interest was on one side, there was a manifest principle on the other—a principle so sacred and so clear as imperatively to demand the sacrifice of men's lives, of their families and their fortune. They resolved to give up everything, not to escape from actual oppression, but to honour a precept of unwritten law. That was the transatlantic discovery in the theory of political duty, the light that came over the ocean. It represented liberty not as a comparative release from tyranny, but as a thing so divine that the existence of society must be staked to prevent even the least constructive infraction of its sovereign right. "A free people," said Dickinson, "can never be too quick in observing nor too firm in opposing the beginnings of alteration either in form or reality, respecting institutions formed for their security. The first kind of alteration leads to the last. As violations of the rights of the governed are commonly not only specious, but small at the beginning, they spread over the multitude in such a manner as to touch individuals but slightly. Every free state should incessantly watch, and instantly take alarm at any addition being made to the power exercised over them." Who are a free people? Not those over whom government is reasonably and equitably exercised; but those who live under a government so constitutionally checked and controlled that proper provision is made against its being otherwise exercised. The contest was plainly a contest of principle, and was conducted entirely on principle by both parties. "The amount of taxes proposed to be raised," said Marshall, the greatest of constitutional lawyers, "was too inconsiderate to interest the people of either country." I will add the words of Daniel Webster, the great expounder of the Constitution, who is the most eloquent of the Americas, and stands, in politics, next to Burke: "The Parliament of Great Britain asserted a right to tax the Colonies in all cases whatsoever; and it was precisely on this question that they made the Revolution turn. The amount of taxation was trifling, but the claim itself was inconsistent with liberty, and that was in their eyes enough. It was against the recital of an act of Parliament, rather than against any suffering under its enactment, that they took up arms. They went to war against a preamble. They fought seven years against a declaration. They saw in the claim of the British Parliament a seminal principle of mischief, the germ of unjust power."

The object of these men was liberty, not independence. Their feeling was expressed by Jay in his address to the people of Great Britain: "Permit us to be as free as yourselves, and we shall ever esteem a union with you to be our greatest glory and our greatest happiness." Before 1775 there was no question of separation. During all the Revolution Adams declared that he would have given everything to restore things as before with security; and both Jefferson and Madison admitted in the presence of the English minister that a few seats in both Houses would have set at rest the whole question.

In their appeal to the higher law the Americans professed the purest Whiggism, and they claimed that their resistance to the House of Commons and the jurisprudence of Westminster only carried forward the eternal conflict between Whig and Tory. By their closer analysis, and their fearlessness of logical consequences, they transformed the doctrine and modified the party. The uprooted Whig, detached from his parchments and precedents, his leading families and historic conditions, exhibited new qualities; and the era of compromise made way for an era of principle. Whilst French diplomacy traced the long hand of the English opposition in the tea riots at Boston, Chatham and Camden were feeling the influence of Dickinson and Otis, without recognising the difference. It appears in a passage of one of Chatham's speeches, in 1775: "This universal opposition to your arbitrary system of taxation might have been foreseen. It was obvious from the nature of things, and from the nature of man, and, above all, from the confirmed habits of thinking, from the spirit of Whiggism flourishing in America. The spirit which now pervades America is the same which formerly opposed loans, benevolences, and ship-money in this country, is the same spirit which roused all England to action at the Revolution, and which established at a remote era your liberties, on the basis of that grand fundamental maxim of the Constitution, that no subject of England shall be taxed but by his own consent. To maintain this principle is the common cause of the Whigs on the other side of the Atlantic, and on this. It is the alliance of God and Nature, immutable, eternal, fixed as the firmament of heaven. Resistance to your acts was necessary as it was just; and your vain declarations of the omnipotence of parliament, and your imperious doctrines of the necessity of submission will be found equally impotent to convince or enslave your fellow-subjects in America."

The most significant instance of the action of America on Europe is Edmund Burke. We think of him as a man who, in early life, rejected all generalities and abstract propositions, and who became the most strenuous and violent of conservatives. But there is an interval when, as the quarrel with the Colonies went on, Burke was as revolutionary as Washington. The inconsistency is not as flagrant as it seems. He had been brought forward by the party of measured propriety and imperative moderation, of compromise and unfinished thought, who claimed the right of taxing, but refused to employ it. When he urged the differences in every situation and every problem, and shrank from the common denominator and the underlying principle, he fell into step with his friends. As an Irishman, who had married into an Irish Catholic family, it was desirable that he should adopt no theories in America which would unsettle Ireland. He had learned to teach government by party as an almost sacred dogma, and party forbids revolt as a breach of the laws of the game. His scruples and his protests, and his defiance of theory, were the policy and the precaution of a man conscious of restraints, and not entirely free in the exertion of powers that lifted him far above his tamer surroundings. As the strife sharpened and the Americans made way, Burke was carried along, and developed views which he never utterly abandoned, but which are difficult to reconcile with much that he wrote when the Revolution had spread to France.

In his address to the Colonists he says: "We do not know how to qualify millions of our countrymen, contending with one heart for an admission to privileges which we have ever thought our own happiness and honour, by odious and unworthy names. On the contrary, we highly revere the principles on which you act. We had much rather see you totally independent of this crown and kingdom, than joined to it by so unnatural a conjunction as that of freedom and servitude. We view the establishment of the English Colonies on principles of liberty, as that which is to render this kingdom venerable to future ages. In comparison of this, we regard all the victories and conquests of our warlike ancestors, or of our own times, as barbarous, vulgar distinctions, in which many nations, whom we look upon with little respect or value, have equalled, if not far exceeded us. Those who have and who hold to that foundation of common liberty, whether on this or on your side of the ocean, we consider as the true and the only true Englishmen. Those who depart from it, whether there or here, are attained, corrupted in blood, and wholly fallen from their original rank and value. They are the real rebels to the fair constitution and just supremacy of England. A long course of war with the administration of this country may be but a prelude to a series of wars and contentions among yourselves, to end at length (as such scenes have too often ended) in a species of humiliating repose, which, nothing but the preceding calamities would reconcile to the dispirited few who survived them. We allow that even this evil is worth the risk to men of honour when national liberty is at stake, as in the present case we confess and lament that it is."

At other times he spoke as follows: "Nothing less than a convulsion that will shake the globe to its centre can ever restore the European nations to that liberty by which they were once so much distinguished. The Western world was the seat of freedom until another, more Western, was discovered; and that other will probably be its asylum when it is hunted down in every other part. Happy it is that the worst of times may have one refuge still left for humanity. If the Irish resisted King William, they resisted him on the very same principle that the English and Scotch resisted King James. The Irish Catholics must have been the very worst and the most truly unnatural of rebels, if they had not supported a prince whom they had seen attacked, not for any designs against their religion or their liberties, but for an extreme partiality for their sect. Princes otherwise meritorious have violated the liberties of the people, and have been lawfully deposed for such violation. I know no human being exempt from the law. I consider Parliament as the proper judge of kings, and it is necessary that they should be amenable to it. There is no such thing as governing the whole body of the people contrary to their inclination. Whenever they have a feeling they commonly are in the right. Christ appeared in sympathy with the lowest of the people, and thereby made it a firm and ruling principle that their welfare was the object of all government.

"In all forms of government the people is the true legislator. The remote and efficient cause is the consent of the people, either actual or implied, and such consent is absolutely essential to its validity. Whiggism did not consist in the support of the power of Parliament or of any other power, but of the rights of the people. If Parliament should become an instrument in invading them, it was no better in any respect, and much worse in some, than any other instrument of arbitrary power. They who call upon you to belong wholly to the people are those who wish you to belong to your proper home, to the sphere of your duty, to the post of your honour. Let the Commons in Parliament assembled be one and the same thing with the Commons at large. I see no other way for the preservation of a decent attention to public interest in the representatives, but the interposition of the body of the people itself, whenever, it shall appear by some flagrant and notorious act, by some capital innovation, that those representatives are going to overleap the fences of the law and to introduce an arbitrary power. This interposition is a most unpleasant remedy; but if it be legal remedy, it is intended on some occasion to be used- to be used then only when it is evident that nothing else can hold the Constitution to its true principles. It is not in Parliament alone that the remedy for parliamentary disorders can be completed; hardly, indeed, can it begin there. Popular origin cannot therefore be the characteristic distinction of a popular representative. This belongs equally to all parts of government, and in all forms. The virtue, spirit, and essence of a House of Commons consists in its being the express image of the feelings of the nation. It was not instituted to be a control upon the people. It was designed as a control for the people. Privilege of the crown and privilege of Parliament are only privilege so long as they are exercised for the benefit of the people. The voice of the people is a voice that is to be heard, and not the votes and resolutions of the House of Commons. He would preserve thoroughly every privilege of the people, because it is a privilege known and written in the law of the land; and he would support it, not against the crown or the aristocratic party only, but against the representatives of the people themselves. This was not a government of balances. It would be a strange thing if two hundred peers should have it in their power to defeat by their negative what had been done by the people of England. I have taken my part in political connections and political quarrels for the purpose of advancing justice and the dominion of reason, and I hope I shall never prefer the means, or any feelings growing out of the use of those means, to the great and substantial end itself. Legislators can do what lawyers can not, for they have no other rules to bind them but the great principles of reason and equity and the general sense of mankind. All human laws are, properly speaking, only declaratory; they may alter the mode and application, but have no power over the substance, of original justice. A conservation and secure enjoyment of our natural rights is the great and ultimate purpose of civil society.

"The great inlet by which a colour for oppression has entered into the world is by one man's pretending to determine concerning the happiness of another. I would give a full civil protection, in which I include an immunity from all disturbance of their public religious worship, and a power of teaching in schools as well as temples, to Jews, Mahometans, and even Pagans. The Christian religion itself arose without establishment, it arose even without toleration, and whilst its own principles were not tolerated, it conquered all the powers of darkness, it conquered all the powers of the world. The moment it began to depart from these principles, it converted the establishment into tyranny, it subverted its foundation from that very hour. It is the power of government to prevent much evil; it can do very little positive good in this, or perhaps in anything else. It is not only so of the State and statesman, but of all the classes and descriptions of the rich: they are the pensioners of the poor, and are maintained by their superfluity They are under an absolute, hereditary, and indefeasible dependence on those who labour and are miscalled the poor. That class of dependent pensioners called the rich is so extremely small that if all their throats were cut, and a distribution made of all they consume in a year, it would not give a bit of bread and cheese for one night's supper to those who labour, and who in reality feed both the pensioners and themselves. It is not in breaking the laws of commerce, which are the laws of nature and consequently the laws of God, that we are to place our hope of softening the divine displeasure. It is the law of nature, which is the law of God."

I cannot resist the inference from these passages that Burke, after 1770, underwent other influences than those of his reputed masters, the Whigs of 1688. And if we find that strain of unwonted thought in a man who afterwards gilded the old order of things and wavered as to toleration and the slave trade, we may expect that the same causes would operate in France.

When the *Letters of a Pennsylvanian Farmer* became known in Europe, Diderot said that it was madness to allow Frenchmen to read such things, as they could not do it without becoming intoxicated and changed into different men. But France was impressed by the event more than by the literature that accompanied it. America had made herself independent under less provocation than had ever been a motive of revolt, and the French Government had acknowledged that her cause was righteous and had gone to war for it. If the king was right in America, he was utterly wrong at home, and if the Americans acted rightly, the argument was stronger, the cause was a hundredfold better, in France itself. All that justified their independence condemned the Government of their French allies. By the principle that taxation without representation is robbery, there was no authority so illegitimate as that of Lewis XVI. The force of that demonstration was irresistible, and it produced its effect where the example of England failed. The English doctrine was repelled at the very earliest stage of the Revolution, and the American was adopted. What the French took from the Americans was their theory of revolution, not their theory of government—their cutting, not their sewing. Many French nobles served in the war, and came home republicans and even democrats by conviction. It was America that converted the aristocracy to the reforming policy, and gave leaders to the Revolution. " The American Revolution," says Washington, "or the peculiar light of the age, seems to have opened the eyes of almost every nation in Europe, and a spirit of equal liberty appears fast to be gaining ground everywhere." When the French officers were leaving, Cooper, of Boston, addressed them in the language of warning: "Do not let your hopes be inflamed by our triumphs on this virgin soil. You will carry our sentiments with you, but if you try to plant them in a country that has been corrupt for centuries, you will encounter obstacles more formidable than ours. Our liberty has been won with blood; you will have to shed it in torrents before liberty can take root in the old world." Adams, after he had been President of the United States, bitterly regretted the Revolution which made them independent, because it had given the example to the French; although he also believed that they had not a single principle in common.

Nothing, on the contrary, is more certain than that American principles profoundly influenced France, and determined the course of the revolution. It is from America that Lafayette derived the saying that created a commotion at the time, that resistance is the most sacred of duties. There also was the theory that political power comes from those over whom it is exercised, and depends upon their will; that every authority not so constituted is illegitimate and precarious; that the past is more a warning than an example; that the earth belongs to those who are upon it, not to those who are underneath. These are characteristics common to both Revolutions.

At one time also the French adopted and acclaimed the American notion that the end of government is liberty, not happiness, or prosperity, or power, or the preservation of an historic inheritance, or the adaptation of national law to national character, or the progress of enlightenment and the promotion of virtue; that the private individual should not feel the pressure of public authority, and should direct his life by the influences that are within him, not around him.

And there was another political doctrine which the Americans transmitted to the French. In old colonial days the executive and the judicial powers were derived from a foreign source, and the common purpose was to diminish them. The assemblies were popular in origin and character, and everything that added to their power seemed to add security to rights. James Wilson, one of the authors and commentators of the constitution, informs us that "at the Revolution the same fond predilection, and the same jealous dislike, existed and prevailed. The executive, and the judicial as well as the legislative authority, was now the child of the people, but to the two former the people behaved like stepmothers. The legislature was still discriminated by excessive partiality." This preference, historic but irrational, led up naturally to a single chamber. The people of America and their delegates in Congress were of opinion that a single Assembly was every way adequate to the management of their federal concerns, and when the Senate was invented, Franklin strongly objected. "As to the two chambers," he wrote, "I am of your opinion that one alone would be better; but, my dear friend, nothing in human affairs and schemes is perfect, and perhaps this is the case of our opinions."

Alexander Hamilton was the ablest as well as the most conservative of the American statesmen. He longed for monarchy, and he desired to establish a national government and to annihilate state rights. The American spirit, as it penetrated France, cannot well be described better than it was by him: "I consider civil liberty, in a genuine, unadulterated sense, as the greatest of terrestrial blessings. I am convinced that the whole human race is entitled to it, and that it can be wrested from no part of them without the blackest and most aggravated guilt. The sacred rights of mankind are not to be rummaged for among old parchments or musty records. They are written, as with a sunbeam, in the whole volume of human nature, by the hand of the Divinity itself, and can never be erased or obscured by mortal power."

But when we speak in the gross of the American Revolution we combine different and discordant things. From the first agitation in 1776 to the Declaration of Independence, and then to the end of the war in 1782, the Americans were aggressive, violent in their language, fond of abstractions, prolific of doctrines universally applicable and universally destructive. It is the ideas of those earlier days that roused the attention of France, and were imported by Lafayette, Noailles, Lameth, and the leaders of the future revolution who had beheld the lowering of the British flag at Yorktown. The America of their experience was the America of James Otis, of Jefferson, of The Rights of Man.

A change followed in 1787, when the Convention drew up the Constitution. It was a period of construction, and every effort was made, every scheme was invented, to curb the inevitable democracy. The members of that assembly were, on the whole, eminently cautious and sensible men. They were not men of extraordinary parts, and the genius of Hamilton failed absolutely to impress them. Some of their most memorable contrivances proceeded from no design, but were merely half measures and mutual concessions. Seward has pointed out this distinction between the revolutionary epoch and the constituent epoch that succeeded: "The rights asserted by our forefathers were not peculiar to themselves. They were the common rights of mankind. The basis of the Constitution was laid broader by far than the superstructure which the conflicting interests and prejudices of the day suffered to be erected. The Constitution and laws of the Federal Government did not practically extend those principles throughout the new system of government; but they were plainly promulgated in the Declaration of Independence."

Now, although France was deeply touched by the American Revolution, it was not affected by the American Constitution. It underwent the disturbing influence, not the conservative.

The Constitution, framed in the summer of 1787, came into operation in March 1789, and nobody knew how it worked, when the crisis came in France. The debates, which explain every intention and combination, remained long ridden from the world. Moreover, the Constitution has become something more than the original printed paper. Besides amendments, it has been interpreted by the courts, modified by opinion, developed in some directions, and tacitly altered in others. Some of its most valued provisions have been acquired in this way, and were not yet visible when the French so greatly needed the guiding lessons of other men's experience. Some of the restrictions on the governing power were not fully established at first.

The most important of these is the action of the Supreme Court in annulling unconstitutional laws. The Duke of Wellington said to Bunsen that by this institution alone the United States made up for all the defects of their government. Since Chief Justice Marshall, the judiciary undoubtedly obtained immense authority, which Jefferson, and others besides, believed to be unconstitutional; for the Constitution itself gives no such power. The idea had grown up in the States, chiefly, I think, in Virginia. At Richmond, in 1781, Judge Wythe said: "Tyranny has been sapped, the departments kept within their own spheres, the citizens protected, and general liberty promoted. But this beneficial result attains to higher perfection when, those who hold the purse and the sword differing as to the powers which each may exercise, the tribunals, who hold neither, are called upon to declare the law impartially between them. If the whole legislature—an event to be deprecated—should attempt to overleap the boundaries prescribed to them by the people, I, in administering the justice of the country, will meet the united powers at my seat in this tribunal, and, pointing to the Constitution, will say to them: 'Here is the limit of your authority; hither shall you go, but no further.'" The Virginian legislature gave way, and repealed the act.

After the Federal Constitution was drawn up, Hamilton, in the seventy-eighth number of the Federalist, argued that the power belonged to the judiciary; but it was not constitutionally recognized until 1801. "This," said Madison, "makes the judiciary department paramount, in fact, to the legislature, which was never intended, and can never be proper. In a government whose vital principle is responsibility, it never will be allowed that the legislative and executive departments should be completely subjected to the judiciary, in which that characteristic feature is so faintly seen." Wilson, on the other hand, justified the practice on the principle of the higher law: "Parliament may, unquestionably, be controlled by natural or revealed law, proceeding from divine authority. Is not this superior authority binding upon the courts of justice? When the courts of justice obey the superior authority, it cannot be said with propriety that they control the inferior one; they only declare, as it is their duty to declare, that this inferior one is controlled by the other, which is superior. They do not repeal an act of Parliament; they pronounce it void, because contrary to an overruling law." Thus the function of the judiciary to be a barrier against democracy, which, according to Tocqueville, it is destined to be, was not apparent. In the same manner religious liberty, which has become so much identified with the United States, is a thing which grew by degrees, and was not to be found imposed by the letter of the law.

The true natural check on absolute democracy is the federal system, which limits the central government by the powers reserved, and the state governments by the powers they have ceded. It is the one immortal tribute of America to political science, for state rights are at the same time the consummation and the guard of democracy. So much so that an officer wrote, a few months before Bull Run: "The people in the south are evidently unanimous in the opinion that slavery is endangered by the current of events, and it is useless to attempt to alter that opinion. As our government is founded on the will of the people, when that will is fixed our government is powerless." Those are the words of Sherman, the man who, by his march through Georgia, cut the Confederacy into two. Lincoln himself wrote, at the same time: "I declare that the maintenance inviolate of the rights of the states, and especially the right of each state to order and control its own domestic institutions according to its own judgment exclusively, is essential to that balance of powers on which the perfection and endurance of our political fabric depend." Such was the force with which state rights held the minds of abolitionists on the eve of the war that bore them down.

At the Revolution there were many Frenchmen who saw in federalism the only way to reconcile liberty and democracy, to establish government on contract, and to rescue the country from the crushing preponderance of Paris and the Parisian populace. I do not mean the Girondins, but men of opinions different from theirs, and, above all, Mirabeau. He planned to save the throne by detaching the provinces from the frenzy of the capital, and he declared that the federal system is alone capable of preserving freedom in any great empire. The idea did not grow up under American influence; for no man was more opposed to it than Lafayette; and the American witness of the Revolution, Morris, denounced federalism as a danger to France.

Apart from the Constitution, the political thought of America influenced the French next to their own. And it was not all speculation, but a system for which men died, which had proved entirely practical, and strong enough to conquer all resistance, with the sanction and encouragement of Europe. It displayed to France a finished model of revolution, both in thought and action, and showed that what seemed extreme and subversive in the old world, was compatible with good and wise government, with respect for social order, and the preservation of national character and custom. The ideas which captured and convulsed the French people were mostly ready-made for them, and much that is familiar to you now, much of that which I have put before you from other than French sources, will meet us again next week with the old faces, when we come to the States-General.

PART III

SELF-, DECENTRALIZED, AND LIMITED GOVERNMENT

James Madison on Responsive Government

James Madison, Federalist No. 46, Jan. 29, 1788.

*James Madison (1751–1836) later became the
fourth President of the United States.*

MADISON
To the People of the State of New York:

RESUMING the subject of the last paper, I proceed to inquire whether the federal government or the State governments will have the advantage with regard to the predilection and support of the people. Notwithstanding the different modes in which they are appointed, we must consider both of them as substantially dependent on the great body of the citizens of the United States. I assume this position here as it respects the first, reserving the proofs for another place. The federal and State governments are in fact but different agents and trustees of the people, constituted with different powers, and designed for different purposes. The adversaries of the Constitution seem to have lost sight of the people altogether in their reasonings on this subject; and to have viewed these different establishments, not only as mutual rivals and enemies, but as uncontrolled by any common superior in their efforts to usurp the authorities of each other. These gentlemen must here be reminded of their error. They must be told that the ultimate authority, wherever the derivative may be found, resides in the people alone, and that it will not depend merely on the comparative ambition or address of the different governments, whether either, or which of them, will be able to enlarge its sphere of jurisdiction at the expense of the other. Truth, no less than decency, requires that the event in every case should be supposed to depend on the sentiments and sanction of their common constituents.

Many considerations, besides those suggested on a former occasion, seem to place it beyond doubt that the first and most natural attachment of the people will be to the governments of their respective States. Into the administration of these a greater number of individuals will expect to rise. From the gift of these a greater number of offices and emoluments will flow. By the superintending care of these, all the more domestic and personal interests of the people will be regulated and provided for. With the affairs of these, the people will be more familiarly and minutely conversant. And with the members of these, will a greater proportion of the people have the ties of personal acquaintance and friendship, and of family and party attachments; on the side of these, therefore, the popular bias may well be expected most strongly to incline.

Experience speaks the same language in this case. The federal administration, though hitherto very defective in comparison with what may be hoped under a better system, had, during the war, and particularly whilst the independent fund of paper emissions was in credit, an activity and importance as great as it can well have in any future circumstances whatever. It was engaged, too, in a course of measures which had for their object the protection of everything that was dear, and the acquisition of everything that could be desirable to the people at large. It was, nevertheless, invariably found, after the transient enthusiasm for the early Congresses was over, that the attention and attachment of the people were turned anew to their own particular governments; that the federal council was at no time the idol of popular favor; and that opposition to proposed enlargements of its powers and importance was the side usually taken by the men who wished to build their political consequence on the prepossessions of their fellow-citizens.

If, therefore, as has been elsewhere remarked, the people should in future become more partial to the federal than to the State governments, the change can only result from such manifest and irresistible proofs of a better administration, as will overcome all their antecedent propensities. And in that case, the people ought not surely to be precluded from giving most of their confidence where they may discover it to be most due; but even in that case the State governments could have little to apprehend, because it is only within a certain sphere that the federal power can, in the nature of things, be advantageously administered.

The remaining points on which I propose to compare the federal and State governments, are the disposition and the faculty they may respectively possess, to resist and frustrate the measures of each other.

It has been already proved that the members of the federal will be more dependent on the members of the State governments, than the latter will be on the former. It has appeared also, that the prepossessions of the people, on whom both will depend, will be more on the side of the State governments, than of the federal government. So far as the disposition of each towards the other may be influenced by these causes, the State governments must clearly have the advantage. But in a distinct and very important point of view, the advantage will lie on the same side. The prepossessions, which the members themselves will carry into the federal government, will generally be favorable to the States; whilst it will rarely happen, that the members of the State governments will carry into the public councils a bias in favor of the general government. A local spirit will infallibly prevail much more in the members of Congress, than a national spirit will prevail in the legislatures of the particular States. Every one knows that a great proportion of the errors committed by the State legislatures proceeds from the disposition of the members to sacrifice the comprehensive and permanent interest of the State, to the particular and separate views of the counties or districts in which they reside. And if they do not sufficiently enlarge their policy to embrace the collective welfare of their particular State, how can it be imagined that they will make the aggregate prosperity of the Union, and the dignity and respectability of its government, the objects of their affections and consultations? For the same reason that the members of the State legislatures will be unlikely to attach themselves sufficiently to national objects, the members of the federal legislature will be likely to attach themselves too much to local objects. The States will be to the latter what counties and towns are to the former. Measures will too often be decided according to their probable effect, not on the national prosperity and happiness, but on the prejudices, interests, and pursuits of the governments and people of the individual States. What is the spirit that has in general characterized the proceedings of Congress? A perusal of their journals, as well as the candid acknowledgments of such as have had a seat in that assembly, will inform us, that the members have but too frequently displayed the character, rather of partisans of their respective States, than of impartial guardians of a common interest; that where on one occasion improper sacrifices have been made of local considerations, to the aggrandizement of the federal government, the great interests of the nation have suffered on a hundred, from an undue attention to the local prejudices, interests, and views of the particular States. I mean not by these reflections to insinuate, that the new federal government will not embrace a more enlarged plan of policy than the existing government may have pursued; much less, that its views will be as confined as those of the State legislatures; but only that it will partake sufficiently of the spirit of both, to be disinclined to invade the rights of the individual States, or the preorgatives of their governments. The motives on the part of the State governments, to augment their prerogatives by defalcations from the federal government, will be overruled by no reciprocal predispositions in the members.

Were it admitted, however, that the Federal government may feel an equal disposition with the State governments to extend its power beyond the due limits, the latter would still have the advantage in the means of defeating such encroachments. If an act of a particular State, though unfriendly to the national government, be generally popular in that State and should not too grossly violate the oaths of the State officers, it is executed immediately and, of course, by means on the spot and depending on the State alone. The opposition of the federal government, or the interposition of federal officers, would but inflame the zeal of all parties on the side of the State, and the evil could not be prevented or repaired, if at all, without the employment of means which must always be resorted to with reluctance and difficulty. On the other hand, should an unwarrantable measure of the federal government be unpopular in particular States, which would seldom fail to be the case, or even a warrantable measure be so, which may sometimes be the case, the means of opposition to it are powerful and at hand. The disquietude of the people; their repugnance and, perhaps, refusal to co-operate with the officers of the Union; the frowns of the executive magistracy of the State; the embarrassments created by legislative devices, which would often be added on such occasions, would oppose, in any State, difficulties not to be despised; would form, in a large State, very serious impediments; and where the sentiments of several adjoining States happened to be in unison, would present obstructions which the federal government would hardly be willing to encounter.

But ambitious encroachments of the federal government, on the authority of the State governments, would not excite the opposition of a single State, or of a few States only. They would be signals of general alarm. Every government would espouse the common cause. A correspondence would be opened. Plans of resistance would be concerted. One spirit would animate and conduct the whole. The same combinations, in short, would result from an apprehension of the federal, as was produced by the dread of a foreign, yoke; and unless the projected innovations should be voluntarily renounced, the same appeal to a trial of force would be made in the one case as was made in the other. But what degree of madness could ever drive the federal government to such an extremity. In the contest with Great Britain, one part of the empire was employed against the other. The more numerous part invaded the rights of the less numerous part. The attempt was unjust and unwise; but it was not in speculation absolutely chimerical. But what would be the contest in the case we are supposing? Who would be the parties? A few representatives of the people would be opposed to the people themselves; or rather one set of representatives would be contending against thirteen sets of representatives, with the whole body of their common constituents on the side of the latter.

The only refuge left for those who prophesy the downfall of the State governments is the visionary supposition that the federal government may previously accumulate a military force for the projects of ambition. The reasonings contained in these papers must have been employed to little purpose indeed, if it could be necessary now to disprove the reality of this danger. That the people and the States should, for a sufficient period of time, elect an uninterupted succession of men ready to betray both; that the traitors should, throughout this period, uniformly

and systematically pursue some fixed plan for the extension of the military establishment; that the governments and the people of the States should silently and
patiently behold the gathering storm, and continue to supply the materials, until
it should be prepared to burst on their own heads, must appear to every one more
like the incoherent dreams of a delirious jealousy, or the misjudged exaggerations of
a counterfeit zeal, than like the sober apprehensions of genuine patriotism.
Extravagant as the supposition is, let it however be made. Let a regular army, fully
equal to the resources of the country, be formed; and let it be entirely at the devotion of the federal government; still it would not be going too far to say, that the
State governments, with the people on their side, would be able to repel the danger.
The highest number to which, according to the best computation, a standing army
can be carried in any country, does not exceed one hundredth part of the whole
number of souls; or one twenty-fifth part of the number able to bear arms. This
proportion would not yield, in the United States, an army of more than twenty-five
or thirty thousand men. To these would be opposed a militia amounting to near
half a million of citizens with arms in their hands, officered by men chosen from
among themselves, fighting for their common liberties, and united and conducted
by governments possessing their affections and confidence. It may well be doubted,
whether a militia thus circumstanced could ever be conquered by such a proportion
of regular troops. Those who are best acquainted with the last successful resistance
of this country against the British arms, will be most inclined to deny the possibility of it. Besides the advantage of being armed, which the Americans possess over
the people of almost every other nation, the existence of subordinate governments,
to which the people are attached, and by which the militia officers are appointed,
forms a barrier against the enterprises of ambition, more insurmountable than any
which a simple government of any form can admit of. Notwithstanding the military establishments in the several kingdoms of Europe, which are carried as far as
the public resources will bear, the governments are afraid to trust the people with
arms. And it is not certain, that with this aid alone they would not be able to shake
off their yokes. But were the people to possess the additional advantages of local
governments chosen by themselves, who could collect the national will and direct
the national force, and of officers appointed out of the militia, by these governments, and attached both to them and to the militia, it may be affirmed with the
greatest assurance, that the throne of every tyranny in Europe would be speedily
overturned in spite of the legions which surround it. Let us not insult the free and
gallant citizens of America with the suspicion, that they would be less able to defend
the rights of which they would be in actual possession, than the debased subjects of
arbitrary power would be to rescue theirs from the hands of their oppressors. Let us

rather no longer insult them with the supposition that they can ever reduce themselves to the necessity of making the experiment, by a blind and tame submission to the long train of insidious measures which must precede and produce it.

The argument under the present head may be put into a very concise form, which appears altogether conclusive. Either the mode in which the federal government is to be constructed will render it sufficiently dependent on the people, or it will not. On the first supposition, it will be restrained by that dependence from forming schemes obnoxious to their constituents. On the other supposition, it will not possess the confidence of the people, and its schemes of usurpation will be easily defeated by the State governments, who will be supported by the people.

On summing up the considerations stated in this and the last paper, they seem to amount to the most convincing evidence, that the powers proposed to be lodged in the federal government are as little formidable to those reserved to the individual States, as they are indispensably necessary to accomplish the purposes of the Union; and that all those alarms which have been sounded, of a meditated and consequential annihilation of the State governments, must, on the most favorable interpretation, be ascribed to the chimerical fears of the authors of them.

Tocqueville on Local Administration

Excerpted from Alexis de Tocqueville, Democracy in America,
Part I (1835), Chap. V and XVI.

Alexis de Tocqueville (1805–1859) was a French political scientist.

"CENTRALIZATION" is a word in general and daily use, without any precise meaning being attached to it. Nevertheless, there exist two distinct kinds of centralization, which it is necessary to discriminate with accuracy.

Certain interests are common to all parts of a nation, such as the enactment of its general laws and the maintenance of its foreign relations. Other interests are peculiar to certain parts of the nation, such, for instance, as the business of the several townships. When the power that directs the former or general interests is concentrated in one place or in the same persons, it constitutes a centralized government. To concentrate in like manner in one place the direction of the latter or local interests, constitutes what may be termed a centralized administration.

Upon some points these two kinds of centralization coincide, but by classifying the objects which fall more particularly within the province of each, they may easily be distinguished.

It is evident that a centralized government acquires immense power when united to centralized administration. Thus combined, it accustoms men to set their own will habitually and completely aside; to submit, not only for once, or upon one point, but in every respect, and at all times. Not only, therefore, does this union of power subdue them compulsorily, but it affects their ordinary habits; it isolates them and then influences each separately.

These two kinds of centralization assist and attract each other, but they must not be supposed to be inseparable. It is impossible to imagine a more completely centralized government than that which existed in France under Louis XIV; when the same individual was the author and the interpreter of the laws, and the representative of France at home and abroad, he was justified in asserting that he constituted the state. Nevertheless, the administration was much less centralized under Louis XIV than it is at the present day.

In England the centralization of the government is carried to great perfection; the state has the compact vigor of one man, and its will puts immense masses in motion and turns its whole power where it pleases. But England, which has done such great things for the last fifty years, has never centralized its administration.

Indeed, I cannot conceive that a nation can live and prosper without a powerful centralization of government. But I am of the opinion that a centralized administration is fit only to enervate the nations in which it exists, by incessantly diminishing their local spirit. Although such an administration can bring together at a given moment, on a given point, all the disposable resources of a people, it injures the renewal of those resources. It may ensure a victory in the hour of strife, but it gradually relaxes the sinews of strength. It may help admirably the transient greatness of a man, but not the durable prosperity of a nation.

Observe that whenever it is said that a state cannot act because it is not centralized, it is the centralization of the government that is spoken of. It is frequently asserted, and I assent to the proposition, that the German Empire has never been able to bring all its powers into action. But the reason is that the state has never been able to enforce obedience to its general laws; the several members of that great body always claimed the right, or found the means, of refusing their co-operation to the representatives of the common authority, even in the affairs that concerned the mass of the people; in other words, there was no centralization of government. The same remark is applicable to the Middle Ages; the cause of all the miseries of feudal society was that the control, not only of administration, but of government, was divided among a thousand hands and broken up in a thousand different ways. The want of a centralized government prevented the nations of Europe from advancing with energy in any straightforward course.

I have shown that in the United States there is no centralized administration and no hierarchy of public functionaries. Local authority has been carried farther than any European nation could endure without great inconvenience, and it has even produced some disadvantageous consequences in America. But in the United States the centralization of the government is perfect; and it would be easy to prove that the national power is more concentrated there than it has ever been in the old nations of Europe. Not only is there but one legislative body in each state, not only does there exist but one source of political authority, but numerous assemblies in districts or counties have not, in general, been multiplied lest they should be tempted to leave their administrative duties and interfere with the government. In America the legislature of each state is supreme; nothing can impede its authority, neither privileges, nor local immunities, nor personal influence, nor even the empire of reason, since it represents that majority which claims to be the sole organ of reason. Its own determination is therefore the only limit to its action. In juxtaposition with it, and under its immediate control, is the representative of the executive power, whose duty it is to constrain the refractory to submit by superior force. The only symptom of weakness lies in certain details of the action of the government. The American republics have no standing armies to intimidate a discontented minority; but as no minority has as yet been reduced to declare open war, the necessity of an army has not been felt. The state usually employs the officers of the township or the county to deal with the citizens. Thus, for instance, in New England the town assessor fixes the rate of taxes; the town collector receives them; the town treasurer transmits the amount to the public treasury; and the disputes that may arise are brought before the ordinary courts of justice. This method of collecting taxes is slow as well as inconvenient, and it would prove a perpetual hindrance to a government whose pecuniary demands were large. It is desirable that, in whatever materially affects its existence, the government should be served by officers of its own, appointed by itself, removable at its pleasure, and accustomed to rapid methods of proceeding. But it will always be easy for the central government, organized as it is in America, to introduce more energetic and efficacious modes of action according to its wants.

The want of a centralized government will not, then, as has often been asserted, prove the destruction of the republics of the New World; far from the American governments being not sufficiently centralized, I shall prove hereafter that they are too much so. The legislative bodies daily encroach upon the authority of the government, and their tendency, like that of the French Convention, is to appropriate it entirely to themselves. The social power thus centralized is constantly changing hands, because it is subordinate to the power of the people. It often forgets the maxims of wisdom and foresight in the consciousness of its strength. Hence arises its danger. Its vigor, and not its impotence, will probably be the cause of its ultimate destruction.

The system of decentralized administration produces several different effects in America. The Americans seem to me to have overstepped the limits of sound policy in isolating the administration of the government; for order, even in secondary affairs, is a matter of national importance. As the state has no administrative functionaries of its own, stationed on different points of its territory, to whom it can give a common impulse, the consequence is that it rarely attempts to issue any general police regulations. The want of these regulations is severely felt and is frequently observed by Europeans. The appearance of disorder which prevails on the surface leads one at first to imagine that society is in a state of anarchy; nor does one perceive one's mistake till one has gone deeper into the subject. Certain undertakings are of importance to the whole state; but they cannot be put in execution, because there is no state administration to direct them. Abandoned to the exertions of the towns or counties, under the care of elected and temporary agents, they lead to no result, or at least to no durable benefit.

The partisans of centralization in Europe are wont to maintain that the government can administer the affairs of each locality better than the citizens can do it for themselves. This may be true when the central power is enlightened and the local authorities are ignorant; when it is alert and they are slow; when it is accustomed to act and they to obey. Indeed, it is evident that this double tendency must augment with the increase of centralization, and that the readiness of the one and the incapacity of the others must become more and more prominent. But I deny that it is so when the people are as enlightened, as awake to their interests, and as accustomed to reflect on them as the Americans are. I am persuaded, on the contrary, that in this case the collective strength of the citizens will always conduce more efficacious to the public welfare than the authority of the government. I know it is difficult to point out with certainty the means of arousing a sleeping population and of giving it passions and knowledge which it does not possess; it is, I am well aware, an arduous task to persuade men to busy themselves about their own affairs. It would frequently be easier to interest them in the punctilios of court etiquette than in the repairs of their common dwelling. But whenever a central administration affects completely to supersede the desirous to mislead. However enlightened and skillfull a central power may be, it cannot of itself embrace all the details of the life of a great nation. Such vigilance exceeds the powers of man. And when it attempts unaided to create and set in motion so many complicated springs, it must submit to a very imperfect result or exhaust itself in bootless efforts.

Centralization easily succeeds, indeed, in subjecting the external actions of men to a certain uniformity, which we come at last to love for its own sake, independently of the objects to which it is applied, like those devotees who worship the statue and forget the deity it represents. Centralization imparts without difficulty an admirable regularity to the routine of business; provides skillfully for the details of the social police; represses small disorders and petty misdemeanors; maintains society in a status quo alike secure from improvement and decline; and perpetuates a drowsy regularity in the conduct of affairs which the heads of the administration are wont to call good order and public tranquillity; in short, it excels in prevention, but not in action. Its force deserts it when society is to be profoundly moved, or accelerated in its course; and if once the co-operation of private citizens is necessary to the furtherance of its measures, the secret of its impotence is disclosed. Even while the centralized power, in its despair, invokes the assistance of the citizens, it says to them: "You shall act just as I please, as much as I please, and in the direction which I please. You are to take charge of the details without aspiring to guide the system; you are to work in darkness; and afterwards you may judge my work by its results." These are not the conditions on which the alliance of the human will is to be obtained; it must be free in its gait and responsible for its acts, or (such is the constitution of man) the citizen had rather remain a passive spectator than a dependent actor in schemes with which he is unacquainted.

It is undeniable that the want of those uniform regulations which control the conduct of every inhabitant of France is not infrequently felt in the United States. Gross instances of social indifference and neglect are to be met with; and from time to time disgraceful blemishes are seen, in complete contrast with the surrounding civilization. Useful undertakings which cannot succeed without perpetual attention and rigorous exactitude are frequently abandoned; for in America, as well as in other countries, the people proceed by sudden impulses and momentary exertions. The European, accustomed to find a functionary always at hand to interfere with all he undertakes, reconciles himself with difficulty to the complex mechanism of the administration of the townships. In general it may be affirmed that the lesser details of the police, which render life easy and comfortable, are neglected in America, but that the essential guarantees of man in society are as strong there as elsewhere. In America the power that conducts the administration is far less regular, less enlightened, and less skillful, but a hundredfold greater than in Europe. In no country in the world do the citizens make such exertions for the common weal. I know of no people who have established schools so numerous and efficacious, places of public worship better suited to the wants of the inhabitants, or roads kept in better repair. Uniformity or permanence of design, the minute arrangement of details, and the perfection of administrative system must not be sought for in the United States; what we find there is the presence of a power which, if it is somewhat wild, is at least robust, and an existence checkered with accidents, indeed, but full of animation and effort.

Granting, for an instant, that the villages and counties of the United States would be more usefully governed by a central authority which they had never seen than by functionaries taken from among them; admitting, for the sake of argument, that there would be more security in America, and the resources of society would be better employed there, if the whole administration centered in a single arm—still the political advantages which the Americans derive from their decentralized system would induce me to prefer it to the contrary plan. It profits me but little, after all, that a vigilant authority always protects the tranquillity of my pleasures and constantly averts all dangers from my path, without my care or concern, if this same authority is the absolute master of my liberty and my life, and if it so monopolizes movement and life that when it languishes everything languishes around it, that when it sleeps everything must sleep, and that when it dies the state itself must perish.

There are countries in Europe where the native considers himself as a kind of settler, indifferent to the fate of the spot which he inhabits. The greatest changes are effected there without his concurrence, and (unless chance may have apprised him of the event) without his knowledge; nay, more, the condition of his village, the police of his street, the repairs of the church or the parsonage, do not concern him; for he looks upon all these things as unconnected with himself and as the property of a powerful stranger whom he calls the government. He has only a life interest in these possessions, without the spirit of ownership or any ideas of improvement. This want of interest in his own affairs goes so far that if his own safety or that of his children is at last endangered, instead of trying to avert the peril, he will fold his arms and wait till the whole nation comes to his aid. This man who has so completely sacrificed his own free will does not, more than any other person, love obedience; he cowers, it is true, before the pettiest officer, but he braves the law with the spirit of a conquered foe as soon as its superior force is withdrawn; he perpetually oscillates between servitude and license.

When a nation has arrived at this state, it must either change its customs and its laws, or perish; for the source of public virtues is dried up; and though it may contain subjects, it has no citizens. Such communities are a natural prey to foreign conquests; and if they do not wholly disappear from the scene, it is only because they are surrounded by other nations similar or inferior to themselves; it is because they still have an indefinable instinct of patriotism; and an involuntary pride in the name of their country, or a vague reminiscence of its bygone fame, suffices to give them an impulse of self-preservation.

Nor can the prodigious exertions made by certain nations to defend a country in which they had lived, so to speak, as strangers be adduced in favor of such a system; for it will be found that in these cases their main incitement was religion. The permanence, the glory, or the prosperity of the nation had become parts of their faith, and in defending their country, they defended also that Holy City of which they were all citizens. The Turkish tribes have never taken an active share in the conduct of their affairs, but they accomplished stupendous enterprises as long as the victories of the Sultan were triumphs of the Mohammedan faith. In the present age they are in rapid decay because their religion is departing and despotism only remains. Montesquieu, who attributed to absolute power an authority peculiar to itself, did it, as I conceive, an undeserved honor; for despotism, taken by itself, can maintain nothing durable. On close inspection we shall find that religion, and not fear, has ever been the cause of the longlived prosperity of an absolute government. Do what you may, there is no true power among men except in the free union of their will; and patriotism and religion are the only two motives in the world that can long urge all the people towards the same end.

Laws cannot rekindle an extinguished faith, but men may be interested by the laws in the fate of their country. It depends upon the laws to awaken and direct the vague impulse of patriotism, which never abandons the human heart; and if it be connected with the thoughts, the passions, and the daily habits of life, it may be consolidated into a durable and rational sentiment. Let it not be said that it is too late to make the experiment; for nations do not grow old as men do, and every fresh generation is a new people ready for the care of the legislator.

It is not the administrative, but the political effects of decentralization that I most admire in America. In the United States the interests of the country are everywhere kept in view; they are an object of solicitude to the people of the whole Union, and every citizen is as warmly attached to them as if they were his own. He takes pride in the glory of his nation; he boasts of its success, to which he conceives himself to have contributed; and he rejoices in the general prosperity by which he profits. The feeling he entertains towards the state is analogous to that which unites him to his family, and it is by a kind of selfishness that he interests himself in the welfare of his country.

To the European, a public officer represents a superior force; to an American, he represents a right. In America, then, it may be said that no one renders obedience to man, but to justice and to law. If the opinion that the citizen entertains of himself is exaggerated, it is at least salutary; he unhesitatingly confides in his own powers, which appear to him to be all-sufficient. When a private individual meditates an undertaking, however directly connected it may be with the welfare of society, he never thinks of soliciting the co-operation of the government; but he publishes his plan, offers to execute it, courts the assistance of other individuals, and struggles manfully against all obstacles. Undoubtedly he is often less successful than the state might have been in his position; but in the end the sum of these private undertakings far exceeds all that the government could have done.

As the administrative authority is within the reach of the citizens, whom in some degree it represents, it excites neither their jealousy nor hatred; as its resources are limited, everyone feels that he must not rely solely on its aid. Thus when the administration thinks fit to act within its own limits, it is not abandoned to itself, as in Europe; the duties of private citizens are not supposed to have lapsed because the state has come into action, but everyone is ready, on the contrary, to guide and support it. This action of individuals, joined to that of the public authorities, frequently accomplishes what the most energetic centralized administration would be unable to do.

It would be easy to adduce several facts in proof of what I advance, but I had rather give only one, with which I am best acquainted. In America the means that the authorities have at their disposal for the discovery of crimes and the arrest of criminals are few. A state police does not exist, and passports are unknown. The criminal police of the United States cannot be compared with that of France; the magistrates and public agents are not numerous; they do not always initiate the measures for arresting the guilty; and the examinations of prisoners are rapid and oral. Yet I believe that in no country does crime more rarely elude punishment. The reason is that everyone conceives himself to be interested in furnishing evidence of the crime and in seizing the delinquent. During my stay in the United States I witnessed the spontaneous formation of committees in a county for the pursuit and prosecution of a man who had committed a great crime. In Europe a criminal is an unhappy man who is struggling for his life against the agents of power, while the people are merely a spectator of the conflict; in America he is looked upon as an enemy of the human race, and the whole of mankind is against him.

I believe that provincial institutions are useful to all nations, but nowhere do they appear to me to be more necessary than among a democratic people. In an aristocracy order can always be maintained in the midst of liberty; and as the rulers have a great deal to lose, order is to them a matter of great interest. In like manner an aristocracy protects the people from the excesses of despotism, because it always possesses an organized power ready to resist a despot. But a democracy without provincial institutions has no security against these evils. How can a populace unaccustomed to freedom in small concerns learn to use it temperately in great affairs? What resistance can be offered to tyranny in a country where each individual is weak and where the citizens are not united by any common interest? Those who dread the license of the mob and those who fear absolute power ought alike to desire the gradual development of provincial liberties.

I am also convinced that democratic nations are most likely to fall beneath the yoke of a centralized administration, for several reasons, among which is the following:

The constant tendency of these nations is to concentrate all the strength of the government in the hands of the only power that directly represents the people; because beyond the people nothing is to be perceived but a mass of equal individuals. But when the same power already has all the attributes of government, it can scarcely refrain from penetrating into the details of the administration, and an opportunity of doing so is sure to present itself in the long run, as was the case in France. In the French Revolution there were two impulses in opposite directions, which must never be confounded; the one was favorable to liberty, the other to despotism. Under the ancient monarchy the king was the sole author of the laws; and below the power of the sovereign certain vestiges of provincial institutions, half destroyed, were still distinguishable. These provincial institutions were incoherent, ill arranged, and frequently absurd; in the hands of the aristocracy they had sometimes been converted into instruments of oppression. The Revolution declared itself the enemy at once of royalty and of provincial institutions; it confounded in indiscriminate hatred all that had preceded it, despotic power and the checks to its abuses; and its tendency was at once to republicanize and to centralize This double character of the French Revolution is a fact which has been adroitly handled by the friends of absolute power. Can they be accused of laboring in the cause of despotism when they are defending that centralized administration which was one of the great innovations of the Revolution? In this manner popularity may be united with hostility to the rights of the people, and the secret slave of tyranny may be the professed lover of freedom.

I have visited the two nations in which the system of provincial liberty has been most perfectly established, and I have listened to the opinions of different parties in those countries. In America I met with men who secretly aspired to destroy the democratic institutions of the Union; in England I found others who openly attacked the aristocracy; but I found no one who did not regard provincial independence as a great good. In both countries I heard a thousand different causes assigned for the evils of the state, but the local system was never mentioned among them. I heard citizens attribute the power and prosperity of their country to a multitude of reasons, but they all placed the advantages of local institutions in the foremost rank.

Am I to suppose that when men who are naturally so divided on religious opinions and on political theories agree on one point (and that one which they can best judge, as it is one of which they have daily experience) they are all in error? The only nations which deny the utility of provincial liberties are those which have fewest of them; in other words, only those censure the institution who do not know it.

I HAVE already pointed out the distinction between a centralized government and a centralized administration. The former exists in America, but the latter is nearly unknown there. If the directing power of the American communities had both these instruments of government at is disposal and united the habit of executing its commands to the right of commanding; if, after having established the general principles of government, it descended to the details of their application; and if, having regulated the great interests of the country, it could descend to the circle of individual interests, freedom would soon be banished from the New World.

But in the United States the majority, which so frequently displays the tastes and the propensities of a despot, is still destitute of the most perfect instruments of tyranny.

In the American republics the central government has never as yet busied itself except with a small number of objects, sufficiently prominent to attract its attention. The secondary affairs of society have never been regulated by its authority; and nothing has hitherto betrayed its desire of even interfering in them. The majority has become more and more absolute, but has not increased the prerogatives of the central government; those great prerogatives have been confined to a certain sphere; and although the despotism of the majority may be galling upon one point, it cannot be said to extend to all. However the predominant party in the nation may be carried away by its passions, however ardent it may be in the pursuit of its projects, it cannot oblige all the citizens to comply with its desires in the same manner and at the same time throughout the country. When the central government which represents that majority has issued a decree, it must entrust the execution of its will to agents over whom it frequently has no control and whom it cannot perpetually direct. The townships, municipal bodies, and counties form so many concealed breakwaters, which check or part the tide of popular determination. If an oppressive law were passed, liberty would still be protected by the mode of executing that law; the majority cannot descend to the details and what may be called the puerilities of administrative tyranny. It does not even imagine that it can do so, for it has not a full consciousness of its authority. It knows only the extent of its natural powers, but is unacquainted with the art of increasing them.

This point deserves attention; for if a democratic republic, similar to that of the United States, were ever founded in a country where the power of one man had previously established a centralized administration and had sunk it deep into the habits and the laws of the people, I do not hesitate to assert that in such a republic a more insufferable despotism would prevail than in any of the absolute monarchies of Europe; or, indeed, than any that could be found on this side of Asia.

Tocqueville on Democratic Despotism

Excerpted from Alexis de Tocqueville Democracy in America Part II *(1840), Book IV, Chapter VI.*

Alexis de Tocqueville (1805-1859) was a French political scientist.

I had remarked during my stay in the United States that a democratic state of society, similar to that of the Americans, might offer singular facilities for the establishment of despotism; and I perceived, upon my return to Europe, how much use had already been made, by most of our rulers, of the notions, the sentiments, and the wants created by this same social condition, for the purpose of extending the circle of their power. This led me to think that the nations of Christendom would perhaps eventually undergo some oppression like that which hung over several of the nations of the ancient world.

A more accurate examination of the subject, and five years of further meditation, have not diminished my fears, but have changed their object.

No sovereign ever lived in former ages so absolute or so powerful as to undertake to administer by his own agency, and without the assistance of intermediate powers, all the parts of a great empire; none ever attempted to subject all his subjects indiscriminately to strict uniformity of regulation and personally to tutor and direct every member of the community. The notion of such an undertaking never occurred to the human mind; and if any man had conceived it, the want of information, the imperfection of the administrative system, and, above all, the natural obstacles caused by the inequality of conditions would speedily have checked the execution of so vast a design.

When the Roman emperors were at the height of their power, the different nations of the empire still preserved usages and customs of great diversity; although they were subject to the same monarch, most of the provinces were separately administered; they abounded in powerful and active municipalities; and although the whole government of the empire was centered in the hands of the Emperor alone and he always remained, in case of need, the supreme arbiter in all matters, yet the details of social life and private occupations lay for the most part beyond his control. The emperors possessed, it is true, an immense and unchecked power, which allowed them to gratify all their whimsical tastes and to employ for that purpose the whole strength of the state. They frequently abused that power arbitrarily to deprive their subjects of property or of life; their tyranny was extremely onerous to the few, but it did not reach the many; it was confined to some few main objects and neglected the rest; it was violent, but its range was limited.

It would seem that if despotism were to be established among the democratic nations of our days, it might assume a different character; it would be more extensive and more mild; it would degrade men without tormenting them. I do not question that, in an age of instruction and equality like our own, sovereigns might more easily succeed in collecting all political power into their own hands and might interfere more habitually and decidedly with the circle of private interests than any sovereign of antiquity could ever do. But this same principle of equality which facilitates despotism tempers its rigor. We have seen how the customs of society become more humane and gentle in proportion as men become more equal and alike. When no member of the community has much power or much wealth, tyranny is, as it were, without opportunities and a field of action. As all fortunes are scanty, the passions of men are naturally circumscribed, their imagination limited, their pleasures simple. This universal moderation moderates the sovereign himself and checks within certain limits the inordinate stretch of his desires.

Independently of these reasons, drawn from the nature of the state of society itself, I might add many others arising from causes beyond my subject; but I shall keep within the limits I have laid down.

Democratic governments may become violent and even cruel at certain periods of extreme effervescence or of great danger, but these crises will be rare and brief. When I consider the petty passions of our contemporaries, the mildness of their manners, the extent of their education, the purity of their religion, the gentleness of their morality, their regular and industrious habits, and the restraint which they almost all observe in their vices no less than in their virtues, I have no fear that they will meet with tyrants in their rulers, but rather with guardians.

I think, then, that the species of oppression by which democratic nations are menaced is unlike anything that ever before existed in the world; our contemporaries will find no prototype of it in their memories. I seek in vain for an expression that will accurately convey the whole of the idea I have formed of it; the old words despotism and tyranny are inappropriate: the thing itself is new, and since I cannot name, I must attempt to define it.

I seek to trace the novel features under which despotism may appear in the world. The first thing that strikes the observation is an innumerable multitude of men, all equal and alike, incessantly endeavoring to procure the petty and paltry pleasures with which they glut their lives. Each of them, living apart, is as a stranger to the fate of all the rest; his children and his private friends constitute to him the whole of mankind. As for the rest of his fellow citizens, he is close to them, but he does not see them; he touches them, but he does not feel them; he exists only in himself and for himself alone; and if his kindred still remain to him, he may be said at any rate to have lost his country.

Above this race of men stands an immense and tutelary power, which takes upon itself alone to secure their gratifications and to watch over their fate. That power is absolute, minute, regular, provident, and mild. It would be like the authority of a parent if, like that authority, its object was to prepare men for manhood; but it seeks, on the contrary, to keep them in perpetual childhood: it is well content that the people should rejoice, provided they think of nothing but rejoicing. For their happiness such a government willingly labors, but it chooses to be the sole agent and the only arbiter of that happiness; it provides for their security, foresees and supplies their necessities, facilitates their pleasures, manages their principal concerns, directs their industry, regulates the descent of property, and subdivides their inheritances: what remains, but to spare them all the care of thinking and all the trouble of living?

Thus it every day renders the exercise of the free agency of man less useful and less frequent; it circumscribes the will within a narrower range and gradually robs a man of all the uses of himself. The principle of equality has prepared men for these things; it has predisposed men to endure them and often to look on them as benefits.

After having thus successively taken each member of the community in its powerful grasp and fashioned him at will, the supreme power then extends its arm over the whole community. It covers the surface of society with a network of small complicated rules, minute and uniform, through which the most original minds and the most energetic characters cannot penetrate, to rise above the crowd. The will of man is not shattered, but softened, bent, and guided; men are seldom forced by it to act, but they are constantly restrained from acting. Such a power does not destroy, but it prevents existence; it does not tyrannize, but it compresses, enervates, extinguishes, and stupefies a people, till each nation is reduced to nothing better than a flock of timid and industrious animals, of which the government is the shepherd.

I have always thought that servitude of the regular, quiet, and gentle kind which I have just described might be combined more easily than is commonly believed with some of the outward forms of freedom, and that it might even establish itself under the wing of the sovereignty of the people.

Our contemporaries are constantly excited by two conflicting passions: they want to be led, and they wish to remain free. As they cannot destroy either the one or the other of these contrary propensities, they strive to satisfy them both at once.

They devise a sole, tutelary, and all-powerful form of government, but elected by the people. They combine the principle of centralization and that of popular sovereignty; this gives them a respite: they console themselves for being in tutelage by the reflection that they have chosen their own guardians. Every man allows himself to be put in leading-strings, because he sees that it is not a person or a class of persons, but the people at large who hold the end of his chain.

By this system the people shake off their state of dependence just long enough to select their master and then relapse into it again. A great many persons at the present day are quite contented with this sort of compromise between administrative despotism and the sovereignty of the people; and they think they have done enough for the protection of individual freedom when they have surrendered it to the power of the nation at large. This does not satisfy me: the nature of him I am to obey signifies less to me than the fact of extorted obedience. I do not deny, however, that a constitution of this kind appears to me to be infinitely preferable to one which, after having concentrated all the powers of government, should vest them in the hands of an irresponsible person or body of persons. Of all the forms that democratic despotism could assume, the latter would assuredly be the worst.

When the sovereign is elective, or narrowly watched by a legislature which is really elective and independent, the oppression that he exercises over individuals is sometimes greater, but it is always less degrading; because every man, when he is oppressed and disarmed, may still imagine that, while he yields obedience, it is to himself he yields it, and that it is to one of his own inclinations that all the rest give way. In like manner, I can understand that when the sovereign represents the nation and is dependent upon the people, the rights and the power of which every citizen is deprived serve not only the head of the state, but the state itself; and that private persons derive some return from the sacrifice of their independence which they have made to the public. To create a representation of the people in every centralized country is, therefore, to diminish the evil that extreme centralization may produce, but not to get rid of it.

I admit that, by this means, room is left for the intervention of individuals in the more important affairs; but it is not the less suppressed in the smaller and more privates ones. It must not be forgotten that it is especially dangerous to enslave men in the minor details of life. For my own part, I should be inclined to think freedom less necessary in great things than in little ones, if it were possible to be secure of the one without possessing the other.

Subjection in minor affairs breaks out every day and is felt by the whole community indiscriminately. It does not drive men to resistance, but it crosses them at every turn, till they are led to surrender the exercise of their own will. Thus their spirit is gradually broken and their character enervated; whereas that obedience which is exacted on a few important but rare occasions only exhibits servitude at certain intervals and throws the burden of it upon a small number of men. It is in vain to summon a people who have been rendered so dependent on the central power to choose from time to time the representatives of that power; this rare and brief exercise of their free choice, however important it may be, will not prevent them from gradually losing the faculties of thinking, feeling, and acting for themselves, and thus gradually falling below the level of humanity.

I add that they will soon become incapable of exercising the great and only privilege which remains to them. The democratic nations that have introduced freedom into their political constitution at the very time when they were augmenting the despotism of their administrative constitution have been led into strange paradoxes. To manage those minor affairs in which good sense is all that is wanted, the people are held to be unequal to the task; but when the government of the country is at stake, the people are invested with immense powers; they are alternately made the play things of their ruler, and his masters, more than kings and less than men. After having exhausted all the different modes of election without finding one to suit their purpose, they are still amazed and still bent on seeking further; as if the evil they notice did not originate in the constitution of the country far more than in that of the electoral body.

It is indeed difficult to conceive how men who have entirely given up the habit of self-government should succeed in making a proper choice of those by whom they are to be governed; and no one will ever believe that a liberal, wise, and energetic government can spring from the suffrages of a subservient people.

A constitution republican in its head and ultra-monarchical in all its other parts has always appeared to me to be a short-lived monster. The vices of rulers and the ineptitude of the people would speedily bring about its ruin; and the nation, weary of its representatives and of itself, would create freer institutions or soon return to stretch itself at the feet of a single master.

Tocqueville on Voluntary Associations

Excerpted from Alexis de Tocqueville, Democracy in America,
Part II (1840), Book II Chap. V.

Alexis de Tocqueville (1805–1859) was a French political scientist.

I do not propose to speak of those political associations by the aid of which men endeavor to defend themselves against the despotic action of a majority or against the aggressions of regal power. That subject I have already treated. If each citizen did not learn, in proportion as he individually becomes more feeble and consequently more incapable of preserving his freedom single-handed, to combine with his fellow citizens for the purpose of defending it, it is clear that tyranny would unavoidably increase together with equality.

Only those associations that are formed in civil life without reference to political objects are here referred to. The political associations that exist in the United States are only a single feature in the midst of the immense assemblage of associations in that country. Americans of all ages, all conditions, and all dispositions constantly form associations. They have not only commercial and manufacturing companies, in which all take part, but associations of a thousand other kinds, religious, moral, serious, futile, general or restricted, enormous or diminutive. The Americans make associations to give entertainments, to found seminaries, to build inns, to construct churches, to diffuse books, to send missionaries to the antipodes; in this manner they found hospitals, prisons, and schools. If it is proposed to inculcate some truth or to foster some feeling by the encouragement of a great example, they form a society. Wherever at the head of some new undertaking you see the government in France, or a man of rank in England, in the United States you will be sure to find an association.

I met with several kinds of associations in America of which I confess I had no previous notion; and I have often admired the extreme skill with which the inhabitants of the United States succeed in proposing a common object for the exertions of a great many men and in inducing them voluntarily to pursue it.

I have since traveled over England, from which the Americans have taken some of their laws and many of their customs; and it seemed to me that the principle of association was by no means so constantly or adroitly used in that country. The English often perform great things singly, whereas the Americans form associations for the smallest undertakings. It is evident that the former people consider association as a powerful means of action, but the latter seem to regard it as the only means they have of acting.

Thus the most democratic country on the face of the earth is that in which men have, in our time, carried to the highest perfection the art of pursuing in common the object of their common desires and have applied this new science to the greatest number of purposes. Is this the result of accident, or is there in reality any necessary connection between the principle of association and that of equality?

Aristocratic communities always contain, among a multitude of persons who by themselves are powerless, a small number of powerful and wealthy citizens, each of whom can achieve great undertakings single-handed. In aristocratic societies men do not need to combine in order to act, because they are strongly held together. Every wealthy and powerful citizen constitutes the head of a permanent and compulsory association, composed of all those who are dependent upon him or whom he makes subservient to the execution of his designs.

Among democratic nations, on the contrary, all the citizens are independent and feeble; they can do hardly anything by themselves, and none of them can oblige his fellow men to lend him their assistance. They all, therefore, become powerless if they do not learn voluntarily to help one another. If men living in democratic countries had no right and no inclination to associate for political purposes, their independence would be in great jeopardy, but they might long preserve their wealth and their cultivation: whereas if they never acquired the habit of forming associations in ordinary life, civilization itself would be endangered. A people among whom individuals lost the power of achieving great things single-handed, without acquiring the means of producing them by united exertions, would soon relapse into barbarism.

Unhappily, the same social condition that renders associations so necessary to democratic nations renders their formation more difficult among those nations than among all others. When several members of an aristocracy agree to combine, they easily succeed in doing so; as each of them brings great strength to the partnership, the number of its members may be very limited; and when the members of an association are limited in number, they may easily become mutually acquainted, understand each other, and establish fixed regulations. The same opportunities do not occur among democratic nations, where the associated members must always be very numerous for their association to have any power.

I am aware that many of my countrymen are not in the least embarrassed by this difficulty. They contend that the more enfeebled and incompetent the citizens become, the more able and active the government ought to be rendered in order that society at large may execute what individuals can no longer accomplish. They believe this answers the whole difficulty, but I think they are mistaken.

A government might perform the part of some of the largest American companies, and several states, members of the Union, have already attempted it; but what political power could ever carry on the vast multitude of lesser undertakings which the American citizens perform every day, with the assistance of the principle of association? It is easy to foresee that the time is drawing near when man will be less and less able to produce, by himself alone, the commonest necessaries of life. The task of the governing power will therefore perpetually increase, and its very efforts will extend it every day. The more it stands in the place of associations, the more will individuals, losing the notion of combining together, require its assistance: these are causes and effects that unceasingly create each other. Will the administration of the country ultimately assume the management of all the manufactures which no single citizen is able to carry on? And if a time at length arrives when, in consequence of the extreme subdivision of landed property, the soil is split into an infinite number of parcels, so that it can be cultivated only by companies of tillers will it be necessary that the head of the government should leave the helm of state to follow the plow? The morals and the intelligence of a democratic people would be as much endangered as its business and manufactures if the government ever wholly usurped the place of private companies. Feelings and opinions are recruited, the heart is enlarged, and the human mind is developed only by the reciprocal influence of men upon one another. I have shown that these influences are almost null in democratic countries; they must therefore be artificially created, and this can only be accomplished by associations.

When the members of an aristocratic community adopt a new opinion or conceive a new sentiment, they give it a station, as it were, beside themselves, upon the lofty platform where they stand; and opinions or sentiments so conspicuous to the eyes of the multitude are easily introduced into the minds or hearts of all around. In democratic countries the governing power alone is naturally in a condition to act in this manner, but it is easy to see that its action is always inadequate, and often dangerous. A government can no more be competent to keep alive and to renew the circulation of opinions and feelings among a great people than to manage all the speculations of productive industry. No sooner does a government attempt to go beyond its political sphere and to enter upon this new track than it exercises, even unintentionally, an insupportable tyranny; for a government can only dictate strict rules, the opinions which it favors are rigidly enforced, and it is never easy to discriminate between its advice and its commands. Worse still will be the case if the government really believes itself interested in preventing all circulation of ideas; it will then stand motionless and oppressed by the heaviness of voluntary torpor. Governments, therefore, should not be the only active powers; associations ought, in democratic nations, to stand in lieu of those powerful private individuals whom the equality of conditions has swept away.

As soon as several of the inhabitants of the United States have taken up an opinion or a feeling which they wish to promote in the world, they look out for mutual assistance; and as soon as they have found one another out, they combine. From that moment they are no longer isolated men, but a power seen from afar, whose actions serve for an example and whose language is listened to. The first time I heard in the United States that a hundred thousand men had bound themselves publicly to abstain from spirituous liquors, it appeared to me more like a joke than a serious engagement, and I did not at once perceive why these temperate citizens could not content themselves with drinking water by their own firesides. I at last understood that these hundred thousand Americans, alarmed by the progress of drunkenness around them, had made up their minds to patronize temperance.

They acted in just the same way as a man of high rank who should dress very plainly in order to inspire the humbler orders with a contempt of luxury. It is probable that if these hundred thousand men had lived in France, each of them would singly have memorialized the government to watch the public houses all over the kingdom.

Nothing, in my opinion, is more deserving of our attention than the intellectual and moral associations of America. The political and industrial associations of that country strike us forcibly; but the others elude our observation, or if we discover them, we understand them imperfectly because we have hardly ever seen anything of the kind. It must be acknowledged, however, that they are as necessary to the American people as the former, and perhaps more so. In democratic countries the science of association is the mother of science; the progress of all the rest depends upon the progress it has made.

Among the laws that rule human societies there is one which seems to be more precise and clear than all others. If men are to remain civilized or to become so, the art of associating together must grow and improve in the same ratio in which the equality of conditions is increased.

PART IV

RELIGION

Tocqueville on Religion

Excerpted from Alexis de Tocqueville, Democracy in America, *Part I (1835), Chap. II and XVII.*

Alexis de Tocqueville (1805–1859) was a French political scientist.

Chapter II
Origin of the Anglo-Americans, and importance of this origin in relation to their future condition

After the birth of a human being his early years are obscurely spent in the toils or pleasures of childhood. As he grows up, the world receives him, when his manhood begins, and he enters into contact with his fellows. He is then studied for the first time, and it is imagined that the germ of the vices and the virtues of his maturer years is then formed.

This, if I am not mistaken, is a great error. We must begin higher up; we must watch the infant in his mother's arms; we must see the first images which the external world casts upon the dark mirror of his mind, the first occurrences that he witnesses, we must hear the first words which awaken the sleeping powers of thought, and stand by his earliest efforts if we would understand the prejudices, the habits, and the passions which will rule his life. The entire man is, so to speak, to be seen in the cradle of the child.

The growth of nations presents something analogous to this; they all bear some marks of their origin. The circumstances that accompanied their birth and contributed to their development affected the whole term of their being.

If we were able to go back to the elements of states and to examine the oldest monuments of their history, I doubt not that we should discover in them the primal cause of the prejudices, the habits, the ruling passions, and, in short, all that constitutes what is called the national character. We should there find the explanation of certain customs which now seem at variance with the prevailing manners; of such laws as conflict with established principles; and of such incoherent opinions as are here and there to be met with in society, like those fragments of broken chains which we sometimes see hanging from the vaults of an old edifice, and supporting nothing. This might explain the destinies of certain nations which seem borne on by an unknown force to ends of which they themselves are ignorant. But hitherto facts have been lacking for such a study: the spirit of analysis has come upon nations only as they matured; and when they at last conceived of contemplating their origin, time had already obscured it, or ignorance and pride had surrounded it with fables behind which the truth was hidden.

America is the only country in which it has been possible to witness the natural and tranquil growth of society, and where the influence exercised on the future condition of states by their origin is clearly distinguishable.

At the period when the peoples of Europe landed in the New World, their national characteristics were already completely formed; each of them had a physiognomy of its own; and as they had already attained that stage of civilization at which men are led to study themselves, they have transmitted to us a faithful picture of their opinions, their manners, and their laws. The men of the sixteenth century are almost as well known to us as our contemporaries. America, consequently, exhibits in the broad light of day the phenomena which the ignorance or rudeness of earlier ages conceals from our researches. The men of our day seem destined to see further than their predecessors into human events; they are close enough to the founding of the American settlements to know in detail their elements, and far enough away from that time already to be able to judge what these beginnings have produced. Providence has given us a torch which our forefathers did not possess, and has allowed us to discern fundamental causes in the history .of the world which the obscurity of the past concealed from them. If we carefully examine the social and political state of America, after having studied its history, we shall remain perfectly convinced that not an opinion, not a custom, not a law, I may even say not an event is upon record which the origin of that people will not explain. The readers of this book will find in the present chapter the germ of all that is to follow and the key to almost the whole work.

The emigrants who came at different periods to occupy the territory now covered by the American Union differed from each other in many respects; their aim was not the same, and they governed themselves on different principles.

These men had, however, certain features in common, and they were all placed in an analogous situation. The tie of language is, perhaps, the strongest and the most durable that can unite mankind. All the emigrants spoke the same language; they were all children of the same people. Born in a country which had been agitated for centuries by the struggles of faction, and in which all parties had been obliged in their turn to place themselves under the protection of the laws, their political education had been perfected in this rude school; and they were more conversant with the notions of right and the principles of true freedom than the greater part of their European contemporaries. At the period of the first emigrations the township system, that fruitful germ of free institutions, was deeply rooted in the habits of the English; and with it the doctrine of the sovereignty of the people had been introduced into the very bosom of the monarchy of the house of Tudor.

The religious quarrels which have agitated the Christian world were then rife. England had plunged into the new order of things with headlong vehemence. The character of its inhabitants, which had always been sedate and reflective, became argumentative and austere. General information had been increased by intellectual contests, and the mind had received in them a deeper cultivation. While religion was the topic of discussion, the morals of the people became more pure. All these national features are more or less discoverable in the physiognomy of those Englishmen who came to seek a new home on the opposite shores of the Atlantic.

Another observation, moreover, to which we shall have occasion to return later, is applicable not only to the English, but to the French, the Spaniards, and all the Europeans who successively established themselves in the New World. All these European colonies contained the elements, if not the development, of a complete democracy. Two causes led to this result. It may be said that on leaving the mother country the emigrants had, in general, no notion of superiority one over another. The happy and the powerful do not go into exile, and there are no surer guarantees of equality among men than poverty and misfortune. It happened, however, on several occasions, that persons of rank were driven to America by political and religious quarrels. Laws were made to establish a gradation of ranks; but it was soon found that the soil of America was opposed to a territorial aristocracy. It was realized that in order to clear this land, nothing less than the constant and self-interested efforts of the owner himself was essential; the ground prepared, it became evident that its produce was not sufficient to enrich at the same time both an owner and a farmer. The land was then naturally broken up into small portions, which the proprietor cultivated for himself. Land is the basis of an aristocracy, which clings to the soil that supports it; for it is not by privileges alone, nor by birth, but by landed property handed down from generation to generation that an aristocracy is constituted. A nation may present immense fortunes and extreme wretchedness; but unless those fortunes are territorial, there is no true aristocracy, but simply the class of the rich and that of the poor.

All the British colonies had striking similarities at the time of their origin. All of them, from their beginning, seemed destined to witness the growth, not of the aristocratic liberty of their mother country, but of that freedom of the middle and lower orders of which the history of the world had as yet furnished no complete example. In this general uniformity, however, several marked divergences could be observed, which it is necessary to point out. Two branches may be distinguished in the great Anglo-American family, which have hitherto grown up without entirely commingling; the one in the South, the other in the North.

Virginia received the first English colony; the immigrants took possession of it in 1607. The idea that mines of gold and silver are the sources of national wealth was at that time singularly prevalent in Europe; a fatal delusion, which has done more to impoverish the European nations who adopted it, and has cost more lives in America, than the united influence of war and bad laws. The men sent to Virginia were seekers of gold, adventurers without resources and without character, whose turbulent and restless spirit endangered the infant colony and rendered its progress uncertain. Artisans and agriculturists arrived afterwards; and, although they were a more moral and orderly race of men, they were hardly in any respect above the level of the inferior classes in England. No lofty views, no spiritual conception, presided over the foundation of these new settlements. The colony was scarcely established when slavery was introduced; this was the capital fact which was to exercise an immense influence on the character, the laws, and the whole future of the South. Slavery, as I shall afterwards show, dishonors labor; it introduces idleness into society, and with idleness, ignorance and pride, luxury and distress. It enervates the powers of the mind and benumbs the activity of man. The influence of slavery, united to the English character, explains the manners and the social condition of the Southern states.

On this same English foundation there developed in the North very different characteristics. Here I may be allowed to enter into some details.

In the English colonies of the North, more generally known as the New England states, the two or three main ideas that now constitute the basis of the social theory of the United States were first combined. The principles of New England spread at first to the neighboring states; they then passed successively to the more distant ones; and at last, if I may so speak, they interpenetrated the whole confederation. They now extend their influence beyond its limits, over the whole American world. The civilization of New England has been like a beacon lit upon a hill, which, after it has diffused its warmth immediately around it, also tinges the distant horizon with its glow.

The foundation of New England was a novel spectacle, and all the circumstances attending it were singular and original. Nearly all colonies have been first inhabited either by men without education and without resources, driven by their poverty and their misconduct from the land which gave them birth, or by speculators and adventurers greedy of gain. Some settlements cannot even boast so honorable an origin; Santo Domingo was founded by buccaneers; and at the present day the criminal courts of England supply the population of Australia.

The settlers who established themselves on the shores of New England all belonged to the more independent classes of their native country. Their union on the soil of America at once presented the singular phenomenon of a society containing neither lords nor common people, and we may almost say neither rich nor poor. These men possessed, in proportion to their number, a greater mass of intelligence than is to be found in any European nation of our own time. All, perhaps without a single exception, had received a good education, and many of them were known in Europe for their talents and their acquirements. The other colonies had been founded by adventurers without families; the immigrants of New England brought with them the best elements of order and morality; they landed on the desert coast accompanied by their wives and children. But what especially distinguished them from all others was the aim of their undertaking. They had not been obliged by necessity to leave their country; the social position they abandoned was one to be regretted, and their means of subsistence were certain. Nor did they cross the Atlantic to improve their situation or to increase their wealth; it was a purely intellectual craving that called them from the comforts of their former homes; and in facing the inevitable sufferings of exile their object was the triumph of an idea.

The immigrants, or, as they deservedly styled themselves, the Pilgrims, belonged to that English sect the austerity of whose principles had acquired for them the name of Puritans. Puritanism was not merely a religious doctrine, but corresponded in many points with the most absolute democratic and republican theories. It was this tendency that had aroused its most dangerous adversaries. Persecuted by the government of the mother country, and disgusted by the habits of a society which the rigor of their own principles condemned, the Puritans went forth to seek some rude and unfrequented part of the world where they could live according to their own opinions and worship God in freedom.

A few quotations will throw more light upon the spirit of these pious adventurers than all that we can say of them. Nathaniel Morton, the historian of the first years of the settlement, thus opens his subject: "Gentle Reader, I have for some lengths of time looked upon it as a duty incumbent especially on the immediate successors of those that have had so large experience of those many memorable and signal demonstrations of God's goodness, viz. the first beginners of this Plantation in New England, to commit to writing his gracious dispensations on that behalf; having so many inducements thereunto, not only otherwise, but so plentifully in the Sacred Scriptures: that so, what we have seen, and what our fathers have told us (Psalm lxxviii. 3,4), we may not hide from our children, showing to the generations to come the praises of the Lord; that especially the seed of Abraham his servant, and the children of Jacob his chosen (Psalm cv. 5, 6), may remember his marvellous works in the beginning and progress of the planting of

New England, his wonders and the judgments of his mouth; how that God brought a vine into this wilderness; that he cast out the heathen, and planted it; that he made room for it and caused it to take deep root; and it filled the land (Psalm lxxx. 8, 9). And not only so, but also that he hath guided his people by his strength to his holy habitation, and planted them in the mountain of his inheritance in respect of precious Gospel enjoyments: and that as especially God may have the glory of all unto whom it is most due; so also some rays of glory may reach the names of those blessed Saints, that were the main instruments and the beginning of this happy enterprise.

The author continues, and thus describes the departure of the first Pilgrims:

"So they left that goodly and pleasant city of Leyden, which had been their resting-place for above eleven years; but they knew that they were pilgrims and strangers here below, and looked not much on these things, but lifted up their eyes to heaven, their dearest country, where God hath prepared for them a city (Heb. xi. 16), and therein quieted their spirits. When they came to Delfs-Haven they found the ship and all things ready; and such of their friends as could not come with them followed after them, and sundry came from Amsterdam to see them shipt, and to take their leaves of them. One night was spent with little sleep with the most, but with friendly entertainment and Christian discourse, and other real expressions of true Christian love. The next day they went on board, and their friends with them, where truly doleful was the sight of that sad and mournful parting, to hear what sighs and sobs and prayers did sound amongst them; what tears did gush from every eye, and pithy speeches pierced each other's heart, that sundry of the Dutch strangers that stood on the Key as spectators could not refrain from tears. But the tide (which stays for no man) calling them away, that were thus loth to depart, their Reverend Pastor, falling down on his knees, and they all with him, with watery cheeks commended them with most fervent prayers unto the Lord and his blessing; and then with mutual embraces and many tears they took their leaves one of another, which proved to be the last leave to many of them."

The emigrants were about 150 in number, including the women and the children. Their object was to plant a colony on the shores of the Hudson; but after having been driven about for some time in the Atlantic Ocean, they were forced to land on the arid coast of New England, at the spot which is now the town of Plymouth. The rock is still shown on which the Pilgrims disembarked.

"But before we pass on," continues our historian, "let the reader with me make a pause, and seriously consider this poor people's present condition, the more to be raised up to admiration of God's goodness towards them in their preservation: for being now passed the vast ocean, and a sea of troubles before them in expectation, they had now no friends to welcome them, no inns to entertain or refresh them, no houses, or much less towns, to repair unto to seek for succour: and for the season it was winter, and they that know the winters of the country know them to be sharp and violent, subject to cruel and fierce storms, dangerous to travel to known places, much more to search unknown coasts. Besides, what could they see but a hideous and desolate wilderness, full of wilde beasts, and wilde men? and what multitudes of them there were, they then knew not: for which way soever they turned their eyes (save upward to Heaven) they could have but little solace or content in respect of any outward object; for summer being ended, all things stand in appearance with a weather-beaten face, and the whole country, full of woods and thickets, represented a wild and savage hew; if they looked behind them, there was the mighty ocean which they had passed, and was now as a main bar or gulph to separate them from all the civil parts of the world."

It must not be imagined that the piety of the Puritans was merely speculative, or that it took no cognizance of the course of worldly affairs. Puritanism, as I have already remarked, was almost as much a political theory as a religious doctrine. No sooner had the immigrants landed on the barren coast described by Nathaniel Morton than it was their first care to constitute a society, by subscribing the following Act: IN THE NAME OF GOD AMEN. We, whose names are underwritten, the loyal subjects of our dread Sovereign Lord King James, &c. &c., Having undertaken for the glory of God, and advancement of the Christian Faith, and the honour of our King and country, a voyage to plant the first colony in the northern parts of Virginia; Do by these presents solemnly and mutually, in the presence of God and one another, covenant and combine ourselves together into a civil body politick, for our better ordering and preservation, and furtherance of the ends aforesaid: and by virtue hereof do enact, constitute, and frame such just and equal laws, ordinances, acts, constitutions, and offices, from time to time, as shall be thought most meet and convenient for the general good of the Colony: unto which we promise all due submission and obedience," etc.

This happened in 1620, and from that time forwards the emigration went on. The religious and political passion which ravaged the British Empire during the whole reign of Charles I drove fresh crowds of sectarians every year to the shores of America. In England the stronghold of Puritanism continued to be in the middle classes; and it was from the middle classes that most of the emigrants came. The population of New England increased rapidly; and while the hierarchy of rank despotically classed the inhabitants of the mother country, the colony approximated more and more the novel spectacle of a community homogeneous in all its parts. A democracy more perfect than antiquity had dared to dream of started in full size and panoply from the midst of an ancient feudal society.

The English government was not dissatisfied with a large emigration which removed the elements of fresh discord and further revolutions. On the contrary, it did everything to encourage it and seemed to have no anxiety about the destiny of those who sought a shelter from the rigor of their laws on the soil of America. It appeared as if New England was a region given up to the dreams of fancy and the unrestrained experiments of innovators.

The English colonies (and this is one of the main causes of their prosperity) have always enjoyed more internal freedom and more political independence than the colonies of other nations; and this principle of liberty was nowhere more extensively applied than in the New England states. It was generally allowed at that period that the territories of the New World belonged to that European nation which had been the first to discover them. Nearly the whole coast of North America thus became a British possession towards the end of the sixteenth century. The means used by the English government to people these new domains were of several kinds: the king sometimes appointed a governor of his own choice, who ruled a portion of the New World in the name and under the immediate orders of the crown; this is the colonial system adopted by the other countries of Europe. Sometimes grants of certain tracts were made by the crown to an individual or to a company, in which case all the civil and political power fell into the hands of one or more persons, who, under the inspection and control of the crown, sold the lands and governed the inhabitants. Lastly, a third system consisted in allowing a certain number of emigrants to form themselves into a political society under the protection of the mother country and to govern themselves in whatever was not contrary to her laws. This mode of colonization, so favorable to liberty, was adopted only in New England.

In 1628 a charter of this kind was granted by Charles I to the emigrants who went to form the colony of Massachusetts. But, in general, charters were not given to the colonies of New England till their existence had become an established fact. Plymouth, Providence, New Haven, Connecticut, and Rhode Island were founded without the help and almost without the knowledge of the mother country. The new settlers did not derive their powers from the head of the empire, although they did not deny its supremacy; they constituted themselves into a society, and it was not till thirty or forty years afterwards, under Charles II, that their existence was legally recognized by a royal charter.

This frequently renders it difficult, in studying the earliest historical and legislative records of New England, to detect the link that connected the emigrants with the land of their forefathers. They continually exercised the rights of sovereignty; they named their magistrates, concluded peace or declared war, made police regulations, and enacted laws, as if their allegiance was due only to God. Nothing can be more curious and at the same time more instructive than the legislation of that period; it is there that the solution of the great social problem which the United States now presents to the world is to be found.

Among these documents we shall notice as especially characteristic the code of laws promulgated by the little state of Connecticut in 1650.

The legislators of Connecticut begin with the penal laws, and, strange to say, they borrow their provisions from the text of Holy Writ.

'Whosoever shall worship any other God than the Lord," says the preamble of the Code, "shall surely be put to death." This is followed by ten or twelve enactments of the same kind, copied verbatim from the books of Exodus, Leviticus, and Deuteronomy. Blasphemy, sorcery, adultery, and rape were punished with death; an outrage offered by a son to his parents was to be expiated by the same penalty. The legislation of a rude and half-civilized people was thus applied to an enlightened and moral community. The consequence was, that the punishment of death was never more frequently prescribed by statute, and never more rarely enforced towards the guilty.

The chief care of the legislators in this body of penal laws was the maintenance of orderly conduct and good morals in the community; thus they constantly invaded the domain of conscience, and there was scarcely a sin which was not subject to magisterial censure. The reader is aware of the rigor with which these laws punished rape and adultery; intercourse between unmarried persons was likewise severely repressed. The judge was empowered to inflict either a pecuniary penalty, a whipping, or marriage on the misdemeanants, and if the records of the old courts of New Haven may be believed, prosecutions of this kind were not infrequent. We find a sentence, bearing the date of May 1, 1660, inflicting a fine and reprimand on a young woman who was accused of using improper language and of allowing herself to be kissed. The Code of 1650 abounds in preventive measures. It punishes idleness and drunkenness with severity. Innkeepers were forbidden to furnish more than a certain quantity of liquor to each consumer; and simple lying, whenever it may be injurious, is checked by a fine or a flogging. In other places the legislator, entirely forgetting the great principles of religious toleration that he had himself demanded in Europe, makes attendance on divine service compulsory, and goes so far as to visit with severe punishment, and even with death, Christians who chose to worship God according to a ritual differing from his own. Sometimes, indeed, the zeal for regulation induces him to descend to the most frivolous particulars: thus a law is to be found in the same code which prohibits the use of tobacco. It must not be forgotten that these fantastic and oppressive laws were not imposed by authority, but that they were freely voted by all the persons interested in them, and that the customs of the community were even more austere and puritanical than the laws. In 1649 a solemn association was formed in Boston to check the worldly luxury of long hair.

These errors are no doubt discreditable to human reason; they attest the inferiority of our nature, which is incapable of laying firm hold upon what is true and just and is often reduced to the alternative of two excesses. In strict connection with this penal legislation, which bears such striking marks of a narrow, sectarian spirit and of those religious passions which had been warmed by persecution and were still fermenting among the people, a body of political laws is to be found which, though written two hundred years ago, is still in advance of the liberties of our age.

The general principles which are the groundwork of modern constitutions, principles which, in the seventeenth century, were imperfectly known in Europe, and not completely triumphant even in Great Britain, were all recognized and established by the laws of New England: the intervention of the people in public affairs, the free voting of taxes, the responsibility of the agents of power, personal liberty, and trial by jury were all positively established without discussion.

These fruitful principles were there applied and developed to an extent such as no nation in Europe has yet ventured to attempt.

In Connecticut the electoral body consisted, from its origin, of the whole number of citizens; and this is readily to be understood. In this young community there was an almost perfect equality of fortune, and a still greater uniformity of opinions. In Connecticut at this period all the executive officials were elected, including the governor of the state. The citizens above the age of sixteen were obliged to bear arms; they formed a national militia, which appointed its own officers, and was to hold itself at all times in readiness to march for the defense of the country.

In the laws of Connecticut, as well as in all those of New England, we find the germ and gradual development of that township independence which is the life and mainspring of American liberty at the present day. The political existence of the majority of the nations of Europe commenced in the superior ranks of society and was gradually and imperfectly communicated to the different members of the social body. In America, on the contrary, it may be said that the township was organized before the county, the county before the state, the state before the union.

In New England, townships were completely and definitely constituted as early as 1650. The independence of the township was the nucleus round which the local interests, passions, rights, and duties collected and clung. It gave scope to the activity of a real political life, thoroughly democratic and republican. The colonies still recognized the supremacy of the mother country; monarchy was still the law of the state; but the republic was already established in every township.

The towns named their own magistrates of every kind, assessed themselves, and levied their own taxes. In the New England town the law of representation was not adopted; but the affairs of the community were discussed, as at Athens, in the marketplace, by a general assembly of the citizens.

In studying the laws that were promulgated at this early era of the American republics, it is impossible not to be struck by the legislator's knowledge of government and advanced theories. The ideas there formed of the duties of society towards its members are evidently much loftier and more comprehensive than those of European legislators at that time; obligations were there imposed upon it which it elsewhere slighted. In the states of New England, from the first, the condition of the poor was provided for; strict measures were taken for the maintenance of roads, and surveyors were appointed to attend to them; records were established in every town, in which the results of public deliberations and the births, deaths, and marriages of the citizens were entered; clerks were directed to keep these records; officers were appointed to administer the properties having no claimants, and others to determine the boundaries of inherited lands, and still others whose principal functions were to maintain public order in the community. The law enters into a thousand various details to anticipate and satisfy a crowd of social wants that are even now very inadequately felt in France.

But it is by the mandates relating to public education that the original character of American civilization is at once placed in the clearest light. "Whereas," says the law, "Satan, the enemy of mankind, finds his strongest weapons in the ignorance of men, and whereas it is important that the wisdom of our fathers shall not remain buried in their tombs, and whereas the education of children is one of the prime concerns of the state, with the aid of the Lord...." Here follow clauses establishing schools in every township and obliging the inhabitants, under pain of heavy fines, to support them. Schools of a superior kind were founded in the same manner in the more populous districts. The municipal authorities were bound to enforce the sending of children to school by their parents; they were empowered to inflict fines upon all who refused compliance; and in cases of continued resistance, society assumed the place of the parent, took possession of the child, and deprived the father of those natural rights which he used to so bad a purpose.[40] The reader will undoubtedly have remarked the preamble of these enactments: in

America religion is the road to knowledge, and the observance of the divine laws leads man to civil freedom.

If, after having cast a rapid glance over the state of American society in 1650, we turn to the condition of Europe, and more especially to that of the Continent, at the same period, we cannot fail to be struck with astonishment. On the continent of Europe at the beginning of the seventeenth century absolute monarchy had everywhere triumphed over the ruins of the oligarchical and feudal liberties of the Middle Ages. Never perhaps were the ideas of right more completely overlooked than in the midst of the splendor and literature of Europe; never was there less political activity among the people; never were the principles of true freedom less widely circulated; and at that very time those principles which were scorned or unknown by the nations of Europe were proclaimed in the deserts of the New World and were accepted as the future creed of a great people. The boldest theories of the human mind were reduced to practice by a community so humble that not a statesman condescended to attend to it; and a system of legislation without a precedent was produced offhand by the natural originality of men's imaginations. In the bosom of this obscure democracy, which had as yet brought forth neither generals nor philosophers nor authors, a man might stand up in the face of a free people, and pronounce with general applause the following fine definition of liberty:

"Concerning liberty, I observe a great mistake in the country about that. There is a twofold liberty, natural (I mean as our nature is now corrupt) and civil or federal. The first is common to man with beasts and other creatures. By this, man, as he stands in relation to man simply, hath liberty to do what he lists; it is a liberty to evil as well as to good. This liberty is incompatible and inconsistent with authority, and cannot endure the least restraint of the most just authority. The exercise and maintaining of this liberty makes men grow more evil, and in time to be worse than brute beasts: omnes sumus licentia deteriores. This is that great enemy of truth and peace, that wild beast, which all the ordinances of God are bent against, to restrain and subdue it. The other kind of liberty I call civil or federal; it may also be termed moral, in reference to the covenant between God and man, in the moral law, and the politic covenants and constitutions, among men themselves. This liberty is the proper end and object of authority, and cannot subsist without it; and it is a liberty to that only which is good, just, and honest. This liberty you are to stand for, with the hazard not only of your goods, but of your lives, if need be. Whatsoever crosseth this, is not authority, but a distemper thereof. This liberty is maintained and exercised in a way of subjection to authority; it is of the same kind of liberty wherewith Christ hath made us free."

I have said enough to put the character of Anglo-American civilization in its true light. It is the result (and this should be constantly kept in mind) of two distinct elements, which in other places have been in frequent disagreement, but which the Americans have succeeded in incorporating to some extent one with the other and combining admirably. I allude to the spirit of religion and the spirit of liberty.

The settlers of New England were at the same time ardent sectarians and daring innovators. Narrow as the limits of some of their religious opinions were, they were free from all political prejudices.

Hence arose two tendencies, distinct but not opposite, which are everywhere discernible in the manners as well as the laws of the country.

Men sacrifice for a religious opinion their friends, their family, and their country; one can consider them devoted to the pursuit of intellectual goals which they came to purchase at so high a price. One sees them, however, seeking with almost equal eagerness material wealth and moral satisfaction; heaven in the world beyond, and well-being and liberty in this one.

Under their hand, political principles, laws, and human institutions seem malleable, capable of being shaped and combined at will. As they go forward, the barriers which imprisoned society and behind which they were born are lowered; old opinions, which for centuries had been controlling the world, vanish; a course almost without limits, a field without horizon, is revealed: the human spirit rushes forward and traverses them in every direction. But having reached the limits of the political world, the human spirit stops of itself; in fear it relinquishes the need of exploration; it even abstains from lifting the veil of the sanctuary; it bows with respect before truths which it accepts without discussion.

Thus in the moral world everything is classified, systematized, foreseen, and decided beforehand; in the political world everything is agitated, disputed, and uncertain. In the one is a passive though a voluntary obedience; in the other, an independence scornful of experience, and jealous of all authority. These two tendencies, apparently so discrepant, are far from conflicting; they advance together and support each other. Religion perceives that civil liberty affords a noble exercise to the faculties of man and that the political world is a field prepared by the Creator for the efforts of mind. Free and powerful in its own sphere, satisfied with the place reserved for it, religion never more surely establishes its empire than when it reigns in the hearts of men unsupported by aught beside its native strength.

Liberty regards religion as its companion in all its battles and its triumphs, as the cradle of its infancy and the divine source of its claims. It considers religion as the safeguard of morality, and morality as the best security of law and the surest pledge of the duration of freedom.

Excerpted from Alexis de Tocqueville, Democracy in America, Part I

Chapter XVII

I have just shown what the direct influence of religion upon politics is in the United States; but its indirect influence appears to me to be still more considerable, and it never instructs the Americans more fully in the art of being free than when it says nothing of freedom.

The sects that exist in the United States are innumerable. They all differ in respect to the worship which is due to the Creator; but they all agree in respect to the duties which are due from man to man. Each sect adores the Deity in its own peculiar manner, but all sects preach the same moral law in the name of God. If it be of the highest importance to man, as an individual, that his religion should be true, it is not so to society. Society has no future life to hope for or to fear; and provided the citizens profess a religion, the peculiar tenets of that religion are of little importance to its interests. Moreover, all the sects of the United States are comprised within the great unity of Christianity, and Christian morality is everywhere the same.

It may fairly be believed that a certain number of Americans pursue a peculiar form of worship from habit more than from conviction. In the United States the sovereign authority is religious, and consequently hypocrisy must be common; but there is no country in the world where the Christian religion retains a greater influence over the souls of men than in America; and there can be no greater proof of its utility and of its conformity to human nature than that its influence is powerfully felt over the most enlightened and free nation of the earth.

I have remarked that the American clergy in general, without even excepting those who do not admit religious liberty, are all in favor of civil freedom; but they do not support any particular political system. They keep aloof from parties and from public affairs. In the United States religion exercises but little influence upon the laws and upon the details of public opinion; but it directs the customs of the community, and, by regulating domestic life, it regulates the state.

I do not question that the great austerity of manners that is observable in the United States arises, in the first instance, from religious faith. Religion is often unable to restrain man from the numberless temptations which chance offers; nor can it check that passion for gain which everything contributes to arouse; but its influence over the mind of woman is supreme, and women are the protectors of morals. There is certainly no country in the world where the tie of marriage is more respected than in America or where conjugal happiness is more highly or worthily appreciated. In Europe almost all the disturbances of society arise from the irregularities of domestic life. To despise the natural bonds and legitimate pleasures of home is to contract a taste for excesses, a restlessness of heart, and fluctuating desires. Agitated by the tumultuous passions that frequently disturb his dwelling, the European is galled by the obedience which the legislative powers of the state exact. But when the American retires from the turmoil of public life to the bosom of his family, he finds in it the image of order and of peace. There his pleasures are simple and natural, his joys are innocent and calm; and as he finds that an orderly life is the surest path to happiness, he accustoms himself easily to moderate his opinions as well as his tastes. While the European endeavors to forget his domestic troubles by agitating society, the American derives from his own home that love of order which he afterwards carries with him into public affairs.

In the United States the influence of religion is not confined to the manners, but it extends to the intelligence of the people. Among the Anglo-Americans some profess the doctrines of Christianity from a sincere belief in them, and others do the same because they fear to be suspected of unbelief. Christianity, therefore, reigns without obstacle, by universal consent; the consequence is, as I have before observed, that every principle of the moral world is fixed and determinate, although the political world is abandoned to the debates and the experiments of men. Thus the human mind is never left to wander over a boundless field; and whatever may be its pretensions, it is checked from time to time by barriers that it cannot surmount. Before it can innovate, certain primary principles are laid down, and the boldest conceptions are subjected to certain forms which retard and stop their completion.

The imagination of the Americans, even in its greatest flights, is circumspect and undecided; its impulses are checked and its works unfinished. These habits of restraint recur in political society and are singularly favorable both to the tranquillity of the people and to the durability of the institutions they have established. Nature and circumstances have made the inhabitants of the United States bold, as is sufficiently attested by the enterprising spirit with which they seek for fortune. If the mind of the Americans were free from all hindrances, they would shortly become the most daring innovators and the most persistent disputants in the world. But the revolutionists of America are obliged to profess an ostensible respect for Christian morality and equity, which does not permit them to violate wantonly the laws that oppose their designs; nor would they find it easy to surmount the scruples of their partisans even if they were able to get over their own. Hitherto no one in the United States has dared to advance the maxim that everything is permissible for the interests of society, an impious adage which seems to have been invented in an age of freedom to shelter all future tyrants. Thus, while the law permits the Americans to do what they please, religion prevents them from conceiving, and forbids them to commit, what is rash or unjust.

Religion in America takes no direct part in the government of society, but it must be regarded as the first of their political institutions; for if it does not impart a taste for freedom, it facilitates the use of it. Indeed, it is in this same point of view that the inhabitants of the United States themselves look upon religious belief. I do not know whether all Americans have a sincere faith in their religion—for who can search the human heart?—but I am certain that they hold it to be indispensable to the maintenance of republican institutions This opinion is not peculiar to a class of citizens or to a party, but it belongs to the whole nation and to every rank of society.

In the United States, if a politician attacks a sect, this may not prevent the partisans of that very sect from supporting him; but if he attacks all the sects together, everyone abandons him, and he remains alone.

While I was in America, a witness who happened to be called at the Sessions of the county of Chester (state of New York) declared that he did not believe in the existence of God or in the immortality of the soul. The judge refused to admit his evidence, on the ground that the witness had destroyed beforehand all the confidence of the court in what he was about to say. The newspapers related the fact without any further comment.

The Americans combine the notions of Christianity and of liberty so intimately in their minds that it is impossible to make them conceive the one without the other; and with them this conviction does not spring from that barren, traditionary faith which seems to vegetate rather than to live in the soul.

I have known of societies formed by Americans to send out ministers of the Gospel into the new Western states, to found schools and churches there, lest religion should be allowed to die away in those remote settlements, and the rising states be less fitted to enjoy free institutions than the people from whom they came. I met with wealthy New Englanders who abandoned the country in which they were born in order to lay the foundations of Christianity and of freedom on the banks of the Missouri or in the prairies of Illinois. Thus religious zeal is perpetually warmed in the United States by the fire of patriotism. These men do not act exclusively from a consideration of a future life; eternity is only one motive of their devotion to the cause. If you converse with these missionaries of Christian civilization, you will be surprised to hear them speak so often of the goods of this world, and to meet a politician . where you expected to find a priest. They will tell you that "all the American republics are collectively involved with each other; if the republics of the West were to fall into anarchy, or to be mastered by a despot, the republican institutions which now flourish upon the shores of the Atlantic Ocean would be in great peril. It is therefore our interest that the new states should be religious, in order that they may permit us to remain free." Such are the opinions of the Americans; and if any hold that the religious spirit which I admire is the very thing most amiss in America, and that the only element wanting to the freedom and happiness of the human race on the other side of the ocean is to believe with Spinoza in the eternity of the world, or with Cabanis that thought is secreted by the brain, I can only reply that those who hold this language have never been in America and that they have never seen a religious or a free nation. When they return from a visit to that country, we shall hear what they have to say. There are persons in France who look upon republican institutions only as a means of obtaining grandeur; they measure the immense space that separates their vices and misery from power and riches, and they aim to fill up this gulf with ruins, that they may pass over it. These men are the condottieri of liberty, and fight for their own advantage, whatever the colors they wear. The republic will stand long enough, they think, to draw them up out of their present degradation. It is not to these that I address myself. But there are others who look forward to a republican form of government as a tranquil and lasting state, towards which modern society is daily impelled by the ideas and manners of the time, and who sincerely desire to prepare men to be free. When these men attack religious opinions, they obey the dictates of their passions and not of their interests. Despotism may govern without faith, but liberty cannot. Religion is much more necessary in the republic which they set forth in glowing colors than in the monarchy which they attack; it is more needed in democratic republics than in any others. How is it possible that society should escape destruction if the moral tie is not strengthened in proportion as the political tie is relaxed? And what can be done with a people who are their own masters if they are not submissive to the Deity?

Principal causes which render religion powerful in America

Care taken by the Americans to separate the church from the state—The laws, public opinion, and even the exertions of the clergy concur to promote this end—Influence of religion upon the mind in the United States attributable to this cause—Reason for this—What is the natural state of men with regard to religion at the present time—What are the peculiar and incidental causes which prevent men, in certain countries, from arriving at this state.

The philosophers of the eighteenth century explained in a very simple manner the gradual decay of religious faith. Religious zeal, said they, must necessarily fail the more generally liberty is established and knowledge diffused. Unfortunately, the facts by no means accord with their theory. There are certain populations in Europe whose unbelief is only equaled by their ignorance and debasement; while in America, one of the freest and most enlightened nations in the world, the people fulfill with fervor all the outward duties of religion.

On my arrival in the United States the religious aspect of the country was the first thing that struck my attention; and the longer I stayed there, the more I perceived the great political consequences resulting from this new state of things. In France I had almost always seen the spirit of religion and the spirit of freedom marching in opposite directions. But in America I found they were intimately united and that they reigned in common over the same country. My desire to discover the causes of this phenomenon increased from day to day. In order to satisfy it questioned the members of all the different sects; I sought especially the society of the clergy, who are the depositaries of the different creeds and are especially interested in their duration. As a member of the Roman Catholic Church, I was more particularly brought into contact with several of its priests, with whom I became intimately acquainted. To each of these men I expressed my astonishment and explained my doubts. I found that they differed upon matters of detail alone, and that they all attributed the peaceful dominion of religion in their country mainly to the separation of church and state. I do not hesitate to affirm that during my stay in America I did not meet a single individual, of the clergy or the laity, who was not of the same opinion on this point.

This led me to examine more attentively than I had hitherto done the station which the American clergy occupy in political society. I learned with surprise that they filled no public appointments; I did not see one of them in the administration, and they are not even represented in the legislative assemblies. In several states the law excludes them from political life; public opinion excludes them in all. And when I came to inquire into the prevailing spirit of the clergy, I found that

| 109 |

most of its members seemed to retire of their own accord from the exercise of power, and that they made it the pride of their profession to abstain from politics.

I heard them inveigh against ambition and deceit, under whatever political opinions these vices might chance to lurk; but I learne from their discourses that men are not guilty in the eye of God for any opinions concerning political government which they may profess with sincerity, any more than they are for their mistakes in building a house or in driving a furrow. I perceived that these ministers of the Gospel eschewed all parties, with the anxiety attendant upon personal interest. These facts convinced me that what I had been told was true; and it then became my object to investigate their causes and to inquire how it happened that the real authority of religion was increased by a state of things which diminished its apparent force. These causes did not long escape my researches.

The short space of threescore years can never content the imagination of man; nor can the imperfect joys of this world satisfy his heart. Man alone, of all created beings, displays a natural contempt of existence, and yet a boundless desire to exist; he scorns life, but he dreads annihilation. These different feelings incessantly urge his soul to the contemplation of a future state, and religion directs his musings thither. Religion, then, is simply another form of hope, and it is no less natural to the human heart than hope itself. Men cannot abandon their religious faith without a kind of aberration of intellect and a sort of violent distortion of their true nature; they are invincibly brought back to more pious sentiments. Unbelief is an accident, and faith is the only permanent state of mankind. If we consider religious institutions merely in a human point of view, they may be said to derive an inexhaustible element of strength from man himself, since they belong to one of the constituent principles of human nature.

I am aware that at certain times religion may strengthen this influence, which originates in itself, by the artificial power of the laws and by the support of those temporal institutions that direct society. Religions intimately united with the governments of the earth have been known to exercise sovereign power founded on terror and faith; but when a religion contracts an alliance of this nature, I do not hesitate to affirm that it commits the same error as a man who should sacrifice his future to his present welfare; and in obtaining a power to which it has no claim, it risks that authority which is rightfully its own. When a religion founds its empire only upon the desire of immortality that lives in every human heart, it may aspire to universal dominion; but when it connects itself with a government, it must adopt maxims which are applicable only to certain nations. Thus, in forming an alliance with a political power, religion augments its authority over a few and forfeits the hope of reigning over all.

As long as a religion rests only upon those sentiments which are the consolation of all affliction, it may attract the affections of all mankind. But if it be mixed up with the bitter passions of the world, it may be constrained to defend allies whom its interests, and not the principle of love, have given to it; or to repel as antagonists men who are still attached to it, however opposed they may be to the powers with which it is allied. The church cannot share the temporal power of the state without being the object of a portion of that animosity which the latter excites.

The political powers which seem to be most firmly established have frequently no better guarantee for their duration than the opinions of a generation, the interests of the time, or the life of an individual. A law may modify the social condition which seems to be most fixed and determinate; and with the social condition everything else must change. The powers of society are more or less fugitive, like the years that we spend upon earth; they succeed each other with rapidity, like the fleeting cares of life; and no government has ever yet been founded upon an invariable disposition of the human heart or upon an imperishable interest.

As long as a religion is sustained by those feelings, propensities, and passions which are found to occur under the same forms at all periods of history, it may defy the efforts of time; or at least it can be destroyed only by another religion. But when religion clings to the interests of the world, it becomes almost as fragile a thing as the powers of earth. It is the only one of them all which can hope for immortality; but if it be connected with their ephemeral power, it shares their fortunes and may fall with those transient passions which alone supported them. The alliance which religion contracts with political powers must needs be onerous to itself, since it does not require their assistance to live, and by giving them its assistance it may be exposed to decay.

The danger which I have just pointed out always exists, but it is not always equally visible. In some ages governments seem to be imperishable; in others the existence of society appears to be more precarious than the life of man. Some constitutions plunge the citizens into a lethargic somnolence, and others rouse them to feverish excitement. When governments seem so strong and laws so stable, men do not perceive the dangers that may accrue from a union of church and state. When governments appear weak and laws inconstant, the danger is self-evident, but it is no longer possible to avoid it. We must therefore learn how to perceive it from afar.

In proportion as a nation assumes a democratic condition of society and as communities display democratic propensities, it becomes more and more dangerous to connect religion with political institutions; for the time is coming when authority will be bandied from hand to hand, when political theories will succeed one another, and when men, laws, and constitutions will disappear or be modified from day to day, and this not for a season only, but unceasingly. Agitation and mutability are inherent in the nature of democratic republics, just as stagnation and sleepiness are the law of absolute monarchies.

If the Americans, who change the head of the government once in four years, who elect new legislators every two years, and renew the state officers every twelve months; if the Americans, who have given up the political world to the attempts of innovators, had not placed religion beyond their reach, where could it take firm hold in the ebb and flow of human opinions? Where would be that respect which belongs to it, amid the struggles of faction? And what would become of its immortality, in the midst of universal decay? The American clergy were the first to perceive this truth and to act in conformity with it. They saw that they must renounce their religious influence if they were to strive for political power, and they chose to give up the support of the state rather than to share its vicissitudes.

In America religion is perhaps less powerful than it has been at certain periods and among certain nations; but its influence is more lasting. It restricts itself to its own resources, but of these none can deprive it; its circle is limited, but it pervades it and holds it under undisputed control.

On every side in Europe we hear voices complaining of the absence of religious faith and inquiring the means of restoring to religion some remnant of its former authority. It seems to me that we must first attentively consider what ought to be the natural state of men with regard to religion at the present time; and when we know what we have to hope and to fear, we may discern the end to which our efforts ought to be directed.

The two great dangers which threaten the existence of religion are schism and indifference. In ages of fervent devotion men sometimes abandon their religion, but they only shake one off in order to adopt another. Their faith changes its objects, but suffers no decline. The old religion then excites enthusiastic attachment or bitter enmity in either party; some leave it with anger, others cling to it with increased devotedness, and although persuasions differ, irreligion is unknown. Such, however, is not the case when a religious belief is secretly undermined by doctrines which may be termed negative, since they deny the truth of one religion without affirming that of any other. Prodigious revolutions then take place in the human mind, without the apparent co-operation of the passions of man, and almost without his knowledge. Men lose the objects of their fondest hopes as if through forgetfulness. They are carried away by an imperceptible current, which they have not the courage to stem, but which they follow with regret, since it bears them away from a faith they love to a skepticism that plunges them into despair.

In ages which answer to this description men desert their religious opinions from lukewarmness rather than from dislike; they are not rejected, but they fall away. But if the unbeliever does not admit religion to be true, he still considers it useful.

Regarding religious institutions in a human point of view, he acknowledges their influence upon manners and legislation. He admits that they may serve to make men live in peace and prepare them gently for the hour of death. He regrets the faith that he has lost; and as he is deprived of a treasure of which he knows the value, he fears to take it away from those who still possess it.

On the other hand, those who continue to believe are not afraid openly to avow their faith. They look upon those who do not share their persuasion as more worthy of pity than of opposition; and they are aware that to acquire the esteem of the unbelieving, they are not obliged to follow their example. They are not hostile, then, to anyone in the world; and as they do not consider the society in which they live as an arena in which religion is bound to face its thousand deadly foes, they love their contemporaries while they condemn their weaknesses and lament their errors.

As those who do not believe conceal their incredulity, and as those who believe display their faith, public opinion pronounces itself in favor of religion: love, support, and honor are bestowed upon it, and it is only by searching the human soul that we can detect the wounds which it has received. The mass of mankind, who are never without the feeling of religion, do not perceive anything at variance with the established faith. The instinctive desire of a future life brings the crowd about the altar and opens the hearts of men to the precepts and consolations of religion.

But this picture is not applicable to us, for there are men among us who have ceased to believe in Christianity, without adopting any other religion; others are in the perplexities of doubt and already affect not to believe; and others, again, are afraid to avow that Christian faith which they still cherish in secret.

Amid these lukewarm partisans and ardent antagonists a small number of believers exists who are ready to brave all obstacles and to scorn all dangers in defense of their faith. They have done violence to human weakness in order to rise superior to public opinion. Excited by the effort they have made, they scarcely know where to stop; and as they know that the first use which the French made of independence was to attack religion, they look upon their contemporaries with dread, and recoil in alarm from the liberty which their fellow citizens are seeking to obtain. As unbelief appears to them to be a novelty, they comprise all that is new in one indiscriminate animosity. They are at war with their age and country, and they look upon every opinion that is put forth there as the necessary enemy of faith.

Such is not the natural state of men with regard to religion at the present day, and some extraordinary or incidental cause must be at work in France to prevent the human mind from following its natural inclination and to drive it beyond the limits at which it ought naturally to stop.

I am fully convinced that this extraordinary and incidental cause is the close connection of politics and religion. The unbelievers of Europe attack the Christians as their political opponents rather than as their religious adversaries; they hate the Christian religion as the opinion of a party much more than as an error of belief; and they reject the clergy less because they are the representatives of the Deity than because they are the allies of government.

In Europe, Christianity has been intimately united to the powers of the earth. Those powers are now in decay, and it is, as it were, buried under their ruins. The living body of religion has been bound down to the dead corpse of superannuated polity; cut but the bonds that restrain it, and it will rise once more. I do not know what could restore the Christian church of Europe to the energy of its earlier days; that power belongs to God alone; but it may be for human policy to leave to faith the full exercise of the strength which it still retains.

PART V

SELF-RELIANCE AND CHARACTER

St. John Crevecoeur, What Is an American

Excerpted from Letter III ("What is an American") of
J. Hector St. John Crevecoeur, Letters from an American Farmer *(1782).*

J. Hector St. John Crevecoeur (1753–1813) was a Frenchman
who immigrated to the U.S., and became a farmer and author.

I wish I could be acquainted with the feelings and thoughts which must agitate
the heart and present themselves to the mind of an enlightened Englishman, when
he first lands on this continent. He must greatly rejoice that he lived at a time to
see this fair country discovered and settled; he must necessarily feel a share of
national pride, when he views the chain of settlements which embellishes these
extended shores. When he says to himself, this is the work of my countrymen,
who, when convulsed by factions, afflicted by a variety of miseries and wants, restless and impatient, took refuge here. They brought along with them their national genius, to which they principally owe what liberty they enjoy, and what substance they possess. Here he sees the industry of his native country displayed in a
new manner, and traces in their works the embrios of all the arts, sciences, and
ingenuity which flourish in Europe. Here he beholds fair cities, substantial villages,
extensive fields, an immense country filled with decent houses, good roads,
orchards, meadows, and bridges, where an hundred years ago all was wild, woody
and uncultivated! What a train of pleasing ideas this fair spectacle must suggest; it
is a prospect which must inspire a good citizen with the most heartfelt pleasure.
The difficulty consists in the manner of viewing so extensive a scene. He is arrived
on a new continent; a modern society offers itself to his contemptation, different
from what he had hitherto seen. It is not composed, as in Europe, of great lords
who possess every thing and of a herd of people who have nothing. Here are no
aristocratical families, no courts, no kings, no bishops, no ecclesiastical dominion,
no invisible power giving to a few a very visible one; no great manufacturers
employing thousands, no great refinements of luxury. The rich and the poor are
not so far removed from each other as they are in Europe. Some few towns excepted, we are all tillers of the earth, from Nova Scotia to West Florida. We are a people of cultivators, scattered over an immense territory communicating with each
other by means of good roads and navigable rivers, united by the silken bands of
mild government, all respecting the laws, without dreading their power, because
they are equitable. We are all animated with the spirit of an industry which is

unfettered and unrestrained, because each person works for himself. If he travels through our rural districts he views not the hostile castle, and the haughty mansion, contrasted with the clay-built hut and miserable cabin, where cattle and men help to keep each other warm, and dwell in meanness, smoke, and indigence. A pleasing uniformity of decent competence appears throughout our habitations. The meanest of our log-houses is a dry and comfortable habitation. Lawyer or merchant are the fairest titles our towns afford; that of a farmer is the only appellation of the rural inhabitants of our country. It must take some time ere he can reconcile himself to our dictionary, which is but short in words of dignity, and names of honour. There, on a Sunday, he sees a congregation of respectable farmers and their wives, all clad in neat homespun, well mounted, or riding in their own humble waggons. There is not among them an esquire, saving the unlettered magistrate. There he sees a parson as simple as his flock, a farmer who does not riot on the labour of others. We have no princes, for whom we toil, starve, and bleed: we are the most perfect society now existing in the world. Here man is free; as he ought to be; nor is this pleasing equality so transitory as many others are. Many ages will not see the shores of our great lakes replenished with inland nations, nor the unknown bounds of North America entirely peopled. Who can tell how far it extends? Who can tell the millions of men whom it will feed and contain? for no European foot has as yet travelled half the extent of this mighty continent!

The next wish of this traveller will be to know whence came all these people? they are mixture of English, Scotch, Irish, French, Dutch, Germans, and Swedes. From this promiscuous breed, that race now called Americans have arisen. The eastern provinces must indeed be excepted, as being the unmixed descendants of Englishmen. I have heard many wish that they had been more intermixed also: for my part, I am no wisher, and think it much better as it has happened. They exhibit a most conspicuous figure in this great and variegated picture; they too enter for a great share in the pleasing perspective displayed in these thirteen provinces. I know it is fashionable to reflect on them, but I respect them for what they have done; for the accuracy and wisdom with which they have settled their territory; for the decency of their manners; for their early love of letters; their ancient college, the first in this hemisphere; for their industry; which to me who am but a farmer, is the criterion of everything. There never was a people, situated as they are, who with so ungrateful a soil have done more in so short a time. Do you think that the monarchical ingredients which are more prevalent in other governments, have purged them from all foul stains? Their histories assert the contrary.

In this great American asylum, the poor of Europe have by some means met together, and in consequence of various causes; to what purpose should they ask one another what countrymen they are? Alas, two thirds of them had no country. Can a wretch who wanders about, who works and starves, whose life is a continual scene of sore affliction or pinching penury; can that man call England or any other kingdom his country? A country that had no bread for him, whose fields procured him no harvest, who met with nothing but the frowns of the rich, the severity of the laws, with jails and punishments; who owned not a single foot of the extensive surface of this planet? No! urged by a variety of motives, here they came. Every thing has tended to regenerate them; new laws, a new mode of living, a new social system; here they are become men: in Europe they were as so many useless plants, wanting vegitative mould, and refreshing showers; they withered, and were mowed down by want, hunger, and war; but now by the power of transplantation, like all other plants they have taken root and flourished! Formerly they were not numbered in any civil lists of their country, except in those of the poor; here they rank as citizens. By what invisible power has this surprising metamorphosis been performed? By that of the laws and that of their industry. The laws, the indulgent laws, protect them as they arrive, stamping on them the symbol of adoption; they receive ample rewards for their labours; these accumulated rewards procure them lands; those lands confer on them the title of freemen, and to that title every benefit is affixed which men can possibly require.

This is the great operation daily performed by our laws. From whence proceed these laws? From our government. Whence the government? It is derived from the original genius and strong desire of the people ratified and confirmed by the crown. This is the great chain which links us all, this is the picture which every province exhibits, Nova Scotia excepted. There the crown has done all; either there were no people who had genius, or it was not much attended to: the consequence is, that the province is very thinly inhabited indeed; the power of the crown in conjunction with the musketos has prevented men from settling there. Yet some parts of it flourished once, and it contained a mild harmless set of people. But for the fault of a few leaders, the whole were banished. The greatest political error the crown ever committed in America, was to cut off men from a country which wanted nothing but men!

What attachment can a poor European emigrant have for a country where he had nothing? The knowledge of the language, the love of a few kindred as poor as himself, were the only cords that tied him: his country is now that which gives him land, bread, protection, and consequence: *Ubi panis ibi patria*, is the motto of all emigrants. What then is the American, this new man? He is either an European, or the descendant of an European, hence that strange mixture of blood, which you will find in no other country. I could point out to you a family whose grandfather was an Englishman, whose wife was Dutch, whose son married a French woman, and whose present four sons have now four wives of different nations. He is an American, who leaving behind him all his ancient prejudices and manners, receives new ones from the new mode of life he has embraced, the new government he obeys, and the new rank he holds

He becomes an American by being received in the broad lap of our great Alma Mater. Here individuals of all nations are melted into a new race of men, whose labours and posterity will one day cause great changes in the world. Americans are the western pilgrims, who are carrying along with them that great mass of arts, sciences, vigour, and industry which began long since in the east; they will finish the great circle. The Americans were once scattered all over Europe; here they are incorporated into one of the finest systems of population which has ever appeared, and which will hereafter become distinct by the power of the different climates they inhabit. The American ought therefore to love this country much better than that wherein either he or his forefathers were born. Here the rewards of his industry follow with equal steps the progress of his labour; his labour is founded on the basis of nature, self-interest; can it want a stronger allurement? Wives and children, who before in vain demanded of him a morsel of bread, now, fat and frolicsome, gladly help their father to clear those fields whence exuberant crops are to arise to feed and to clothe them all; without any part being claimed, either by a despotic prince, a rich abbot, or a mighty lord. Here religion demands but little of him; a small voluntary salary to the minister, and gratitude to God; can he refuse these? The American is a new man, who acts upon new principles; he must therefore entertain new ideas, and form new opinions. From involuntary idleness, servile dependence, penury, and useless labour, he has passed to toils of a very different nature, rewarded by ample subsistence. —This is an American.

British America is divided into many provinces, forming a large association, scattered along a coast 1,500 miles extent and about 200 wide. This society I would fain examine, at least such as it appears in the middle provinces; if it does not afford that variety of tinges and gradations which may be observed in Europe, we have colours peculiar to ourselves. For instance, it is natural to conceive that those who live near the sea, must be very different from those who live in the woods; the intermediate space will afford a separate and distinct class.

Men are like plants; the goodness and flavour of the fruit proceeds from the peculiar soil and exposition in which they grow. We are nothing but what we derive from the air we breathe, the climate we inhabit, the government we obey, the system of religion we profess, and the nature of our employment. Here you will find but few crimes; these have acquired as yet no root among us. I wish I were able to trace all my ideas; if my ignorance prevents me from describing them properly, I hope I shall be able to delineate a few of the outlines, which are all I propose.

Those who live near the sea, feed more on fish than on flesh, and often encounter that boisterous element. This renders them more bold and enterprising; this leads them to neglect the confined occupations of the land. They see and converse with a variety of people; their intercourse with mankind becomes extensive. The sea inspires them with a love of traffic, a desire of transporting produce from one place to another; and leads them to a variety of resources which supply the place of labour. Those who inhabit the middle settlements, by far the most numerous, must be very different; the simple cultivation of the earth purifies them, but the indulgences of the government, the soft remonstrances of religion, the rank of independent freeholders, must necessarily inspire them with sentiments, very little known in Europe among people of the same class. What do I say? Europe has no such class of men; the early knowledge they acquire, the early bargains they make, give them a great degree of sagacity. As freemen they will be litigious; pride and obstinacy are often the cause of law suits; the nature of our laws and governments may be another. As citizens it is easy to imagine, that they will carefully read the newspapers, enter into every political disquisition, freely blame or censure governors and others. As farmers they will be careful and anxious to get as much as they can, because what they get is their own. As northern men they will love the cheerful cup. As Christians, religion curbs them not in their opinions; the general indulgence leaves every one to think for themselves in spiritual matters; the laws inspect our actions, our thoughts are left to God. Industry, good living, selfishness, litigiousness, country politics, the pride of freemen, religious indifference, are their characteristics. If you recede still farther from the sea, you will come into more modern settlements; they exhibit the same strong lineaments, in a ruder appearance. Religion seems to have still less influence, and their manners are less improved.

Now we arrive near the great woods, near the last inhabited districts; there men seem to be placed still farther beyond the reach of government, which in some measure leaves them to themselves. How can it pervade every corner; as they were driven there by misfortunes, necessity of beginnings, desire of acquiring large tracks of land, idleness, frequent want of economy, ancient debts; the re-union of such people does not afford a very pleasing spectacle. When discord, want of unity and friendship; when either drunkenness or idleness prevail in such remote districts; contention, inactivity, and wretchedness must ensue. There are not the same remedies to these evils as in a long established community. The few magistrates they have, are in general little better than the rest; they are often in a perfect state of war; that of man against man, sometimes decided by blows, sometimes by means of the law; that of man against every wild inhabitant of these venerable woods, of which they are come to dispossess them. There men appear to be no better than carnivorous animals of a superior rank, living on the flesh of wild animals when they can catch them, and when they are not able, they subsist on grain. He who wish to see America in its proper light, and have a true idea of its feeble beginnings barbarous rudiments, must visit our extended line of frontiers where the last settlers dwell, and where he may see the first labours of the mode of clearing the earth, in their different appearances; where men are wholly left dependent on their native tempers, and on the spur of uncertain industry, which often fails when not sanctified by the efficacy of a few moral rules. There, remote from the power of example, and check of shame, many families exhibit the most hideous parts of our society. They are a kind of forlorn hope, preceding by ten or twelve years the most respectable army of veterans which come after them. In that space, prosperity will polish some, vice and the law will drive off the rest, who uniting again with others like themselves will recede still farther; making room for more industrious people, who will finish their improvements, convert the loghouse into a convenient habitation, and rejoicing that the first heavy labours are finished, will change in a few years that hitherto barbarous country into a fine fertile, well regulated district. Such is our progress, such is the march of the Europeans toward the interior parts of this continent. In all societies there are off-casts; this impure part serves as our precursors or pioneers; my father himself was one of that class, but he came upon honest principles, and was therefore one of the few who held fast; by good conduct and temperance, he transmitted to me his fair inheritance, when not above one in fourteen of his contemporaries had the same good fortune. Forty years ago this smiling country was thus inhabited; it is now purged, a general decency of manners prevails throughout, and such has been the fate of our best countries.

Exclusive of those general characteristics, each province has its own, founded on the government, climate, mode of husbandry, customs, and peculiarity of circumstances. Europeans submit insensibly to these great powers, and become, in the course of a few generations, not only Americans in general, but either Pennsylvanians, Virginians, or provincials under some other name. Whoever traverses the continent must easily observe those strong differences, which will grow more evident in time. The inhabitants of Canada, Massachusetts, the middle provinces, the southern ones will be as different as their climates; their only points of unity will be those of religion and language.

As I have endeavoured to shew you how Europeans become Americans; it may

not be disagreeable to shew you likewise how the various Christian sects introduced, wear out, and how religious indifference becomes prevalent. When any
considerable number of a particular sect happen to dwell contiguous to each other,
they immediately erect a temple, and there worship the Divinity agreeably to their
own peculiar ideas. Nobody disturbs them. If any new sect springs up in Europe,
it may happen that many of its professors will come and settle in America. As they
bring their zeal with them, they are at liberty to make proselytes if they can, and
to build a meeting and to follow the dictates of their consciences; for neither the
government nor any other power interferes. If they are peaceable subjects, and are
industrious, what is it to their neighbours how and in what manner they think fit
to address their prayers to the Supreme Being? But if the sectaries are not settled
close together, if they are mixed with other denominations, their zeal will cool for
want of fuel, and will be extinguished in a little time. Then the Americans become
as to religion, what they are as to country, allied to all. In them the name of
Englishman, Frenchman, and European is lost, and in like manner, the strict
modes of Christianity as practised in Europe are lost also. This effect will extend
itself still farther hereafter, and though this may appear to you as a strange idea, yet
it is a very true one. I shall be able perhaps hereafter to explain myself better, in
the meanwhile, let the following example serve as my first justification.

Let us suppose you and I to be travelling; we observe that in this house, to the
right, lives a Catholic, who prays to God as he has been taught, and believes in
transubstantion; he works and raises wheat, he has a large family of children, all
hale and robust; his belief, his prayers offend nobody. About one mile farther on
the same road, his next neighbour may be a good honest plodding German
Lutheran, who addresses himself to the same God, the God of all, agreeably to the
modes he has been educated in, and believes in consubstantiation; by so doing he
scandalizes nobody; he also works in his fields, embellishes the earth, clears
swamps, etc. What has the world to do with his Lutheran principles? He persecutes
nobody, and nobody persecutes him, he visits his neighbours, and his neighbours
visit him. Next to him lives a seceder, the most enthusiastic of all sectaries; his zeal
is hot and fiery, but separated as he is from others of the same complexion, he has
no congregation of his own to resort to, where he might cabal and mingle religious
pride with worldly obstinacy. He likewise raises good crops, his house is hand-
somely painted, his orchard is one of the fairest in the neighbourhood. How does
it concern the welfare of the country, or of the province at large, what this man's
religious sentiments are, or really whether he has any at all? He is a good farmer,
he is a sober, peaceable, good citizen: William Penn himself would not wish for
more. This is the visible character, the invisible one is only guessed at, and is

nobody's business. Next again lives a Low Dutchman, who implicitly believes the rules laid down by the synod of Dort. He conceives no other idea of a clergyman than that of an hired man; if he does his work well he will pay him the stipulated sum; if not he will dismiss him, and do without his sermons, and let his church be shut up for years. But notwithstanding this coarse idea, you will find his house and farm to be the neatest in all the country; and you will judge by his waggon and fat horses, that he thinks more of the affairs of this world than of those of the next. He is sober and laborious, therefore he is all he ought to be as to the affairs of this life; as for those of the next, he must trust to the great Creator. Each of these people instruct their children as well as they can, but these instructions are feeble compared to those which are given to the youth of the poorest class in Europe. Their children will therefore grow up less zealous and more indifferent in matters of religion than their parents. The foolish vanity, or rather the fury of making Proselytes, is unknown here; they have no time. The seasons call for all their attention, and thus in a few years, this mixed neighbourhood will exhibit a strange religious medley, that will be neither pure Catholicism nor pure Calvinism. A very perceptible indifference even in the first generation, will become apparent; and it may happen that the daughter of the Catholic will marry the son of the seceder, and settle by themselves at a distance from their parents. What religious education will they give their children? A very imperfect one. If there happens to be in the neighbourhood any place of worship, we will suppose a Quaker's meeting; rather than not show their fine clothes, they will go to it, and some of them may perhaps attach themselves to that society. Others will remain in a perfect state of indifference; the children of these zealous parents will not be able to tell what their religious principles are, and their grandchildren still less. The neighborhood of a place of worship generally leads them to it, and the action of going thither, is the strongest evidence they can give of their attachment to any sect. The Quakers are the only people who retain a fondness for their own mode of worship; for be they ever so far separated from each other, they hold a sort of communion with the society, and seldom depart from its rules, at least in this country. Thus all sects are mixed as well as all nations; thus religious indifference is imperceptibly disseminated from one end of the continent to the other; which is at present one of the strongest characteristics of the Americans. Where this will reach no one can tell, perhaps it may leave a vacuum fit to receive other systems. Persecution, religious pride, the love of contradiction, are the food of what the world commonly calls religion. These motives have ceased here: zeal in Europe is confined; here it evaporates in the great distance it has to travel; there it is a grain of powder inclosed, here it burns away in the open air, and consumes without effect.

But to return to our back settlers. I must tell you, that there is something in the proximity of the woods, which is very singular. It is with men as it is with the plants and animals that grow and live in the forests; they are entirely different from those that live in the plains. I will candidly tell you all my thoughts but you are not to expect that I shall advance any reasons. By living in or near the woods, their actions are regulated by the wildness of the neighbourhood. The deer often come to eat their grain, the wolves to destroy their sheep, the bears to kill their hogs, the foxes to catch their poultry. This surrounding hostility, immediately puts the gun into their hands; they watch these animals, they kill some; and thus by defending their property, they soon become professed hunters; this is the progress; once hunters, farewell to the plough. The chase renders them ferocious, gloomy, and unsociable; a hunter wants no neighbour, he rather hates them, because he dreads the competition. In a little time their success in the woods makes them neglect their tillage. They trust to the natural fecundity of the earth, and therefore do little; carelessness in fencing, often exposes what little they sow to destruction; they are not at home to watch; in order therefore to make up the deficiency, they go oftener to the woods. That new mode of life brings along with it a new set of manners, which I cannot easily describe. These new manners being grafted on the old stock, produce a strange sort of lawless profligacy, the impressions of which are indelible.

The manners of the Indian natives are respectable, compared with this European medley. Their wives and children live in sloth and inactivity; and having no proper pursuits, you may judge what education the latter receive. Their tender minds have nothing else to contemplate but the example of their parents; like them they grow up a mongrel breed, half civilized, half savage, except nature stamps on them some constitutional propensities. That rich, that voluptuous sentiment is gone that struck them so forcibly; the possession of their freeholds no longer conveys to their minds the same pleasure and pride. To all these reasons you must add, their lonely situation, and you cannot imagine what an effect on manners the great distances they live from each other has I Consider one of the last settlements in its first view: of what is it composed? Europeans who have not that sufficient share of knowledge they ought to have, in order to prosper; people who have suddenly passed from oppression, dread of government, and fear of laws, into the unlimited freedom of the woods. This sudden change must have a very great effect on most men, and on that class particularly. Eating of wild meat, what ever you may think, tends to alter their temper though all the proof I can adduce, is, that I have seen it: and having no place of worship to resort to, what little society this might afford, is denied them. The Sunday meetings, exclusive of religious benefits, were the only social bonds that might have inspired them with some degree of emulation in neatness. Is it then surprising to see men thus situated, immersed in great and heavy labours, degenerate a little? It is rather a wonder the effect is not more diffusive. The Moravians and the Quakers are the only instances in exception to what I have advanced. The first never settle singly, it is a colony of the society which emigrates; they carry with them their forms, worship, rules, and decency: the others never begin so hard, they are always able to buy improvements, in which there is a great advantage, for by that time the country is recovered from its first barbarity. Thus our bad people are those who are half cultivators and half hunters; and the worst of them are those who have degenerated altogether into the hunting state. As old ploughmen and new men of the woods, as Europeans and new made Indians, they contract the vices of both; they adopt the moroseness and ferocity of a native, without his mildness, or even his industry at home. If manners are not refined, at least they are rendered simple and inoffensive by tilling the earth; all our wants are supplied by it, our time is divided between labour and rest, and leaves none for the commission of great misdeeds. As hunters it is divided between the toil of the chase, the idleness of repose, or the indulgence of inebriation Hunting is but a licentious idle life, and if it does not always pervert good dispositions; yet, when it is united with bad luck, it leads to want: want stimulates that propensity to rapacity and injustice, too natural to needy men, which is the fatal gradation. After this explanation of the effects which follow by living in the woods, shall we yet vainly flatter ourselves with the hope of converting the Indians? We should rather begin with converting our back-settlers; and now if I dare mention the name of religion, its sweet accents would be lost in the immensity of these woods. Men thus placed, are not fit either to receive or remember its mild instructions; they want temples and ministers, but as soon as men cease to remain at home, and begin to lead an erratic life, let them be either tawny or white, they cease to be its disciples.

Thus have I faintly and imperfectly endeavoured to trace our society from the sea to our woods ! Yet you must not imagine that every person who moves back, acts upon the same principles, or falls into the same degeneracy. Many families carry with them all their decency of conduct, purity of morals, and respect of religion; but these are scarce, the power of example is sometimes irresistible. Even among these back-settlers, their depravity is greater or less, according to what nation or province they belong. Were I to adduce proofs of this, I might be accused of partiality. If there happens to be some rich intervals, some fertile bottoms, in those remote districts, the people will there prefer tilling the land to hunting, and will attach themselves to it; but even on these fertile spots you may plainly perceive the inhabitants to acquire a great degree of rusticity and selfishness. It is in consequence of this straggling situation, and the astonishing power it has on manners, that the back-settlers of both the Carolinas, Virginia, and many other parts, have been long a set of lawless people; it has been even dangerous to travel among them. Government can do nothing in so extensive a country, better it should wink at these irregularities, than that it should use means inconsistent with its usual mildness. Time will efface those stains: in proportion as the great body of population approaches them they will reform, and become polished and subordinate. Whatever has been said of the four New England provinces, no such degeneracy of manners has ever tarnished their annals; their back-settlers have been kept within the bounds of decency, and government, by means of wise laws, and by the influence of religion. What a detestable idea such people must have given to the natives of the Europeans They trade with them, the worst of people are permitted to do that which none but persons of the best characters should be employed in. They get drunk with them, and often defraud the Indians. Their avarice, removed from the eyes of their superiors, knows no bounds; and aided by a little superiority of knowledge, these traders deceive them, and even sometimes shed blood. Hence those shocking violations, those sudden devastations which have so often stained our frontiers, when hundreds of innocent people have been sacrificed for the crimes of a few. It was in consequence of such behaviour, that the Indians took the hatchet against the Virginians in 1774. Thus are our first steps trod, thus are our first trees felled, in general, by the most vicious of our people and thus the path is opened for the arrival of a second and better class, the true American freeholders; the most respectable set of people in this part of the world: respectable for their industry, their happy independence, the great share of freedom they possess, the good regulation of their families, and for extending the trade and the dominion of our mother country. Europe contains hardly any other distinctions but lords and tenants; this fair country alone is settled by freeholders, the possessors of the soil they cultivate, members of the government they obey, and the framers of their own laws, by means of their representatives. This is a thought which you have taught me to cherish; our difference from Europe, far from diminishing, rather adds to our usefulness and consequence as men and subjects. Had our forefathers remained there, they would only have crowded it, and perhaps prolonged those convulsions which had shook it so long. Every industrious European who transports himself here may be compared to a sprout growing at the foot of a great tree; it enjoys and draws but a little portion of sap; wrench it from the parent roots, transplant it, and it will become a tree bearing fruit also. Colonists are therefore entitled to the consideration due to the most useful subjects; a hundred families barely existing in some parts of Scotland, will here in six years, cause an annual exportation of 10,000 bushels of wheat: 100 bushels being but a common quantity for an industrious family to sell, if they cultivate good land. It is here then that the idle may be employed, the useless be- come useful, and the poor become rich; but by riches I do not mean gold and silver, we have but little of those metals; I mean a better sort of wealth, cleared lands, cattle, good houses, good cloaths, and an increase of people to enjoy them.

It is no wonder that this country has so many charms, and presents to Europeans so many temptations to remain in it. A traveller in Europe becomes a stranger as soon as he quits his own kingdom; but it is otherwise here. We know, properly speaking, no strangers; this is every person's country; the variety of our soils, situations, climates, governments, and produce, hath something which must please every body. No sooner does an European arrive, no matter of what condition, than his eyes are opened upon the fair prospect; he hears his language spoke, he retraces many of his own country manners, he perpetually hears the names of families and towns with which he is acquainted; he sees happiness and prosperity in all places disseminated; he meets with hospitality, kindness, and plenty every where; he beholds hardly any poor, he seldom hears of punishments and executions; and he wonders at the elegance of our towns, those miracles of industry and freedom. He cannot admire enough our rural districts, our convenient roads, good taverns, and our many accommodations; he involuntarily loves a country where every thing is so lovely. When in England, he was a mere Englishman; here he stands on a larger portion of the globe, not less than its fourth part, and may see the productions of the north, in iron and naval stores; the provisions of Ireland, the grain of Egypt, the indigo, the rice of China. He does not find, as in Europe, a crowded society, where every place is over-stocked; he does not feel that perpetual collision of parties, that difficulty of beginning, that contention which oversets so many. There is room for every body in America; has he any particular talent, or industry? he exerts it in order to procure a livelihood, and it succeeds. Is he a merchant? the avenues of trade are infinite; is he eminent in any respect? he will be employed and respected. Does he love a country life ? pleasant farms present themselves; he may purchase what he wants, and thereby become an American farmer. Is he a labourer, sober and industrious? he need not go many miles, nor receive many informations before he will be hired, well fed at the table of his employer, and paid four or five times more than he can get in Europe. Does he want uncultivated lands? Thousands of acres present themselves, which he may purchase cheap. Whatever be his talents or inclinations, if they are moderate, he may satisfy them. I do not mean that every one who comes will grow rich in a little time;

no, but he may procure an easy, decent maintenance, by his industry. Instead of starving he will be fed, instead of being idle he will have employment; and these are riches enough for such men as come over here. The rich stay in Europe, it is only the middling and the poor that emigrate. Would you wish to travel in independent idleness, from north to south, you will find easy access, and the most chearful reception at every house; society without ostentation, good cheer without pride, and every decent diversion which the country affords, with little expence. It is no wonder that the European who has lived here a few years, is desirous to remain; Europe with all its pomp, is not to be compared to this continent, for men of middle stations, or labourers.

An European, when he first arrives, seems limited in his intentions, as well as in his views; but he very suddenly alters his scale; two hundred miles formerly appeared a very great distance, it is now but a trifle; he no sooner breathes our air than he forms schemes, and embarks in designs he never would have thought of in his own country. There the plenitude of society confines many useful ideas, and often extinguishes the most laudable schemes which here ripen into maturity. Thus Europeans become Americans.

But how is this accomplished in that crowd of low, indigent people, who flock here every year from all parts of Europe? I will tell you; they no sooner arrive than they immediately feel the good effects of that plenty of provisions we possess: they fare on our best food, and they are kindly entertained; their talents, character, and peculiar industry are immediately inquired into; they find countrymen everywhere disseminated, let them come from whatever part of Europe. Let me select one as an epitome of the rest; he is hired, he goes to work, and works moderately; instead of being employed by a haughty person, he finds himself with his equal, placed at the substantial table of the farmer, or else at an inferior one as good; his wages are high, his bed is not like that bed of sorrow on which he used to lie: if he behaves with propriety, and is faithful, he is caressed, and becomes as it were a member of the family. He begins to feel the effects of a sort of resurrection; hitherto he had not lived, but simply vegetated; he now feels himself a man, because he is treated as such; the laws of his own country had overlooked him in his insignificancy; the laws of this cover him with their mantle. Judge what an alteration there must arise in the mind and thoughts of this man; he begins to forget his former servitude and dependence, his heart involuntarily swells and glows; this first swell inspires him with those new thoughts which constitute an American. What love can he entertain for a country where his existence was a burthen to him; if he is a generous good man, the love of this new adoptive parent will sink deep into his heart. He looks around, and sees many a prosperous person, who but a few years before was as poor as himself. This encourages him much, he begins to form some little scheme, the first, alas, he ever formed in his life. If he is wise he thus spends two or three years, in which time he acquires knowledge, the use of tools, the modes of working the lands, felling trees, etc. This prepares the foundation of a good name, the most useful acquisition he can make. He is encouraged, he has gained friends; he is advised and directed, he feels bold, he purchases some land; he gives all the money he has brought over, as well as what he has earned, and trusts to the God of harvests for the discharge of the rest. His good name procures him credit. He is now possessed of the deed, conveying to him and his posterity the fee simple and absolute property of two hundred acres of land, situated on such a river. What an epocha in this man's life! He is become a freeholder, from perhaps a German boor—he is now an American, a Pennsylvanian, an English subject. He is naturalized, his name is enrolled with those of the other citizens of the province. Instead of being a vagrant, he has a place of residence; he is called the inhabitant of such a county, or of such a district, and for the first time in his life counts for something; for hitherto he has been a cypher. I only repeat what I have heard man say, and no wonder their hearts should glow, and be agitated with a multitude of feelings, not easy to describe. From nothing to start into being; from a servant to the rank of a master; from being the slave of some despotic prince, to become a free man, invested with lands, to which every municipal blessing is annexed! What a change indeed! It is in consequence of that change that he becomes an American. This great metamorphosis has a double effect, it extinguishes all his European prejudices, he forgets that mechanism of subordination, that servility of disposition which poverty had taught him; and sometimes he is apt to forget too much, often passing from one extreme to the other. If he is a good man, he forms schemes of future prosperity, he proposes to educate his children better than he has been educated himself; he thinks of future modes of conduct, feels an ardor to labour he never felt before. Pride steps in and leads him to everything that the laws do not forbid: he respects them; with a heartfelt gratitude he looks toward the east, toward that insular government from whose wisdom all his new felicity is derived, and under whose wings and protection he now lives. These reflections constitute him the good man and the good subject. Ye poor Europeans, ye, who sweat, and work for the great—-ye, who are obliged to give so many sheaves to the church, so many to your lords, so many to your government, and have hardly any left for yourselves—ye, who are held in less estimation than favourite hunters or useless lapdogs—ye, who only breathe the air of nature, because it cannot be withheld from you; it is here that ye can conceive the possibility of those feelings I have been describing; it is here the laws of naturalization invite everyone to partake of our great labours and felicity, to till unrented untaxed lands! Many, corrupted beyond the power of amendment, have brought with them all their vices, and disregarding the advantages held to them, have gone on in their former career of iniquity, until they have been overtaken and punished by our laws. It is not every emigrant who succeeds; no, it is only the sober, the honest, and industrious: happy those to whom this transition has served as a powerful spur to labour, to prosperity, and to the good establishment of children, born in the days of their poverty; and who had no other portion to expect but the rags of their parents, had it not been for their happy emigration. Others again, have been led astray by this enchanting scene; their new pride, instead of leading them to the fields, has kept them in idleness; the idea of possessing lands is all that satisfies them—though surrounded with fertility, they have mouldered away their time in inactivity, misinformed husbandry, and ineffectual endeavours. How much wiser, in general, the honest Germans than almost all other Europeans; they hire themselves to some of their wealthy landsmen, and in that apprenticeship learn everything that is necessary. They attentively consider the prosperous industry of others, which imprints in their minds a strong desire of possessing the same advantages. This forcible idea never quits them, they launch forth, and by dint of sobriety, rigid parsimony, and the most persevering industry, they commonly succeed. Their astonishment at their first arrival from Germany is very great—it is to them a dream; the contrast must be powerful indeed they observe their countrymen flourishing in every place; they travel through whole counties where not a word of English is spoken; and in the names and the language of the people, they retrace Germany. They have been an useful acquisition to this continent, and to Pennsylvania in particular; to them it owes some share of its prosperity: to their mechanical knowledge and patience, it owes the finest mills in all America, the best teams of horses, and many other advantages. The recollection of their former poverty and slavery never quits them as long as they live. The Scotch and the Irish might have lived in their own country perhaps as poor, but enjoying more civil advantages, the effects of their new situation do not strike them so forcibly, nor has it so lasting an effect. From whence the difference arises I know not, but out of twelve families of emigrants of each country, generally seven Scotch will succeed, nine German, and four Irish. The Scotch are frugal and laborious, but their wives cannot work so hard as German women, who on the contrary vie with their husbands, and often share with them the most severe toils of the field, which they understand better. They have therefore nothing to struggle against, but the common casualties of nature. The Irish do not prosper so well; they love to drink and to quarrel; they are litigious, and soon take to the gun, which is the ruin of everything; they seem beside to labour under a greater degree of ignorance in husbandry than the others; perhaps it is that their industry had less scope, and was less exercised at home. I have heard many relate, how the land was parcelled out in that kingdom; their ancient conquest has been a great detriment to them, by oversetting their landed property. The lands possessed by a few, are leased down ad infinitum, and the occupiers often pay five guineas an acre. The poor are worse lodged there than anywhere else in Europe; their potatoes, which are easily raised, are perhaps an inducement to laziness: their ages are too low and their whisky too cheap.

There is no tracing observations of this kind, without making at the same time very great allowances, as there are everywhere to be found, a great many exceptions. The Irish themselves, from different parts of that kingdom, are very different. It is difficult to account for this surprising locality, one would think on so small an island an Irishman must be an Irishman: yet it is not so, they are different in their aptitude to, and in their love of labour.

The Scotch on the contrary are all industrious and saving; they want nothing more than a field to exert themselves in, and they are commonly sure of succeeding. The only difficulty they labour under is, that technical American knowledge which requires some time to obtain; it is not easy for those who seldom saw a tree, to conceive how it is to be felled, cut up, and split into rails and posts. As I am fond of seeing and talking of prosperous families, I intend to finish this letter by relating to you the history of an honest Scotch Hebridean, who came here in 1774, which will shew you in epitome, what the Scotch can do, wherever they have room for the exertion of their industry.

Whenever I hear of any new settlement, I pay it a visit once or twice a year, on purpose to observe the different steps each settler takes, the gradual improvements, the different tempers of each family, on which their prosperity in a great nature depends; their different modifications of industry, their ingenuity, and contrivance; for being all poor, their life requires sagacity and prudence. In an evening I love to hear them tell their stories, they furnish me with new ideas; I sit still and listen to their ancient misfortunes, observing in many of them a strong degree of gratitude to God, and the government. Many a well meant sermon have I preached to some of them. When I found laziness and inattention to prevail, who could refrain from wishing well to these new countrymen after having undergone so many fatigues. Who could withhold good advice? What a happy change it must be, to descend from the high, sterile, bleak lands of Scotland, where every thing is barren and cold, to rest on some fertile farms in these middle provinces! Such a transition must have afforded the most pleasing satisfaction.

The following dialogue passed at an outsettlement, where I lately paid a visit:

Well, friend, how do you do now; I am come fifty odd miles on purpose to see you; how do you go on with your new cutting and slashing? Very well, good Sir, we learn the use of the axe bravely, we shall make it out; we have a belly full of victuals every day, our cows run about, and come home full of milk, our hogs get fat of themselves in the woods: Oh, this is a good country ! God bless the king, and William Penn; we shall do very well by and by, if we keep our healths.

Your loghouse looks neat and light, where did you get these shingles? One of our neighbours is a New England man, and he showed us how to split them out of chestnut trees. Now for a barn, but all in good time, here are fine trees to build with. Who is to frame it, sure you don't understand that work yet?

A countryman of ours who has been in America these ten years, offers to wait for his money until the second crop is lodged in it. What did you give for your land? Thirty-five shillings per acre, payable in seven years. How many acres have you got? An hundred and fifty. That is enough to begin with; is not your land pretty hard to clear? Yes, Sir, hard enough, but it would be harder still if it was ready cleared, for then we should have no timber, and I love the woods much; the land is nothing without them. Have not you found out any bees yet? No, Sir; and if we had we should not know what to do with them. I will tell you by and by. You are very kind. Farewell, honest man, God prosper you; whenever you travel toward, enquire for J.S. He will entertain you kindly, provided you bring him good tidings from your family and farm. In this manner I often visit them, and carefully examine their houses, their modes of ingenuity, their different ways; and make them all relate all they know, and describe all they feel. These are scenes which I believe you would willingly share with me. I well remember your philanthropic turn of mind. Is it not better to contemplate under these humble roofs, the rudiments of future wealth and population, than to behold the accumulated bundles of litigious papers in the office of a lawyer? To examine how the world is gradually settled, how the howling swamp is converted into a pleasing meadow, the rough ridge into a fine field; and to hear the cheerful whistling, the rural song, where there was no sound heard before, save the yell of the savage, the screech of the owl, or the hissing of the snake? Here an European, fatigued with luxury, riches, and pleasures, may find a sweet relaxation in a series of interesting scenes, as affecting as they are new. England, which now contains so many domes, so many castles, was once like this; a place woody and marshy; its inhabitants, now the favourite nation for arts and commerce, were once painted like our neighbours. The country will flourish in its turn, and the same observations will be made which I have just delineated. Posterity will look back with avidity and pleasure, to trace, if possible, the era of this or that particular settlement. Pray, what is the reason that the Scots are in general more religious, more faithful, more honest, and industrious than the Irish? I do not mean to insinuate national reflections, God forbid! If ill becomes any man, and much less an American; but as I know men are nothing of themselves, and that they owe all their different modifications either to government or other local circumstances, there must be some powerful causes which constitute this great national difference. Agreeable to the account which several Scotchmen have given me of the north of Britain, of the Orkneys, and the Hebride Islands, they seem, on many accounts, to be unfit for the habitation of men; they appear to be calculated only for great sheep pastures. Who then can blame the inhabitants of these countries for transporting themselves hither? This great continent must in time absorb the poorest part of Europe; and this will happen in proportion as it becomes better known; and as war, taxation, oppression, and misery increase there. The Hebrides appear to be fit only for the residence of malefactors, and it would be much better to send felons there than either to Virginia or Maryland. What a strange compliment has our mother country paid to two of the finest provinces in America! England has entertained in that respect very mistaken ideas; what was intended as a punishment, is become the good fortune of several; many of those who have been transported as felons, are now rich, and strangers to the stings of those wants that urged them to violations of the law: they are become industrious, exemplary, and useful citizens. The English government should purchase the most northern and barren of those islands; it should send over to us the honest, primitive Hebrideans, settle them here on good lands, as a reward for their virtue and ancient poverty; and replace them with a colony of her wicked sons. The severity of the climate, the inclemency of the seasons, the sterility of the soil, the tempestuousness of the sea, would afflict and punish enough. Could there be found a spot better adapted to retaliate the injury it had received by their crimes? Some of those islands might be considered as the hell of Great Britain, where all evil spirits should be sent. Two essential ends would be answered by this simple operation. The good people, by emigration, would be rendered happier; the bad ones would be placed where they ought to be. In a few years the dread of being sent to that wintry region would have a much stronger effect, than that of transportation. This is no place of punishment; were I a poor hopeless, breadless Englishman, and not restrained by the power of shame, I should be very thankful for the passage. It is of very little importance how, and in what manner an indigent man arrives; for if he is but sober, honest, and industrious, he has nothing more to ask of heaven. Let him go to work, he will have opportunities enough to earn a comfortable support, and even the means of procuring some land; which ought to be the utmost wish of every person who has health and hands to work. I knew a man who came to this country, in the literal sense of the expression, stark naked; I think he was a Frenchman and a sailor on board an English man of war.

Being discontented, he had stripped himself and swam ashore; where finding clothes and friends, he settled afterwards at Maraneck, In the county of Chester, in the province of New York: he married and left a good farm to each of his sons. I knew another person who was but twelve years old when he was taken on the frontiers of Canada, by the Indians; at his arrival at Albany he was purchased by a gentleman, who generously bound him apprentice to a tailor. He lived to the age of ninety, and left behind him a fine estate and a numerous family, all well settled; many of them I am acquainted with. Where is then the industrious European who ought to despair? After a foreigner from any part of Europe is arrived, and become a citizen; let him devoutly listen to the voice of our great parent, which says to him, "Welcome to my shores, distressed European; bless the hour in which thou didst see my verdant fields, my fair navigable rivers, and my green mountains! If thou wilt work, I have bread for thee; if thou wilt be honest, sober, and industrious, I have greater rewards to confer on thee—ease and independence. I will give thee fields to feed and clothe thee; a comfortable fireside to sit by, and tell thy children by what means thou hast prospered; and a decent bed to repose on. I shall endow thee beside with the immunities of a freeman. If thou wilt carefully educate thy children, teach them gratitude to God, and reverence to that government, that philanthropic government, which has collected here so many men and made them happy. I will also provide for thy progeny; and to every good man this ought to be the most holy, the most powerful, the most earnest wish he can possibly form, as well as the most consolatory prospect when he dies. Go thou and work and till; thou shalt prosper, provided thou be just, grateful, and industrious."

Benjamin Franklin, To Those Who Would Remove to America

Benjamin Franklin, "Information to Those Who Would Remove to America," February 1784

Benjamin Franklin (1706–1790) was a statesman and a philosopher.

Many Persons in Europe having directly or by Letters, express'd to the Writer of this, who is well acquainted with North-America, their Desire of transporting and establishing themselves in that Country; but who appear to him to have formed thro' Ignorance, mistaken Ideas & Expectations of what is to be obtained there; he thinks it may be useful, and prevent inconvenient, expensive & fruitless Removals and Voyages of improper Persons, if he gives some clearer & truer Notions of that Part of the World than appear to have hitherto prevailed.

He finds it is imagined by Numbers that the Inhabitants of North America are rich, capable of rewarding, and disposed to reward all sorts of Ingenuity; that they are at the same time ignorant of all the Sciences; & consequently that strangers possessing Talents in the Belles-Letters, Fine Arts, &c. must be highly esteemed, and so well paid as to become easily rich themselves; that there are also abundance of profitable Offices to be disposed of, which the Natives are not qualified to fill; and that having few Persons of Family among them, Strangers of Birth must be greatly respected, and of course easily obtain the best of those Offices, which will make all their Fortunes: that the Governments too, to encourage Emigrations from Europe, not only pay the expence of personal Transportation, but give Lands gratis to Strangers, with Negroes to work for them, Utensils of Husbandry, & Stocks of Cattle. These are all wild Imaginations; and those who go to America with Expectations founded upon them, will surely find themselves disappointed.

The Truth is, that tho' there are in that Country few People so miserable as the Poor of Europe, there are also very few that in Europe would be called rich: it is rather a general happy Mediocrity that prevails. There are few great Proprietors of the Soil, and few Tenants; most People cultivate their own Lands, or follow some Handicraft or Merchandise; very few rich enough to live idly upon their Rents or Incomes; or to pay the high Prices given in Europe, for Paintings, Statues, Architecture and the other Works of Art that are more curious than useful. Hence the natural Geniuses that have arisen in America, with such Talents, have uniformly quitted that Country for Europe, where they can be more suitably rewarded. It is true that Letters and mathematical Knowledge are in Esteem there, but they are at the same time more common than is apprehended; there being already existing nine Colleges or Universities, viz. four in New England, and one in each of the Provinces of New York, New Jersey, Pennsylvania, Maryland and Virginia, all furnish'd with learned Professors; besides a number of smaller Academies: These educate many of their Youth in the Languages and those Sciences that qualify Men for the Professions of Divinity, Law or Physick. Strangers indeed are by no means excluded from exercising those Professions, and the quick Increase of Inhabitants every where gives them a Chance of Employ, which they have in common with the Natives. Of civil Offices or Employments there are few; no superfluous Ones as in Europe; and it is a Rule establish'd in some of the States, that no Office should be so profitable as to make it desirable. The 36 Article of the Constitution of Pennsylvania, runs expressly in these Words: *As every Freeman, to preserve his Independence, (if he has not a sufficient Estate) ought to have some Profession, Calling, Trade or Farm, whereby he may honestly subsist, there can be no Necessity for, nor Use in, establishing Offices of Profit; the usual Effects of which are Dependance and Servility, unbecoming Freemen, in the Possessors and Expectants; Faction, Contention, Corruption, and Disorder among the People. Wherefore whenever an Office, thro' Increase of Fees or otherwise, becomes so profitable as to occasion many to apply for it, the Profits ought to be lessened by the Legislature.*

These Ideas prevailing more or less in all the United States, it cannot be worth any Man's while, who has a means of Living at home, to expatriate himself in hopes of obtaining a profitable civil Office in America; and as to military Offices, they are at an End with the War; the Armies being disbanded. Much less is it adviseable for a Person to go thither who has no other Quality to recommend him but his Birth. In Europe it has indeed its Value, but it is a Commodity that cannot be carried to a worse Market than to that of America, where People do not enquire concerning a Stranger, What IS he? but What can he DO? If he has any useful Art, he is welcome; and if he exercises it and behaves well, he will be respected by all that know him; but a mere Man of Quality, who on that Account wants to live upon the Public, by some Office or Salary, will be despis'd and disregarded. The Husbandman is in honor there, & even the Mechanic, because their Employments are useful. The People have a Saying, that God Almighty is himself a Mechanic, the greatest in the Universe; and he is respected and admired more for the Variety, Ingenuity and Utility of his Handiworks, than for the Antiquity of his Family. They are pleas'd with the Observation of a Negro, and frequently mention it, that Boccarorra (meaning the Whiteman) make de Blackman workee, make de

Horse workee, make de Ox workee, make ebery ting workee; only de Hog. He de Hog, no workee; he eat, he drink, he walk about, he go to sleep when he please, he libb like a Gentleman. According to these Opinions of the Americans, one of them would think himself more oblig'd to a Genealogist, who could prove for him that his Ancestors & Relations for ten Generations had been Ploughmen, Smiths, Carpenters, Turners, Weavers, Tanners, or even Shoemakers, & consequently that they were useful Members of Society; than if he could only prove that they were Gentlemen, doing nothing of Value, but living idly on the Labour of others, mere fruges consumere nati* , and otherwise good for nothing, till by their Death, their Estates like the Carcase of the Negro's Gentleman-Hog, come to be cut up.

[*There are a Number of us born / Merely to eat up the Corn. Watts.]

With Regard to Encouragements for Strangers from Government, they are really only what are derived from good Laws & Liberty. Strangers are welcome because there is room enough for them all, and therefore the old Inhabitants are not jealous of them; the Laws protect them sufficiently, so that they have no need of the Patronage of great Men; and every one will enjoy securely the profits of his Industry. But if he does not bring a Fortune with him, he must work and be industrious to live. One or two Years Residence give him all the Rights of a Citizen; but the Government does not at present, whatever it may have done in former times, hire People to become Settlers, by Paying their Passages, giving Land, Negroes, Utensils, Stock, or any other kind of Emolument whatsoever. In short America is the Land of Labour, and by no means what the English call Lubberland, and the French Pays de Cocagne, where the Streets are said to be pav'd with half-peck Loaves, the Houses til'd with Pancakes, and where the Fowls fly about ready roasted, crying, Come eat me!

Who then are the kind of Persons to whom an Emigration to America may be advantageous? And what are the Advantages they may reasonably expect?

Land being cheap in that Country, from the vast Forests still void of Inhabitants, and not likely to be occupied in an Age to come, insomuch that the Propriety of an hundred Acres of fertile Soil full of Wood may be obtained near the Frontiers in many Places for eight or ten Guineas, hearty young Labouring Men, who understand the Husbandry of Corn and Cattle, which is nearly the same in that Country as in Europe, may easily establish themselves there. A little Money sav'd of the good Wages they receive there while they work for others, enables them to buy the Land and begin their Plantation, in which they are assisted by the Good Will of their Neighbours and some Credit. Multitudes of poor People from England, Ireland, Scotland and Germany, have by this means in a few Years become wealthy Farmers, who in their own Countries, where all the Lands are fully occupied, and the Wages of Labour low, could never have emerged from the mean Condition wherein they were born.

From the Salubrity of the Air, the Healthiness of the Climate, the Plenty of good Provisions, and the Encouragement to early Marriages, by the certainty of Subsistance in cultivating the Earth, the Increase of Inhabitants by natural Generation is very rapid in America, and becomes still more so by the Accession of Strangers; hence there is a continual Demand for more Artisans of all the necessary and useful kinds, to supply those Cultivators of the Earth with Houses, and with Furniture & Utensils of the grosser Sorts which cannot so well be brought from Europe. Tolerably good Workmen in any of those mechanic Arts, are sure to find Employ, and to be well paid for their Work, there being no Restraints preventing Strangers from exercising any Art they understand, nor any Permission necessary. If they are poor, they begin first as Servants or Journeymen; and if they are sober, industrious & frugal, they soon become Masters, establish themselves in Business, marry, raise Families, and become respectable Citizens.

Also, Persons of moderate Fortunes and Capitals, who having a Number of Children to provide for, are desirous of bringing them up to Industry, and to secure Estates for their Posterity, have Opportunities of doing it in America, which Europe does not afford. There they may be taught & practice profitable mechanic Arts, without incurring Disgrace on that Account; but on the contrary acquiring Respect by such Abilities. There small Capitals laid out in Lands, which daily become more valuable by the Increase of People, afford a solid Prospect of ample Fortunes thereafter for those Children. The Writer of this has known several Instances of large Tracts of Land, bought on what was then the Frontier of Pensilvania, for ten Pounds per hundred Acres, which, after twenty Years, when the Settlements had been extended far beyond them, sold readily, without any Improvement made upon them, for three Pounds per Acre. The Acre in America is the same with the English Acre or the Acre of Normandy.

Those who desire to understand the State of Government in America, would do well to read the Constitutions of the several States, and the Articles of Confederation that bind the whole together for general Purposes under the Direction of one Assembly called the Congress. These Constitutions have been printed by Order of Congress in America; two Editions of them have also been printed in London, and a good Translation of them into French has lately been published at Paris.

Several of the Princes of Europe having of late Years, from an Opinion of Advantage to arise by producing all Commodities & Manufactures within their own Dominions, so as to diminish or render useless their Importations, have endeavoured to entice workmen from other Countries, by high Salaries, Privileges, &c. Many Persons pretending to be skilled in various great manufactures, imagining that

America must be in Want of them, and that the Congress would probably be dis-pos'd to imitate the Princes above mentioned, have proposed to go over, on Condition of having their Passages paid, Lands given, Salaries appointed, exclusive Privileges for Terms of Years, etc. Such Persons on reading the Articles of Confederation will find that the Congress have no Power committed to them, or Money put into their Hands, for such purposes; and that if any such Encouragement is given, it must be by the Government of some separate State. This however has rarely been done in America; and when it has been done it has rarely succeeded, so as to establish a Manufacture which the Country was not yet so ripe for as to encourage private Persons to set it up; Labour being generally too dear there, & Hands difficult to be kept together, every one desiring to be a Master, and the Cheapness of Land enclining many to leave Trades for Agriculture. Some indeed have met with Success, and are carried on to Advantage; but they are generally such as require only a few Hands, or wherein great Part of the Work is perform'd by Machines. Goods that are bulky, & of so small Value as not well to bear the Expence of Freight, may often be made cheaper in the Country than they can be imported; and the Manufacture of such Goods will be profitable wherev-er there is a sufficient Demand. The Farmers in America produce indeed a good deal of Wool & Flax; and none is exported, it is all work'd up; but it is in the Way of Domestic Manufacture for the Use of the Family. The buying up Quantities of Wool & Flax with the Design to employ Spinners, Weavers, &c. and form great Establishments, producing Quantities of Linen and Woollen Goods for Sale, has been several times attempted in different Provinces; but those Projects have gener-ally failed, Goods of equal Value being imported cheaper. And when the Governments have been solicited to support such Schemes by Encouragements, in Money, or by imposing Duties on Importation of such Goods, it has been gener-ally refused, on this Principle, that if the Country is ripe for the Manufacture, it may be carried on by private Persons to Advantage; and if not, it is a Folly to think of forceing Nature. Great Establishments of Manufacture, require great Numbers of Poor to do the Work for small Wages; these Poor are to be found in Europe, but will not be found in America, till the Lands are all taken up and cultivated, and the excess of People who cannot get Land, want Employment. The Manufacture of Silk, they say, is natural in France, as that of Cloth in England, because each Country produces in Plenty the first Material: But if England will have a Manufacture of Silk as well as that of Cloth, and France one of Cloth as well as that of Silk, these unnatural Operations must be supported by mutual Prohibitions or high Duties on the Importation of each others Goods, by which means the Workmen are enabled to tax the home-Consumer by greater Prices, while the higher Wages they receive makes them neither happier nor richer, since they only drink more and work less. Therefore the Governments in America do nothing to encourage such Projects. The People by this Means are not impos'd on, either by the Merchant or Mechanic; if the Merchant demands too much Profit on imported Shoes, they buy of the Shoemaker: and if he asks too high a Price, they take them of the Merchant: thus the two Professions are Checks on each other. The Shoemaker however has on the whole a considerable Profit upon his Labour in America, beyond what he had in Europe, as he can add to his Price a Sum nearly equal to all the Expences of Freight & Commission, Risque or Insurance, &c. necessarily charged by the Merchant. And the Case is the same with the Workmen in every other Mechanic Art. Hence it is that Artisans generally live better and more easily in America than in Europe, and such as are good Economists make a comfortable Provision for Age, & for their Children. Such may therefore remove with Advantage to America.

In the old longsettled Countries of Europe, all Arts, Trades, Professions, Farms, &c. are so full that it is difficult for a poor Man who has Children, to place them where they may gain, or learn to gain a decent Livelihood. The Artisans, who fear creating future Rivals in Business, refuse to take Apprentices, but upon Conditions of Money, Maintenance or the like, which the Parents are unable to comply with. Hence the Youth are dragg'd up in Ignorance of every gainful Art, and oblig'd to become Soldiers or Servants or Thieves, for a Subsistance. In America the rapid Increase of Inhabitants takes away that Fear of Rivalship, & Artisans willingly receive Apprentices from the hope of Profit by their Labour during the Remainder of the Time stipulated after they shall be instructed. Hence it is easy for poor Families to get their Children instructed; for the Artisans are so desirous of Apprentices, that many of them will even give Money to the Parents to have Boys from ten to fifteen Years of Age bound Apprentices to them till the Age of twenty one; and many poor Parents have by that means, on their Arrival in the Country, raised Money enough to buy Land sufficient to establish themselves, and to subsist the rest of their Family by Agriculture. These Contracts for Apprentices are made before a Magistrate, who regulates the Agreement according to Reason and Justice; and having in view the Formation of a future useful Citizen, obliges the Master to engage by a written Indenture, not only that during the time of Service stipulated, the Apprentice shall be duly provided with Meat, Drink, Apparel, washing & Lodging, and at its Expiration with a compleat new suit of Clothes, but also that he shall be taught to read, write & cast Accompts, & that he shall be well instructed in the Art or Profession of his Master, or some other, by which he may afterwards gain a Livelihood, and be able in his turn to raise a Family. A Copy of this Indenture is given to the Apprentice or his Friends, & the Magistrate keeps a Record of it, to which Recourse may be had, in case of Failure by the Master in any Point of Performance. This Desire among the Masters to have more Hands employ'd in working for them, induces them to pay the Passages of young Persons, of both Sexes, who on their Arrival agree to serve them one, two, three or four Years; those who have already learnt a Trade agreeing for a shorter Term in Proportion to their Skill and the consequent immediate Value of their Service; and those who have none, agreeing for a longer Term, in Consideration of being taught an Art their Poverty would not permit them to acquire in their own Country.

The almost general Mediocrity of Fortune that prevails in America, obliging its People to follow some Business for Subsistance, those Vices that arise usually from Idleness are in a great Measure prevented. Industry and constant Employment are great Preservatives of the Morals and Virtue of a Nation. Hence bad Examples to Youth are more rare in America, which must be a comfortable Consideration to Parents. To this may be truly added, that serious Religion under its various Denominations, is not only tolerated but respected and practised. Atheism is unknown there, Infidelity rare & secret, so that Persons may live to a great Age in that Country without having their Piety shock'd by meeting with either an Atheist or an Infidel. And the Divine Being seems to have manifested his Approbation of the mutual Forbearance and Kindness with which the different Sects treat each other, by the remarkable Prosperity with which he has been pleased to favour the whole Country.

H.L. Mencken, On Being An American

*The following two newspaper stories written by H.L. Mencken,
"The American,"* The New York Evening Mail, *May 3, 1918, and
"On Being an American,"* The Baltimore Evening Sun, *Oct. 11, 1920
are reprinted by permission of the Enoch Pratt Free Library of Baltimore,
in accordance with the terms of the will of H.L. Mencken.*

H.L. Mencken (1880–1956) was a journalist and editor.

The American

The notion that Americans are a sordid money-grubbing people, with no thought above the dollar, is a favorite delusion of continentals, and even the English, on occasion, dally with it. It has, in fact, little solid basis. The truth is that Americans, as a race, set relatively little store by money; surely all of their bitterest critics are at least as eager for it. This is probably the only country in the world, save Russia under the Bolsheviki, in which a rich man is *ipso facto* a scoundrel and *ferae naturae*, with no rights that any slanderer is bound to respect. It would be a literal impossibility for an Englishman worth $100,000,000 to avoid public office and public honor; it would be equally impossible for an American worth $100,000,000 to obtain either. The moment he showed his head the whole pack would be upon him.

Americans, true enough, are richer than most. Their country yields more than other countries; they get more cash for their labor; they jingle more money in their pockets. But they also spend more, and with less thought of values. Whatever is gaudy and showy gets their dollars; they are, so to speak, constantly on holiday, their eyes alert to get rid of their change. The only genuinely thrifty people among us, in the sense that a Frenchman is thrifty, are foreigners. This is why they are ousting the natives in New England and in large areas of the middle West. But as soon as they become Americanized they begin to draw their money out of the savings banks and to buy phonographs, Fords, boiled shirts, yellow shoes, cuckoo clocks and the works of Bulwer-Lytton.

The character that actually marks off the American is not money-hunger at all; it is what might be called, at the risk of misunderstanding; social aspiration. That is to say, he is forever trying to improve his position; to break down some barrier of caste, to secure the acceptance of his betters. Money, of course, usually helps him in this endeavor, and so he values it — but not for its own sake, not as a thing in itself. On the contrary, he is always willing to pay it out lavishly for what he wants. Nothing is too expensive if it helps him to make a better showing in the world, to raise himself above what he has been.

It is the opportunity that founds the aspiration. The cause of all this unanimous pushing is plainly the fact that every American's position is always more or less insecure—that he is free to climb upward almost infinitely, and that, by the same token, he is in steady danger of slipping back. This keeps him in a state of social timorousness; he is never absolutely safe and never absolutely contented. Such a thing as a secure position is practically unknown among us. There is no American who cannot hope to lift himself another notch—if he is good. And there is no American who doesn't have to keep on fighting for whatever position he has got. All our cities are full of aristocrats whose grandfathers were day laborers, and clerks whose grandfathers were aristocrats.

The oldest societies of Europe protect caste lines more resolutely. A grandee of Spain, for example, is quite as secure in his class as a dog is in his. Nothing he can do in this world can raise him above it, and nothing he can do can bounce him out of it. Once, a long while ago, I met a Spanish count who wore celluloid cuffs, was drunk every afternoon and borrowed money for a living. Yet he remained a count in perfectly good standing, and all lesser Spaniards deferred to him and envied him. He knew that he was quite safe, and so he gave no thought to appearances. In the same way he knew that he had reached his limit. He was a grandee, but he had no hope whatever of making the next step; he knew that he could never be royal.

No American is ever so securely lodged. There is always something just ahead of him, beckoning him and tantalizing him, and there is always something just behind him, menacing him and causing him to sweat. The preposterous doings of what we call our fashionable society are all based on this uncertainty. The elect are surrounded by hordes of pushers, all full of envy, but the elect themselves are by no means safe. The result is a constant maneuvering, an incessant effort to get a firmer hold. It is this effort which inspires so many rich girls to shanghai foreigners of title, A title, however paltry, is still of genuine value. It represents a social status that cannot be changed by the rise of rivals, or by personal dereliction, or by mere accident. It is a policy of insurance against dangers that it is very difficult to meet otherwise.

The mention of social aspiration always suggests the struggle to be accepted as fashionable, but it is really quite as earnest and quite as widespread on all lower planes. Every men's club, even the worst, has a waiting list of men who are eager to get in but have not yet demonstrated that they are up to it. The huge fraternal orders are surrounded by the same swarms of aspirants; there are thousands of men who look forward eagerly to election to the Masons, the Odd Fellows or the Knights of Pythias. And among women – but let us keep away from women. The dominating emotion of almost every normal woman is envy of some other woman. Put beside this grand passion her deep, delirious affection for her husband, and even for her children, fades to a mere phosphoresence.

As I have said, the fruit of all this appetite to get on, this desire to cut a better figure, is not the truculence that might be imagined, but rather timorousness. The desire itself is bold and insatiable, but its satisfaction demands discretion, prudence, a politic and ingratiating habit. The walls are not to be stormed, they must be wooed to a sort of Jerishoan fall. Success takes the form of a series of waves of protective coloration; failure is a succession of unmaskings. The aspirant must first imitate exactly the aspects and behavior of the class he yearns to penetrate. There follows notice. There follows confusion. There follows recognition and acceptance.

Thus the hog murderer's or soap boiler's wife horns into the fashionable society of Chicago or New York, and thus the whiskey drummer insinuates himself into the Elks, and the rising retailer wins the toleration of wholesalers, and the rich peasant becomes a planter, and the servant girl penetrates the movies, and the shyster lawyer becomes a statesman, and Schmidt turns into Smith, and all of us Yankees creep up, up, up. The business is not to be accomplished by headlong assault; it must be done quietly, insidiously, pianissimo. Above all, it must be done without exciting alarm and opposition lest the portcullis fall. Above all, the manner of a Jenkins must be got into it.

It seems to me that this necessity is responsible for one of the characters that observers often note in the average American, to wit, the character of orthodory, of eager conformity–in brief, the fear to give offense. "More than any other people," said Wendell Phillips one blue day, "we Americans are afraid of one another." The saying seems harsh. It goes counter to the national delusion of uncompromising independence and limitless personal freedom. It wars upon the national vanity. But all the same there is a good deal of truth in it.

What is often mistaken for an independent spirit in dealing with the national traits, is not more than a habit of crying with the pack. The American is not a joiner for nothing. He joins something, whether it be a political party, a church or a tin-pot fraternal order, because joining gives him the feeling of security–because it makes him a part of something larger and safer than he is–because it gives him a chance to work off his steam within prudent limits. Beyond lie the national taboos. Beyond lies true independence–and the heavy penalties that go therewith. Once over the border, and the whole pack is on the heretic.

The taboos that I have mentioned are extraordinarily harsh and numerous. They stand around nearly every subject that is genuinely important to man; they hedge in free opinion and experimentation on all sides. Consider, for example, the matter of religion. It is debated freely and furiously in almost every country in the world save the United States. Here the debate, save it keep to the superficial, is frowned upon. Let an individual uncover the fundamentals of the thing, and he is denounced as a disturber of the public peace. Let a journal cut loose and at once an effort if made to bar if from the mails. The result is that all religions are equally safeguarded against criticism and that all of them lose vitality. We protect the status quo, and so make steady war upon revision and improvement.

Nor is our political discussion much more free and thorough. It concerns itself, in the overwhelming main, with non-essentials; time and again the two chief parties of the country, warring over details, have come so close together that it has been almost impossible to distinguish them. Whenever a stray heretic essays to grapple with essentials he finds himself denounced for his contumacy. Thus the discussion of the capital problem of industrial organization, is so far as it has gone on at all, has gone on under the surface, and almost furtively. Now, suddenly bursting out in war time, it takes on an aspect of the sinister, and causes justifiable alarm. That alarm might have been avoided by threshing out the thing in the days of peace.

Behind all this timorousness, of course, there is a sound discretion. With a population made up of widely various and often highly antagonistic elements, many of them without political experience, the dangers of a "too free" gabbling needn't be pointed out. But at the same time it would be useless to deny the disadvantages of the current system of taboos. It tends to substitute mere complacency for alertness and information. It gives a false importance to the occasional rebel. It sets up a peace that is full of dynamite.

On Being an American
I

Apparently there are those who begin to find it disagreeable. One of them unburdened his woes in this place last Tuesday, under the heading of "Is America Fit to Live In?" Let me confess at once that this elegy filled me with great astonishment. I had labored under the impression that this Republic was wholly satisfactory to all 100% Americans—that any proposal to fumigate and improve it was as personally offensive to them as a proposal to improve the looks of their wives. Yet here was a 100% American ranting against it like a Bolshevik on a soap box. And here was I, less than $^1/_2$ of 1% American by volume, standing aghast. A curious experience, indeed. Can it be that all the 100% Americans are preparing to throw up their hands and move out, leaving the land that the Fathers sweated and bled for to us Huns?

God forbid! I'd as lief have some poor working girl (mistaking the street number) leave twins on my doorstep. No one would weep saltier tears than I when the huge fleet of Mayflowers sailed away, bound for some land of liberty. For what makes America charming is precisely the Americans–that is, those above 50%, those above proof. They are, by long odds, the most charming people that I have ever encountered in this world. They have the same charm that one so often notes in a young girl, say of seventeen or eighteen, and perhaps it is grounded upon the same qualities; artlessness, great seriousness, extreme self-consciousness, a fresh and innocent point of view, a disarming and ingratiating ignorance. They are culturally speaking the youngest of white races, and they have all the virtues that go with youngness. It is easy to excite them. It is easy to fool them. But it is very hard to dislike them.

Perhaps there is something deeper than the qualities I have rehearsed. I grope for it vaguely, and decide that it is probably a naïve fidelity to good intentions. The Americans do everything with the best of motives, and with all the solemnity that goes therewith. And they get the reward that the jocose gods invariably bestow. I recall a scene in a low burlesque show, witnessed for hire in my days as a dramatic critic. A chorus girl executes a fall on the stage, and Krausemeyer, the Swiss comedian, rushes to her aid. As he stoops painfully to pick her up, Irving Rabinovitz, the Zionist comedian, fetches him a fearful clout across the cofferdam with a slapstick. Here, in brief, is the history of the United States, particularly in recent years. Say what you will against it, I maintain to the last that it is diverting—that it affords stimulating entertainment to a civilized man.

II

Where, indeed, is there a better show in the world? Where has there been a better show since the Reformation? It goes on daily, not in three rings, but in three hundred rings, and in each one of them whole battalions of acrobats tie themselves into fabulous knots, and the handsomest gals in Christendom pirouette upon the loveliest and most skittish horses, and clowns of unbelievable limberness and humor perform inordinate monkey shines. Consider, for example, the current campaign for the Presidency. Would it be possible to imagine anything more stupendously grotesque—a deafening, nerve-wracking battle to the death between Tweedledum and Tweedledee—the impossible, with fearful snorts, gradually swallowing the inconceivable? I defy anyone to match it elsewhere on this earth. In other lands, at worst, there are at least issues, ideas, personalities. Somebody says something intelligible, and somebody replies. It is important to somebody that the thing go this way or that way. But here, having perfected democracy, we lift the whole combat to a gaudy symbolism, to a disembodied transcendentalism, to metaphysics, that sweet nirvana. Here we load a pair of palpably tin cannons with blank cartridges charged with talcum powder, and so let fly. Here one may howl over the show without an uneasy reminder that someone is being hurt.

I hold that this exhibition is peculiarly American—that nowhere else on this disreputable ball has the art of the sham-battle been developed to such fineness. Two late experiences in point: A few weeks back a Berlin paper reprinted an article of mine from the *Evening Sunpaper*, with an explanatory preface. In this preface the editor was at pains to explain that no intelligent man in the United States regarded the result of an election as important and to warn the Germans against getting into "feverish sweats" over such combats. Last week, I had dinner with an Englishman. From cocktails to bromo seltzer he bewailed the political lassitude of the English populace—its growing indifference to the whole political buffoonery. Here we have two typical foreign attitudes; the Germans make politics too harsh and implacable, and the English take politics too lightly. Both attitudes make for bad shows. Observing a German election, one is uncomfortably harassed and stirred up; observing an English election, one falls asleep. In the United States the thing is better done. Here it is purged of all menace, all sinister quality, all genuine significance—and stuffed with such gorgeous humors, such extravagant imbecilities, such uproarious farce that one comes to the end of it with one's midriff in tatters.

III

But feeling better for the laugh. As the 100% *pleurour* said last Tuesday, the human soul craves joy. It is necessary to happiness, to health. Well, here is the land of joy. Here the show never stops. What could be more steadily mirth-provoking than the endless battle of the Puritans to make this joy unlawful and impossible? The effort is itself a greater joy to one standing on the sidelines than any or all of the joys that it combats. If I had to choose between hanging Dr. Kelly and closing all of the theatres in Baltimore, I'd surely shut up the theatres, for nine times out of ten their laborious struggles to amuse me merely bore me, whereas Dr. Kelly fetches me every time. He is, it seems to me, the eternal American, ever moved by good intentions, ever lifting me to yells with the highest of motives, ever stooping á la Krausemeyer to pick up a foundered chorus girl and ever getting a thumping clout from the Devil.

I am sinful, and such spectacles delight me. If the slapstick were a sash-weight the show would be cruel, and I'd probably go to the rescue of Dr. Kelly. As it is I know that he is not hurt. On the contrary, it does him good; it helps to get him into Heaven. As for me, it helps to divert me from my sorrows, of which there are many. More, it makes me a better American. One man likes the republic because it pays better wages than Bulgaria. Another because it has laws to keep him sober, pious and faithful to his wife. Another because the Woolworth Building is higher than the cathedral at Chartres. Another because there is a warrant out for him somewhere else. Me, I like it because it amuses me. I never get tired of the show. It is worth every cent it costs.

IV

I have never heard of such a show in any other country. Perhaps one goes on in Russia, but, as the European *Advocates Diaboli* said last Tuesday, it is difficult to be happy when one is hungry. Here one always gets plenty to eat, even in the midst of war, and despite Prohibition, quite enough to drink. I remember many post-praedial felicities, inconceivable in Europe, Asia, Africa or Oceania. Four nights, for example, at the Bill Sunday circus; one night in particular. I had got down a capital dinner, with three or four coffin-varnish cocktails and half a bottle of Beni Carlo. (Ah, those days!) Proceeding to the holy place, I witnessed the incomparable spectacle of a governor of Maryland, the president of a bank and the president of the Western Maryland Railroad moaning and puffing in a bull-ring together. Match it in Europe if you can! I defy you to name the country. The governor, prefect, lord lieutenant, *Oberpräsident* of an ancient and imperial province sobbing out his sins in the presence of 20,000 neckstretchers, the while a florid man with an elkborn mustache played "Throw Out the Lifeline" on a trombone!

Another memory. The other day in New York, I gave ear to a publisher soured and made hopeless by the incessant forays of the Comstocks—*The "Genius"* and *Jurgen* suppressed out of hand, half a dozen other good books killed abornin' the national letters hamstrung and knee-haltered by a violent arbitrary and unintelligible despotism. That night I went to the Winter Garden to see the new show. During the first part, 40 or 50 head of girls with their legs bare marched down a runway into the audience, passing within four or five centimeters of my popping eyes. During the second part two comedians came out and began to make jokes about what Havelock Ellis calls inversion. Revolve the thing in your mind. Here was I, an innocent young yoke, forbidden by law to read *Jurgen*, and yet it was quite lawful to beguile me with a herd of half-naked vampires and to divert me with jests proper only to banquets of internes at the Phipps' Clinic. After the show I met Ernest A. Boyd. He told me that he had a fearful beer thirst and would gladly give $5 for a Humpen of 2 3/4%. I raised him $1, but we found that malt was forbidden. But down in Greenwich Village we found plenty of 100-proof Scotch at 65 cents a drink.

V

Let the 100% viewer with alarm stay his tears. If this is not joy, then what is?

Ralph Waldo Emerson, Self-Reliance

Unabridged text of Ralph Waldo Emerson, Self-Reliance *(1841).*

Ralph Waldo Emerson (1803–1882) was an American essayist and poet.

"Ne te quaesiveris extra."

"Man is his own star; and the soul that can
Render an honest and a perfect man,
Commands all light, all influence, all fate;
Nothing to him falls early or too late.
Our acts our angels are, or good or ill,
Our fatal shadows that walk by us still."

Epilogue to Beaumont and Fletcher's Honest Man's Fortune

Cast the bantling on the rocks,
Suckle him with the she-wolf's teat;
Wintered with the hawk and fox,
Power and speed be hands and feet.

I read the other day some verses written by an eminent painter which were original and not conventional. The soul always hears an admonition in such lines, let the subject be what it may. The sentiment they instil is of more value than any thought they may contain. To believe your own thought, to believe that what is true for you in your private heart is true for all men,— that is genius. Speak your latent conviction, and it shall be the universal sense; for the inmost in due time becomes the outmost,—and our first thought is rendered back to us by the trumpets of the Last Judgment. Familiar as the voice of the mind is to each, the highest merit we ascribe to Moses, Plato, and Milton is, that they set at naught books and traditions, and spoke not what men but what they thought. A man should learn to detect and watch that gleam of light which flashes across his mind from within, more than the lustre of the firmament of bards and sages. Yet he dismisses without notice his thought, because it is his. In every work of genius we recognize our own rejected thoughts: they come back to us with a certain alienated majesty. Great works of art have no more affecting lesson for us than this. They teach us to abide by our spontaneous impression with good-humored inflexibility then most when the whole cry of voices is on the other side. Else, tomorrow a stranger will say with masterly good sense precisely what we have thought and felt all the time, and we shall be forced to take with shame our own opinion from another.

There is a time in every man's education when he arrives at the conviction that envy is ignorance; that imitation is suicide; that he must take himself for better, for worse, as his portion; that though the wide universe is full of good, no kernel of nourishing corn can come to him but through his toil bestowed on that plot of ground which is given to him to till. The power which resides in him is new in nature, and none but he knows what that is which he can do, nor does he know until he has tried. Not for nothing one face, one character, one fact, makes much impression on him, and another none. This sculpture in the memory is not without preestablished harmony. The eye was placed where one ray should fall, that it might testify of that particular ray. We but half express ourselves, and are ashamed of that divine idea which each of us represents. It may be safely trusted as proportionate and of good issues, so it be faithfully imparted, but God will not have his work made manifest by cowards. A man is relieved and gay when he has put his heart into his work and done his best; but what he has said or done otherwise, shall give him no peace. It is a deliverance which does not deliver. In the attempt his genius deserts him; no muse befriends; no invention, no hope.

Trust thyself: every heart vibrates to that iron string. Accept the place the divine providence has found for you, the society of your contemporaries, the connection of events. Great men have always done so, and confided themselves childlike to the genius of their age, betraying their perception that the absolutely trustworthy was seated at their heart, working through their hands, predominating in all their being. And we are now men, and must accept in the highest mind the same transcendent destiny; and not minors and invalids in a protected corner, not cowards fleeing before a revolution, but guides, redeemers, and benefactors, obeying the Almighty effort, and advancing on Chaos and the Dark.

What pretty oracles nature yields us on this text, in the face and behaviour of children, babes, and even brutes! That divided and rebel mind, that distrust of a sentiment because our arithmetic has computed the strength and means opposed to our purpose, these have not. Their mind being whole, their eye is as yet unconquered, and when we look in their faces, we are disconcerted. Infancy conforms to nobody: all conform to it, so that one babe commonly makes four or five out of the adults who prattle and play to it. So God has armed youth and puberty and manhood no less with its own piquancy and charm, and made it enviable and gracious and its claims not to be put by, if it will stand by itself. Do not think the youth has no force, because he cannot speak to you and me. Hark! in the next room his voice is sufficiently clear and emphatic. It seems he knows how to speak to his contemporaries. Bashful or bold, then, he will know how to make us seniors very unnecessary.

The nonchalance of boys who are sure of a dinner, and would disdain as much as a lord to do or say aught to conciliate one, is the healthy attitude of human nature. A boy is in the parlour what the pit is in the playhouse; independent, irresponsible, looking out from his corner on such people and facts as pass by, he tries and sentences them on their merits, in the swift, summary way of boys, as good, bad, interesting, silly, eloquent, troublesome. He cumbers himself never about consequences, about interests: he gives an independent, genuine verdict. You must court him: he does not court you. But the man is, as it were, clapped into jail by his consciousness. As soon as he has once acted or spoken with eclat, he is a committed person, watched by the sympathy or the hatred of hundreds, whose affections must now enter into his account. There is no Lethe for this. Ah, that he could pass again into his neutrality! Who can thus avoid all pledges, and having observed, observe again from the same unaffected, unbiased, unbribable, unaffrighted innocence, must always be formidable. He would utter opinions on all passing affairs, which being seen to be not private, but necessary, would sink like darts into the ear of men, and put them in fear.

These are the voices which we hear in solitude, but they grow faint and inaudible as we enter into the world. Society everywhere is in conspiracy against the manhood of every one of its members. Society is a joint-stock company, in which the members agree, for the better securing of his bread to each shareholder, to surrender the liberty and culture of the eater. The virtue in most request is conformity. Self-reliance is its aversion. It loves not realities and creators, but names and customs.

Whoso would be a man must be a nonconformist. He who would gather immortal palms must not be hindered by the name of goodness, but must explore if it be goodness. Nothing is at last sacred but the integrity of your own mind. Absolve you to yourself, and you shall have the suffrage of the world. I remember an answer which when quite young I was prompted to make to a valued adviser, who was wont to importune me with the dear old doctrines of the church. On my saying, What have I to do with the sacredness of traditions, if I live wholly from within? my friend suggested, — "But these impulses may be from below, not from above." I replied, "They do not seem to me to be such; but if I am the Devil's child, I will live then from the Devil." No law can be sacred to me but that of my nature. Good and bad are but names very readily transferable to that or this; the only right is what is after my constitution, the only wrong what is against it.

A man is to carry himself in the presence of all opposition, as if every thing were titular and ephemeral but he. I am ashamed to think how easily we capitulate to badges and names, to large societies and dead institutions. Every decent and well-spoken individual affects and sways me more than is right. I ought to go upright and vital, and speak the rude truth in all ways. If malice and vanity wear the coat of philanthropy, shall that pass? If an angry bigot assumes this bountiful cause of Abolition, and comes to me with his last news from Barbadoes, why should I not say to him, 'Go love thy infant; love thy wood-chopper: be good-natured and modest: have that grace; and never varnish your hard, uncharitable ambition with this incredible tenderness for black folk a thousand miles off. Thy love afar is spite at home.' Rough and graceless would be such greeting, but truth is handsomer than the affectation of love. Your goodness must have some edge to it, — else it is none. The doctrine of hatred must be preached as the counteraction of the doctrine of love when that pules and whines. I shun father and mother and wife and brother, when my genius calls me. I would write on the lintels of the door-post, Whim. I hope it is somewhat better than whim at last, but we cannot spend the day in explanation. Expect me not to show cause why I seek or why I exclude company. Then, again, do not tell me, as a good man did today, of my obligation to put all poor men in good situations. Are they my poor? I tell thee, thou foolish philanthropist, that I grudge the dollar, the dime, the cent, I give to such men as do not belong to me and to whom I do not belong. There is a class of persons to whom by all spiritual affinity I am bought and sold; for them I will go to prison, if need be; but your miscellaneous popular charities; the education at college of fools; the building of meeting-houses to the vain end to which many now stand; alms to sots; and the thousand-fold Relief Societies; — though I confess with shame I sometimes succumb and give the dollar, it is a wicked dollar which by and by I shall have the manhood to withhold.

Virtues are, in the popular estimate, rather the exception than the rule. There is the man and his virtues. Men do what is called a good action, as some piece of courage or charity, much as they would pay a fine in expiation of daily non-appearance on parade. Their works are done as an apology or extenuation of their living in the world, — as invalids and the insane pay a high board. Their virtues are penances. I do not wish to expiate, but to live. My life is for itself and not for a spectacle. I much prefer that it should be of a lower strain, so it be genuine and equal, than that it should be glittering and unsteady. I wish it to be sound and sweet, and not to need diet and bleeding. I ask primary evidence that you are a man, and refuse this appeal from the man to his actions. I know that for myself it makes no difference whether I do or forbear those actions which are reckoned excellent. I cannot consent to pay for a privilege where I have intrinsic right. Few and mean as my gifts may be, I actually am, and do not need for my own assurance or the assurance of my fellows any secondary testimony.

What I must do is all that concerns me, not what the people think. This rule, equally arduous in actual and in intellectual life, may serve for the whole distinction between greatness and meanness. It is the harder, because you will always find those who think they know what is your duty better than you know it. It is easy in the world to live after the world's opinion; it is easy in solitude to live after our own; but the great man is he who in the midst of the crowd keeps with perfect sweetness the independence of solitude.

The objection to conforming to usages that have become dead to you is, that it scatters your force. It loses your time and blurs the impression of your character. If you maintain a dead church, contribute to a dead Bible-society, vote with a great party either for the government or against it, spread your table like base housekeepers, — under all these screens I have difficulty to detect the precise man you are. And, of course, so much force is withdrawn from your proper life. But do your work, and I shall know you. Do your work, and you shall reinforce yourself. A man must consider what a blindman's-buff is this game of conformity. If I know your sect, I anticipate your argument. I hear a preacher announce for his text and topic the expediency of one of the institutions of his church. Do I not know beforehand that not possibly can he say a new and spontaneous word? Do I not know that, with all this ostentation of examining the grounds of the institution, he will do no such thing? Do I not know that he is pledged to himself not to look but at one side, — the permitted side, not as a man, but as a parish minister? He is a retained attorney, and these airs of the bench are the emptiest affectation. Well, most men have bound their eyes with one or another handkerchief, and attached themselves to some one of these communities of opinion. This conformity makes them not false in a few particulars, authors of a few lies, but false in all particulars. Their every truth is not quite true. Their two is not the real two, their four not the real four; so that every word they say chagrins us, and we know not where to begin to set them right. Meantime nature is not slow to equip us in the prison-uniform of the party to which we adhere. We come to wear one cut of face and figure, and acquire by degrees the gentlest asinine expression. There is a mortifying experience in particular, which does not fail to wreak itself also in the general history; I mean "the foolish face of praise," the forced smile which we put on in company where we do not feel at ease in answer to conversation which does not interest us. The muscles, not spontaneously moved, but moved by a low usurping wilfulness, grow tight about the outline of the face with the most disagreeable sensation.

For nonconformity the world whips you with its displeasure. And therefore a man must know how to estimate a sour face. The by-standers look askance on him in the public street or in the friend's parlour. If this aversation had its origin in contempt and resistance like his own, he might well go home with a sad countenance; but the sour faces of the multitude, like their sweet faces, have no deep cause, but are put on and off as the wind blows and a newspaper directs. Yet is the discontent of the multitude more formidable than that of the senate and the college. It is easy enough for a firm man who knows the world to brook the rage of the cultivated classes. Their rage is decorous and prudent, for they are timid as being very vulnerable themselves. But when to their feminine rage the indignation of the people is added, when the ignorant and the poor are aroused, when the unintelligent brute force that lies at the bottom of society is made to growl and mow, it needs the habit of magnanimity and religion to treat it godlike as a trifle of no concernment.

The other terror that scares us from self-trust is our consistency; a reverence for our past act or word, because the eyes of others have no other data for computing our orbit than our past acts, and we are loath to disappoint them.

But why should you keep your head over your shoulder? Why drag about this corpse of your memory, lest you contradict somewhat you have stated in this or that public place? Suppose you should contradict yourself; what then? It seems to be a rule of wisdom never to rely on your memory alone, scarcely even in acts of pure memory, but to bring the past for judgment into the thousand-eyed present, and live ever in a new day. In your metaphysics you have denied personality to the Deity: yet when the devout motions of the soul come, yield to them heart and life, though they should clothe God with shape and color. Leave your theory, as Joseph his coat in the hand of the harlot, and flee.

A foolish consistency is the hobgoblin of little minds, adored by little statesmen and philosophers and divines. With consistency a great soul has simply nothing to do. He may as well concern himself with his shadow on the wall. Speak what you think now in hard words, and tomorrow speak what tomorrow thinks in hard words again, though it contradict every thing you said today. — 'Ah, so you shall be sure to be misunderstood.' — Is it so bad, then, to be misunderstood? Pythagoras was misunderstood, and Socrates, and Jesus, and Luther, and Copernicus, and Galileo, and Newton, and every pure and wise spirit that ever took flesh. To be great is to be misunderstood.

I suppose no man can violate his nature. All the sallies of his will are rounded in by the law of his being, as the inequalities of Andes and Himmaleh are insignificant in the curve of the sphere. Nor does it matter how you gauge and try him. A character is like an acrostic or Alexandrian stanza; — read it forward, backward, or across, it still spells the same thing. In this pleasing, contrite wood-life which God allows me, let me record day by day my honest thought without prospect or retrospect, and, I cannot doubt, it will be found symmetrical, though I mean it not, and see it not. My book should smell of pines and resound with the hum of insects. The swallow over my window should interweave that thread or straw he carries in his bill into my web also. We pass for what we are. Character teaches above our wills. Men imagine that they communicate their virtue or vice only by overt actions, and do not see that virtue or vice emit a breath every moment.

There will be an agreement in whatever variety of actions, so they be each honest and natural in their hour. For of one will, the actions will be harmonious, however unlike they seem. These varieties are lost sight of at a little distance, at a little height of thought. One tendency unites them all. The voyage of the best ship is a zigzag line of a hundred tacks. See the line from a sufficient distance, and it straightens itself to the average tendency. Your genuine action will explain itself, and will explain your other genuine actions. Your conformity explains nothing. Act singly, and what you have already done singly will justify you now. Greatness appeals to the future. If I can be firm enough to-day to do right, and scorn eyes, I must have done so much right before as to defend me now. Be it how it will, do right now. Always scorn appearances, and you always may. The force of character is cumulative. All the foregone days of virtue work their health into this. What makes the majesty of the heroes of the senate and the field, which so fills the imagination? The consciousness of a train of great days and victories behind. They shed an united light on the advancing actor. He is attended as by a visible escort of angels. That is it which throws thunder into Chatham's voice, and dignity into Washington's port, and America into Adams's eye. Honor is venerable to us because it is no ephemeris. It is always ancient virtue. We worship it to-day because it is not of to-day. We love it and pay it homage, because it is not a trap for our love and homage, but is self-dependent, self-derived, and therefore of an old immaculate pedigree, even if shown in a young person.

I hope in these days we have heard the last of conformity and consistency. Let the words be gazetted and ridiculous henceforward. Instead of the gong for dinner, let us hear a whistle from the Spartan fife. Let us never bow and apologize more. A great man is coming to eat at my house. I do not wish to please him; I wish that he should wish to please me. I will stand here for humanity, and though I would make it kind, I would make it true. Let us affront and reprimand the smooth mediocrity and squalid contentment of the times, and hurl in the face of custom, and trade, and office, the fact which is the upshot of all history, that there is a great responsible Thinker and Actor working wherever a man works; that a true man belongs to no other time or place, but is the centre of things. Where he is, there is nature. He measures you, and all men, and all events. Ordinarily, every body in society reminds us of somewhat else, or of some other person. Character, reality, reminds you of nothing else; it takes place of the whole creation. The man must be so much, that he must make all circumstances indifferent. Every true man is a cause, a country, and an age; requires infinite spaces and numbers and time fully to accomplish his design; — and posterity seem to follow his steps as a train of clients. A man Caesar is born, and for ages after we have a Roman Empire. Christ is born, and millions of minds so grow and cleave to his genius, that he is confounded with virtue and the possible of man. An institution is the lengthened shadow of one man; as, Monachism, of the Hermit Antony; the Reformation, of Luther; Quakerism, of Fox; Methodism, of Wesley; Abolition, of Clarkson. Scipio, Milton called "the height of Rome"; and all history resolves itself very easily into the biography of a few stout and earnest persons.

Let a man then know his worth, and keep things under his feet. Let him not peep or steal, or skulk up and down with the air of a charity-boy, a bastard, or an interloper, in the world which exists for him. But the man in the street, finding no worth in himself which corresponds to the force which built a tower or sculptured a marble god, feels poor when he looks on these. To him a palace, a statue, or a costly book have an alien and forbidding air, much like a gay equipage, and seem to say like that, 'Who are you, Sir?' Yet they all are his, suitors for his notice, petitioners to his faculties that they will come out and take possession. The picture waits for my verdict: it is not to command me, but I am to settle its claims to praise. That popular fable of the sot who was picked up dead drunk in the street, carried to the duke's house, washed and dressed and laid in the duke's bed, and, on his waking, treated with all obsequious ceremony like the duke, and assured that he had been insane, owes its popularity to the fact, that it symbolizes so well the state of man, who is in the world a sort of sot, but now and then wakes up, exercises his reason, and finds himself a true prince.

Our reading is mendicant and sycophantic. In history, our imagination plays us false. Kingdom and lordship, power and estate, are a gaudier vocabulary than private John and Edward in a small house and common day's work; but the things of life are the same to both; the sum total of both is the same. Why all this deference to Alfred, and Scanderbeg, and Gustavus? Suppose they were virtuous; did they wear out virtue? As great a stake depends on your private act to-day, as followed their public and renowned steps. When private men shall act with original views, the lustre will be transferred from the actions of kings to those of gentlemen.

The world has been instructed by its kings, who have so magnetized the eyes of nations. It has been taught by this colossal symbol the mutual reverence that is due from man to man. The joyful loyalty with which men have everywhere suffered the king, the noble, or the great proprietor to walk among them by a law of his own, make his own scale of men and things, and reverse theirs, pay for benefits not with money but with honor, and represent the law in his person, was the hieroglyphic by which they obscurely signified their consciousness of their own right and comeliness, the right of every man.

The magnetism which all original action exerts is explained when we inquire the reason of self-trust. Who is the Trustee? What is the aboriginal Self, on which a universal reliance may be grounded? What is the nature and power of that science-baffling star, without parallax, without calculable elements, which shoots a ray of beauty even into trivial and impure actions, if the least mark of independence appear? The inquiry leads us to that source, at once the essence of genius, of virtue, and of life, which we call Spontaneity or Instinct. We denote this primary wisdom as Intuition, whilst all later teachings are tuitions. In that deep force, the last fact behind which analysis cannot go, all things find their common origin. For, the sense of being which in calm hours rises, we know not how, in the soul, is not diverse from things, from space, from light, from time, from man, but one with them, and proceeds obviously from the same source whence their life and being also proceed. We first share the life by which things exist, and afterwards see them as appearances in nature, and forget that we have shared their cause. Here is the fountain of action and of thought. Here are the lungs of that inspiration which giveth man wisdom, and which cannot be denied without impiety and atheism. We lie in the lap of immense intelligence, which makes us receivers of its truth and organs of its activity. When we discern justice, when we discern truth, we do nothing of ourselves, but allow a passage to its beams. If we ask whence this comes, if we seek to pry into the soul that causes, all philosophy is at fault. Its presence or its absence is all we can affirm. Every man discriminates between the voluntary acts of his mind, and his involuntary perceptions, and knows that to his involuntary perceptions a perfect faith is due. He may err in the expression of them, but he knows that these things are so, like day and night, not to be disputed. My wilful actions and acquisitions are but roving; — the idlest reverie, the faintest native emotion, command my curiosity and respect. Thoughtless people contradict as readily the statement of perceptions as of opinions, or rather much more readily; for, they do not distinguish between perception and notion. They fancy that I choose to see this or that thing. But perception is not whimsical, but fatal. If I see a trait, my children will see it after me, and in course of time, all mankind, — although it may chance that no one has seen it before me. For my perception of it is as much a fact as the sun.

The relations of the soul to the divine spirit are so pure, that it is profane to seek to interpose helps. It must be that when God speaketh he should communicate, not one thing, but all things; should fill the world with his voice; should scatter forth light, nature, time, souls, from the centre of the present thought; and new date and new create the whole. Whenever a mind is simple, and receives a divine wisdom, old things pass away, — means, teachers, texts, temples fall; it lives now, and absorbs past and future into the present hour. All things are made sacred by relation to it, — one as much as another. All things are dissolved to their centre by their cause, and, in the universal miracle, petty and particular miracles disappear. If, therefore, a man claims to know and speak of God, and carries you backward to the phraseology of some old mouldered nation in another country, in another world, believe him not. Is the acorn better than the oak which is its fulness and completion? Is the parent better than the child into whom he has cast his ripened being? Whence, then, this worship of the past? The centuries are conspirators against the sanity and authority of the soul. Time and space are but physiological colors which the eye makes, but the soul is light; where it is, is day; where it was, is night; and history is an impertinence and an injury, if it be any thing more than a cheerful apologue or parable of my being and becoming.

Man is timid and apologetic; he is no longer upright; he dares not say 'I think,' 'I am,' but quotes some saint or sage. He is ashamed before the blade of grass or the blowing rose. These roses under my window make no reference to former roses or to better ones; they are for what they are; they exist with God to-day. There is no time to them. There is simply the rose; it is perfect in every moment of its existence. Before a leaf-bud has burst, its whole life acts; in the full-blown flower there is no more; in the leafless root there is no less. Its nature is satisfied, and it satisfies nature, in all moments alike. But man postpones or remembers; he does not live in the present, but with reverted eye laments the past, or, heedless of the riches that surround him, stands on tiptoe to foresee the future. He cannot be happy and strong until he too lives with nature in the present, above time.

This should be plain enough. Yet see what strong intellects dare not yet hear God himself, unless he speak the phraseology of I know not what David, or Jeremiah, or Paul. We shall not always set so great a price on a few texts, on a few lives. We are like children who repeat by rote the sentences of grandames and tutors, and, as they grow older, of the men of talents and character they chance to see, — painfully recollecting the exact words they spoke; afterwards, when they come into the point of view which those had who uttered these sayings, they understand them, and are willing to let the words go; for, at any time, they can use words as good when occasion comes. If we live truly, we shall see truly. It is as easy for the strong man to be strong, as it is for the weak to be weak. When we have new perception, we shall gladly disburden the memory of its hoarded treasures as old rubbish. When a man lives with God, his voice shall be as sweet as the murmur of the brook and the rustle of the corn.

And now at last the highest truth on this subject remains unsaid; probably cannot be said; for all that we say is the far-off remembering of the intuition. That thought, by what I can now nearest approach to say it, is this. When good is near you, when you have life in yourself, it is not by any known or accustomed way; you shall not discern the foot-prints of any other; you shall not see the face of man; you shall not hear any name;—the way, the thought, the good, shall be wholly strange and new. It shall exclude example and experience. You take the way from man, not to man. All persons that ever existed are its forgotten ministers. Fear and hope are alike beneath it. There is somewhat low even in hope. In the hour of vision, there is nothing that can be called gratitude, nor properly joy. The soul raised over passion beholds identity and eternal causation, perceives the self-existence of Truth and Right, and calms itself with knowing that all things go well. Vast spaces of nature, the Atlantic Ocean, the South Sea, — long intervals of time, years, centuries, — are of no account. This which I think and feel underlay every former state of life and circumstances, as it does underlie my present, and what is called life, and what is called death.

Life only avails, not the having lived. Power ceases in the instant of repose; it resides in the moment of transition from a past to a new state, in the shooting of the gulf, in the darting to an aim. This one fact the world hates, that the soul becomes; for that for ever degrades the past, turns all riches to poverty, all reputation to a shame, confounds the saint with the rogue, shoves Jesus and Judas equally aside. Why, then, do we prate of self-reliance? Inasmuch as the soul is present, there will be power not confident but agent. To talk of reliance is a poor external way of speaking. Speak rather of that which relies, because it works and is. Who has more obedience than I masters me, though he should not raise his finger. Round him I must revolve by the gravitation of spirits. We fancy it rhetoric, when we speak of eminent virtue. We do not yet see that virtue is Height, and that a man or a company of men, plastic and permeable to principles, by the law of nature must overpower and ride all cities, nations, kings, rich men, poets, who are not.

This is the ultimate fact which we so quickly reach on this, as on every topic, the resolution of all into the ever-blessed ONE. Self-existence is the attribute of the Supreme Cause, and it constitutes the measure of good by the degree in which it enters into all lower forms. All things real are so by so much virtue as they contain. Commerce, husbandry, hunting, whaling, war, eloquence, personal weight, are somewhat, and engage my respect as examples of its presence and impure action. I see the same law working in nature for conservation and growth. Power is in nature the essential measure of right. Nature suffers nothing to remain in her kingdoms which cannot help itself. The genesis and maturation of a planet, its poise and orbit, the bended tree recovering itself from the strong wind, the vital resources of every animal and vegetable, are demonstrations of the self-sufficing, and therefore self-relying soul.

Thus all concentrates: let us not rove; let us sit at home with the cause. Let us stun and astonish the intruding rabble of men and books and institutions, by a simple declaration of the divine fact. Bid the invaders take the shoes from off their feet, for God is here within. Let our simplicity judge them, and our docility to our own law demonstrate the poverty of nature and fortune beside our native riches.

But now we are a mob. Man does not stand in awe of man, nor is his genius admonished to stay at home, to put itself in communication with the internal ocean, but it goes abroad to beg a cup of water of the urns of other men. We must go alone. I like the silent church before the service begins, better than any preaching. How far off, how cool, how chaste the persons look, begirt each one with a precinct or sanctuary! So let us always sit. Why should we assume the faults of our friend, or wife, or father, or child, because they sit around our hearth, or are said to have the same blood? All men have my blood, and I have all men's. Not for that will I adopt their petulance or folly, even to the extent of being ashamed of it. But your isolation must not be mechanical, but spiritual, that is, must be elevation. At times the whole world seems to be in conspiracy to importune you with emphatic trifles. Friend, client, child, sickness, fear, want, charity, all knock at once at thy closet door, and say, — 'Come out unto us.' But keep thy state; come not into their confusion. The power men possess to annoy me, I give them by a weak curiosity. No man can come near me but through my act. "What we love that we have, but by desire we bereave ourselves of the love."

If we cannot at once rise to the sanctities of obedience and faith, let us at least resist our temptations; let us enter into the state of war, and wake Thor and Woden, courage and constancy, in our Saxon breasts. This is to be done in our smooth times by speaking the truth. Check this lying hospitality and lying affection. Live no longer to the expectation of these deceived and deceiving people with whom we converse. Say to them, O father, O mother, O wife, O brother, O friend, I have lived with you after appearances hitherto. Henceforward I am the truth's. Be it known unto you that henceforward I obey no law less than the eternal law. I will have no covenants but proximities. I shall endeavour to nourish my parents, to support my family, to be the chaste husband of one wife, — but these relations I must fill after a new and unprecedented way. I appeal from your customs. I must be myself. I cannot break myself any longer for you, or you. If you can love me for what I am, we shall be the happier. If you cannot, I will still seek to deserve that you should. I will not hide my tastes or aversions. I will so trust that what is deep is holy, that I will do strongly before the sun and moon whatever inly rejoices me, and the heart appoints. If you are noble, I will love you; if you are not, I will not hurt you and myself by hypocritical attentions. If you are true, but not in the same truth with me, cleave to your companions; I will seek my own. I do this not selfishly, but humbly and truly. It is alike your interest, and mine, and all men's, however long we have dwelt in lies, to live in truth. Does this sound harsh to-day? You will soon love what is dictated by your nature as well as mine, and, if we follow the truth, it will bring us out safe at last. — But so you may give these friends pain. Yes, but I cannot sell my liberty and my power, to save their sensibility. Besides, all persons have their moments of reason, when they look out into the region of absolute truth; then will they justify me, and do the same thing.

The populace think that your rejection of popular standards is a rejection of all standard, and mere antinomianism; and the bold sensualist will use the name of philosophy to gild his crimes. But the law of consciousness abides. There are two confessionals, in one or the other of which we must be shriven. You may fulfil your round of duties by clearing yourself in the direct, or in the reflex way. Consider whether you have satisfied your relations to father, mother, cousin, neighbour, town, cat, and dog; whether any of these can upbraid you. But I may also neglect this reflex standard, and absolve me to myself. I have my own stern claims and perfect circle. It denies the name of duty to many offices that are called duties. But if I can discharge its debts, it enables me to dispense with the popular code. If any one imagines that this law is lax, let him keep its commandment one day.

And truly it demands something godlike in him who has cast off the common motives of humanity, and has ventured to trust himself for a taskmaster. High be his heart, faithful his will, clear his sight, that he may in good earnest be doctrine, society, law, to himself, that a simple purpose may be to him as strong as iron necessity is to others!

If any man consider the present aspects of what is called by distinction *society*, he will see the need of these ethics. The sinew and heart of man seem to be drawn out, and we are become timorous, desponding whimperers. We are afraid of truth, afraid of fortune, afraid of death, and afraid of each other. Our age yields no great and perfect persons. We want men and women who shall renovate life and our social state, but we see that most natures are insolvent, cannot satisfy their own wants, have an ambition out of all proportion to their practical force, and do lean and beg day and night continually. Our housekeeping is mendicant, our arts, our occupations, our marriages, our religion, we have not chosen, but society has chosen for us. We are parlour soldiers. We shun the rugged battle of fate, where strength is born.

If our young men miscarry in their first enterprises, they lose all heart. If the young merchant fails, men say he is ruined. If the finest genius studies at one of our colleges, and is not installed in an office within one year afterwards in the cities or suburbs of Boston or New York, it seems to his friends and to himself that he is right in being disheartened, and in complaining the rest of his life. A sturdy lad from New Hampshire or Vermont, who in turn tries all the professions, who teams it, farms it, peddles, keeps a school, preaches, edits a newspaper, goes to Congress, buys a township, and so forth, in successive years, and always, like a cat, falls on his feet, is worth a hundred of these city dolls. He walks abreast with his days, and feels no shame in not 'studying a profession,' for he does not postpone his life, but lives already. He has not one chance, but a hundred chances. Let a Stoic open the resources of man, and tell men they are not leaning willows, but can and must detach themselves; that with the exercise of self-trust, new powers shall appear; that a man is the word made flesh, born to shed healing to the nations, that he should be ashamed of our compassion, and that the moment he acts from himself, tossing the laws, the books, idolatries, and customs out of the window, we pity him no more, but thank and revere him, — and that teacher shall restore the life of man to splendor, and make his name dear to all history.

It is easy to see that a greater self-reliance must work a revolution in all the offices and relations of men; in their religion; in their education; in their pursuits; their modes of living; their association; in their property; in their speculative views.

1. In what prayers do men allow themselves! That which they call a holy office is not so much as brave and manly. Prayer looks abroad and asks for some foreign addition to come through some foreign virtue, and loses itself in endless mazes of natural and supernatural, and mediatorial and miraculous. Prayer that craves a particular commodity, — any thing less than all good, — is vicious. Prayer is the contemplation of the facts of life from the highest point of view. It is the soliloquy of a beholding and jubilant soul. It is the spirit of God pronouncing his works good. But prayer as a means to effect a private end is meanness and theft. It supposes dualism

and not unity in nature and consciousness. As soon as the man is at one with God, he will not beg. He will then see prayer in all action. The prayer of the farmer kneeling in his field to weed it, the prayer of the rower kneeling with the stroke of his oar, are true prayers heard throughout nature, though for cheap ends. Caratach, in Fletcher's Bonduca, when admonished to inquire the mind of the god Audate, replies, —

"His hidden meaning lies in our endeavours;

Our valors are our best gods."

Another sort of false prayers are our regrets. Discontent is the want of self-reliance: it is infirmity of will. Regret calamities, if you can thereby help the sufferer; if not, attend your own work, and already the evil begins to be repaired. Our sympathy is just as base. We come to them who weep foolishly, and sit down and cry for company, instead of imparting to them truth and health in rough electric shocks, putting them once more in communication with their own reason. The secret of fortune is joy in our hands. Welcome evermore to gods and men is the self-helping man. For him all doors are flung wide: him all tongues greet, all honors crown, all eyes follow with desire. Our love goes out to him and embraces him, because he did not need it. We solicitously and apologetically caress and celebrate him, because he held on his way and scorned our disapprobation. The gods love him because men hated him. "To the persevering mortal," said Zoroaster, "the blessed Immortals are swift."

As men's prayers are a disease of the will, so are their creeds a disease of the intellect. They say with those foolish Israelites, 'Let not God speak to us, lest we die. Speak thou, speak any man with us, and we will obey.' Everywhere I am hindered of meeting God in my brother, because he has shut his own temple doors, and recites fables merely of his brother's, or his brother's brother's God. Every new mind is a new classification. If it prove a mind of uncommon activity and power, a Locke, a Lavoisier, a Hutton, a Bentham, a Fourier, it imposes its classification on other men, and lo! a new system. In proportion to the depth of the thought, and so to the number of the objects it touches and brings within reach of the pupil, is his complacency. But chiefly is this apparent in creeds and churches, which are also classifications of some powerful mind acting on the elemental thought of duty, and man's relation to the Highest. Such is Calvinism, Quakerism, Swedenborgism. The pupil takes the same delight in subordinating every thing to the new terminology, as a girl who has just learned botany in seeing a new earth and new seasons thereby. It will happen for a time, that the pupil will find his intellectual power has grown by the study of his master's mind. But in all unbalanced minds, the classification is idolized, passes for the end, and not for a speedily exhaustible means, so that the walls of the system blend to their eye in the remote horizon with the walls of the universe; the luminaries of heaven seem to them hung on the arch their master built. They cannot imagine how you aliens have any right to see, — how you can see; 'It must be somehow that you stole the light from us.' They do not yet perceive, that light, unsystematic, indomitable, will break into any cabin, even into theirs. Let them chirp awhile and call it their own. If they are honest and do well, presently their neat new pinfold will be too strait and low, will crack, will lean, will rot and vanish, and the immortal light, all young and joyful, million-orbed, million-colored, will beam over the universe as on the first morning.

2. It is for want of self-culture that the superstition of Travelling, whose idols are Italy, England, Egypt, retains its fascination for all educated Americans. They who made England, Italy, or Greece venerable in the imagination did so by sticking fast where they were, like an axis of the earth. In manly hours, we feel that duty is our place. The soul is no traveller; the wise man stays at home, and when his necessities, his duties, on any occasion call him from his house, or into foreign lands, he is at home still, and shall make men sensible by the expression of his countenance, that he goes the missionary of wisdom and virtue, and visits cities and men like a sovereign, and not like an interloper or a valet.

I have no churlish objection to the circumnavigation of the globe, for the purposes of art, of study, and benevolence, so that the man is first domesticated, or does not go abroad with the hope of finding somewhat greater than he knows. He who travels to be amused, or to get somewhat which he does not carry, travels away from himself, and grows old even in youth among old things. In Thebes, in Palmyra, his will and mind have become old and dilapidated as they. He carries ruins to ruins.

Travelling is a fool's paradise. Our first journeys discover to us the indifference of places. At home I dream that at Naples, at Rome, I can be intoxicated with beauty, and lose my sadness. I pack my trunk, embrace my friends, embark on the sea, and at last wake up in Naples, and there beside me is the stern fact, the sad self, unrelenting, identical, that I fled from. I seek the Vatican, and the palaces. I affect to be intoxicated with sights and suggestions, but I am not intoxicated. My giant goes with me wherever I go.

3. But the rage of travelling is a symptom of a deeper unsoundness affecting the whole intellectual action. The intellect is vagabond, and our system of education fosters restlessness. Our minds travel when our bodies are forced to stay at home. We imitate; and what is imitation but the travelling of the mind? Our houses are built with foreign taste; our shelves are garnished with foreign ornaments; our opinions, our tastes, our faculties, lean, and follow the Past and the Distant. The soul created the arts wherever they have flourished. It was in his own mind that the artist

sought his model. It was an application of his own thought to the thing to be done and the conditions to be observed. And why need we copy the Doric or the Gothic model? Beauty, convenience, grandeur of thought, and quaint expression are as near to us as to any, and if the American artist will study with hope and love the precise thing to be done by him, considering the climate, the soil, the length of the day, the wants of the people, the habit and form of the government, he will create a house in which all these will find themselves fitted, and taste and sentiment will be satisfied also.

Insist on yourself; never imitate. Your own gift you can present every moment with the cumulative force of a whole life's cultivation; but of the adopted talent of another, you have only an extemporaneous, half possession. That which each can do best, none but his Maker can teach him. No man yet knows what it is, nor can, till that person has exhibited it. Where is the master who could have taught Shakspeare? Where is the master who could have instructed Franklin, or Washington, or Bacon, or Newton? Every great man is a unique. The Scipionism of Scipio is precisely that part he could not borrow. Shakspeare will never be made by the study of Shakspeare. Do that which is assigned you, and you cannot hope too much or dare too much. There is at this moment for you an utterance brave and grand as that of the colossal chisel of Phidias, or trowel of the Egyptians, or the pen of Moses, or Dante, but different from all these. Not possibly will the soul all rich, all eloquent, with thousand-cloven tongue, deign to repeat itself; but if you can hear what these patriarchs say, surely you can reply to them in the same pitch of voice; for the ear and the tongue are two organs of one nature. Abide in the simple and noble regions of thy life, obey thy heart, and thou shalt reproduce the Foreworld again.

4. As our Religion, our Education, our Art look abroad, so does our spirit of society. All men plume themselves on the improvement of society, and no man improves.

Society never advances. It recedes as fast on one side as it gains on the other. It undergoes continual changes; it is barbarous, it is civilized, it is christianized, it is rich, it is scientific; but this change is not amelioration. For every thing that is given, something is taken. Society acquires new arts, and loses old instincts. What a contrast between the well-clad, reading, writing, thinking American, with a watch, a pencil, and a bill of exchange in his pocket, and the naked New Zealander, whose property is a club, a spear, a mat, and an undivided twentieth of a shed to sleep under! But compare the health of the two men, and you shall see that the white man has lost his aboriginal strength. If the traveller tell us truly, strike the savage with a broad axe, and in a day or two the flesh shall unite and heal as if you struck the blow into soft pitch, and the same blow shall send the white to his grave.

The civilized man has built a coach, but has lost the use of his feet. He is supported on crutches, but lacks so much support of muscle. He has a fine Geneva watch, but he fails of the skill to tell the hour by the sun. A Greenwich nautical almanac he has, and so being sure of the information when he wants it, the man in the street does not know a star in the sky. The solstice he does not observe; the equinox he knows as little; and the whole bright calendar of the year is without a dial in his mind. His note-books impair his memory; his libraries overload his wit; the insurance-office increases the number of accidents; and it may be a question whether machinery does not encumber; whether we have not lost by refinement some energy, by a Christianity entrenched in establishments and forms, some vigor of wild virtue. For every Stoic was a Stoic; but in Christendom where is the Christian?

There is no more deviation in the moral standard than in the standard of height or bulk. No greater men are now than ever were. A singular equality may be observed between the great men of the first and of the last ages; nor can all the science, art, religion, and philosophy of the nineteenth century avail to educate greater men than Plutarch's heroes, three or four and twenty centuries ago. Not in time is the race progressive. Phocion, Socrates, Anaxagoras, Diogenes, are great men, but they leave no class. He who is really of their class will not be called by their name, but will be his own man, and, in his turn, the founder of a sect. The arts and inventions of each period are only its costume, and do not invigorate men. The harm of the improved machinery may compensate its good. Hudson and Behring accomplished so much in their fishing-boats, as to astonish Parry and Franklin, whose equipment exhausted the resources of science and art. Galileo, with an opera-glass, discovered a more splendid series of celestial phenomena than any one since. Columbus found the New World in an undecked boat. It is curious to see the periodical disuse and perishing of means and machinery, which were introduced with loud laudation a few years or centuries before. The great genius returns to essential man. We reckoned the improvements of the art of war among the triumphs of science, and yet Napoleon conquered Europe by the bivouac, which consisted of falling back on naked valor, and disencumbering it of all aids. The Emperor held it impossible to make a perfect army, says Las Casas, "without abolishing our arms, magazines, commissaries, and carriages, until, in imitation of the Roman custom, the soldier should receive his supply of corn, grind it in his hand-mill, and bake his bread himself."

Society is a wave. The wave moves onward, but the water of which it is composed does not. The same particle does not rise from the valley to the ridge. Its unity is only phenomenal. The persons who make up a nation to-day, next year die, and their experience with them.

And so the reliance on Property, including the reliance on governments which protect it, is the want of self-reliance. Men have looked away from themselves and at things so long, that they have come to esteem the religious, learned, and civil institutions as guards of property, and they deprecate assaults on these, because they feel them to be assaults on property. They measure their esteem of each other by what each has, and not by what each is. But a cultivated man becomes ashamed of his property, out of new respect for his nature. Especially he hates what he has, if he see that it is accidental, — came to him by inheritance, or gift, or crime; then he feels that it is not having; it does not belong to him, has no root in him, and merely lies there, because no revolution or no robber takes it away. But that which a man is does always by necessity acquire, and what the man acquires is living property, which does not wait the beck of rulers, or mobs, or revolutions, or fire, or storm, or bankruptcies, but perpetually renews itself wherever the man breathes. "Thy lot or portion of life," said the Caliph Ali, "is seeking after thee; therefore be at rest from seeking after it." Our dependence on these foreign goods leads us to our slavish respect for numbers. The political parties meet in numerous conventions; the greater the concourse, and with each new uproar of announcement, The delegation from Essex! The Democrats from New Hampshire! The Whigs of Maine! the young patriot feels himself stronger than before by a new thousand of eyes and arms. In like manner the reformers summon conventions, and vote and resolve in multitude. Not so, O friends! will the God deign to enter and inhabit you, but by a method precisely the reverse. It is only as a man puts off all foreign support, and stands alone, that I see him to be strong and to prevail. He is weaker by every recruit to his banner. Is not a man better than a town? Ask nothing of men, and in the endless mutation, thou only firm column must presently appear the upholder of all that surrounds thee. He who knows that power is inborn, that he is weak because he has looked for good out of him and elsewhere, and so perceiving, throws himself unhesitatingly on his thought, instantly rights himself, stands in the erect position, commands his limbs, works miracles; just as a man who stands on his feet is stronger than a man who stands on his head.

So use all that is called Fortune. Most men gamble with her, and gain all, and lose all, as her wheel rolls. But do thou leave as unlawful these winnings, and deal with Cause and Effect, the chancellors of God. In the Will work and acquire, and thou hast chained the wheel of Chance, and shalt sit hereafter out of fear from her rotations. A political victory, a rise of rents, the recovery of your sick, or the return of your absent friend, or some other favorable event, raises your spirits, and you think good days are preparing for you. Do not believe it. Nothing can bring you peace but yourself. Nothing can bring you peace but the triumph of principles.

PART VI

THE FRONTIER

Ole Rölvaag, Giants in the Earth

Excerpted from Ole Rölvaag, Giants in the Earth *(1927),*
about Norwegian pioneers in the Dakota Territory.

Ole Rölvaag (1876–1931) was born in Norway and emigrated to
South Dakota to work on his uncle's farm.

Book I, Chapter II
Home-Founding
VI

As Per Hansa lay there dreaming of the future it seemed to him that hidden springs of energy, "hitherto unsuspected even by himself, were welling up in his heart. He felt as if his strength were inexhaustible. And so he commenced his labours with a fourteen-hour day; but soon, as the plans grew clearer, he began to realize how little could be accomplished in that short span of time, with so much work always ahead of him; he accordingly lengthened the day to sixteen hours, and threw in another hour for good measure; at last he found himself wondering if a man couldn't get along with only five hours of rest, in this fine summer weather.

His waking dreams passed unconsciously into those of sleep; all that night a pleasant buoyancy seemed to be lifting him up and carrying him along; at dawn, when he opened his eyelids, morning was there to greet him—the morning of a glorious new day. … He saw that it was already broad daylight; with a guilty start, he came wide awake. Heavens! He might have overslept himself—on this morning!… He jumped into his clothes, and found some cold porridge to quiet his hunger for the time being; then he hurried out, put the yoke on the oxen, and went across to Hans Olsa's to fetch the plow. … Over there no life was stirring yet. Well, maybe they could afford to sleep late in the morning; but he had arrived five days behind the others, and had just been delayed for two days more; they had a big start over him already. His heart sang as he thought how he would have to hurry! … He led the oxen carefully, trying to make as little noise around the tent as possible.

Dragging the plow, he drove out for some distance toward the hillock, then stopped and looked around. This was as good a place as anywhere to start breaking. … He straightened up the plow, planted the share firmly in the ground and spoke to the oxen: "Come now, move along, you lazy rascals!" He had meant to speak gruffly, but the thrill of joy that surged over him as he sank the plow in his own land for the first time, threw such an unexpected tone of gentleness into his voice that the oxen paid no attention to it; he found that he would have to resort to more powerful encouragement; but even with the goad it was hard to make them bend to the yoke so early in the: morning. After a little, however, they began to stretch their muscles. Then they were off the plow moved…sank deeper… the first furrow was breaking. …

It would have gone much easier now if Ole had only been there to drive the oxen, so that he could have given his whole attention to the plow. But never mind that! . . . The boy ought to sleep for at least another hour; the day would be plenty long enough for him, before it was through. … Young bulls have tender sinews—though for one of his age, Ole was an exceptionally able youngster.

That first furrow turned out very crooked for Per Hansa; he made a long one of it, too. When he thought he had gone far enough and halted the oxen, the furrow came winding up behind him like a snake. He turned around, drove the oxen back in the opposite direction, and laid another furrow up against the one he had already struck

At the starting point again, he surveyed his work ruefully. Well, the second furrow wasn't any crookeder than the first, at all events!… When he had made another round he let the oxen stand awhile; taking the spade which he had brought out, he began to cut the sod on one side of the breaking into strips that could be handled. This was to be his building material. … Field for planting on the one hand, sods for a house on the other—that was the way to plow!… Leave it to Per Hansa—he was the fellow to have everything figured out beforehand!

By breakfast time he had made a fine start. No sooner had he swallowed the last morsel than he ordered both the boys to turn to, hitched the oxen to the old home-made wagon, and off they all went together toward the field, Per Hansa leading the way. … "You'd better cook the kettles full today!" He shouted back, as they were leaving. "We're going to punish a lot of food when we come in!"

Now Per Hansa began working in real earnest. He and Store-Hans, with plow and oxen, broke up the land; Ole used the hoe, but the poor fellow was having a hard time of it. The sod, which had been slumbering there undisturbed for countless ages, was tough of fibre and would not give up its hold on the earth without a struggle. It almost had to be turned by main strength, piece by piece; it was a dark brownish colour on the under side—a rich, black mould that gave promise of wonderful fertility; it actually gleamed and glistened under the rays of the morning sun, where the plow had carved and polished its upturned face. … Ole toiled on, settling and straightening the furrows as best he could, now and then cutting out the clods that fell unevenly. When Per Hansa had made a couple of rounds, he let the oxen stand awhile to catch their breath, and came over to Ole to instruct him. "This is the way to do it!" he said, seizing the hoe. "Watch me, now—like this!" He chewed away till the clods were flying around him. ...

When they quit work at noon a good many furrows lay stretched out on the slope, smiling up at the sun; they were also able to bring home with them a full wagonload of building material; at coffee time they brought another; at supper time another. But when, arriving home at the end of the day, they found that supper was not quite ready, Per Hansa felt that he must go after still another load; they had better make use of every minute of time!

VII

He began building the house that same evening. "You ought to rest, Per Hansa!" Beret pleaded. "Please use a little common sense!"

"Rest—of course! That's just what I propose to do!... Come along, now, all hands of you; you can't imagine what fun this is going to be. ... Just think of it—a new house on our own estate! I don't mean that you've got to work, you know; but come along and watch the royal mansion rise!"

They all joined in, nevertheless . . . couldn't have kept their hands off. It gave them such keen enjoyment that they worked away until they could no longer see to place the strips of sod. Then Per Hansa called a halt—that was enough for one day. They had laboured hard and faithfully; well, they would get their wages in due time, every last one of them—but he couldn't bother with such trifles just now! That night sleep overpowered him at once; he was too tired even to dream.

From now on Per Hansa worked on the house every morning before breakfast, and every evening as soon as he had finished supper. The whole family joined in the task when they had nothing else to do; it seemed like a fascinating game.

To the eyes of Tonseten and Hans Olsa, it appeared as if nothing short of witchcraft must be at work on Per Hansa's quarter section; in spite of the fact that he and his entire family were breaking ground in the fields the whole day long, a great sod house shot up beside the wagon, like an enormous mushroom.

Per Hansa plowed and harrowed, delved and dug; he built away at the house, and he planted the potatoes; he had such a zest for everything and thought it all such fun that he could hardly bear to waste a moment in stupid sleep. It was Beret who finally put a check on him. One morning, as he threw off the blanket at dawn, on the point of jumping up in his reckless way, she lay there awake, waiting for him. The moment he stirred, she put her arms lovingly around him and told him that he must stay in bed awhile longer. This would never do, she said; he ought to remember that he was only a human being. … She begged him so gently and soothingly that he gave in at last and stayed in bed with her. But he was ill at ease over the loss of time. It wouldn't take long to lay a round of sod, and every round helped. … This Beret-girl of his meant well enough, but she didn't realize the multitude of things that weighed on his mind, things that couldn't wait, that had to be attended to immediately!

… Yes, she was an exceptional woman, this Beret of his; he didn't believe that her like existed anywhere else under the sun. During the last two days she had hurried through her housework, and then, taking And-Ongen by the hand, had come out in the field with them; she had let the child roam around and play in the grass while she herself had joined in their labour; she had pitched in beside them and taken her full term like any man.

It had all been done to make things easier for him … and now she was lying awake here, just to look after him!

… He thought of other things she had done. When they had harrowed and hoed sufficient seed ground, Beret had looked over her bundles and produced all kinds of seeds—he couldn't imagine how or where she got them—turnips, and carrots, and onions, and tomatoes, and melons, even! … What a wife she was! … Well, he had better stay in bed and please her this time, when she had been so clever and thoughtful about everything.

However it was accomplished, on Per Hansa's estate they had a field all broken and harrowed and seeded down, and a large house ready for thatching, by the time that Hans Olsa and the Solum boys had barely finished thatching their houses and started the plowing. Tonseten, though, was ahead of him with the breaking—and was now busy planting his potatoes. But Syvert had every reason to be in the lead; his house had been all ready to move into when they had arrived. That little stable which he had built wasn't more than a decent day's work for an able man. And he had horses, too. … Of course, such things gave him a big advantage!

They finished planting the big field at Per Hansa's late one afternoon; all the potatoes that he had brought home from Sioux Falls had been cut up in small pieces and tucked away in the ground. "Only one eye to each piece!" he had warned Beret as she sat beside him, cutting them up. "That's enough for such rich soil." … The older seed, which she had provided with such splendid forethought, had also been planted. The field looked larger than it really was. It stood out clearly against the fresh verdure of the hillside; from a little distance it appeared as if some one had sewn a dark brown patch on a huge green cloth. … That patch looked mighty good to Per Hansa as he stood surveying the scene, his whole being filled with the sense of completed effort. Here he had barely arrived in a new country; yet already he had got more seed into the ground than in any previous year since Beret and he had started out for themselves. ... Just wait." What couldn't he do another year!

"Well, Beret-girl," he said, "we've cleaned up a busy spring season, all right! Tonight we ought to have an extra-fine dish of porridge, to bless what has been put into the ground." He stood there with sparkling eyes, admiring his wonderful field.

Beret was tired out with the labour she had undergone; her back ached as if it would break. She, too, was looking at the field, but the joy he felt found no response in her.

... I'm glad that he is happy, she thought, sadly. Perhaps in time I will learn to like it, too...But she did not utter the thought; she merely took the child by the hand, turned away, and went back to their wagon-home. There she measured out half of the milk that Rosie had given that morning, dipped some grits from the bag and prepared the porridge, adding water until it was thin enough. Before she served it up she put a small dab of butter in each dish, like a tiny eye that would hardly keep open; then she sprinkled over the porridge a small portion of sugar; this was all the luxury she could afford. Indeed, her heart began to reproach her even for this extravagance. But when she saw the joyful faces of the boys, and heard Per Hansa's exclamations over her merits as a housekeeper, she brightened up a little, cast her fears to the wind, and sprinkled on more sugar from the bag. ... Then she sat down among them, smiling and happy; she was glad that she hadn't told them how her back was aching.

...They all worked at the house building that night as long as they could see.

Book I, Chapter V
Facing the Great Desolation
I

In the beginning of October a memorable event stirred the little Spring Creek settlement. This, the greatest happening of the year, chose an opportune moment for its arrival.

It was shortly after dinner. In the early morning Per Hansa, Hans Olsa, and Henry Solum had gone east to the Sioux River after wood; Tonseten was so sorely troubled by rheumatism that he hadn't been able to go along; anyway, he had wood enough on hand to last until after Christmas, and hauling would be easier on the snow. He did want some trees for planting; but as it was getting so late in the fall, with little likelihood of their taking root, he had given up the project.

Beret sat by the window at home; she was knitting some sort of a round affair—something so tiny that Store-Hans had asked her whether it was a new thumb for one of dad's mittens? …His mother had given him a queer smile, and answered, maybe it was. …

Beret had grown more sober as the autumn came, more locked up within herself; a heavy heart lay all the time in her bosom, but she tried her best to hide it from her husband. …Her knitting needles worked rapidly, with an involuntary rhythm; but her mind was not on her task; she barely glanced at the knitting as she emptied a needle; her gaze constantly wandered out-of-doors, flitting back and forth over the section of the plain that lay in her view. Her face wore that weary, abandoned expression which had now become habitual to it whenever she was left alone; a sense of such deep melancholy lay upon her, that her whole appearance seemed to reflect a never-ending struggle with unreality. …Round after round was added to the knitting; her gaze continued to wander.

…Without volition, it fastened on an object somewhere out there—and stayed. The knitting sank to her lap; she sat and gazed for a long time, motionless, self-absorbed. Deep compassion was mingled with her melancholy, as in the heart of one who would gladly give up life to save another from destruction.

…There must be many in that caravan! …She leaned forward, trying to count the wagons. …No, she could not make them out; the wagon train had already crossed the sky line and had come some distance toward her, settling into the blue-green stillness that lay over the intervening prairie.

…Some one else has gone astray! …Poor folks—poor folks!

Suddenly a strong impulse took hold of her to do something to save these people; she felt as if she ought to go and tell them to turn back; yes, turn back—turn back—before they had strayed any farther into destruction! …

She laid her knitting on the table, went outside, and stood at the door to look at them more clearly. …Were there five wagons in the caravan? …That meant a good many people.

… "Almighty God!" she sighed, "show mercy now to the children of men! Let not these folks be altogether lost in the trackless wilderness. …For it is only I who have sinned so sorely against Thee!"

Ole had gone to the woods with his father; Store-Hans at that moment came riding up from the creek, where he had been to water the pony; he saw his mother standing outside the door in an attitude of constrained attention, and rode rapidly toward her.

"What do you want, Mother? …What are you looking at?"

His words brought her out of her deep abstraction; she took a few steps forward, then halted again. …What was the use of trying? She couldn't even speak the language of these people! … A feeling of unfathomable loneliness settled upon her; the cruelty of her fate suddenly took on fanciful proportions. ... Here she was, an exile in an unknown desert; even when human beings passed, their own kind, she could not talk with them! How could the Lord have found it in His heart to smite a soul so heavily? ... Beret put her hand up under her breast, where her own heart was beating, and pressed convulsively. ...

"What is it, Mother—what is it?"

"Ride ... ride over to them and see if you can't do something ... help them out!"

The boy was suddenly all aglow with life; he wheeled the pony around, followed the direction of his mother's gaze, and immediately discovered the caravan.

"We must tell Syvert at once!" ... Store-Hans turned his head, waiting for his mother's opinion.

... "Syvert?" ... A shadow spread over her face. ... What possible help could Syvert be to these poor people in their grievous need. She sighed in hopeless impotence. ... "No, just ride over and ask them if you can do anything... Tell them your father isn't at home."

Store-Hans couldn't remember when he had ever heard his mother talk so sensibly; he straightened himself in the saddle, sitting like a grown man; then he spoke to the pony, gave it a slap with the flat of his hand, and shouted to his mother "Now I'm off! ... You had better go and tell Syvert!"

But other eyes than hers had wandered across the prairie to the eastern sky line that day. All at once Sam came running to tell the news; he stopped only an instant, then continued on toward Ton Seten's. Beret went into the house, roused And Ongen, who was asleep on the bed, and took her along to tell Sorine; she, too, would be glad over a bit of news. ...On the way over she prayed fervently to the Lord for these people, that they should not be lost in the blue-green endlessness. ... She felt secretly glad because her husband was away from home.

Book II, Chapter I
On the Border of Utter Darkness
IX

Sunday afternoon... a dim, lurid day... a pale sun flickering through the drifting snow...an everlasting wind...the whole prairie a foaming, storm-beaten sea. ... Nothing else, to the very ends of the world. ... The sun dogs were still on guard, one ahead of the sun, the other following...

The whole settlement was gathered in Tonseten's hut that afternoon; a gloomy restlessness hat taken hold of them, so that they could not stay at home. Per Hansa had bundled the newcomer up and taken him over; that completed the roll call.

...Kjersti was serving potato coffee, with potato cakes; but for the coffee today she had fresh cow's milk, which made it not so bad, and her store of loaf sugar wasn't entirely gone. ...Inside the hut the lurid daylight cast a pale, sickly gleam. From out the stove, with its crackling fire, bright streamers of warmer light played about the room.

A heavy mood lay on the folk—too heavy for potato coffee to dispel. ...It was such a terrible, hopeless day out-of-doors...and all the days were alike. ...

Under the strain of this winter the courage of the men was slowly ebbing away. ...As they sat cooped up in Tonseten's house, they were discussing the question of how this place would look in two years, or maybe in four years—or even after six years had passed. See how many had come last year—this roomful, where the year before there wasn't a living soul! Wouldn't it be reasonable to expect that an equal number of new settlers would turn up another year? They began to figure it out on this basis: next year so many, in four years such a number; until at last the country would be filled up and the folk would stretch, neighbour to neighbour, clear out to the Rocky Mountains! They foresaw the whole process and calculated correctly— but no one in that company believed in the calculation! They heard themselves speak, and listened to one another, but all realized that there was no fire in their words!

"I don't believe Per Hansa is ready himself to swallow that story," thought Hans Olsa, but he raised no objection. ... "God save them from making mistakes in their figuring!" ran through Kjersti's mind, as she listened in awe to Per Hansa and Syvert rolling up the total; but she was careful to throw no cold water on the dream.

...On a day like this it was impossible to believe in such fine fancies; they all felt it, deep down in their hearts.

But here came Tonseten with a question that made them forget everything else for a while. The conversation had died of its own inertia; no one could find a thought that seemed worth expressing. Then Tonseten straightened up where he sat on the chest, demanding to know what names Hans Olsa and Per Hansa intended to adopt when they took out the title deeds to their land.

"Names?"

"Yes, names! ...That point would have to be settled clearly beforehand," Tonseten explained. "When the deeds were taken out, their names would then be written into the law of the land, and thereafter would be as unchangeable as the Constitution itself!"

...But they all had been baptized! How about Tonseten himself? asked Per Hansa, irritably. He couldn't understand why the name Peder Hansen would not be good enough even for the United States Constitution. ... This snobbish fastidiousness of Syvert's didn't fit the case.

Tonseten bridled at once and said that sarcasm was uncalled for. He was only, in the capacity of an old American citizen, giving good advice on matters which he understood perfectly…"That's all!" …And when Tonseten threw the phrase, "That's all!" into his conversation, they knew that he was offended. …Besides, he went on stiffly, it seemed as if anyone ought to be able to understand this much: Hans Olsen and Peder Hansen—why, either a Greek or a Hebrew might bear those names! It would never occur to anyone who heard them that they were carried by Norwegian people!

Hans Olsa laughed good-naturedly, and said with quiet humour: "Then perhaps I had better call myself Olav Trygvason. …Wasn't there some one of that name?"

This made everyone laugh: Hans Olsa's shaft had suddenly torn a rift in their mood of depression.

"Well, well," chuckled Per Hansa, "if you want to be Olav Trygvason, I'll be Peter Tordenskjold!

But then we'll have to rechristen Syvert, too …St. Olaf or Tore Hund. How would that do, Hans Olsa? …If that wouldn't proclaim to both Jew and Gentile that we are good Norwegians, then I'm certainly up a stump!" …They were all laughing so hard now that Tonseten had to join them in spite of himself. …Then Kjersti and Sorine took up the question; the Solum boys chimed in and expressed their opinions; while the children were busy discussing it among themselves. But Beret sat quietly rocking the baby on her lap, and said nothing.

An earnest liveliness crept into the conversation. Opinions flew thick and fast. At last Sorine spoke up resolutely, as if she had made up her mind, saying that if she had her choice she would rather be called Mrs. Vaag, from their place name in Norway, than Mrs. Olsen.

This sounded so sensible and practical that all the others had to try the idea at once, with their own place names.

"But, look here, Sorrina," objected Per Hansa, "that wouldn't do for my wife! Your notion would make her Mrs. Skarvholmen [holm of the cormorant]—and that nobody shall call her! I warn you!"

"No, that certainly wouldn't do for a Christian woman!" cried Kjersti with a hearty laugh.

"No, I suppose not," admitted Sorine, unwilling to give up. "But how about Mrs. Holm? That seems to me both pretty and practical. …I say, Beret, shall we all turn Baptists for a while?" …Sorine was laughing in her jolly way, immensely taken up with the idea

Beret sat rocking the child. She had listened absently all the while, humming a quiet melody to herself. When Sorine addressed her directly she stopped singing and answered that it made little difference to her, if—she choked, and went on— if it was right for a person to take a name other than the one given in baptism. ... But it made no difference to her.

Sorine grew serious over this point.

"I agree with you, Beret. ...But here in this country we can't bear our fathers' names, anyway. It wouldn't do for me to sign my name as Sorine Sakkarias'-Daughter!"

"No," cried Tonseten, excitedly, "not if you want to be Hans Olsa's wife!" ... Remarkable what a bright head sat on Sorrina's shoulders!

This matter of names brought on a long discussion. Hans Olsa, like the others, decided that his wife had made a practical suggestion; Per Hansa found little to say, but his face had a look of quiet elation. ...He must speak to Beret about this, alone and right away! ...He sat there trying the name over in his mind, first on her, then on himself, finally on each of the children. As he ran them over, the radiant light in his face grew stronger...Mrs. Holm, that sounded well; Peder Holm, that had a fine ring! ...Ole Haldor Holm! ...Hans-Kristian Holm! ...Peder Holm—no, Peder Victorious Holm! ... Peder Victorious Holm! ... He rolled the name on his tongue, biting it off in three distinct parts, as if to enjoy the sound; then he got up suddenly, grasped the waistband of his trousers, and gave them a hitch.

... "Sörine has got it right—that name is both pretty and practical. What do you say, boys— shall we adopt the plan?"

Per Hansa was plainly in a towering humour now; the note of it rang in his voice. There was no opposing him. ...After that day, each of the two families in question had a pair of surnames. Among themselves they always used the old names, but among strangers they were Vaag and Holm— though Hans Olsa invariably wrote it with a "W" instead of a "V."

Book II, Chapter II
The Power of Evil in High Places
V

Foggy weather had now been hanging over the prairie for three whole days; a warm mist of rain drizzled continuously out of the low sky. Toward evening of the third day, the fog lifted and clear sky again appeared; the setting sun burst through the cloud banks rolling up above the western horizon, and transformed them into marvellous fairy castles. ...While this was going on, over to the northeast of the Solum boys' place a lonely wagon had crept into sight; it had almost reached the creek before anyone had noticed it, for the Solum boys were visiting among the Sognings, where there were many young people. But as Beret sat out in the yard, milking, the wagon crossed her view. When she brought in the milk, she remarked in her quiet manner that they were going to have company, at which tidings the rest of the family had to run out and see who might be coming at this time of day.

There was only one wagon, with two cows following behind; on the left side walked a brown-whiskered, stooping man—he was doing the driving; close behind him came a half-grown boy, dragging his feet heavily. The wagon at last crawled up the hill and came to a stop in Per Hansa's yard, where the whole family stood waiting.

"I don't suppose there are any Norwegians in this settlement? No, that would be too much to expect," said the man in a husky, worn-out voice.

"If you're looking for Norwegians, you have found the right place, all right! We sift the people as they pass through here—keep our own, and let the others go!" ... Per Hansa wanted to run on, for he felt in high spirits; but he checked himself, observing that the man looked as if he stood on the very brink of the grave.

—Was there any chance of putting up here for the night?

"Certainly! certainly!" cried Per Hansa, briskly, "provided they were willing to take things as they were."

The man didn't answer, but walked instead to the wagon and spoke to some one inside:

"Kari, now; you must brace up and come down. Here we have found Norwegians at last!" As if fearing a contradiction, he added: "Ya, they are real Norwegians. I've talked with them."

On top of his words there came out of the wagon, first a puny boy with a hungry face, somewhat smaller than the other boy; then a girl of about the same size, but looking much older. She helped to get down another boy, about six years old, who evidently had been sleeping and looked cross and tired. That seemed to be all.

The man stepped closer to the wagon. "Aren't you coming, Kari?" A groan sounded within canvas. The girl grabbed hold of her father's arm. "You must untie the rope! Can't you remember *anything*?" she whispered, angrily.

"Ya, that's right! Wait a minute till I come and help you."

An irresistible curiosity took hold of Per-Hansa; in two jumps he stood on the tongue of the wagon. The sight that met his eyes sent chills running down his spine. Inside sat a woman on a pile of clothes, with her back against a large immigrant chest; around her wrists and leading to the handles of the chest a strong rope was tied; her face was drawn and unnatural. Per Hansa trembled so violently that he had to catch hold of the wagon box, but inwardly he was swearing a steady stream. To him it looked as if the woman was crucified.

… "For God's sake, man!"

The stranger paid no attention; he was pottering about and pleading: "Come down now, Kari. … Ya, all right, I'll help you! Everything's going to be all right— I know it will! … Can you manage to get up?" He had untied the rope, and the woman had risen to her knees.

"O God!" she sighed, putting her hands to her head.

"Please come. That's right; I'll help you!" pleaded the man, as if he were trying to persuade a child.

She came down unsteadily. "Is this the place Jakob?" she asked in a bewildered way. But now, Beret ran up and put her arm around her; the women looked into each other's eyes and instantly a bond of understanding had been established. "You come with me!" urged Beret. … "O God! This isn't the place, either!" wailed the woman; but she followed Beret submissively into the house.

"Well, well!" sighed the man as he began to unhitch the horses. "Life isn't easy— no, it certainly isn't." Per Hansa watched him anxiously, hardly knowing what to do. Both the boys kept close to him. Then an idea flashed through his mind: "You boys run over to Hans Olsa's and tell him not to go to bed until I come. … No, I don't want him here. And you two stay over there tonight. Now run along!"

Turning to the man, he asked, "Aren't there anymore in your party?"

"No, not now. We were five, you see, to begin with—five in all—but the others had to go on. … Haven't they been by here yet? Well, they must be somewhere over to the westward. …No, life isn't easy." …The man wandered on in his monotonous, blurred tone; he sounded all the time as if he were half sobbing.

"Where do you come from?" Per Hansa demanded, gruffly.

The man didn't give a direct answer, but continued to ramble on in the same mournful way, stretching his story out interminably. …They had been wandering over the prairie for nearly six weeks…Ya, it was a hard life. When they had started from Houston County, Minnesota, there had been five wagons in all. Strange that the others hadn't turned up here. Where could they be? It seemed to him as if he had travelled far enough to reach the ends of the earth! … Good God, what a nightmare life was! If he had only—only known! …

"Did the others go away and leave you?" Per Hansa hadn't intended to ask that question, but it had slipped out before he realized what he was saying. He wondered if there could be anything seriously wrong. …

"They couldn't possibly wait for us—couldn't have been expected to. Everything went wrong, you see, and I didn't know when I would be able to start again. …Turn the horses loose, John," he said to the boy. "Take the pail and see if you can squeeze some milk out of the cows. Poor beasts, they don't give much now!" Then he turned to Per Hansa again. "I don't know what would have become of us if we hadn't reached this place tonight! We'd have been in a bad hole, that I assure you! Women folk can't bear up…" the man stopped and blew his nose.

Per Hansa dreaded what might be coming next. "You must have got off your course, since you are coming down from the north?"

The man shook his head he}plessly. "To tell the truth, I don't know where we've been these last few days. We couldn't see the sun."

"Haven't you got a compass?"

"Compass? No! I tried to steer with a rope, but the one I had wasn't long enough."

"Like hell you did!" exclaimed Per Hansa, excitedly, full of a sudden new interest.

"Ya, I tried that rope idea—hitched it to the back of the wagon, and let it drag in the wet grass. But it didn't work—I couldn't steer straight with it. The rope was so short, and kept kinking around so much, that it didn't leave any wake."

"Uh-huh!" nodded Per Hansa wisely. "You must be a seafaring man, to have tried that trick!"

"No, I'm no sailor. But fisher-folk out here have told me that it's possible to steer by a rope. …I had to try something."

"Where did you cross the Sioux?"

"How do I know where I crossed it? We came to a river a long way to the east of here—that must have been the Sioux. We hunted and hunted before we could find a place shallow enough to cross…God! this has certainly been a wandering in the desert for me! … But if Kari only gets better, I won't complain—though I never dreamed that life could be so hard." …

"Is she—is she *sick*, that woman of yours?"

The man did not answer this question immediately; he wiped his face with the sleeve of his shirt. When he spoke again, his voice had grown even more blurred and indistinct: "Physically she seems to be as well as ever—as far as I can see. She certainly hasn't overworked since we've been travelling. I hope there's nothing wrong with her…But certain things are hard to bear—I suppose it's worse for the mother, too—though the Lord knows it hasn't been easy for me, either! …You see, we had to leave our youngest boy out there on the prairie…"

"Leave him?" … These were the only two words that came to Per Hansa's mind.

"Ya, there he lies, our little boy!… I never saw a more promising man—you know what I mean— when he grew up…But now—oh, well…"

Per Hansa felt faint in the pit of his stomach; his throat grew dry; his voice became as husky as that of the other; he came closer up to him. "Tell me— how did this happen?"

The man shook his head again, in a sort of dumb despair. Then he cleared his throat and continued with great effort: "I can't tell how it happened!

Fate just willed it so. Such things are not to be explained…The boy had been ailing for some time—we knew that, but didn't pay much attention. We had other things to think of…Then he began to fail fast. We were only one day's journey this side of Jackson; so we went back. That was the time when the others left us. I don't blame them much—it was uncertain when we could go on…The doctor we found wasn't a capable man —I realize it now. He spoke only English and couldn't under-stand what I was saying. He had no idea what was wrong with the boy—I could see that plainly enough… Ya, well—so we started again… It isn't any use to fight against Fate; that's an old saying, and a true one, too, I guess… Before long we saw that the boy wasn't going to recover. So we hurried on, day and night, trying to catch our neighbors… Well, that's about all of it. One night he was gone—just as if you had blown out a candle. Ya, let me see—that was five nights ago."

"Have you got him there in the wagon?" demanded Per Hansa, grabbing the man by the arm.

"No, no," he muttered huskily. "We buried him out there by a big stone—no coffin or anything. But Kari took the best skirt she had and wrapped it all around him—we had to do something, you know… But," he continued, suddenly straight-ening up, "Paul cannot lie there! As soon as I find my neighbors, I'll go and get him. Otherwise Kari…" The man paused between the sobs that threatened to choke him. "I have had to tie her up the last few days. She insisted on getting out and going back to Paul. I don't think she has had a wink of sleep for over a week… It's just as I was saying—some people can't stand things." …

Per Hansa leaned heavily against the wagon. "Has she gone crazy?" he asked, hoarsely.

"She isn't much worse than the rest of us. I don't believe … Kari is really a well-balanced woman … but you can imagine how it feels to leave a child that way …"

The boy, John, had finished milking. He had put the pail down and was stand-ing a little way off, listening to his father's story; suddenly he threw himself on the ground, sobbing as if in convulsions.

"John! John!" admonished the father. "Aren't you ashamed of-yourself—a grown-up man like you! Take the milk and carry it into the house!"

"That's right!" echoed Per Hansa, pulling himself together. "We'd better all go in. There's shelter here, and plenty to eat."

Beret was bustling around the room when they entered; she had put the woman to bed, and now was tending her. "Where are the boys?" she asked. Per Hansa told her that he had sent them to Hans Olsa's for the night.

"That was hardly necessary; we could have made room here somewhere." Beret's voice carried a note of keen reproach.

The man had paused at the door; now he came over to the bed, took the limp hand, and muttered:

"Poor soul! ... Why, I believe she's asleep already!"

Beret came up and pushed him gently aside. "Be careful! Don't wake her. She needs the rest."

"Ya, I don't doubt it—not I! She hasn't slept for a week, you see—the poor soul!" With a loud sniff, he turned and left the room.

When supper time came the woman seemed to be engulfed in a stupefying sleep. Beret did not join the others at the supper table, but busied herself, instead, by trying to make the woman more comfortable; she loosened her clothes, took off her shoes, and washed her face in warm water; during all this the stranger never stirred. That done, Beret began to fix up sleeping quarters for the strangers, in the barn. She carried in fresh hay and brought out all the bedding she had; she herself would take care of the woman, in case she awoke and needed attention. Beret did little talking, but she went about these arrangements with a firmness and confidence that surprised her husband.

Per Hansa came in from the barn, after helping the strangers settle themselves for the night. Beret was sitting on the edge of the bed, dressing the baby for the night; she had put And-Ongen to bed beside the distracted woman.

"Did she tell you much?" he asked in a low voice.

Beret glanced toward the other bed before she answered: "Only that she had had to leave one of her children on the way. She wasn't able to talk connectedly."

"It's a terrible thing!" he said, looking away from his wife. "I think I'll go over to Hans Olsa's for a minute. I want to talk this matter over with him."

"Talk it over with him?" she repeated, coldly.

"I don't suppose Hans Olsa knows everything!"

"No, of course not. But these people have got to be helped, and we can't do it all alone." He hesitated for a minute, as if waiting for her consent. "Well, I won't be gone long," he said as he went out the door.

When he returned, an hour later, she was still sitting on the edge of the bed, with the baby asleep on her lap. They sat in silence for a long while; at last he began to undress. She waited until he was in bed, then turned the lamp low and lay down herself, but without undressing... The lamp shed only a faint light. It was so quiet in the room that one could hear the breathing of all the others. Beret lay there listening; though the room was still, it seemed alive to her with strange movements; she forced herself to open her eyes and look around.

Noticing that Per Hansa wasn't asleep, either, she asked:

"Did you look after the boys?"

"Nothing the matter with them! They were fast asleep in Sofie's bed."

"You told them everything, at Hans Olsa's?"

"Of course!"

"What did they think of it?"

Per Hansa raised himself on his elbows and glanced at the broken creature lying in the bed back of theirs. The woman, apparently, had not stirred a muscle. "It's a bad business," he said. "We must try to get together a coffin and find the boy. We can't let him lie out there—that way." ... As Beret made no answer, he briefly narrated the story that the man had told him. "The fellow is a good-for-nothing, stupid fool, I'm sure of that," concluded Per Hansa.

She listened to him in silence. For some time she brooded over her thoughts; then in a bitter tone she suddenly burst out: "Now you can see that this kind of a life is impossible! It's beyond human endurance."

He had not the power to read her thoughts; he did not want to know them; tonight every nerve in his body was taut with apprehension and dismay. But he tried to say, reassuringly: "Hans Olsa and I will both go with the man, as soon as the day breaks. If we only had something to make the coffin of! The few pieces of board that I've got here will be hardly enough. ... Now let's go to sleep. Be sure and call me if you need anything!"

He turned over resolutely, as if determined to sleep; but she noticed that he was a long time doing it. ... I wonder what's going through his mind? she thought. She was glad to have him awake, just the same; tonight there were strange things abroad in the room. ...

Book II, Chapter IV
The Great Plain Drinks the Blood
of Christian Men and is Satisfied
I

Many and incredible are the tales the grandfathers tell from those days when the wilderness was yet untamed, and when they, unwittingly, founded the Kingdom. There was the Red Son of the Great Prairie, who hated the Palefaces with a hot hatred; stealthily he swooped down upon them, tore up and laid waste the little settlements. Great was the terror he spread; bloody the saga concerning him.

But more to be dreaded than this tribulation was the strange spell of sadness which the unbroken solitude cast upon the minds of some. Many took their own lives; asylum after asylum was filled with disordered beings who had once been human. It is hard for the eye to wander from sky line to sky line, year in and year out, without finding a resting place! ...

Then, too, there were the years of pestilence— toil and travail, famine and disease. God knows how human beings could endure it all. And many did not—they lay down and died. "There is nothing to do about that," said they who survived. "We are all destined to die—that's certain. Some must go now; others will have to go later. It's all the same, is it not?" The poor could find much wherewith to console themselves. And whisky was cheap in those days, and easy to get. ...

And on the hot summer days terrible storms might come. In the twinkling of an eye they would smash to splinters the habitations which man had built for himself, so that they resembled nothing so much as a few stray hairs on a wornout pelt. Man have power? Breathe it not, for that is to tempt the Almighty...

Some feared most the prairie fire. Terrible, too, it was, before people had learned how to guard against it.

Others remembered best the trips to town. They were the jolliest days, said some; no, they were the worst of all, said the others. It may be that both were right. ...The oxen moved slowly—whether the distance was thirty miles or ninety made little difference. In the sod house back there, somewhere along the horizon, life got on your nerves at times. There sat a wife with a flock of starving children; she had grown very pale of late, and the mouths of the children were always open—always crying for food. ...But in the town it was cheerful and pleasant. There one could get a drink; there one could talk with people who spoke with enthusiasm and certainty about the future. This was the land of promise, they said. Sometimes one met these people in the saloons; and then it was more fascinating to listen to them than to any talk about the millennium. Their words lay like embers in the mind during the whole of the interminable, jolting journey homeward, and made it less long. ... It helps so much to have something pleasant to think about, say the Old.

And it was as if nothing affected people in those days. They threw themselves blindly into the impossible, and accomplished the Unbelievable. If anyone succumbed in the struggle—and that happened often—another would come and take his place. Youth was in the race; the unknown, the untried, the unheard-of, was in the air; people caught it, were intoxicated by it, threw themselves away, and laughed at the cost. Of course it was possible - everything was possible out here. There was no such thing as the Impossible any more. The human race has not known such faith and such self-confidence since history began. ...And so had been the Spirit since the day the first settlers landed on the eastern shores; it would rise and fall at intervals, would swell and surge on again - with every new wave of settlers that rolled westward into the unbroken solitude.

Mark Twain, Old Times on the Mississippi

Excerpted from Mark Twain, Old Times on the Mississippi *(1875),*
which originally appeared as a series of seven short stories
in The Atlantic Monthly.

Mark Twain was the pen name of American novelist
Samuel Langhorne Clemens (1835-1910).

I

When I was a boy, there was but one permanent ambition among my comrades in our village [Hannibal, Missouri] on the west bank of the Mississippi River. That was, to be a steamboatman. We had transient ambitions of other sorts, but they were only transient. When a circus came and went, it left us all burning to become clowns; the first negro minstrel show that came to our section left us all suffering to try that kind of life; now and then we had a hope that if we lived and were good, God would permit us to be pirates. These ambitions faded out, each in its turn; but the ambition to be a steamboatman always remained.

Once a day a cheap, gaudy packet arrived upward from St. Louis, and another downward from Keokuk. Before these events had transpired, the day was glorious with expectancy; after they had transpired, the day was a dead and empty thing. Not only the boys, but the whole village, felt this. After all these years I can picture that old time to myself now, just as it was then: the white town drowsing in the sun-shine of a summer's morning; the streets empty, or pretty nearly so; one or two clerks in front of the Water Street stores, with their splint-bottomed chairs tilted back against the wall, chins on breasts, hats slouched over their faces, asleep—with shingle-shavings enough around to show what broke them down; a sow and a litter of pigs loafing along the sidewalk, doing a good business in water-melon rinds and seeds; two or three lonely little freight piles scattered about the "levee"; a pile of "skids" on the slope of the stone-paved wharf, and the fragrant town drunkard asleep in the shadow of them; two or three wood flats at the head of the wharf, but nobody to listen to the peaceful lapping of the wavelets against them; the great Mississippi, the majestic, the magnificent Mississippi, rolling its mile-wide tide along, shining in the sun; the dense forest away on the other side; the "point" above the town, and the "point" below, bounding the river-glimpse and turning it into a sort of sea, and withal a very still and brilliant and lonely one. Presently a film of dark smoke appears above one of those remote "points"; instantly a negro drayman, famous for his quick eye and prodigious voice, lifts up the cry, "S-t-e-a-m-boat a-comin'!" and the scene changes! The town drunkard stirs, the clerks wake up, a furious clatter of drays follows, every house and store pours out a human contribution, and all in a twinkling the dead town is alive and moving. Drays, carts, men, boys, all go hurrying from many quarters to a common centre, the wharf. Assembled there, the people fasten their eyes upon the coming boat as upon a wonder they are seeing for the first time. And the boat is rather a handsome sight, too. She is long and sharp and trim and pretty; she has two tall, fancy-topped chimneys, with a gilded device of some kind swung between them; a fanciful pilot-house, all glass and "gingerbread," perched on top of the "texas" deck behind them; the paddle-boxes are gorgeous with a picture or with gilded rays above the boat's name; the boiler deck, the hurricane deck, and the texas deck are fenced and ornamented with clean white railings; there is a flag gallantly flying from the jack-staff; the furnace doors are open and the fires flaring bravely; the upper decks are black with passengers; the captain stands by the big bell, calm, imposing, the envy of all; great volumes of the blackest smoke are rolling and tumbling out of the chimneys—a husbanded grandeur created with a bit of pitch pine just before arriving at a town; the crew are grouped on the forecastle; the broad stage is run far out over the port bow, and an envied deck-hand stands picturesquely on the end of it with a coil of rope in his hand; the pent steam is screaming through the gauge-cocks; the captain lifts his hand, a bell rings, the wheels stop; then they turn back, churning the water to foam, and the steamer is at rest. Then such a scramble as there is to get aboard, and to get ashore, and to take in freight and to discharge freight, all at one and the same time; and such a yelling and cursing as the mates facilitate it all with! Ten minutes later the steamer is under way again, with no flag on the jack-staff and no black smoke issuing from the chimneys. After ten more minutes the town is dead again, and the town drunkard asleep by the skids once more.

My father was a justice of the peace, and I supposed he possessed the power of life and death over all men and could hang anybody that offended him. This was distinction enough for me as a general thing; but the desire to be a steamboatman kept intruding, nevertheless. I first wanted to be a cabin-boy, so that I could come out with a white apron on and shake a table-cloth over the side, where all my old comrades could see me; later I thought I would rather be the deck-hand who stood on the end of the stage-plank with the coil of rope in his hand, because he was particularly conspicuous. But these were only day-dreams— they were too heavenly to be contemplated as real possibilities. By and by one of our boys went away. He was not heard of for a long time. At last he turned up as apprentice engineer or "striker" on a steamboat. This thing shook the bottom out of all my Sunday-school teachings. That boy had been notoriously worldly, and I just the reverse, yet he was exalted to this eminence, and I left in obscurity and misery. There was nothing generous about this fellow in his greatness. He would always manage to have a rusty bolt to scrub while his boat tarried at our town, and he would sit on the inside guard and scrub it, where we could all see him and envy him and loathe him. And whenever his boat was laid up he would come home and swell around the town in his blackest and greasiest clothes, so that nobody could help remembering that he was a steamboatman; and he used all sorts of steamboat technicalities in his talk, as if he were so used to them that he forgot common people could not understand them. He would speak of the "labboard" side of a horse in an easy, natural way that would make one wish he was dead. And he was always talking about "St. Looy" like an old citizen, he would refer casually to occasions when he "was coming down Fourth Street," or when he was "passing by the Planter's House," or when there was a fire and he took a turn on the brakes of "the old Big Missouri;" and then he would go on and lie about how many towns the size of ours were burned down there that day. Two or three of the boys had long been persons of consideration among us because they had been to St. Louis once and had a vague general knowledge of its wonders, but the day of their glory was over now. They lapsed into a humble silence, and learned to disappear when the ruthless "cub"-engineer approached. This fellow had money, too, and hair oil. Also an ignorant silver watch and a showy brass watch chain. He wore a leather belt and used no suspenders. If ever a youth was cordially admired and hated by his comrades, this one was. No girl could withstand his charms. He "cut out" every boy in the village. When his boat blew up at last, it diffused a tranquil contentment among us such as we had not known for months. But when he came home the next week, alive, renowned, and appeared in church all battered up and bandaged, a shining hero, stared at and wondered over by everybody, it seemed to us that the partiality of Providence for an undeserving reptile had reached a point where it was open to criticism.

This creature's career could produce but one result, and it speedily followed. Boy after boy managed to get on the river. The minister's son became an engineer. The doctor's and the postmaster's sons became "mud clerks"; the wholesale liquor dealer's son became a barkeeper on a boat; four sons of the chief merchant, and two sons of the county judge, became pilots. Pilot was the grandest position of all. The pilot, even in those days of trivial wages, had a princely salary—from a hundred and fifty to two hundred and fifty dollars a month, and no board to pay. Two months of his wages would pay a preacher's salary for a year. Now some of us were left disconsolate. We could not get on the river—at least our parents would not let us.

So, by and by, I ran away. I said I never would come home again till I was a pilot and could come in glory. But somehow I could not manage it. I went meekly aboard a few of the boats that lay packed together like sardines at the long St. Louis wharf, and very humbly inquired for the pilots, but got only a cold shoulder and short words from mates and clerks. I had to make the best of this sort of treatment for the time being, but I had comforting day-dreams of a future when I should be a great and honored pilot, with plenty of money, and could kill some of these mates and clerks and pay for them.

Months afterward the hope within me struggled to a reluctant death, and I found myself without an ambition. But I was ashamed to go home. I was in Cincinnati, and I set to work to map out a new career. I had been reading about the recent exploration of the river Amazon by an expedition sent out by our government. It was said that the expedition, owing to difficulties, had not thoroughly explored a part of the country lying about the headwaters, some four thousand miles from the mouth of the river. It was only about fifteen hundred miles from Cincinnati to New Orleans, where I could doubtless get a ship. I had thirty dollars left; I would go and complete the exploration of the Amazon. This was all the thought I gave to the subject. I never was great in matters of detail. I packed my valise, and took passage on an ancient tub called the Paul Jones, for New Orleans. For the sum of sixteen dollars I had the scarred and tarnished splendors of "her" main saloon principally to myself, for she was not a creature to attract the eye of wiser travelers.

When we presently got under way and went poking down the broad Ohio, I became a new being, and the subject of my own admiration. I was a traveler! A word never had tasted so good in my mouth before. I had an exultant sense of being bound for mysterious lands and distant climes which I never have felt in so uplifting a degree since. I was in such a glorified condition that all ignoble feelings departed out of me, and I was able to look down and pity the untraveled with a compassion that had hardly a trace of contempt in it. Still, when we stopped at villages and wood-yards, I could not help lolling carelessly upon the railings of the boiler deck to enjoy the envy of the country boys on the bank. If they did not seem to discover me, I presently sneezed to attract their attention, or moved to a position where they could not help seeing me. And as soon as I knew they saw me I gaped and stretched, and gave other signs of being mightily bored with traveling.

I kept my hat off all the time, and stayed where the wind and the sun could strike me, because I wanted to get the bronzed and weather-beaten look of an old traveler. Before the second day was half gone, I experienced a joy which filled me with the purest gratitude; for I saw that the skin had begun to blister and peel off my face and neck. I wished that the boys and girls at home could see me now.

We reached Louisville in time—at least the neighborhood of it. We stuck hard and fast on the rocks in the middle of the river and lay there four days. I was now beginning to feel a strong sense of being a part of the boat's family, a sort of infant son to the captain and younger brother to the officers. There is no estimating the pride I took in this grandeur, or the affection that began to swell and grow in me for those people. I could not know how the lordly steamboatman scorns that sort of presumption in a mere landsman. I particularly longed to acquire the least trifle of notice from the big stormy mate, and I was on the alert for an opportunity to do him a service to that end. It came at last. The riotous powwow of setting a spar was going on down on the forecastle, and I went down there and stood around in the way—or mostly skipping out of it— till the mate suddenly roared a general order for somebody to bring him a capstan bar. I sprang to his side and said: "Tell me where it is—I'll fetch it!"

If a rag-picker had offered to do a diplomatic service for the Emperor of Russia, the monarch could not have been more astounded than the mate was. He even stopped swearing. He stood and stared down at me. It took him ten seconds to scrape his disjointed remains together again. Then he said impressively: "Well, if this don't beat hell!" and turned to his work with the air of a man who had been confronted with a problem too abstruse for solution.

I crept away, and courted solitude for the rest of the day. I did not go to dinner; I stayed away from supper until everybody else had finished. I did not feel so much like a member of the boat's family now as before. However, my spirits returned, in installments, as we pursued our way down the river. I was sorry I hated the mate so, because it was not in (young) human nature not to admire him. He was huge and muscular, his face was bearded and whiskered all over; he had a red woman and a blue woman tattooed on his right arm—one on each side of a blue anchor with a red rope to it; and in the matter of profanity he was perfect. When he was getting out cargo at a landing, I was always where I could see and hear. He felt all the sublimity of his great position, and made the world feel it, too. When he gave even the simplest order, he discharged it like a blast of lightning, and sent a long, reverberating peal of profanity thundering after it. I could not help contrasting the way in which the average landsman would give an order, with the mate's way of doing it. If the landsman should wish the gang-plank moved a foot farther forward, he would probably say: "James, or William, one of you push that plank forward, please;" but put the mate in his place, and he would roar out: "Here, now, start that gang-plank for'ard! Lively, now! What're you about! Snatch it! snatch it! There! there! Aft again! aft again! Don't you hear me? Dash it to dash! are you going to sleep over it! 'Vast heaving. 'Vast heaving, I tell you! Going to heave it clear astern? Where're you going with that barrel! for'ard with it 'fore I make you swallow it, you dash-dash-dash-dashed split between a tired mud-turtle and a crippled hearse-horse!"

I wished I could talk like that.

When the soreness of my adventure with the mate had somewhat worn off, I began timidly to make up to the humblest official connected with the boat— the night watchman. He snubbed my advances at first, but I presently ventured to offer him a new chalk pipe, and that softened him. So he allowed me to sit with him by the big bell on the hurricane deck, and in time he melted into conversation. He could not well have helped it, I hung with such homage on his words and so plainly showed that I felt honored by his notice. He told me the names of dim capes and shadowy islands as we glided by them in the solemnity of the night, under the winking stars, and by and by got to talking about himself. He seemed over-sentimental for a man whose salary was six dollars a week—or rather he might have seemed so to an older person than I. But I drank in his words hungrily, and with a faith that might have moved mountains if it had been applied judiciously. What was it to me that he was soiled and seedy and fragrant with gin? What was it to me that his grammar was bad, his construction worse, and his profanity so void of art that it was an element of weakness rather than strength in his conversation? He was a wronged man, a man who had seen trouble, and that was enough for me. As he mellowed into his plaintive history his tears dripped upon the lantern in his lap, and I cried, too, from sympathy. He said he was the son of an English nobleman—either an earl or an alderman, he could not remember which, but believed he was both; his father, the nobleman, loved him, but his mother hated him from the cradle; and so while he was still a little boy he was sent to "one of them old, ancient colleges"— he couldn't remember which; and by and by his father died and his mother seized the property and "shook" him, as he phrased it. After his mother shook him, members of the nobility with whom he was acquainted used their influence to get him the position of "loblolly-boy in a ship"; and from that point my watchman threw off all trammels of date and locality and branched out into a narrative that bristled all along with incredible adventures; a narrative that was so reeking with bloodshed and so crammed with hair-breadth escapes and the most engaging and unconscious personal villainies, that I sat speechless, enjoying, shuddering, wondering, worshiping.

It was a sore blight to find out afterwards that he was a low, vulgar, ignorant, sentimental, half-witted humbug, an untraveled native of the wilds of Illinois, who had absorbed wildcat literature and appropriated its marvels, until in time he had woven odds and ends of the mess into this yarn, and then gone on, telling it to fledgelings like me, until he had come to believe it himself.

II

WHAT with lying on the rocks four days at Louisville, and some other delays, the poor old Paul Jones fooled away about two weeks in making the voyage from Cincinnati to New Orleans. This gave me a chance to get acquainted with one of the pilots, and he taught me how to steer the boat, and thus made the fascination of river life more potent than ever for me.

It also gave me a chance to get acquainted with a youth who had taken deck passage—more's the pity; for he easily borrowed six dollars of me on a promise to return to the boat and pay it back to me the day after we should arrive. But he probably died or forgot, for he never came. It was doubtless the former, since he had said his parents were wealthy, and he only traveled deck passage because it was cooler.

I soon discovered two things. One was that a vessel would not be likely to sail for the mouth of the Amazon under ten or twelve years; and the other was that the nine or ten dollars still left in my pocket would not suffice for so imposing an exploration as I had planned, even if I could afford to wait for a ship. Therefore it followed that I must contrive a new career. The Paul Jones was now bound for St. Louis. I planned a siege against my pilot, and at the end of three hard days he surrendered. He agreed to teach me the Mississippi River from New Orleans to St. Louis for five hundred dollars, payable out of the first wages I should receive after graduating. I entered upon the small enterprise of "learning" twelve or thirteen hundred miles of the great Mississippi River with the easy confidence of my time of life. If I had really known what I was about to require of my faculties, I should not have had the courage to begin. I supposed that all a pilot had to do was to keep his boat in the river, and I did not consider that that could be much of a trick, since it was so wide.

The boat backed out from New Orleans at four in the afternoon, and it was "our watch" until eight. Mr. Bixby, my chief, "straightened her up," plowed her along past the sterns of the other boats that lay at the Levee, and then said, "Here, take her; shave those steamships as close as you'd peel an apple." I took the wheel, and my heart went down into my boots; for it seemed to me that we were about to scrape the side off every ship in the line, we were so close. I held my breath and began to claw the boat away from the danger; and I had my own opinion of the pilot who had known no better than to get us into such peril, but I was too wise to express it. In half a minute I had a wide margin of safety intervening between the Paul Jones and the ships; and within ten seconds more I was set aside in disgrace, and Mr. Bixby was going into danger again and flaying me alive with abuse of my cowardice. I was stung, but I was obliged to admire the easy confidence with which my chief loafed from side to side of his wheel, and trimmed the ships so closely that disaster seemed ceaselessly imminent. When he had cooled a little he told me that the easy water was close ashore and the current outside, and therefore we must hug the bank, up-stream, to get the benefit of the former, and stay well out, down-stream, to take advantage of the latter. In my own mind I resolved to be a down-stream pilot and leave the up-streaming to people dead to prudence.

Now and then Mr. Bixby called my attention to certain things. Said he, "This is Six-Mile Point." I assented. It was pleasant enough information, but I could not see the bearing of it. I was not conscious that it was a matter of any interest to me. Another time he said, "This is Nine-Mile Point." Later he said, "This is Twelve-Mile Point." They were all about level with the water's edge; they all looked about alike to me; they were monotonously unpicturesque. I hoped Mr. Bixby would change the subject. But no; he would crowd up around a point, hugging the shore with affection, and then say: "The slack water ends here, abreast this bunch of Chinatrees; now we cross over." So he crossed over. He gave me the wheel once or twice, but I had no luck. I either came near chipping off the edge of a sugar plan-tation, or else I yawed too far from shore, and so I dropped back into disgrace again and got abused.

The watch was ended at last, and we took supper and went to bed. At midnight the glare of a lantern shone in my eyes, and the night watchman said:

"Come, turn out!"

And then he left. I could not understand this extraordinary procedure; so I presently gave up trying to, and dozed off to sleep. Pretty soon the watchman was back again, and this time he was gruff. I was annoyed. I said:

"What do you want to come bothering around here in the middle of the night for? Now as like as not I'll not get to sleep again to-night."

The watchman said:—

"Well, if this ain't good, I'm blest."

The "off-watch" was just turning in, and I heard some brutal laughter from them, and such remarks as "Hello, watchman! ain't the new cub turned out yet? He's delicate, likely. Give him some sugar in a rag and send for the chambermaid to sing rock-a-by-baby to him."

About this time Mr. Bixby appeared on the scene. Something like a minute later I was climbing the pilot-house steps with some of my clothes on and the rest in my arms. Mr. Bixby was close behind, commenting. Here was something fresh— this thing of getting up in the middle of the night to go to work. It was a detail in piloting that had never occurred to me at all. I knew that boats ran all night, but somehow I had never happened to reflect that somebody had to get up out of a warm bed to run them. I began to fear that piloting was not quite so romantic as I had imagined it was; there was something very real and work-like about this new phase of it.

It was a rather dingy night, although a fair number of stars were out. The big mate was at the wheel, and he had the old tub pointed at a star and was holding her straight up the middle of the river. The shores on either hand were not much more than a mile apart, but they seemed wonderfully far away and ever so vague and indistinct. The mate said:

"We've got to land at Jones's plantation, sir."

The vengeful spirit in me exulted. I said to myself, I wish you joy of your job, Mr. Bixby; you'll have a good time finding Mr. Jones's plantation such a night as this; and I hope you never will find it as long as you live.

Mr. Bixby said to the mate:

"Upper end of the plantation, or the lower?"

"Upper."

"I can't do it. The stumps there are out of water at this stage. It's no great distance to the lower, and you'll have to get along with that."

"All right, sir. If Jones don't like it he'll have to lump it, I reckon."

And then the mate left. My exultation began to cool and my wonder to come up. Here was a man who not only proposed to find this plantation on such a night, but to find either end of it you preferred. I dreadfully wanted to ask a question, but I was carrying about as many short answers as my cargo-room would admit of, so I held my peace. All I desired to ask Mr. Bixby was the simple question whether he was ass enough to really imagine he was going to find that plantation on a night when all plantations were exactly alike and all the same color. But I held in. I used to have fine inspirations of prudence in those days.

Mr. Bixby made for the shore and soon was scraping it, just the same as if it had been daylight. And not only that, but singing:

"Father in heaven the day is declining," etc. It seemed to me that I had put my life in the keeping of a peculiarly reckless outcast. Presently he turned on me and said:

"What's the name of the first point above New Orleans?"

I was gratified to be able to answer promptly, and I did. I said I didn't know.

"Don't know?"

This manner jolted me. I was down at the foot again, in a moment. But I had to say just what I had said before.

"Well, you're a smart one," said Mr. Bixby. "What's the name of the next point?" Once more I didn't know.

"Well this beats anything. Tell me the name of any point or place I told you."

I studied a while and decided that I couldn't.

"Look-a-here! What do you start out from, above Twelve-Mile Point, to cross over?"

"I—I—don't know."

"You—you—don't know?" mimicking my drawling manner of speech. "What do you know?"

"I—I—nothing, for certain."

"By the great Caesar's ghost I believe you! You're the stupidest dunderhead I ever saw or ever heard of, so help me Moses! The idea of you being a pilot —you! Why, you don't know enough to pilot a cow down a lane."

Oh, but his wrath was up! He was a nervous man, and he shuffled from one side of his wheel to the other as if the floor was hot. He would boil a while to himself, and then overflow and scald me again.

"Look-a-here! What do you suppose I told you the names of those points for?"

I tremblingly considered a moment, and then the devil of temptation provoked me to say:

"Well—to—to—be entertaining, I thought."

This was a red rag to the bull. He raged and stormed so (he was crossing the river at the time) that I judge it made him blind, because he ran over the steering-oar of a trading-scow. Of course the traders sent up a volley of red-hot profanity. Never was a man so grateful as Mr. Bixby was: because he was brim full, and here were subjects who would talk back. He threw open a window, thrust his head out; and such an irruption followed as I never had heard before. The fainter and farther away the scowmen's curses drifted, the higher Mr. Bixby lifted his voice and the weightier his adjectives grew. When he closed the window he was empty. You could have drawn a seine through his system and not caught curses enough to disturb your mother with. Presently he said to me in the gentlest way:

"My boy, you must get a little memorandum-book, and every time I tell you a thing, put it down right away. There's only one way to be a pilot, and that is to get this entire river by heart. You have to know it just like A B C."

That was a dismal revelation to me; for my memory was never loaded with anything but blank cartridges. However, I did not feel discouraged long. I judged that it was best to make some allowances, for doubtless Mr. Bixby was "stretching." Presently he pulled a rope and struck a few strokes on the big bell. The stars were all gone now, and the night was as black as ink. I could hear the wheels churn along the bank, but I was not entirely certain that I could see the shore. The voice of the invisible watchman called up from the hurricane deck:

"What's this, sir?"

"Jones's plantation."

I said to myself, I wish I might venture to offer a small bet that it isn't. But I did not chirp. I only waited to see. Mr. Bixby handled the engine bells, and in due time the boat's nose came to the land, a torch glowed from the forecastle, a man skipped ashore, a darky's voice on the bank said. "Gimme de k'yarpet-bag, Mass' Jones," and the next moment we were standing up the river again, all serene. I reflected deeply a while, and then said,—but not aloud,—Well, the finding of that plantation was the luckiest accident that ever happened; but it couldn't happen again in a hundred years. And I fully believed it was an accident, too.

By the time we had gone seven or eight hundred miles up the river, I had learned to be a tolerably plucky up-stream steersman in daylight, and before we reached St. Louis I had made a trifle of progress in night-work, but only a trifle. I had a note-book that fairly bristled with the names of towns, "points," bars, islands, bends, reaches, etc.: but the information was to be found only in the note-book— none of it was in my head. It made my heart ache to think I had only got half of the river set down; for as our watch was four hours off and four hours on, day and night, there was a long four-hour gap in my book for every time I had slept since the voyage began.

My chief was presently hired to go on a big New Orleans boat, and I packed my satchel and went with him. She was a grand affair. When I stood in her pilot-house I was so far above the water that I seemed perched on a mountain; and her decks stretched so far away, fore and aft, below me, that I wondered how I could ever have considered the little Paul Jones a large craft. There were other differences, too. The Paul Jones's pilot-house was a cheap, dingy, battered rattletrap, cramped for room: but here was a sumptuous glass temple; room enough to have a dance in; showy red and gold window-curtains; an imposing sofa; leather cushions and a back to the high bench where visiting pilots sit, to spin yarns and "look at the river;" bright, fanciful "cuspadores" instead of a broad wooden box filled with sawdust; nice new oilcloth on the floor; a hospitable big stove for winter; a wheel as high as my head, costly with inlaid work; a wire tiller-rope; bright brass knobs for the bells; and a tidy, white-aproned, black "texas-tender," to bring up tarts and ices and coffee during mid-watch, day and night. Now this was "something like"; and so I began to take heart once more to believe that piloting was a romantic sort of occupation after all. The moment we were under way I began to prowl about the great steamer and fill myself with joy. She was as clean and as dainty as a drawing-room; when I looked down her long, gilded saloon, it was like gazing through a splendid tunnel; she had an oil-picture, by some gifted sign-painter, on every state-room door; she glittered with no end of prism-fringed chandeliers; the clerk's office was elegant, the bar was marvelous, and the bar-keeper had been barbered and upholstered at incredible cost. The boiler deck (i. e., the second story of the boat, so to speak) was as spacious as a church, it seemed to me; so with the forecastle; and there was no pitiful handful of deckhands, firemen, and roustabouts down there, but a whole battalion of men. The fires were fiercely glaring from a long row of furnaces, and over them were eight huge boilers! This was unutterable pomp. The mighty engines— but enough of this. I had never felt so fine before. And when I found that the regiment of natty servants respectfully "sir'd" me, my satisfaction was complete.

When I returned to the pilot-house St. Louis was gone and I was lost. Here was a piece of river which was all down in my book, but I could make neither head nor tail of it: you understand, it was turned around. I had seen it, when coming upstream, but I had never faced about to see how it looked when it was behind me. My heart broke again, for it was plain that I had got to learn this troublesome river both ways.

The pilot-house was full of pilots, going down to "look at the river." What is called the "upper river" (the two hundred miles between St. Louis and Cairo, where the Ohio comes in) was low; and the Mississippi changes its channel so constantly that the pilots used to always find it necessary to run down to Cairo to take a fresh look, when their boats were to lie in port a week, that is, when the water was at a low stage. A deal of this "looking at the river" was done by poor fellows who seldom had a berth, and whose only hope of getting one lay in their being always freshly posted and therefore ready to drop into the shoes of some reputable pilot, for a single trip, on account of such pilot's sudden illness, or some other necessity. And a good many of them constantly ran up and down inspecting the river, not because they ever really hoped to get a berth, but because (they being guests of the boat) it was cheaper to "look at the river" than stay ashore and pay board. In time these fellows grew dainty in their tastes, and only infested boats that had an established reputation for setting good tables. All visiting pilots were useful, for they were always ready and willing, winter or summer, night or day, to go out in the yawl and help buoy the channel or assist the boat's pilots in any way they could. They were likewise welcome because all pilots are tireless talkers, when gathered together, and as they talk only about the river they are always understood and are always interesting. Your true pilot cares nothing about anything on earth but the river, and his pride in his occupation surpasses the pride of kings.

We had a fine company of these river inspectors along, this trip. There were eight or ten; and there was abundance of room for them in our great pilot-house. Two or three of them wore polished silk hats, elaborate shirt-fronts, diamond breastpins, kid gloves, and patent-leather boots. They were choice in their English, and bore themselves with a dignity proper to men of solid means and prodigious reputation as pilots. The others were more or less loosely clad, and wore upon their heads tall felt cones that were suggestive of the days of the Commonwealth.

I was a cipher in this august company, and felt subdued, not to say torpid. I was not even of sufficient consequence to assist at the wheel when it was necessary to put the tiller hard down in a hurry; the guest that stood nearest did that when occasion required— and this was pretty much all the time, because of the crookedness of the channel and the scant water. I stood in a corner; and the talk I listened to took the hope all out of me. One visitor said to another:

"Jim, how did you run Plum Point, coming up?"

"It was in the night, there, and I ran it the way one of the boys on the Diana told me; started out about fifty yards above the wood pile on the false point, and held on the cabin under Plum Point till I raised the reef quarter less twain—then straightened up for the middle bar till I got well abreast the old one-limbed cottonwood in the bend, then got my stern on the cottonwood and head on the low place above the point, and came through a-booming —nine and a half."

"Pretty square crossing, an't it?"

"Yes, but the upper bar's working down fast."

Another pilot spoke up and said:—

"I had better water than that, and ran it lower down; started out from the false point—mark twain—raised the second reef abreast the big snag in the bend, and had quarter less twain."

One of the gorgeous ones remarked: "I don't want to find fault with your leadsmen, but that's a good deal of water for Plum Point, it seems to me."

There was an approving nod all around as this quiet snub dropped on the boaster and "settled" him. And so they went on talk-talk-talking. Meantime, the thing that was running in my mind was, "Now if my ears hear aright, I have not only to get the names of all the towns and islands and bends, and so on, by heart, but I must even get up a warm personal acquaintanceship with every old snag and one-limbed cottonwood and obscure wood pile that ornaments the banks of this river for twelve hundred miles; and more than that, I must actually know where these things are in the dark, unless these guests are gifted with eyes that can pierce through two miles of solid blackness; I wish the piloting business was in Jericho and I had never thought of it."

At dusk Mr. Bixby tapped the big bell three times (the signal to land), and the captain emerged from his drawing-room in the forward end of the texas, and looked up inquiringly. Mr. Bixby said:

"We will lay up here all night, captain."

"Very well, sir."

That was all. The boat came to shore and was tied up for the night. It seemed to me a fine thing that the pilot could do as he pleased without asking so grand a captain's permission. I took my supper and went immediately to bed, discouraged by my day's observations and experiences. My late voyage's note-booking was but a confusion of meaningless names. It had tangled me all up in a knot every time I had looked at it in the daytime. I now hoped for respite in sleep; but no, it reveled all through my head till sunrise again, a frantic and tireless nightmare.

Next morning I felt pretty rusty and low-spirited. We went booming along, taking a good many chances, for we were anxious to "get out of the river" (as getting out to Cairo was called) before night should overtake us. But Mr. Bixby's partner, the other pilot, presently grounded the boat, and we lost so much time getting her off that it was plain the darkness would overtake us a good long way above the mouth. This was a great misfortune, especially to certain of our visiting pilots, whose boats would have to wait for their return, no matter how long that might be. It sobered the pilot-house talk a good deal. Coming up-stream, pilots did not mind low water or any kind of darkness: nothing stopped them but fog. But down-stream work was different; a boat was too nearly helpless, with a stiff current pushing behind her; so it was not customary to run down-stream at night in low water.

There seemed to be one small hope, however: if we could get through the intricate and dangerous Hat Island crossing before night, we could venture the rest, for we would have plainer sailing and better water. But it would be insanity to attempt Hat Island at night. So there was a deal of looking at watches all the rest of the day, and a constant ciphering upon the speed we were making; Hat Island was the eternal subject; sometimes hope was high and sometimes we were delayed in a bad crossing, and down it went again. For hours all hands lay under the burden of this suppressed excitement; it was even communicated to me, and I got to feeling so solicitous about Hat Island, and under such an awful pressure of responsibility, that I wished I might have five minutes on shore to draw a good, full, relieving breath, and start over again. We were standing no regular watches. Each of our pilots ran such portions of the river as he had run when coming up-stream, because of his greater familiarity with it; but both remained in the pilot-house constantly.

An hour before sunset, Mr. Bixby took the wheel and Mr. W— stepped aside. For the next thirty minutes every man held his watch in his hand and was restless, silent, and uneasy. At last somebody said, with a doomful sigh:

"Well, yonder's Hat Island—and we can't make it."

All the watches closed with a snap, everybody sighed and muttered something about its being "too bad, too bad—ah, if we could only have got here half an hour sooner!" and the place was thick with the atmosphere of disappointment. Some started to go out, but loitered, hearing no bell-tap to land. The sun dipped behind the horizon, the boat went on. Inquiring looks passed from one guest to another; and one who had his hand on the doorknob, and had turned it, waited, then presently took away his hand and let the knob turn back again. We bore steadily down the bend. More looks were exchanged, and nods of surprised admiration— but no words. Insensibly the men drew together behind Mr. Bixby as the sky darkened and one or two dim stars came out. The dead silence and sense of waiting became oppressive. Mr. Bixby pulled the cord, and two deep, mellow notes from the big bell floated off on the night. Then a pause, and one more note was struck. The watchman's voice followed, from the hurricane deck:

"Labboard lead, there! Stabboard lead!"

The cries of the leadsmen began to rise out of the distance, and were gruffly repeated by the word-passers on the hurricane deck.

"M-a-r-k three! M-a-r-k three! Quarter-less-three! Half twain! Quarter twain! M-a-r-k twain! Quarter-less."

Mr. Bixby pulled two bell-ropes, and was answered by faint jinglings far below in the engine-room, and our speed slackened. The steam began to whistle through the gauge-cocks. The cries of the leadsmen went on—and it is a weird sound, always, in the night. Every pilot in the lot was watching, now, with fixed eyes, and talking under his breath. Nobody was calm and easy but Mr. Bixby. He would put his wheel down and stand on a spoke, and as the steamer swung into her (to me) utterly invisible marks —for we seemed to be in the midst of a wide and gloomy sea—he would meet and fasten her there. Talk was going on, now, in low voices:

"There; she's over the first reef all right!"

After a pause, another subdued voice:

"Her stern's coming down just exactly right, by George! Now she's in the marks; over she goes!"

Somebody else muttered:

"Oh, it was done beautiful—beautiful!" The engines were stopped altogether, and we drifted with the current. Not that I could see the boat drift, for I could not, the stars being all gone by this time. This drifting was the dismalest work; it held one's heart still. Presently I discovered a blacker gloom than that which surrounded us. It was the head of the island. We were closing right down upon it. We entered its deeper shadow, and so imminent seemed the peril that I was likely to suffocate;

and I had the strongest impulse to do something, anything, to save the vessel. But still Mr. Bixby stood by his wheel, silent, intent as a cat, and all the pilots stood shoulder to shoulder at his back.

"She'll not make it!" somebody whispered.

The water grew shoaler and shoaler by the leadsmen's cries, till it was down to—

"Eight-and-a-half! E-i-g-h-t feet! E-i-g-h-t feet! Seven-and"—

Mr. Bixby said warningly through his speaking tube to the engineer:—

"Stand by, now!"

"Aye-aye, sir."

"Seven-and-a-half! Seven feet! Six-and"—

We touched bottom! Instantly Mr. Bixby set a lot of bells ringing, shouted through the tube, "Now let her have it—every ounce you've got!" then to his partner, "Put her hard down! snatch her! snatch her!" The boat rasped and ground her way through the sand, hung upon the apex of disaster a single tremendous instant, and then over she went! And such a shout as went up at Mr. Bixby's back never loosened the roof of a pilot-house before!

There was no more trouble after that. Mr. Bixby was a hero that night; and it was some little time, too, before his exploit ceased to be talked about by river men.

Fully to realize the marvelous precision required in laying the great steamer in her marks in that murky waste of water, one should know that not only must she pick her intricate way through snags and blind reefs, and then shave the head of the island so closely as to brush the overhanging foliage with her stern, but at one place she must pass almost within arm's reach of a sunken and invisible wreck that would snatch the hull timbers from under her if she should strike it, and destroy a quarter of a million dollars' worth of steamboat and cargo in five minutes, and maybe a hundred and fifty human lives into the bargain.

The last remark I heard that night was a compliment to Mr. Bixby, uttered in soliloquy and with unction by one of our guests. He said:

"By the Shadow of Death, but he's a lightning pilot!"

PART VII

THE SPIRIT OF LIBERTY

Thomas Jefferson, The Spirit of Resistance

Thomas Jefferson, Letter to William Smith, Nov. 13, 1787.

Thomas Jefferson (1743–1826) was one of the
main founders of the American Republic.

DEAR SIR, — I am now to acknowledge the receipt of your favors of October the 4th, 8th, & 26th. In the last you apologise for your letters of introduction to Americans coming here. It is so far from needing apology on your part, that it calls for thanks on mine. I endeavor to shew civilities to all the Americans who come here, & will give me opportunities of doing it: and it is a matter of comfort to know from a good quarter what they are, & how far I may go in my attentions to them. Can you send me Woodmason's bills for the two copying presses for the M. de la Fayette, & the M. de Chastellux? The latter makes one article in a considerable account, of old standing, and which I cannot present for want of this article. — I do not know whether it is to yourself or Mr. Adams I am to give my thanks for the copy of the new constitution. I beg leave through you to place them where due. It will be yet three weeks before I shall receive them from America. There are very good articles in it: & very bad. I do not know which preponderate. What we have lately read in the history of Holland, in the chapter on the Stadtholder, would have sufficed to set me against a chief magistrate eligible for a long duration, if I had ever been disposed towards one: & what we have always read of the elections of Polish kings should have forever excluded the idea of one continuable for life. Wonderful is the effect of impudent & persevering lying. The British ministry have so long hired their gazetteers to repeat and model into every form lies about our being in anarchy, that the world has at length believed them, the English nation has believed them, the ministers themselves have come to believe them, & what is more wonderful, we have believed them ourselves. Yet where does this anarchy exist? Where did it ever exist, except in the single instance of Massachusetts? And can history produce an instance of rebellion so honourably conducted? I say nothing of it's motives. They were founded in ignorance, not wickedness. God forbid we should ever be 20 years without such a rebellion. The people cannot be all, & always, well informed. The part which is wrong will be discontented in proportion to the importance of the facts they misconceive. If they remain quiet under such misconceptions it is a lethargy, the forerunner of death to the public liberty. We have had 13. states independent 11. years. There has been one rebellion. That comes to one rebellion in a century & a half for each state. What country before ever existed a century & half without a rebellion? & what country can preserve it's liberties if their rulers are not warned from time to time that their people preserve the spirit of resistance? Let them take arms. The remedy is to set them right as to facts, pardon & pacify them. What signify a few lives lost in a century or two? The tree of liberty must be refreshed from time to time with the blood of patriots & tyrants. It is it's natural manure. Our Convention has been too much impressed by the insurrection of Massachusetts: and in the spur of the moment they are setting up a kite to keep the hen-yard in order. I hope in God this article will be rectified before the new constitution is accepted. — You ask me if any thing transpires here on the subject of S. America? Not a word. I know that there are combustible materials there, and that they wait the torch only. But this country probably will join the extinguishers. — The want of facts worth communicating to you has occasioned me to give a little loose to dissertation. We must be contented to amuse, when we cannot inform.

Henry David Thoreau, Civil Disobedience

Unabridged text of Henry David Thoreau, Civil Disobedience
(Boston: 1849).

*Henry David Thoreau (1817–1862) was a philosopher
and the author of* Walden *among other works.*

I heartily accept the motto, "That government is best which governs least"; and I should like to see it acted up to more rapidly and systematically. Carried out, it finally amounts to this, which also I believe—"That government is best which governs not at all"; and when men are prepared for it, that will be the kind of government which they will have. Government is at best but an expedient; but most governments are usually, and all governments are sometimes, inexpedient. The objections which have been brought against a standing army, and they are many and weighty, and deserve to prevail, may also at last be brought against a standing government. The standing army is only an arm of the standing government. The government itself, which is only the mode which the people have chosen to execute their will, is equally liable to be abused and perverted before the people can act through it. Witness the present Mexican war, the work of comparatively a few individuals using the standing government as their tool; for in the outset, the people would not have consented to this measure.

This American government—what is it but a tradition, though a recent one, endeavoring to transmit itself unimpaired to posterity, but each instant losing some of its integrity? It has not the vitality and force of a single living man; for a single man can bend it to his will. It is a sort of wooden gun to the people themselves. But it is not the less necessary for this; for the people must have some complicated machinery or other, and hear its din, to satisfy that idea of government which they have. Governments show thus how successfully men can be imposed upon, even impose on themselves, for their own advantage. It is excellent, we must all allow. Yet this government never of itself furthered any enterprise, but by the alacrity with which it got out of its way. It does not keep the country free. It does not settle the West. It does not educate. The character inherent in the American people has done all that has been accomplished; and it would have done somewhat more, if the government had not sometimes got in its way. For government is an expedient, by which men would fain succeed in letting one another alone; and, as has been said, when it is most expedient, the governed are most let alone by it. Trade and commerce, if they were not made of india-rubber, would never manage to bounce over obstacles which legislators are continually putting in their way; and if one were to judge these men wholly by the effects of their actions and not partly by their intentions, they would deserve to be classed and punished with those mischievous persons who put obstructions on the railroads.

But, to speak practically and as a citizen, unlike those who call themselves no-government men, I ask for, not at once no government, but at once a better government. Let every man make known what kind of government would command his respect, and that will be one step toward obtaining it.

After all, the practical reason why, when the power is once in the hands of the people, a majority are permitted, and for a long period continue, to rule is not because they are most likely to be in the right, nor because this seems fairest to the minority, but because they are physically the strongest. But a government in which the majority rule in all cases can not be based on justice, even as far as men understand it. Can there not be a government in which the majorities do not virtually decide right and wrong, but conscience?—in which majorities decide only those questions to which the rule of expediency is applicable? Must the citizen ever for a moment, or in the least degree, resign his conscience to the legislator? Why has every man a conscience then? I think that we should be men first, and subjects afterward. It is not desirable to cultivate a respect for the law, so much as for the right. The only obligation which I have a right to assume is to do at any time what I think right. It is truly enough said that a corporation has no conscience; but a corporation of conscientious men is a corporation with a conscience. Law never made men a whit more just; and, by means of their respect for it, even the well-disposed are daily made the agents of injustice. A common and natural result of an undue respect for the law is, that you may see a file of soldiers, colonel, captain, corporal, privates, powder-monkeys, and all, marching in admirable order over hill and dale to the wars, against their wills, ay, against their common sense and consciences, which makes it very steep marching indeed, and produces a palpitation of the heart. They have no doubt that it is a damnable business in which they are concerned; they are all peaceably inclined. Now, what are they? Men at all? or small movable forts and magazines, at the service of some unscrupulous man in power? Visit the Navy Yard, and behold a marine, such a man as an American government can make, or such as it can make a man with its black arts—a mere shadow and reminiscence of humanity, a man laid out alive and standing, and already, as one may say, buried under arms with funeral accompaniment, though it may be,

> "Not a drum was heard, not a funeral note,
> As his corse to the rampart we hurried;

Not a soldier discharged his farewell shot
O'er the grave where our hero was buried."

The mass of men serve the state thus, not as men mainly, but as machines, with their bodies. They are the standing army, and the militia, jailers, constables, posse comitatus, etc. In most cases there is no free exercise whatever of the judgement or of the moral sense; but they put themselves on a level with wood and earth and stones; and wooden men can perhaps be manufactured that will serve the purpose as well. Such command no more respect than men of straw or a lump of dirt. They have the same sort of worth only as horses and dogs. Yet such as these even are commonly esteemed good citizens. Others—as most legislators, politicians, lawyers, ministers, and office-holders—serve the state chiefly with their heads; and, as they rarely make any moral distinctions, they are as likely to serve the devil, without intending it, as God. A very few—as heroes, patriots, martyrs, reformers in the great sense, and men—serve the state with their consciences also, and so necessarily resist it for the most part; and they are commonly treated as enemies by it. A wise man will only be useful as a man, and will not submit to be "clay," and "stop a hole to keep the wind away," but leave that office to his dust at least:

"I am too high born to be propertied,
To be a second at control,
Or useful serving-man and instrument
To any sovereign state throughout the world."

He who gives himself entirely to his fellow men appears to them useless and self-ish; but he who gives himself partially to them is pronounced a benefactor and phi-lanthropist.

How does it become a man to behave toward the American government today? I answer, that he cannot without disgrace be associated with it. I cannot for an instant recognize that political organization as my government which is the slave's government also.

All men recognize the right of revolution; that is, the right to refuse allegiance to, and to resist, the government, when its tyranny or its inefficiency are great and unendurable. But almost all say that such is not the case now. But such was the case, they think, in the Revolution of '75. If one were to tell me that this was a bad gov-ernment because it taxed certain foreign commodities brought to its ports, it is most probable that I should not make an ado about it, for I can do without them. All machines have their friction; and possibly this does enough good to counter-bal-ance the evil. At any rate, it is a great evil to make a stir about it. But when the friction comes to have its machine, and oppression and robbery are organized, I say, let us not have such a machine any longer. In other words, when a sixth of the population of a nation which has undertaken to be the refuge of liberty are slaves, and a whole country is unjustly overrun and conquered by a foreign army, and subjected to military law, I think that it is not too soon for honest men to rebel and revolutionize. What makes this duty the more urgent is that fact that the country so overrun is not our own, but ours is the invading army.

Paley, a common authority with many on moral questions, in his chapter on the "Duty of Submission to Civil Government," resolves all civil obligation into expediency; and he proceeds to say that "so long as the interest of the whole society requires it, that it, so long as the established government cannot be resisted or changed without public inconveniency, it is the will of God. . .that the established government be obeyed—and no longer. This principle being admitted, the justice of every particular case of resistance is reduced to a computation of the quantity of the danger and grievance on the one side, and of the probability and expense of redressing it on the other." Of this, he says, every man shall judge for himself. But Paley appears never to have contemplated those cases to which the rule of expediency does not apply, in which a people, as well as an individual, must do justice, cost what it may. If I have unjustly wrested a plank from a drowning man, I must restore it to him though I drown myself. This, according to Paley, would be inconvenient. But he that would save his life, in such a case, shall lose it. This people must cease to hold slaves, and to make war on Mexico, though it cost them their existence as a people.

In their practice, nations agree with Paley; but does anyone think that Massachusetts does exactly what is right at the present crisis?

"A drab of stat, a cloth-o'-silver slut, To have her train borne up, and her soul trail in the dirt."

Practically speaking, the opponents to a reform in Massachusetts are not a hundred thousand politicians at the South, but a hundred thousand merchants and farmers here, who are more interested in commerce and agriculture than they are in humanity, and are not prepared to do justice to the slave and to Mexico, cost what it may. I quarrel not with far-off foes, but with those who, neat at home, co-operate with, and do the bidding of, those far away, and without whom the latter would be harmless. We are accustomed to say, that the mass of men are unprepared; but improvement is slow, because the few are not as materially wiser or better than the many. It is not so important that many should be good as you, as that there be some absolute goodness somewhere; for that will leaven the whole lump. There are thousands who are in opinion opposed to slavery and to the war, who yet in effect do nothing to put an end to them; who, esteeming themselves children of Washington and Franklin, sit down with their hands in their pockets, and say that they know not what to do, and do nothing; who even postpone the question of freedom to the question of free trade, and quietly read the prices-current along with the latest advices from Mexico, after dinner, and, it may be, fall asleep over them both. What is the price-current of an honest man and patriot today? They hesitate, and they regret, and sometimes they petition; but they do nothing in earnest and with effect. They will wait, well disposed, for others to remedy the evil, that they may no longer have it to regret. At most, they give up only a cheap vote, and a feeble countenance and Godspeed, to the right, as it goes by them. There are nine hundred and ninety-nine patrons of virtue to one virtuous man. But it is easier to deal with the real possessor of a thing than with the temporary guardian of it.

All voting is a sort of gaming, like checkers or backgammon, with a slight moral tinge to it, a playing with right and wrong, with moral questions; and betting naturally accompanies it. The character of the voters is not staked. I cast my vote, perchance, as I think right; but I am not vitally concerned that that right should prevail. I am willing to leave it to the majority. Its obligation, therefore, never exceeds that of expediency. Even voting for the right is doing nothing for it. It is only expressing to men feebly your desire that it should prevail. A wise man will not leave the right to the mercy of chance, nor wish it to prevail through the power of the majority. There is but little virtue in the action of masses of men. When the majority shall at length vote for the abolition of slavery, it will be because they are indifferent to slavery, or because there is but little slavery left to be abolished by their vote. They will then be the only slaves. Only his vote can hasten the abolition of slavery who asserts his own freedom by his vote.

I hear of a convention to be held at Baltimore, or elsewhere, for the selection of a candidate for the Presidency, made up chiefly of editors, and men who are politicians by profession; but I think, what is it to any independent, intelligent, and respectable man what decision they may come to? Shall we not have the advantage of this wisdom and honesty, nevertheless? Can we not count upon some independent votes? Are there not many individuals in the country who do not attend conventions? But no: I find that the respectable man, so called, has immediately drifted from his position, and despairs of his country, when his country has more reasons to despair of him. He forthwith adopts one of the candidates thus selected as the only available one, thus proving that he is himself available for any purposes of the demagogue. His vote is of no more worth than that of any unprincipled foreigner or hireling native, who may have been bought. O for a man who is a man, and, and my neighbor says, has a bone is his back which you cannot pass your hand through! Our statistics are at fault: the population has been returned too large. How many men are there to a square thousand miles in the country? Hardly one. Does not America offer any inducement for men to settle here? The American has dwindled into an Odd Fellow—one who may be known by the development of his organ of gregariousness, and a manifest lack of intellect and cheerful self-reliance; whose first and chief concern, on coming into the world, is to see that the almshouses are in good repair; and, before yet he has lawfully donned the virile garb, to collect a fund to the support of the widows and orphans that may be; who, in short, ventures to live only by the aid of the Mutual Insurance company, which has promised to bury him decently.

It is not a man's duty, as a matter of course, to devote himself to the eradication of any, even to most enormous, wrong; he may still properly have other concerns to engage him; but it is his duty, at least, to wash his hands of it, and, if he gives it no thought longer, not to give it practically his support. If I devote myself to other pursuits and contemplations, I must first see, at least, that I do not pursue them sitting upon another man's shoulders. I must get off him first, that he may pursue his contemplations too. See what gross inconsistency is tolerated. I have heard some of my townsmen say, "I should like to have them order me out to help put down an insurrection of the slaves, or to march to Mexico—see if I would go"; and yet these very men have each, directly by their allegiance, and so indirectly, at least, by their money, furnished a substitute. The soldier is applauded who refuses to serve in an unjust war by those who do not refuse to sustain the unjust government which makes the war; is applauded by those whose own act and authority he disregards and sets at naught; as if the state were penitent to that degree that it hired one to scourge it while it sinned, but not to that degree that it left off sinning for a moment. Thus, under the name of Order and Civil Government, we are all made at last to pay homage to and support our own meanness. After the first blush of sin comes its indifference; and from immoral it becomes, as it were, unmoral, and not quite unnecessary to that life which we have made.

The broadest and most prevalent error requires the most disinterested virtue to sustain it. The slight reproach to which the virtue of patriotism is commonly liable, the noble are most likely to incur. Those who, while they disapprove of the character and measures of a government, yield to it their allegiance and support are undoubtedly its most conscientious supporters, and so frequently the most serious obstacles to reform. Some are petitioning the State to dissolve the Union, to disregard the requisitions of the President. Why do they not dissolve it themselves—the union between themselves and the State—and refuse to pay their quota into its treasury? Do not they stand in same relation to the State that the State does to the

Union? And have not the same reasons prevented the State from resisting the Union which have prevented them from resisting the State?

How can a man be satisfied to entertain an opinion merely, and enjoy it? Is there any enjoyment in it, if his opinion is that he is aggrieved? If you are cheated out of a single dollar by your neighbor, you do not rest satisfied with knowing you are cheated, or with saying that you are cheated, or even with petitioning him to pay you your due; but you take effectual steps at once to obtain the full amount, and see to it that you are never cheated again. Action from principle, the perception and the performance of right, changes things and relations; it is essentially revolutionary, and does not consist wholly with anything which was. It not only divided States and churches, it divides families; ay, it divides the individual, separating the diabolical in him from the divine.

Unjust laws exist: shall we be content to obey them, or shall we endeavor to amend them, and obey them until we have succeeded, or shall we transgress them at once? Men, generally, under such a government as this, think that they ought to wait until they have persuaded the majority to alter them. They think that, if they should resist, the remedy would be worse than the evil. But it is the fault of the government itself that the remedy is worse than the evil. It makes it worse. Why is it not more apt to anticipate and provide for reform? Why does it not cherish its wise minority? Why does it cry and resist before it is hurt? Why does it not encourage its citizens to put out its faults, and do better than it would have them? Why does it always crucify Christ and excommunicate Copernicus and Luther, and pronounce Washington and Franklin rebels?

One would think, that a deliberate and practical denial of its authority was the only offense never contemplated by its government; else, why has it not assigned its definite, its suitable and proportionate, penalty? If a man who has no property refuses but once to earn nine shillings for the State, he is put in prison for a period unlimited by any law that I know, and determined only by the discretion of those who put him there; but if he should steal ninety times nine shillings from the State, he is soon permitted to go at large again.

If the injustice is part of the necessary friction of the machine of government, let it go, let it go: perchance it will wear smooth—certainly the machine will wear out. If the injustice has a spring, or a pulley, or a rope, or a crank, exclusively for itself, then perhaps you may consider whether the remedy will not be worse than the evil; but if it is of such a nature that it requires you to be the agent of injustice to another, then I say, break the law. Let your life be a counter-friction to stop the machine. What I have to do is to see, at any rate, that I do not lend myself to the wrong which I condemn.

As for adopting the ways which the State has provided for remedying the evil, I know not of such ways. They take too much time, and a man's life will be gone. I have other affairs to attend to. I came into this world, not chiefly to make this a good place to live in, but to live in it, be it good or bad. A man has not everything to do, but something; and because he cannot do everything, it is not necessary that he should be petitioning the Governor or the Legislature any more than it is theirs to petition me; and if they should not hear my petition, what should I do then? But in this case the State has provided no way: its very Constitution is the evil. This may seem to be harsh and stubborn and unconcilliatory; but it is to treat with the utmost kindness and consideration the only spirit that can appreciate or deserves it. So is all change for the better, like birth and death, which convulse the body.

I do not hesitate to say, that those who call themselves Abolitionists should at once effectually withdraw their support, both in person and property, from the government of Massachusetts, and not wait till they constitute a majority of one, before they suffer the right to prevail through them. I think that it is enough if they have God on their side, without waiting for that other one. Moreover, any man more right than his neighbors constitutes a majority of one already.

I meet this American government, or its representative, the State government, directly, and face to face, once a year—no more—in the person of its tax-gatherer; this is the only mode in which a man situated as I am necessarily meets it; and it then says distinctly, Recognize me; and the simplest, the most effectual, and, in the present posture of affairs, the indispensablest mode of treating with it on this head, of expressing your little satisfaction with and love for it, is to deny it then. My civil neighbor, the tax-gatherer, is the very man I have to deal with—for it is, after all, with men and not with parchment that I quarrel—and he has voluntarily chosen to be an agent of the government. How shall he ever know well that he is and does as an officer of the government, or as a man, until he is obliged to consider whether he will treat me, his neighbor, for whom he has respect, as a neighbor and well-disposed man, or as a maniac and disturber of the peace, and see if he can get over this obstruction to his neighborlines without a ruder and more impetuous thought or speech corresponding with his action. I know this well, that if one thousand, if one hundred, if ten men whom I could name—if ten honest men only—ay, if one HONEST man, in this State of Massachusetts, ceasing to hold slaves, were actually to withdraw from this co-partnership, and be locked up in the county jail therefor, it would be the abolition of slavery in America. For it matters not how small the beginning may seem to be: what is once well done is done forever. But we love better to talk about it: that we say is our mission. Reform keeps many scores of newspapers in its service, but not one man. If my esteemed neighbor, the State's ambassador, who will devote his days to the settlement of the question of human rights in the Council Chamber, instead of being threatened with the prisons of Carolina, were to sit down the prisoner of Massachusetts, that State which is so anxious to foist the sin of slavery upon her sister—though at present she can discover only an act of inhospitality to be the ground of a quarrel with her—the Legislature would not wholly waive the subject of the following winter.

Under a government which imprisons unjustly, the true place for a just man is also a prison. The proper place today, the only place which Massachusetts has provided for her freer and less despondent spirits, is in her prisons, to be put out and locked out of the State by her own act, as they have already put themselves out by their principles. It is there that the fugitive slave, and the Mexican prisoner on parole, and the Indian come to plead the wrongs of his race should find them; on that separate but more free and honorable ground, where the State places those who are not with her, but against her—the only house in a slave State in which a free man can abide with honor. If any think that their influence would be lost there, and their voices no longer afflict the ear of the State, that they would not be as an enemy within its walls, they do not know by how much truth is stronger than error, nor how much more eloquently and effectively he can combat injustice who has experienced a little in his own person. Cast your whole vote, not a strip of paper merely, but your whole influence. A minority is powerless while it conforms to the majority; it is not even a minority then; but it is irresistible when it clogs by its whole weight. If the alternative is to keep all just men in prison, or give up war and slavery, the State will not hesitate which to choose. If a thousand men were not to pay their tax bills this year, that would not be a violent and bloody measure, as it would be to pay them, and enable the State to commit violence and shed innocent blood. This is, in fact, the definition of a peaceable revolution, if any such is possible. If the tax-gatherer, or any other public officer, asks me, as one has done, "But what shall I do?" my answer is, "If you really wish to do anything, resign your office." When the subject has refused allegiance, and the officer has resigned from office, then the revolution is accomplished. But even suppose blood shed when the conscience is wounded? Through this wound a man's real manhood and immortality flow out, and he bleeds to an everlasting death. I see this blood flowing now.

I have contemplated the imprisonment of the offender, rather than the seizure of his goods—though both will serve the same purpose—because they who assert the purest right, and consequently are most dangerous to a corrupt State, commonly have not spent much time in accumulating property. To such the State renders comparatively small service, and a slight tax is wont to appear exorbitant, particularly if they are obliged to earn it by special labor with their hands. If there were one who lived wholly without the use of money, the State itself would hesitate to demand it of him. But the rich man—not to make any invidious comparison—is always sold to the institution which makes him rich. Absolutely speaking, the more money, the less virtue; for money comes between a man and his objects, and obtains them for him; it was certainly no great virtue to obtain it. It puts to rest many questions which he would otherwise be taxed to answer; while the only new question which it puts is the hard but superfluous one, how to spend it. Thus his moral ground is taken from under his feet. The opportunities of living are diminished in proportion as what are called the "means" are increased. The best thing a man can do for his culture when he is rich is to endeavor to carry out those schemes which he entertained when he was poor. Christ answered the Herodians according to their condition. "Show me the tribute-money," said he—and one took a penny out of his pocket—if you use money which has the image of Caesar on it, and which he has made current and valuable, that is, if you are men of the State, and gladly enjoy the advantages of Caesar's government, then pay him back some of his own when he demands it. "Render therefore to Caesar that which is Caesar's and to God those things which are God's"—leaving them no wiser than before as to which was which; for they did not wish to know.

When I converse with the freest of my neighbors, I perceive that, whatever they may say about the magnitude and seriousness of the question, and their regard for the public tranquillity, the long and the short of the matter is, that they cannot spare the protection of the existing government, and they dread the consequences to their property and families of disobedience to it. For my own part, I should not like to think that I ever rely on the protection of the State. But, if I deny the authority of the State when it presents its tax bill, it will soon take and waste all my property, and so harass me and my children without end. This is hard. This makes it impossible for a man to live honestly, and at the same time comfortably, in outward respects. It will not be worth the while to accumulate property; that would be sure to go again. You must hire or squat somewhere, and raise but a small crop, and eat that soon. You must live within yourself, and depend upon yourself always tucked up and ready for a start, and not have many affairs. A man may grow rich in Turkey even, if he will be in all respects a good subject of the Turkish government. Confucius said: "If a state is governed by the principles of reason, poverty and misery are subjects of shame; if a state is not governed by the principles of reason, riches and honors are subjects of shame." No: until I want the protection of Massachusetts to be extended to me in some distant Southern port, where my liberty is endangered, or until I am bent solely on building up an estate at home by peaceful enterprise, I can afford to refuse allegiance to Massachusetts, and her right to my property and life. It costs me less in every sense to incur the penalty of disobedience to the State than it would to obey. I should feel as if I were worth less in that case.

Some years ago, the State met me in behalf of the Church, and commanded me to pay a certain sum toward the support of a clergyman whose preaching my father attended, but never I myself. "Pay," it said, "or be locked up in the jail." I declined to pay. But, unfortunately, another man saw fit to pay it. I did not see why the schoolmaster should be taxed to support the priest, and not the priest the schoolmaster; for I was not the State's schoolmaster, but I supported myself by voluntary subscription. I did not see why the lyceum should not present its tax bill, and have the State to back its demand, as well as the Church. However, at the request of the selectmen, I condescended to make some such statement as this in writing: "Know all men by these presents, that I, Henry Thoreau, do not wish to be regarded as a member of any society which I have not joined." This I gave to the town clerk; and he has it. The State, having thus learned that I did not wish to be regarded as a member of that church, has never made a like demand on me since; though it said that it must adhere to its original presumption that time. If I had known how to name them, I should then have signed off in detail from all the societies which I never signed on to; but I did not know where to find such a complete list.

I have paid no poll tax for six years. I was put into a jail once on this account, for one night; and, as I stood considering the walls of solid stone, two or three feet thick, the door of wood and iron, a foot thick, and the iron grating which strained the light, I could not help being struck with the foolishness of that institution which treated my as if I were mere flesh and blood and bones, to be locked up. I wondered that it should have concluded at length that this was the best use it could put me to, and had never thought to avail itself of my services in some way. I saw that, if there was a wall of stone between me and my townsmen, there was a still more difficult one to climb or break through before they could get to be as free as I was. I did not for a moment feel confined, and the walls seemed a great waste of stone and mortar. I felt as if I alone of all my townsmen had paid my tax. They plainly did not know how to treat me, but behaved like persons who are underbred. In every threat and in every compliment there was a blunder; for they thought that my chief desire was to stand the other side of that stone wall. I could not but smile to see how industriously they locked the door on my meditations, which followed them out again without let or hindrance, and they were really all that was dangerous. As they could not reach me, they had resolved to punish my body; just as boys, if they cannot come at some person against whom they have a spite, will abuse his dog. I saw that the State was half-witted, that it was timid as a lone woman with her silver spoons, and that it did not know its friends from its foes, and I lost all my remaining respect for it, and pitied it.

Thus the state never intentionally confronts a man's sense, intellectual or moral, but only his body, his senses. It is not armed with superior wit or honesty, but with superior physical strength. I was not born to be forced. I will breathe after my own fashion. Let us see who is the strongest. What force has a multitude? They only can force me who obey a higher law than I. They force me to become like themselves. I do not hear of men being forced to live this way or that by masses of men. What sort of life were that to live? When I meet a government which says to me, "Your money our your life," why should I be in haste to give it my money? It may be in a great strait, and not know what to do: I cannot help that. It must help itself; do as I do. It is not worth the while to snivel about it. I am not responsible for the successful working of the machinery of society. I am not the son of the engineer. I perceive that, when an acorn and a chestnut fall side by side, the one does not remain inert to make way for the other, but both obey their own laws, and spring and grow and flourish as best they can, till one, perchance, overshadows and destroys the other. If a plant cannot live according to nature, it dies; and so a man.

The night in prison was novel and interesting enough. The prisoners in their shirtsleeves were enjoying a chat and the evening air in the doorway, when I entered. But the jailer said, "Come, boys, it is time to lock up"; and so they dispersed, and I heard the sound of their steps returning into the hollow apartments. My roommate was introduced to me by the jailer as "a first-rate fellow and clever man." When the door was locked, he showed me where to hang my hat, and how he managed matters there. The rooms were whitewashed once a month; and this one, at least, was the whitest, most simply furnished, and probably neatest apartment in town. He naturally wanted to know where I came from, and what brought me there; and, when I had told him, I asked him in my turn how he came there, presuming him to be an honest man, of course; and as the world goes, I believe he was. "Why," said he, "they accuse me of burning a barn; but I never did it." As near as I could discover, he had probably gone to bed in a barn when drunk, and smoked his pipe there; and so a barn was burnt. He had the reputation of being a clever man, had been there some three months waiting for his trial to come on, and would have to wait as much longer; but he was quite domesticated and contented, since he got his board for nothing, and thought that he was well treated.

He occupied one window, and I the other; and I saw that if one stayed there long, his principal business would be to look out the window. I had soon read all the tracts that were left there, and examined where former prisoners had broken out, and where a grate had been sawed off, and heard the history of the various occupants of that room; for I found that even there there was a history and a gossip which never circulated beyond the walls of the jail. Probably this is the only house in the town where verses are composed, which are afterward printed in a circular form, but not published. I was shown quite a long list of young men who had been detected in an attempt to escape, who avenged themselves by singing them.

I pumped my fellow-prisoner as dry as I could, for fear I should never see him again; but at length he showed me which was my bed, and left me to blow out the lamp.

It was like travelling into a far country, such as I had never expected to behold, to lie there for one night. It seemed to me that I never had heard the town clock strike before, not the evening sounds of the village; for we slept with the windows open, which were inside the grating. It was to see my native village in the light of the Middle Ages, and our Concord was turned into a Rhine stream, and visions of knights and castles passed before me. They were the voices of old burghers that I heard in the streets. I was an involuntary spectator and auditor of whatever was done and said in the kitchen of the adjacent village inn—a wholly new and rare experience to me. It was a closer view of my native town. I was fairly inside of it. I never had seen its institutions before. This is one of its peculiar institutions; for it is a shire town. I began to comprehend what its inhabitants were about.

In the morning, our breakfasts were put through the hole in the door, in small oblong-square tin pans, made to fit, and holding a pint of chocolate, with brown bread, and an iron spoon. When they called for the vessels again, I was green enough to return what bread I had left, but my comrade seized it, and said that I should lay that up for lunch or dinner. Soon after he was let out to work at haying in a neighboring field, whither he went every day, and would not be back till noon; so he bade me good day, saying that he doubted if he should see me again.

When I came out of prison—for some one interfered, and paid that tax—I did not perceive that great changes had taken place on the common, such as he observed who went in a youth and emerged a gray-headed man; and yet a change had come to my eyes over the scene—the town, and State, and country, greater than any that mere time could effect. I saw yet more distinctly the State in which I lived. I saw to what extent the people among whom I lived could be trusted as good neighbors and friends; that their friendship was for summer weather only; that they did not greatly propose to do right; that they were a distinct race from me by their prejudices and superstitions, as the Chinamen and Malays are that in their sacrifices to humanity they ran no risks, not even to their property; that after all they were not so noble but they treated the thief as he had treated them, and hoped, by a certain outward observance and a few prayers, and by walking in a particular straight though useless path from time to time, to save their souls. This may be to judge my neighbors harshly; for I believe that many of them are not aware that they have such an institution as the jail in their village.

It was formerly the custom in our village, when a poor debtor came out of jail, for his acquaintances to salute him, looking through their fingers, which were crossed to represent the jail window, "How do ye do?" My neighbors did not thus salute me, but first looked at me, and then at one another, as if I had returned from a long journey. I was put into jail as I was going to the shoemaker's to get a shoe which was mended. When I was let out the next morning, I proceeded to finish my errand, and, having put on my mended shoe, joined a huckleberry party, who were impatient to put themselves under my conduct; and in half an hour—for the horse was soon tackled—was in the midst of a huckleberry field, on one of our highest hills, two miles off, and then the State was nowhere to be seen.

This is the whole history of "My Prisons."

I have never declined paying the highway tax, because I am as desirous of being a good neighbor as I am of being a bad subject; and as for supporting schools, I am doing my part to educate my fellow countrymen now. It is for no particular item in the tax bill that I refuse to pay it. I simply wish to refuse allegiance to the State, to withdraw and stand aloof from it effectually. I do not care to trace the course of my dollar, if I could, till it buys a man a musket to shoot one with—the dollar is innocent—but I am concerned to trace the effects of my allegiance. In fact, I quietly declare war with the State, after my fashion, though I will still make use and get what advantages of her I can, as is usual in such cases.

If others pay the tax which is demanded of me, from a sympathy with the State, they do but what they have already done in their own case, or rather they abet injustice to a greater extent than the State requires. If they pay the tax from a mistaken interest in the individual taxed, to save his property, or prevent his going to jail, it is because they have not considered wisely how far they let their private feelings interfere with the public good.

This, then is my position at present. But one cannot be too much on his guard in such a case, lest his actions be biased by obstinacy or an undue regard for the opinions of men. Let him see that he does only what belongs to himself and to the hour.

I think sometimes, Why, this people mean well, they are only ignorant; they would do better if they knew how: why give your neighbors this pain to treat you as they are not inclined to? But I think again, This is no reason why I should do as they do, or permit others to suffer much greater pain of a different kind. Again, I sometimes say to myself, When many millions of men, without heat, without ill will, without personal feelings of any kind, demand of you a few shillings only, without the possibility, such is their constitution, of retracting or altering their present demand, and without the possibility, on your side, of appeal to any other millions, why expose yourself to this overwhelming brute force? You do not resist cold and hunger, the winds and the waves, thus obstinately; you quietly submit to a thousand similar necessities. You do not put your head into the fire. But just in proportion as I regard this as not wholly a brute force, but partly a human force, and consider that I have relations to those millions as to so many millions of men, and not of mere brute or inanimate things, I see that appeal is possible, first and instantaneously, from them to the Maker of them, and, secondly, from them to themselves. But if I put my head deliberately into the fire, there is no appeal to fire or to the Maker of fire, and I have only myself to blame. If I could convince myself that I have any right to be satisfied with men as they are, and to treat them accordingly, and not according, in some respects, to my requisitions and expectations of what they and I ought to be, then, like a good Mussulman and fatalist, I should endeavor to be satisfied with things as they are, and say it is the will of God. And, above all, there is this difference between resisting this and a purely brute or natural force, that I can resist this with some effect; but I cannot expect, like Orpheus, to change the nature of the rocks and trees and beasts.

I do not wish to quarrel with any man or nation. I do not wish to split hairs, to make fine distinctions, or set myself up as better than my neighbors. I seek rather, I may say, even an excuse for conforming to the laws of the land. I am but too ready to conform to them. Indeed, I have reason to suspect myself on this head; and each year, as the tax-gatherer comes round, I find myself disposed to review the acts and position of the general and State governments, and the spirit of the people to discover a pretext for conformity.

I believe that the State will soon be able to take all my work of this sort out of my hands, and then I shall be no better patriot than my fellow-countrymen. Seen from a lower point of view, the Constitution, with all its faults, is very good; the law and the courts are very respectable; even this State and this American government are, in many respects, very admirable, and rare things, to be thankful for, such as a great many have described them; seen from a higher still, and the highest, who shall say what they are, or that they are worth looking at or thinking of at all?

However, the government does not concern me much, and I shall bestow the fewest possible thoughts on it. It is not many moments that I live under a government, even in this world. If a man is thought-free, fancy-free, imagination-free, that which is not never for a long time appearing to be to him, unwise rulers or reformers cannot fatally interrupt him.

I know that most men think differently from myself; but those whose lives are by profession devoted to the study of these or kindred subjects content me as little as any. Statesmen and legislators, standing so completely within the institution, never distinctly and nakedly behold it. They speak of moving society, but have no resting-place without it. They may be men of a certain experience and discrimination, and have no doubt invented ingenious and even useful systems, for which we sincerely thank them; but all their wit and usefulness lie within certain not very wide limits. They are wont to forget that the world is not governed by policy and expediency. Webster never goes behind government, and so cannot speak with authority about it. His words are wisdom to those legislators who contemplate no essential reform in the existing government; but for thinkers, and those who legislate for all time, he never once glances at the subject. I know of those whose serene and wise speculations on this theme would soon reveal the limits of his mind's range and hospitality. Yet, compared with the cheap professions of most reformers, and the still cheaper wisdom and eloquence of politicians in general, his are almost the only sensible and valuable words, and we thank Heaven for him. Comparatively, he is always strong, original, and, above all, practical. Still, his quality is not wisdom, but prudence. The lawyer's truth is not Truth, but consistency or a consistent expediency. Truth is always in harmony with herself, and is not concerned chiefly to reveal the justice that may consist with wrong-doing. He well deserves to be called, as he has been called, the Defender of the Constitution. There are really no blows to be given him but defensive ones. He is not a leader, but a follower. His leaders are the men of '87. "I have never made an effort," he says, "and never propose to make an effort; I have never countenanced an effort, and never mean to countenance an effort, to disturb the arrangement as originally made, by which various States came into the Union." Still thinking of the sanction which the Constitution gives to slavery, he says, "Because it was part of the original compact—let it stand." Notwithstanding his special acuteness and ability, he is unable to take a fact out of its merely political relations, and behold it as it lies absolutely to be disposed of by the intellect—what, for instance, it behooves a man to do here in America today with regard to slavery—but ventures, or is driven, to make some such desperate answer to the following, while professing to speak absolutely, and as a private man—from which what new and singular code of social duties might be inferred? "The manner," says he, "in which the governments of the States where slavery exists are to regulate it is for their own consideration, under the responsibility to their constituents, to the general laws of propriety, humanity, and justice, and to God. Associations formed elsewhere, springing from a feeling of humanity, or any other cause, have nothing whatever to do with it. They have never received any encouragement from me and they never will.

They who know of no purer sources of truth, who have traced up its stream no higher, stand, and wisely stand, by the Bible and the Constitution, and drink at it there with reverence and humanity; but they who behold where it comes trickling into this lake or that pool, gird up their loins once more, and continue their pilgrimage toward its fountainhead.

No man with a genius for legislation has appeared in America. They are rare in the history of the world. There are orators, politicians, and eloquent men, by the thousand; but the speaker has not yet opened his mouth to speak who is capable of settling the much-vexed questions of the day. We love eloquence for its own sake, and not for any truth which it may utter, or any heroism it may inspire. Our legislators have not yet learned the comparative value of free-trade and of freed, of union, and of rectitude, to a nation. They have no genius or talent for comparatively humble questions of taxation and finance, commerce and manufactures and agriculture. If we were left solely to the wordy wit of legislators in Congress for our guidance, uncorrected by the seasonable experience and the effectual complaints of the people, America would not long retain her rank among the nations. For eighteen hundred years, though perchance I have no right to say it, the New Testament has been written; yet where is the legislator who has wisdom and practical talent enough to avail himself of the light which it sheds on the science of legislation.

The authority of government, even such as I am willing to submit to—for I will cheerfully obey those who know and can do better than I, and in many things even those who neither know nor can do so well—is still an impure one: to be strictly just, it must have the sanction and consent of the governed. It can have no pure right over my person and property but what I concede to it. The progress from an absolute to a limited monarchy, from a limited monarchy to a democracy, is a progress toward a true respect for the individual. Even the Chinese philosopher was wise enough to regard the individual as the basis of the empire. Is a democracy, such as we know it, the last improvement possible in government? Is it not possible to take a step further towards recognizing and organizing the rights of man? There will never be a really free and enlightened State until the State comes to recognize the individual as a higher and independent power, from which all its own power and authority are derived, and treats him accordingly. I please myself with imagining a State at last which can afford to be just to all men, and to treat the individual with respect as a neighbor; which even would not think it inconsistent with its own repose if a few were to live aloof from it, not meddling with it, nor embraced by it, who fulfilled all the duties of neighbors and fellow men. A State which bore this kind of fruit, and suffered it to drop off as fast as it ripened, would prepare the way for a still more perfect and glorious State, which I have also imagined, but not yet anywhere seen.

Voltairine de Cleyre,
Anarchism and American Traditions

Unabridged text of Voltairine de Cleyre, Anarchism and American
Traditions *(Chicago: Free Society Group, 1932).*
This essay first appeared in Mother Earth *in 1909.*

*Voltairine de Cleyre (1866–1912) was an American anarchist
and feminist author.*

American traditions, begotten of religious rebellion, small self-sustaining communities, isolated conditions, and hard pioneer life, grew during the colonization period of one hundred and seventy years from the settling of Jamestown to the outburst of the Revolution. This was in fact the great constitution-making epoch, the period of charters guaranteeing more or less of liberty, the general tendency of which is well described by Wm. Penn in speaking of the charter for Pennsylvania: "I want to put it out of my power, or that of my successors, to do mischief."

The revolution is the sudden and unified consciousness of these traditions, their loud assertion, the blow dealt by their indomitable will against the counter force of tyranny, which has never entirely recovered from the blow, but which from then till now has gone on remolding and regrappling the instruments of governmental power, that the Revolution sought to shape and hold as defenses of liberty.

To the average American of today, the Revolution means the series of battles fought by the patriot army with the armies of England. The millions of school children who attend our public schools are taught to draw maps of the siege of Boston and the siege of Yorktown, to know the general plan of the several campaigns, to quote the number of prisoners of war surrendered with Burgoyne; they are required to remember the date when Washington crossed the Delaware on the ice; they are told to "Remember Paoli," to repeat "Molly Stark's a widow," to call General Wayne "Mad Anthony Wayne," and to execrate Benedict Arnold; they know that the Declaration of Independence was signed on the Fourth of July, 1776, and the Treaty of Paris in 1783; and then they think they have learned the Revolution—blessed be George Washington! They have no idea why it should have been called a "revolution" instead of the "English War," or any similar title: it's the name of it, that's all. And name-worship, both in child and man, has acquired such mastery of them, that the name "American Revolution" is held sacred, though it means to them nothing more than successful force, while the name "Revolution" applied to a further possibility, is a spectre detested and abhorred. In neither case have they any idea of the content of the word, save that of armed force. That has already happened, and long happened, which Jefferson foresaw when he wrote:

"The spirit of the times may alter, will alter. Our rulers will become corrupt, our people careless. A single zealot may become persecutor, and better men be his victims. It can never be too often repeated that the time for fixing every essential right, on a legal basis, is while our rulers are honest, ourselves united. From the conclusion of this war we shall be going down hill. It will not then be necessary to resort every moment to the people for support. They will be forgotten, therefore, and their rights disregarded. They will forget themselves in the sole faculty of making money, and will never think of uniting to effect a due respect for their rights. The shackles, therefore, which shall not be knocked off at the conclusion of this war, will be heavier and heavier, till our rights shall revive or expire in a convulsion."

To the men of that time, who voiced the spirit of that time, the battles that they fought were the least of the Revolution; they were the incidents of the hour, the things they met and faced as part of the game they were playing; but the stake they had in view, before, during, and after the war, the real Revolution, was a change in political institutions which should make of government not a thing apart, a superior power to stand over the people with a whip, but a serviceable agent, responsible, economical, and trustworthy (but never so much trusted as not to be continually watched), for the transaction of such business as was the common concern and to set the limits of the common concern at the line of where one man's liberty would encroach upon another's.

They thus took their starting point for deriving a minimum of government upon the same sociological ground that the modern Anarchist derives the no-government theory; viz., that equal liberty is the political ideal. The difference lies in the belief, on the one hand, that the closest approximation to equal liberty might be best secured by the rule of the majority in those matters involving united action of any kind (which rule of the majority they thought it possible to secure by a few simple arrangements for election), and, on the other hand, the belief that majority rule is both impossible and undesirable; that any government, no matter what its forms, will be manipulated by a very small minority, as the development of the States and United States governments has strikingly proved; that candidates will loudly profess allegiance to platforms before elections, which as officials in power they will openly disregard, to do as they please; and that even if the majority will could be imposed, it would also be subversive of equal liberty, which may be best secured by leaving to the voluntary association of those interested in the management of matters of common concern, without coercion of the uninterested or the opposed.

Among the fundamental likeness between the Revolutionary Republicans and the Anarchists is the recognition that the little must precede the great; that the local must be the basis of the general; that there can be a free federation only when there are free communities to federate; that the spirit of the latter is carried into the councils of the former, and a local tyranny may thus become an instrument for general enslavement. Convinced of the supreme importance of ridding the municipalities of the institutions of tyranny, the most strenuous advocates of independence, instead of spending their efforts mainly in the general Congress, devoted themselves to their home localities, endeavoring to work out of the minds of their neighbors and fellow-colonists the institutions of entailed property, of a State-Church, of a class-divided people, even the institution of African slavery itself. Though largely unsuccessful, it is to the measure of success they did achieve that we are indebted for such liberties as we do retain, and not to the general government. They tried to inculcate local initiative and independent action. The author of the Declaration of Independence, who in the fall of '76 declined a re-election to Congress in order to return to Virginia and do his work in his own local assembly, in arranging there for public education which he justly considered a matter of "common concern," said his advocacy of public schools was not with any "view to take its ordinary branches out of the hands of private enterprise, which manages so much better the concerns to which it is equal"; and in endeavoring to make clear the restrictions of the Constitution upon the functions of the general government, he likewise said:

"Let the general government be reduced to foreign concerns only, and let our affairs be disentangled from those of all other nations, except as to commerce, which the merchants will manage for themselves, and the general government may be reduced to a very simple organization, and a very inexpensive one; a few plain duties to be performed by a few servants."

This then was the American tradition, that private enterprise manages better all that to which it IS equal. Anarchism declares that private enterprise, whether individual or cooperative, is equal to all the undertakings of society. And it quotes the particular two instances, Education and Commerce, which the governments of the States and of the United States have undertaken to manage and regulate, as the very two which in operation have done more to destroy American freedom and equality, to warp and distort American tradition, to make of government a mighty engine of tyranny, than any other cause, save the unforeseen developments of Manufacture.

It was the intention of the Revolutionists to establish a system of common education, which should make the teaching of history one of its principal branches; not with the intent of burdening the memories of our youth with the dates of battles or the speeches of generals, nor to make the Boston Tea Party Indians the one sacrosanct mob in all history, to be revered but never on any account to be imitated, but with the intent that every American should know to what conditions the masses of people had been brought by the operation of certain institutions, by what means they had wrung out their liberties, and how those liberties had again and again been filched from them by the use of governmental force, fraud, and privilege. Not to breed security, laudation, complacent indolence, passive acquiescence in the acts of a government protected by the label "home-made," but to beget a wakeful jealousy, a never-ending watchfulness of rulers, a determination to squelch every attempt of those entrusted with power to encroach upon the sphere of individual action - this was the prime motive of the revolutionists in endeavoring to provide for common education.

"Confidence," said the revolutionists who adopted the Kentucky Resolutions, "is everywhere the parent of despotism; free government is founded in jealousy, not in confidence; it is jealousy, not confidence, which prescribes limited constitutions to bind down those whom we are obliged to trust with power; our Constitution has accordingly fixed the limits to which, and no further, our confidence may go. ...In questions of power, let no more be heard of confidence in man, but bind him down from mischief by the chains of the Constitution."

These resolutions were especially applied to the passage of the Alien laws by the monarchist party during John Adams' administration, and were an indignant call from the State of Kentucky to repudiate the right of the general government to assume undelegated powers, for said they, to accept these laws would be "to be bound by laws made, not with our. consent, but by others against our consent—that is, to surrender the form of government we have chosen, and to live under one deriving its powers from its own will, and not from our authority." Resolutions identical in spirit were also passed by Virginia, the following month; in those days the States still considered themselves supreme, the general government subordinate.

To inculcate this proud spirit of the supremacy of the people over their governors was to be the purpose of public education! Pick up today any common school history, and see how much of this spirit you will find therein. On the contrary, from cover to cover you will find nothing but the cheapest sort of patriotism, the inculcation of the most unquestioning acquiescence in the deeds of government, a lullaby of rest, security, confidence—the doctrine that the Law can do no wrong, a Te Deum in praise of the continuous encroachments of the powers of the general government upon the reserved rights of the States, shameless falsification of all acts of rebellion, to put the government in the right and the rebels in the wrong, pyrotechnic glorifications of union, power, and force, and a complete ignoring of the essential liberties to maintain which was the purpose of the revolutionists. The anti-Anarchist law of post-McKinley passage, a much worse law than the Alien and Sedition acts which roused the wrath of Kentucky and Virginia to the point of threatened rebellion, is exalted as a wise provision of our All-Seeing Father in Washington.

Such is the spirit of government-provided schools. Ask any child what he knows about Shays' rebellion, and he will answer, "Oh, some of the farmers couldn't pay their taxes, and Shays led a rebellion against the court-house at Worcester, so they could burn up the deeds; and when Washington heard of it he sent over an army quick and taught 'em a good lesson"— "And what was the result of it?" "The result? Why—why—the result was—Oh yes, I remember—the result was they saw the need of a strong federal government to collect the taxes and pay the debts." Ask if he knows what was said on the other side of the story, ask if he knows that the men who had given their goods and their health and their strength for the freeing of the country now found themselves cast into prison for debt, sick, disabled, and poor, facing a new tyranny for the old; that their demand was that the land should become the free communal possession of those who wished to work it, not subject to tribute, and the child will answer "No." Ask him if he ever read Jefferson's letter to Madison about it, in which he says:

"Societies exist under three forms, sufficiently distinguishable. 1. Without government, as among our Indians. 2. Under government wherein the will of every one has a just influence; as is the case in England in a slight degree, and in our States in a great one. 3. Under government of force, as is the case in all other monarchies, and in most of the other republics. To have an idea of the curse of existence in these last, they must be seen. It is a government of wolves over sheep. It is a problem not clear in my mind that the first condition is not the best. But I believe it to be inconsistent with any great degree of population. The second state has a great deal of good in it. …It has its evils too, the principal of which is the turbulence to which it is subject. …But even this evil is productive of good. It prevents the degeneracy of government, and nourishes a general attention to public affairs. I hold that a little rebellion now and then is a good thing."

Or to another correspondent:

"God forbid that we should ever be twenty years without such a rebellion!

…What country can preserve its liberties if its rulers are not warned from time to time that the people preserve the spirit of resistance? Let them take up arms. …The tree of liberty must be refreshed from time to time with the blood of patriots and tyrants. It is its natural manure."

Ask any school child if he was ever taught that the author of the Declaration of Independence, one of the great founders of the common school, said these things, and he will look at you with open mouth and unbelieving eyes. Ask him if he ever heard that the man who sounded the bugle note in the darkest hour of the Crisis, who roused the courage of the soldiers when Washington saw only mutiny and despair ahead, ask him if he knows that this man also wrote, "Government at best is a necessary evil, at worst an intolerable one," and if he is a little better informed than the average he will answer, "Oh well, he [Tom Paine] was an infidel!" Catechize him about the merits of the Constitution which he has learned to repeat like a poll-parrot, and you will find his chief conception is not of the powers withheld from Congress, but of the powers granted.

Such are the fruits of government schools. We, the Anarchists, point to them and say: If the believers in liberty wish the principles of liberty taught, let them never entrust that instruction to any government; for the nature of government is to become a thing apart, an institution existing for its own sake, preying upon the people, and teaching whatever will tend to keep it secure in its seat. As the fathers said of the governments of Europe, so say we of this government also after a century and a quarter of independence: "The blood of the people has become its inheritance, and those who fatten on it will not relinquish it easily."

Public education, having to do with the intellect and spirit of a people, is probably the most subtle and far-reaching engine for molding the course of a nation; but commerce, dealing as it does with material things and producing immediate effects, was the force that bore down soonest upon the paper barriers of constitutional restriction, and shaped the government to its requirements. Here, indeed, we arrive at the point where we, looking over the hundred and twenty five years of independence, can see that the simple government conceived by the revolutionary republicans was a foredoomed failure. It was so because of: (1) the essence of government itself; (2) the essence of human nature; (3) the essence of Commerce and Manufacture.

Of the essence of government, I have already said, it is a thing apart, developing its own interests at the expense of what opposes it; all attempts to make it anything else fail. In this Anarchists agree with the traditional enemies of the Revolution, the monarchists, federalists, strong government believers, the Roosevelts of today, the Jays, Marshalls, and Hamiltons of then—that Hamilton, who, as Secretary of the Treasury, devised a financial system of which we are the unlucky heritors, and whose objects were twofold: To puzzle the people and make public finance obscure to those that paid for it; to serve as a machine for corrupting the legislatures; "for he avowed the opinion that man could be governed by two motives only, force or interest"; force being then out of the question, he laid hold of interest, the greed of the legislators, to set going an association of persons having an entirely separate welfare from the welfare of their electors, bound together by mutual corruption and mutual desire for plunder. The Anarchist agrees that Hamilton was logical, and understood the core of government; the difference is, that while strong governmentalists believe this is necessary and desirable, we choose the opposite conclusion, No Government Whatsoever.

As to the essence of human nature, what our national experience has made plain is this, that to remain in a continually exalted moral condition is not human nature. That has happened which was prophesied: we have gone down hill from the Revolution until now; we are absorbed in "mere money-getting." The desire for material ease long ago vanquished the spirit of '76. What was that spirit? The spirit that animated the people of Virginia, of the Carolinas, of Massachusetts, of New York, when they refused to import goods from England; when they preferred (and stood by it) to wear coarse, homespun cloth, to drink the brew of their own growths, to fit their appetites to the home supply, rather than submit to the taxation of the imperial ministry. Even within the lifetime of the revolutionists, the spirit decayed. The love of material ease has been, in the mass of men and permanently speaking, always greater than the love of liberty. Nine hundred and ninety nine women out of a thousand are more interested in the cut of a dress than in the independence of their sex; nine hundred and ninety nine men out of a thousand are more interested in drinking a glass of beer than in questioning the tax that is laid on it; how many children are not willing to trade the liberty to play for the promise of a new cap or a new dress? That it is which begets the complicated mechanism of society; that it is which, by multiplying the concerns of government, multiplies the strength of government and the corresponding weakness of the people; this it is which begets indifference to public concern, thus making the corruption of government easy.

As to the essence of Commerce and Manufacture, it is this: to establish bonds between every corner of the earth's surface and every other corner, to multiply the needs of mankind, and the desire for material possession and enjoyment.

The American tradition was the isolation of the States as far as possible. Said they: We have won our liberties by hard sacrifice and struggle unto death. We wish now to be let alone and to let others alone, that our principles may have time for trial; that we may become accustomed to the exercise of our rights; that we may be kept free from the contaminating influence of European gauds, pageants, distinctions. So richly did they esteem the absence of these that they could in all fervor write: "We shall see multiplied instances of Europeans coming to America, but no man living will ever seen an instance of an American removing to settle in Europe, and continuing there." Alas! In less than a hundred years the highest aim of a "Daughter of the Revolution" was, and is, to buy a castle, a title, and rotten lord, with the money wrung from American servitude! And the commercial interests of America are seeking a world empire!

In the earlier days of the revolt and subsequent independence, it appeared that the "manifest destiny" of America was to be an agricultural people, exchanging food stuffs and raw materials for manufactured articles. And in those days it was written: "We shall be virtuous as long as agriculture is our principal object, which will be the case as long as there remain vacant lands in any part of America. When we get piled upon one another in large cities, as in Europe, we shall become corrupt as in Europe, and go to eating one another as they do there." Which we are doing, because of the inevitable development of Commerce and Manufacture, and the concomitant development of strong government. And the parallel prophecy is likewise fulfilled: "If ever this vast country is brought under a single government, it will be one of the most extensive corruption, indifferent and incapable of a wholesome care over so wide a spread of surface." There is not upon the face of the earth today a government so utterly and shamelessly corrupt as that of the United States of America. There are others more cruel, more tyrannical, more devastating; there is none so utterly venal.

And yet even in the very days of the prophets, even with their own consent, the first concession to this later tyranny was made. It was made when the Constitution was made; and the Constitution was made chiefly because of the demands of Commerce. Thus it was at the outset a merchant's machine, which the other interests of the country, the land and labor interests, even then foreboded would destroy their liberties. In vain their jealousy of its central power made enact the first twelve amendments. In vain they endeavored to set bounds over which the federal power dare not trench. In vain they enacted into general law the freedom of speech, of the press, of assemblage and petition. All of these things we see ridden roughshod upon every day, and have so seen with more or less intermission since the beginning of the nineteenth century. At this day, every police lieutenant considers himself, and rightly so, as more powerful than the General Law of the Union; and that one who told Robert Hunter that he held in his fist something stronger than the Constitution, was perfectly correct. The right of assemblage is an American tradition which has gone out of fashion; the police club is now the mode. And it is so in virtue of the people's indifference to liberty, and the steady progress of constitutional interpretation towards the substance of imperial government.

It is an American tradition that a standing army is a standing menace to liberty; in Jefferson's presidency the army was reduced to 3,000 men. It is American tradition that we keep out of the affairs of other nations. It is American practice that we meddle with the affairs of everybody else from the West to the East Indies, from Russia to Japan; and to do it we have a standing army of 83,251 men.

It is American tradition that the financial affairs of a nation should be transacted on the same principles of simple honesty that an individual conducts his own business; viz., that debt is a bad thing, and a man's first surplus earning should be applied to his debts; that offices and office holders should be few. It is American practice that the general government should always have millions [of dollars] of debt, even if a panic or a war has to be forced to prevent its being paid off; and as to the application of its income office holders come first. And within the last administration it is reported that 99,000 offices have been created at an annual expense of 63,000,000. Shades of Jefferson! "How are vacancies to be obtained? Those by deaths are few; by resignation none." [Theodore] Roosevelt cuts the knot by making 99,000 new ones! And few will die - and none resign. They will beget sons and daughters, and Taft will have to create 99,000 more! Verily a simple and a serviceable thing is our general government.

It is American tradition that the Judiciary shall act as a check upon the impetuosity of Legislatures, should these attempt to pass the bounds of constitutional limitation. It is American practice that the Judiciary justifies every law which trenches on the liberties of the people and nullifies every act of the Legislature by which the people seek to regain some measure of their freedom. Again, in the words of Jefferson: "The Constitution is a mere thing of wax in the hands of the Judiciary, which they may twist and shape in any form they please." Truly, if the men who fought the good fight for the triumph of simple, honest, free life in that day, were now to look upon the scene of their labors, they would cry out together with him who said:

"I regret that I am now to die in the belief that the useless sacrifices of themselves by the generation of '76 to acquire self-government and happiness to their country, is to be thrown away by the unwise and unworthy passions of their sons, and that my only consolation is to be that I shall not live to see it."

And now, what has Anarchism to say to all this, this bankruptcy of republicanism, this modern empire that has grown up on the ruins of our early freedom? We say this, that the sin our fathers sinned was that they did not trust liberty wholly. They thought it possible to compromise between liberty and government, believing the latter to be "a necessary evil," and the moment the compromise was made, the whole misbegotten monster of our present tyranny began to grow. Instruments which are set up to safeguard rights become the very whip with which the free are struck.

Anarchism says, Make no laws whatever concerning speech, and speech will be free; so soon as you make a declaration on paper that speech shall be free, you will have a hundred lawyers proving that "freedom does not mean abuse, nor liberty license"; and they will define and define freedom out of existence. Let the guarantee of free speech be in every man's determination to use it, and we shall have no need of paper declarations. On the other hand, so long as the people do not care to exercise their freedom, those who wish to tyrannize will do so; for tyrants are active and ardent, and will devote themselves in the name of any number of gods, religious and otherwise, to put shackles upon sleeping men.

The problem then becomes, Is it possible to stir men from their indifference? We have said that the spirit of liberty was nurtured by colonial life; that the elements of colonial life were the desire for sectarian independence, and the jealous watchfulness incident thereto; the isolation of pioneer communities which threw each individual strongly on his own resources, and thus developed all-around men, yet at the same time made very strong such social bonds as did exist; and, lastly, the comparative simplicity of small communities.

All this has disappeared. As to sectarianism, it is only by dint of an occasional idiotic persecution that a sect becomes interesting; in the absence of this, out-landish sects play the fool's role, are anything but heroic, and have little to do with either the name or the substance of liberty. The old colonial religious parties have gradually become the "pillars of society," their animosities have died out, their offensive peculiarities have been effaced, they are as like one another as beans in a pod, they build churches - and sleep in them.

As to our communities, they are hopelessly and helplessly interdependent, as we ourselves are, save that continuously diminishing proportion engaged in all around farming; and even these are slaves to mortgages. For our cities, probably there is not one that is provisioned to last a week, and certainly there is none which would not be bankrupt with despair at the proposition that it produce its own food. In response to this condition and its correlative political tyranny, Anarchism affirms the economy of self-sustenance, the disintegration of the great communities, the use of the earth.

I am not ready to say that I see clearly that this will take place; but I see clearly that this must take place if ever again men are to be free. I am so well satisfied that the mass of mankind prefer material possessions to liberty, that I have no hope that they will ever, by means of intellectual or moral stirrings merely, throw off the yoke of oppression fastened on them by the present economic system, to institute free societies. My only hope is in the blind development of the economic system and political oppression itself. The great characteristic looming factor in this gigantic power is Manufacture. The tendency of each nation is to become more and more a manufacturing one, an exporter of fabrics, not an importer. If this tendency follows its own logic, it must eventually circle round to each community producing for itself. What then will become of the surplus product when the manufacturer shall have no foreign market? Why, then mankind must face the dilemma of sitting down and dying in the midst of it, or confiscating the goods.

Indeed, we are partially facing this problem even now; and so far we are sitting down and dying. I opine, however, that men will not do it forever, and when once by an act of general expropriation they have overcome the reverence and fear of property, and their awe of government, they may waken to the consciousness that things are to be used, and therefore men are greater than things. This may rouse the spirit of liberty.

If, on the other hand, the tendency of invention to simplify, enabling the advantages of machinery to be combined with smaller aggregations of workers, shall also follow its own logic, the great manufacturing plants will break up, population will go after the fragments, and there will be seen not indeed the hard, self-sustaining, isolated pioneer communities of early America, but thousands of small communities stretching along the lines of transportation, each producing very largely for its own needs, able to rely upon itself, and therefore able to be independent. For the same rule holds good for societies as for individuals—those may be free who are able to make their own living.

In regard to the breaking up of that vilest creation of tyranny, the standing army and navy, it is clear that so long as men desire to fight, they will have armed force in one form or another. Our fathers thought they had guarded against a standing army by providing for the voluntary militia. In our day we have lived to see this militia declared part of the regular military force of the United States, and subject to the same demands as the regulars. Within another generation we shall probably see its members in the regular pay of the general government. Since any embodiment of the fighting spirit, any military organization, inevitably follows the same line of centralization, the logic of Anarchism is that the least objectionable form of armed force is that which springs up voluntarily, like the minute men of Massachusetts, and disbands as soon as the occasion which called it into existence is past: that the really desirable thing is that all men—not Americans only—should be at peace; and that to reach this, all peaceful persons should withdraw their support from the army, and require that all who make war shall do so at their own cost and risk; that neither pay nor pensions are to be provided for those who choose to make man-killing a trade.

As to the American tradition of non-meddling, Anarchism asks that it be carried down to the individual himself. It demands no jealous barrier of isolation; it knows that such isolation is undesirable and impossible; but it teaches that by all men's strictly minding their own business, a fluid society, freely adapting itself to mutual needs, wherein all the world shall belong to all men, as much as each has need or desire, will result.

And when Modern Revolution has thus been carried to the heart of the whole world—if it ever shall be, as I hope it will—then may we hope to see a resurrection of that proud spirit of our fathers which put the simple dignity of Man above the gauds of wealth and class, and held that to be an American was greater than to be a king.

In that day there shall be neither kings nor Americans, only Men; over the whole earth, MEN.

PART VIII

OPEN AMERICA

Emma Lazarus,
Poem on the Statue of Liberty

This poem by Emma Lazarus, was written in 1883
to help raise money for the construction of
the Statue of Liberty's pedestal, and later inscribed on it.

Emma Lazarus (1849–1887) was an American poet.

The New Colossus

Not like the brazen giant of Greek fame,
With conquering limbs astride from land to land;

Here at our sea-washed, sunset gates shall stand
A mighty woman with a torch, whose flame
Is the imprisoned lightning, and her name Mother of Exiles.
From her beacon-hand glows world-wide welcome;
Her mild eyes command the air-bridged harbor that twin cities frame.

"Keep ancient lands, your storied pomp!" cries she with silent lips.

"Give me your tired, your poor, your huddled masses
yearning to breathe free
The wretched refuse of your teeming shore.

Send these, the homeless, tempest-tost to me,
I lift my lamp beside the golden door!"

John Quincy Adams on Foreign Policy

Excerpted from a speech of July 4, 1821, given before the House of Representatives by Secretary of State John Quincy Adams (1767–1848).

Warning Against the Search for Monsters to Destroy

And now, friends and countrymen, if the wise and learned philosophers of the elder world, the first observers of nutation and aberration, the discoverers of maddening ether and invisible planets, the inventors of Congreve rockets and Shrapnel shells, should find their hearts disposed to enquire what has America done for the benefit of mankind? Let our answer be this: America, with the same voice which spoke herself into existence as a nation, proclaimed to mankind the inextinguishable rights of human nature, and the only lawful foundations of government. America, in the assembly of nations, since her admission among them, has invariably, though often fruitlessly, held forth to them the hand of honest friendship, of equal freedom, of generous reciprocity. She has uniformly spoken among them, though often to heedless and often to disdainful ears, the language of equal liberty, of equal justice, and of equal rights. She has, in the lapse of nearly half a century, without a single exception, respected the independence of other nations while asserting and maintaining her own. She has abstained from interference in the concerns of others, even when conflict has been for principles to which she clings, as to the last vital drop that visits the heart.

She has seen that probably for centuries to come, all the contests of that Aceldama the European world, will be contests of inveterate power, and emerging right. Wherever the standard of freedom and Independence has been or shall be unfurled, there will her heart, her benedictions and her prayers be. But she goes not abroad, in search of monsters to destroy. She is the well-wisher to the freedom and independence of all. She is the champion and vindicator only of her own. She will commend the general cause by the countenance of her voice, and the benignant sympathy of her example. She well knows that by once enlisting under other banners than her own, were they even the banners of foreign independence, she would involve herself beyond the power of extrication, in all the wars of interest and intrigue, of individual avarice, envy, and ambition, which assume the colors and usurp the standard of freedom. The fundamental maxims of her policy would insensibly change from liberty to force. ...She might become the dictatress of the world. She would be no longer the ruler of her own spirit. ...

[America's] glory is not dominion, but liberty. Her march is the march of the mind. She has a spear and a shield: but the motto upon her shield is, Freedom, Independence, Peace. This has been her Declaration: this has been, as far as her necessary intercourse with the rest of mankind would permit, her practice.

The Daily Reckoning is a free daily e-letter
written by William Bonner.

It offers a "refreshingly witty, erudite, and sensible"
look at the day's stock news.

One reader says *The Daily Reckoning* offers
"more sense in one e-mail than a month of CNBC."

www.dailyreckoning.com

The Metaphor of Chance

BERT G. HORNBACK, *1935 -*

→ The Metaphor of Chance

Vision and Technique in the Works of Thomas Hardy

OHIO UNIVERSITY PRESS / *Athens, Ohio*

FOR MY MOTHER AND FATHER

Acknowledgments

This study of Thomas Hardy grows out of what was originally a doctoral dissertation presented at the University of Notre Dame. In its evolution from that state to this, my work has been generously supported by a faculty research fellowship and a travel grant from the Horace H. Rackham School of the University of Michigan.

In the preparation of this book I have made use of almost all of the extant Hardy manuscripts, and wish to express my thanks to the appropriate persons and institutions for permission to work with and quote from them: Miss Irene Cooper-Willis, trustee of the Hardy estate; Mr. Roger N. R. Peers, curator of the Dorset County Museum, Dorchester; Mr. T. C. Skeat, keeper of manuscripts at the British Museum; Miss Phyllis M. Giles, librarian of the Fitzwilliam Museum, Cambridge University; Mr. Donald Bond, librarian of the Houghton Library, Harvard University; Mr. David C. Mearns, custodian of manuscripts at the Library of Congress; and Miss Eileen Power, librarian at University College, Dublin. Quotations from the poems of Thomas Hardy are with the permission of The Macmillan Company; those quotations from other of Hardy's works and *The Life of Thomas Hardy* are courtesy of Macmillan and Company, Limited.

I also wish to thank some of the many people who have assisted me: Professor Joseph M. Duffy, Jr., who directed my graduate work at the University of Notre Dame; Professor Ernest E. Sandeen of the University of Notre Dame and Professor John T. Frederick, now of the University of Iowa, my long-time mentors; Professors Donald Hall, Ejner J. Jensen, Warner G. Rice, and John W. Wright, all of the University of Michigan; Professor Arthur J. Carr, now of Williams College; Professor Gwenn Davis of Bryn Mawr College; Professor Vernon T. Hornback and Professor Ellen R. Smith, both of Sacramento State College; and Susan Schulman, my very helpful editor for Ohio University Press.

Finally, I wish to acknowledge the numbers of students, colleagues, and friends who have listened, talked, and argued Hardy with me over the years. They will recognize our ideas as they read, perhaps, and will remember their own noble patience.

Bert G. Hornback
Ann Arbor, Michigan
December 31, 1969

Contents

The Metaphor of Chance

I

INTRODUCTION

It was one of those sequestered spots outside the
gates of the world . . . where, from time to time,
dramas of a grandeur and unity truly Sophoclean
are enacted in the real, by virtue of the concen-
trated passions and closely-knit interdependence
of the lives therein.

THE WOODLANDERS
1887

Thomas Hardy is first of all a storyteller, a "teller
of tales," an "Ancient Mariner."[1] It is the plan
of this book to approach Hardy's work by describing what is particularly
Hardyean about his tales and about the way he tells them. It is impossible, of course, to separate the two: like every artist, Hardy is his art.
If one may speak of his vision as concerned with certain details or characteristics of life—coincidence, for example—then one may speak also
of his technique as involving the use of those same characteristics. He
writes about what he sees, and in the way that he sees it. His country—
the world of his novels and, for the most part, of his poems—is Wessex,
and its rules are not only the rules that lives are lived by, they are also
to a large extent the rules by which Hardy's tales are told. To deal with
this world of Wessex, as it affects both vision and technique in Hardy's
work, will be the major concern of this book.

I do not propose to elaborate a complete, preemptive appreciation of
Hardy—to deal with themes ranging from physical love to agriculture,

3

or generally with characters and characterization, or with Hardy as a social critic. My focus is limited, and particular. My plan is to examine Hardy's setting, in space and in time, as it exists in itself, as it supports the major characters, and as it is used to establish the literal (physical) and metaphorical environment for his themes. My approach to Hardy's work is generally chronological because it seems that both his vision of the world and the artistic techniques he invents in order to represent that vision grow and develop through the course of his career.

There are several elements of Hardy's philosophical and aesthetic character to be set out here, and discussed in detail later with reference to particular works. On the philosophic side we have what has so often been called Hardy's fatalism, his ideas concerning chance and, more importantly, coincidence. These arguments lead to Hardy's theory of the intensity of experience, his concern with time as an idea, his notion of history, and finally to his idea of heroism. On the aesthetic side, there is the representation of this world-view through reference to the general and universal history of man. Hardy's use of history and pre-history is not only philosophically descriptive of that vision, however; it also supports and justifies aesthetically what otherwise must be grotesque coincidences in the affairs of the world and the lives of men. Coincidence is frequently Hardy's way of expressing, dramatically, the idea of the intensity of experience; involved with this is his denial of time passing as a valid measure of experience, and the manipulation of time-as-history to emphasize and expand the significance of the coincidental event.

Though Hardy was influenced by Periclean and Elizabethan drama, and had a strong sense of classical form and its appropriateness, his interest is never in obviously great men and great events. His heroes are mayors of small county towns, not kings, and peasants descended from extinct aristocratic ancestors, and obscure yeomen. His concern, generally, is with simple people living rather basic lives. Their drama is generated from within this simplicity, and requires a close, compassionate understanding if it is to be appreciated. Hardy is concerned with the commonest and most human aspects of humanity, and he believes that in these are to be found our heroism, our tragedy, and our dignity. Even when he looks beyond simple people and their affairs— as he does in *The Dynasts* or in the various poems which are in some way about a God or the Immanent Will—his thematic focus is still finally on basic human qualities. Napoleon, who begins as an historical

4

character, is transformed into a Hardyean hero by the end of *The Dynasts.* Many of the various conscious God-figures in the poems, though their sympathy is usually laden with heavy irony, see and sympathize with what is most human about humanity. The Immanent Will, the unconscious God, reduces everything to the common denominator by its pervasive web-like linking of all the phenomena of the vital world, so that what we see is man, stripped of all trappings and pretense, acting out his character in tension with his environment.

Hardy's vision of the world prohibited his acceptance of the conventions of goodness, success, and order which his Victorian background offered him. As he saw the world it was Tess's "blighted apple," and its most characteristic aspect that of invulnerable, unsympathetic, unresponsive, hard and alien Egdon Heath. Yet this vision is not pessimistic, just because it rejects Victorian optimism. Hardy characterized his "view" as "evolutionary meliorism," which he claimed "to underlie the Gospel scheme, and even to permeate the Greek drama." As a meliorist, Hardy looked forward to "amendment and not madness" in the future, when "pain . . . shall be kept down to a minimum by loving-kindness."[2] This "loving-kindness" is the highest expression, for Hardy, of man's freedom. It can be argued easily enough, and rightly enough, that Hardy is not a determinist or a fatalist. Still, Hardy does not discount as positive and pervasive "the mighty necessitating forces" of the natural universe. Man is free—but he is free within his environment; and he must come to terms both with himself and with his environment. The more successful he is the closer will be their identification. Clym Yeobright's sympathetic self-identification with the heath is the best example of this success.

Much has been said about Hardy's ideas of freedom and determinism, and much has been written associating his ideas with those of Spencer, von Hartmann, and Schopenhauer. It is not my purpose to trace further Hardy's philosophical debts and allegiances;[3] however, I do wish to invoke Schopenhauer briefly. His *"Wille"*—"which, considered purely in itself, is without knowledge, and is merely a blind incessant impulse"[4]—is the basis, surely, for Hardy's Immanent Will. Schopenhauer says in discussing the Will that though man *"acts* with strict necessity," he *"exists* and is what [he] is by virtue of [his] *freedom."*[5] In Hardy, this freedom is the freedom of character, of what the dramatist deals with as being. The necessity is the moral necessity of consequence, an "incessant impulse" which shows itself dramatically in patterns of intense coincidental recurrence in the lives of free men.

Coincidence is Hardy's convention. This statement has been made before in the history of Hardy criticism, but it has never seemed to lead us anywhere. Taken philosophically, it has led critics to cry "Fate" with a capital "F." Taken aesthetically, it has led critics to apologize for its clumsiness and crudity. Coincidence is the central problem for almost every critic who has had reservations about Hardy's art—and this is so because coincidence is at the center of his vision and his technique. From his philosophical acceptance of the interdependence and interaction of all vital phenomena, Hardy develops the idea of necessary co-incidents. Because he is committed to a dramatic view of life—and this comes from his respect for living—he sees these moments of crisis as the essence of human existence. "Experience," he says, "is as to intensity";[6] it is significantly dramatic "by virtue of the concentrated passions and closely-knit interdependence of the lives" so intensified.[7]

Coincidences come about either as chance occurrences or through the operation of causal relationships. An example of the first is Tess's placing a note under the door and Angel's failing to find it because it has slipped—by accident—under the carpet. The fates haven't willed this, Hardy has: and he says frankly that, after all, such things do happen. More interesting, however, is such coincidence as that of the height of Michael Henchard's ambitions being crossed by the return of the wife he sold to realize those ambitions. Henchard deserves Susan's return—causes it, in a moral sense. The coincidence is not just in Susan's finding him again after twenty years, not just in her reintroduction into his life; more importantly, the coincidence is in the juxtaposition of cause and consequence, in the introduction of the guilty past which Henchard has tried to escape into his successful present. Repetition, thus, is a kind of coincidence—a kind of moral coincidence.

In Hardy's world, nature in itself is neither moral nor immoral. And the Will is neither sympathetic nor malevolent in its attitudes toward man. But there is a stern and unyielding morality at work in the lives of men, operating through the Will in the form of cause and consequence. Frequently this morality derives its support—not philosophically, but aesthetically—from the natural world. A world of dramatic action needs a set, a place, a stage. The setting Hardy creates is Wessex.

6

Setting, even in its simplest form, is always the creation or re-creation of a background. This background helps to bring the story into reality, to establish mood, and to affirm the characters by giving them something against which they can act and develop. Wessex and its most particular parts—Egdon Heath, Maumbury Ring, the Vales of Blackmore and Froom, Mai Dun, Stonehenge—function this way. These stages are more than background, however, and the effect they produce is more than mood. The background is finally mythic in its suggestiveness, and the effect is metaphor rather than mood. Setting for Hardy is a matter of space—or place—and, more importantly, a matter of time. Lionel Johnson, the first of Hardy's serious critics, notes the importance of descriptive setting in the novels and points out Hardy's interest in "the pageant of the Past" as "a dramatic meditation upon the earth's antiquity."[8] Though he doesn't provide an answer to the basic question one must ask about Hardy's use of the past—a simple "why?" question— Johnson does insist that the uses of history and the ancient past in descriptive passages are parts of the whole, "duly subordinate to his design."[9]

The historical aspect of Wessex, the country of Lear,[10] the world of prehistoric ruins and Roman skeletons, is the first and most obvious part of Hardy's description. Wessex is re-created out of England's past as the substantial soil of a new world. Its historic and prehistoric context serves first to establish a pervasive mood of bleakness, of an unchanging world so much larger than the lives and works of any single generation of men. It also serves to establish a sense of continuity in the ages of men—what I want to call the mythic element in Hardy's work. So many points in history are representative ones because we keep enacting—pathetically, usually, and often tragically—the same dramas. But Hardy is not willing to rest with this vision of man, of his inadequacy and minority. Hardy's challenge for himself is to discover for man a sufficient dramatic dignity to enable him to act as a hero in this enlarged, symbolic world. The pattern of repetition is the oppressive element. While history, or history-as-recurrence, seems to make Hardy's central characters representative men, it also denies them freedom. They cannot escape their own pasts, for which they are immediately responsible, and they cannot escape the pasts of history which we all share: "the winds, and rains," he says, "And Earth's old glooms and pains/Are still the same, and Life and Death are neighbours nigh."

7

What men have to do, for Hardy, is come to terms with these oppressions in order to find their freedom and their dignity. Circumstances may limit man, but will, as consciousness, fulfills him. Space and time are both larger than man is, but man has consciousness, which is potentially larger than space and time.

Men—even heroes—cannot change the world. The myth of history and the vagaries of chance combine to frustrate the ambitions of such extravagant self-assertion. But men can revise the patterns of their lives by asserting their wills, by understanding themselves in relation to the world and thus averting the pathetic disaster of dumb defeat. The significance of this kind of assertion—Michael Henchard's "my punishment is *not* greater than I can bear," or Tess's "It is as it should be"—is reinforced by the mythic context in which it is made. The expanded temporal and spatial dimensions of the world finally support Hardy's heroes rather than diminish them, making the understanding they arrive at seem a climax of human achievement.[11]

Another aspect of this support, more important than the mythic and more peculiarly Hardy's, is what I want to call the metaphorical, in a large but rather special sense of that term. As we usually think of it, metaphor involves the thematic or conceptual juxtaposition of things or ideas which are not ordinarily considered together; the end of this juxtaposition, if the metaphor works, is our discovery of "the before unapprehended relations of things," to use Shelley's phrase. The truth of metaphor, then, exists in the imagination, as the product of the juxtaposition rather than as the juxtaposition itself. For Hardy, the important truth he wishes to communicate—that his art seems committed to, dramatically—is this metaphoric truth. For him, the truth of experience does not exist in circumstance, or even in the juxtaposition of circumstances and events, but in the crisis which ensues.[12] Setting becomes metaphoric in this sense, in the juxtaposition of past and present. The truth that emerges from the juxtaposition is a terribly intense time, a moment reinforced by its extension in history; and this, then, is the time appropriate for heroic action.

Though we are talking about setting and setting described, space is unimportant. The significance of space, or place, is almost always its historical or temporal aspect for Hardy. The important map of Wessex represents time as it is described in the physical world. Hardy so manipulates the idea and the measure of time that actions of but a moment expand to take place in the context of the full lapse of history, and actions literally years apart impose upon each other as though time has ceased to exist. In creating a setting that embodies history and time in this way, Hardy establishes a stage for his dramas which supports the kind of action that takes place. The setting stands for intensity, repetition, and coincidence; it elaborates them as myth and metaphor in the background, marking out the patterns the action will take. As myth the setting makes the action of the novel, or poem, representative action; as metaphor, it suggests the dramatic significance of that action.

All of Hardy's art is guided by these several interrelated philosophical and aesthetic ideas. In the following chapters I have undertaken a detailed consideration of the novels, the poetry, and *The Dynasts* from the perspective of these theoretical abstractions. The theory can be demonstrated briefly through a rather simple analysis of two short works of Hardy's, "The Three Strangers" and "The Convergence of the Twain," which are typical and, indeed, exemplary of both his vision and technique.

"The Convergence of the Twain" has nothing of the mythic use of the past about it, though it is concerned with coincidence. It is a dramatic poem, and at the same time almost allegorically argumentative. The drama is that of "the loss of the 'Titanic,'" as Hardy sees it; and the argument is about that moral relationship between man and the cosmos which so many critics have called Fate.

"The Convergence of the Twain" is a carefully structured and formal poem. Its first five stanzas ask why the Titanic sank; the middle stanza introduces the Immament Will; and the last five stanzas explain the sinking. But it is not just in its form that the poem is carefully made; its language is precisely chosen, and its complex theme is rigorously presented. Hardy's writing of this poem comes not from any interest in the sinking of a ship; and though he may well have felt sympathy for all those who drowned, that sympathy is not what makes the poem. "The Convergence of the Twain" is a philosophical poem in its concern with the Immanent Will; and as that concern is dramatized in the story of the Titanic, the poem becomes almost a moral allegory.

The allegory is in the reason why the Titanic sank and the significance of that sinking. The reason is given directly, it seems, in the five stanzas that answer the question, "What does this vaingloriousness down

9

here?" But this reason cannot be understood without reference to the description of the ship given in the opening stanzas. To understand that description we must establish a definition of irony—a definition which Hardy elaborates, in fact, in the poem. "The Convergence of the Twain" may not seem like an ironic poem, perhaps, but it is so essentially and emphatically. Irony involves the frustration of expectations, or the substitution of the unexpected for the expected in a meeting or combination. What converges in the poem is not just ship and iceberg, but expectation (the ship is unsinkable) and its opposite (a hole is gashed in the side).

The first five stanzas of the poem are concerned with the ironic fact of the Titanic's sinking. In each of these stanzas there is an indirect but obvious reference to the principle of irony: in the first, the Titanic lies at the bottom of the sea, contrary to what was "planned" for her; in the second, furnaces "turn" in these circumstances to water chambers; in the third, slimy sea-worms use the "mirrors meant/To glass the opulent"; in the fourth, jewels "designed" to sparkle are dull and lightless; and in the fifth, climaxing all these observations, the question is asked, "What does this vaingloriousness down here?" One part of the answer is given in this question. Hardy is not writing a poem about fate, but rather a poem about the essential moral relationship between cause and consequence. The description of the ship is summarized as "vaingloriousness." We are told earlier that the Titanic was planned by "human vanity," by "the Pride of Life." Advertised as unsinkable, presumptuously manned and equipped inadequately for emergency, and brazenly sailing a dangerous northern route without even an iceberg watch on duty, the Titanic is an example of man's proud, overreaching stupidity. It is a symbol of *hubris*, as Hardy sees it, and his morality says that such presumption must be paid for.

It is at this point in the poem that the Immanent Will is introduced, to execute the truth and the justice of the matter. The influence of the Will—it "stirs and urges everything"—is to insure that consequence follows upon cause. As the Will "Prepared a sinister mate / For her . . . / . . . for the time far and dissociate," it was not calculating malignly; it was doing what is natural, making an iceberg. It is the human decision to send the ship, unguarded, on the North Atlantic that makes the disastrous choice of the meeting. Iceberg and ship are originally "dissociate," not matched by fate—and Hardy avoids the rhyme of "fate" with "mate" and "great," choosing instead the opposite word, "dissociate." Iceberg and ship are originally distant; "Alien they seemed to be." But then they meet, on "paths coincident," and become "twin halves of one august event." The coincidence is not a matter of chance, nor is it a matter of arbitrarily determined fate. The poem makes it quite clear, from start to finish, that this significant coincidence is the ironic climax of man's folly, man's pride. Although coincidence is not always or necessarily ironic, it becomes so when men ignore the urgent morality of cause-and-effect relationships:

> Till the Spinner of the Years
> Said "Now!" And each one hears,
> And consummation comes, and jars two hemispheres.

The Will fulfills itself, in ship and iceberg. As we come to understand this convergence as a "consummation," as a fulfillment, we can understand the poem. When they come together these two alien-seeming things have a totally new composite and metaphoric meaning. Neither of them possessed this significance, neither could know or demonstrate this ironic truth, before their convergence. By itself the iceberg was a typically dangerous but natural iceberg; the Titanic was a new ship about which numerous boasts were made. When they meet, the result is metaphoric: a truth different from that of either iceberg or ship is dramatized. It is this truth, of the attendance of consequence upon cause, dramatically, morally, philosophically, and aesthetically, that "jars two hemispheres."

The sinking of the Titanic does not in itself have such a momentous effect, of course, except as people on both sides of the Atlantic may grieve at the loss. The meaning of that sinking, however, as Hardy explains it, has a genuine universal significance. The enforced recognition of this meaning would, perhaps, "jar two hemispheres."

"The Three Strangers," written in 1883 and published in 1888 in Hardy's first volume of short stories, *Wessex Tales*, presents a macabre and grotesque theme of coincidence. At a house which is the scene of a christening party, three strangers knock, one after another. The first man is an escapee, scheduled to be hanged in Casterbridge the next day. The second man is coming to Casterbridge to serve as hangman. The third is the brother of the first, coming to say his last good-byes. The

11

coincidence of this complex meeting seems outrageous and gratuitous, and the irony unrelated to either life or truth. Yet Hardy makes the story real and credible, and he makes its irony and its commentary on man and his world incisive and true.

The technique Hardy uses to make his success in "The Three Strangers" is the introduction of historical reference to create a metaphor of time. Hardy begins by setting the story in a specific location and giving that place some basic dramatic significance. Then, through the use of historical allusion and the collapsing of time, Hardy establishes the place as one prepared for intense and coincidental occurrences. The story opens:

> Among the few features of agricultural England which retain an appearance but little modified by the lapse of centuries may be reckoned the high, grassy and furzy downs, coombs, or enclaves, as they are indifferently called, that fill a large area of certain counties in the south and southwest. (3)

Although the paragraph is one of general description, the reference to the past and the suggestion of present antiquity begin to establish the mood of the story. A cottage is introduced: "Fifty years ago such a lovely cottage stood on such a down, and may possibly still be standing there now"—and isolated both in space and in time:

> Five miles of irregular upland, during the long inimical seasons, with their sleets, snows, rains, and mists, afford withdrawing space enough to isolate a Timon or Nebuchadnezzar. (3)

The isolation, however, is only from what is familiar, thus suggesting the possibility of these strange and bizarre events. The seemingly inaccessible place is actually on "the crossing of two footpaths at right angles hard by, which may have crossed there and thus for a good five hundred years" (pp. 3–4). And though the time references take one back to Nebuchadnezzar, through "the lapse of centuries" and "five hundred years," through Hastings and Crecy, by "Some old earthen camp or barrow, . . . some starved fragment of ancient hedge" (p. 3), simultaneously there is an insistence upon a real existence at the time of the story—"fifty years ago"—and upon that story's continuing existence "as well-known as ever" (p. 29) in the present.

The purpose of this opening description is to prepare the reader to accept and understand the large ironies and the coincidence of events to come. To make these acceptable and meaningful Hardy sets the story in the actual time of a particular moment in history, "The night of March 28, 182–," and in time expanded to include the long past of history. The setting in actual time insists on factual reality and affirms the story as something more than mere fantasy. Then the joining of this actual present with the extended past creates a metaphoric continuance of the past in the present, condensing and compressing the strength and significance of all time into the factual but coincidental reality of this one night. The crossing footpaths next to the cottage indicate the marked center of the stage on which the events of this world, dramatically foreshortened to express the highest intensity of human existence, will take place.

In the end of the story, Hardy discharges the fiction somewhat, insisting on its vitality in the present, but suggesting also a sort of legendary existence for it:

> The grass has long been green on the graves of Shepherd Fennel and his frugal wife; the guests who made up the christening party have mainly followed their entertainers to the tomb; the baby in whose honour they all had met is a matron in the sere and yellow leaf. But the arrival of the three strangers at the shepherd's that night, and the details connected therewith, is a story as well known as ever in the country about Higher Crowstairs. (29)

From the heightened world of the meetings in the shepherd's cottage, the story is allowed to fall back to an easier, perspective view. During its dramatization, the story's insistence on coincidence represents man in conflict, struggling with his bizarre fate; in its conclusion, the story points up the small and insignificant transience of men and their actions in relation to the unresponsive, unchanging, and timeless physical world.

"The Three Strangers" dramatizes in small the technique Hardy uses throughout his work to legitimize coincidence aesthetically and to create an intensity of experience by surrounding its moment with an enlarged time. "The Convergence of the Twain" is an example of his thematic use of coincidence and its philosophical interpretation in terms of morality. Both technique and theme are formed out of a metaphorical conception of experience, in these short pieces as in most of Hardy's works. Missing here, however, is what is most impressive in Hardy's art: the vision that comes from theme and technique, marked by compassion, love, and a sense of the necessity of heroism.

NOTES TO CHAPTER I

1. Florence Emily Hardy, *The Life of Thomas Hardy* (New York, 1962), p. 252. This biography was originally published as *The Early Life of Thomas Hardy* (London, 1928) and *The Later Years of Thomas Hardy* (London, 1930).

2. Thomas Hardy, "Apology" to *Late Lyrics and Earlier*, in *Collected Poems of Thomas Hardy* (New York, 1961), p. 527. References throughout to Hardy's works are to this edition of the poetry, to the Macmillan Library Edition (London, 1951–1961) of the fiction, and to *The Dynasts and the Queen of Cornwall* (London, 1931).

3. There are several books which treat these matters, the best among them being William R. Rutland, *Thomas Hardy: A Study of his Writings and their Background* (Oxford, 1938) and Harvey C. Webster, *On a Darkling Plain* (Chicago, 1947). Cf. also Ernest Brennecke, Jr., *Thomas Hardy: A Study of a Poet's Mind* (London, 1924) and Helen Garwood, *Thomas Hardy: An Illustration of the Philosophy of Schopenhauer* (Philadelphia, 1911).

4. Arthur Schopenhauer, *The World as Will and Idea*, trans. R. B. Haldane and J. Kemp, 3 vols. (London, 1907), 1:354. This translation, first published in 1883, is the one that Hardy bought and read; see Rutland, *Thomas Hardy*, p. 93.

5. Schopenhauer, *World as Will and Idea*, 3:68.

6. *Tess of the D'Urbervilles*, p. 160.

7. *The Woodlanders*, pp. 4–5.

8. *The Art of Thomas Hardy* (London, 1923), p. 49. Johnson's book was first published in 1894.

9. Ibid., p. 48.

10. See the 1895 preface to *The Return of the Native*, the 1892 preface to *Tess of the D'Urbervilles*, and "The Withered Arm" in *Wessex Tales*, p. 87.

11. Harold Child, in *Thomas Hardy* (New York, 1916), p. 21, sees that "the enormous past is always present to him as a moment of time." He continues: "Man would not be worth writing about, were it not for one of Mr. Hardy's distinctive gifts as novelist and dramatist—what might be called his double vision. It is a peculiar gift; there is no author in whom it is so highly developed. If he sees the littleness, he also sees the greatness. Watching from infinity, he sees human life as futile and trivial. Down in the stress and the turmoil, looking out from the very heart of some farmer or milkmaid, he shows human life heroically grand."

12. This idea of metaphor and the metaphoric use of setting to support action might be relatable to John Stuart Mill's idea of "embodied symbol" in Tennyson's early poetry, to the Pre-Raphaelite ideas of descriptive intensity, and even to T. S. Eliot's idea of the "objective correlative." See also Benjamin Sankey, "Hardy's Plotting," *Twentieth Century Literature* (July 1965):91: "Certain of Hardy's procedures can be thought of . . . as supplying 'analogues' for the main action. This is true . . . of much of Hardy's natural description."

II

THE RETURN OF THE NATIVE

The age of a modern man is to be measured by the intensity of his history.

THE RETURN OF THE NATIVE
1878

The Return of the Native used often to be called Hardy's masterpiece. The first serious assertion of this was Lionel Johnson's, in 1894: "I readily confess, that I can as little question the pre-eminence of *The Return of the Native*, among Mr. Hardy's works, as that of *King Lear* among Shakespeare's plays." Johnson's reason for according this novel the first place among Hardy's works was its "singleness and simplicity of effect," the "simple truth" of its setting and descriptive detail.[1] Egdon Heath is neither simple as a setting, nor is it single in its effect. Still, the heath is what must first impress any reader of *The Return of the Native*—and that seeming "singleness and simplicity of effect" is the basic challenge of the novel. Throughout the history of criticism of *The Return of the Native*, reviewers, essayists, and critics have been impressed by that "vast tract of unenclosed wild," that "obscure, obsolete, superseded country"[2] which is Egdon. It is right that they should be impressed, of course; however, many readers have been over-impressed by Egdon, and the existence of the heath has been appreciated while what happens on it has been neglected.[3]

H. C. Duffin begins his discussion of *The Return of the Native* by calling it "the book of Egdon Heath," and argues that "without Egdon it would not hold together. . . . Egdon influences all the human characters, moving them to love or to hate, to despair or to the philosophic mind."

15

The heath is "the protagonist of the novel" for Duffin as it was "one of the *dramatis personae*" for an early reviewer. Joseph Warren Beach speaks of the heath in terms of "the novelistic unity of place," and asserts that Hardy "had very distinctly imagined and went about very deliberately to evoke, the atmosphere with which to envelope his tragedy." For Beach, "plot and setting . . . are one"; yet when it comes to the point of explaining either what this means or how it is achieved, he finds that "the effect is obtained . . . by means too subtle for analysis." D. H. Lawrence finds "the real sense of tragedy . . . the great, tragic power" of *The Return of the Native* in Egdon, and William R. Rutland calls it "the principal character in the book." And though Albert Guerard is "repelled or left indifferent" by Hardy's "pretentious meditation on Egdon Heath," Evelyn Hardy blithely asserts that "As everyone knows, the Heath is the great protagonist of the drama."[4]

One of Hardy's most recent critics, Richard Carpenter, comes perhaps closest of all to understanding the use of this symbolic setting. Carpenter begins his discussion of the novel saying, "The most massive and compelling image of the timeless that Hardy ever created is Egdon Heath, the setting of *The Return of the Native*."[5] He continues:

> The heath is not, however, simply an image; it is also a most functional setting for Hardy's purposes. By confining nearly all his action to its terrain he achieves a unity of place which markedly aids in the creation of dramatic effects.[6]

He then falls back upon nearly ninety years of traditional interpretation, and concludes:

> Egdon's function goes beyond its timelessness and its physical topography in the way it is characterized and personified. Hardy quite clearly wanted us to think of it as acting as a character in the novel, as a complex symbol of alien and indifferent nature.[7]

To read *The Return of the Native* correctly one must see Egdon in its proper place. The heath is the setting of the novel in a very large sense, as critics have always said; but unless one understands what its contribution is to the effect and order of the whole, one cannot understand what is more important than the setting, the characters and what they do. What the most significant of them—Clym Yeobright—does is to come to understand Egdon Heath. In doing so he takes the novel away from Eustacia Vye, who is destroyed on but not by the heath, and he puts the whole novel into the proper perspective for its readers. Indeed, one might say that as Clym comes to understand Egdon Heath, Hardy's world in this novel, he establishes the true philosophical perspective for all of Hardy's art.

The first chapter of *The Return of the Native* is entitled "A Face on which Time makes but Little Impression." The opening description, then, is of the immutability of eternal Egdon. This "vast tract of unenclosed wild" is the world, of course, as well as the world of the novel. As a setting, Egdon is not just a somber, unfeeling, and harsh representative of an unkind world; more importantly, it functions in the novel as the intensifier of time and space, and thus of character and action. In the second paragraph of the opening chapter the narrator describes the face of the heath, insisting on those qualities which allow it to distort and intensify time and space. The purpose of the description is to prepare for the dramatic elements of the story to come:

> The face of the heath by its mere complexion added half an hour to evening; it could in like manner retard the dawn, sadden noon, anticipate the frowning of storms scarcely generated, and intensify the opacity of a moonless midnight to a cause of shaking and dread. (3)

Egdon has existed "from prehistoric times as unaltered as the stars overhead" (p. 7), and the "ancient lineal measure . . . of Egdon down to the present day has but little diminished" (p. 6). "The untameable, Ishmaelitish thing that Egdon now was it always had been . . . and ever since the beginning of vegetation its soil had worn the same antique brown dress" (p. 6). It is a "great inviolate place," of "ancient permanence which the sea cannot claim" (p. 7), whose boundary "in one direction extended an unlimited number of miles" (p. 30). Though all else—seas, fields, rivers in their courses as well as in their running currents, villages and people—change, "yet Egdon remained" (p. 7).

The heath is set as unlimited and immutable, and thus eternal. It is not just a microcosmic representation of the physical world of the novelist's or his novel's time, but is rather a microcosm, both in space and in time, of the total history of the world, compressed through its description into an immediate and present existence. As this compression is accomplished, the actual time and place of the novel are transcended suggesting that the action will be of universal significance, involving characters large enough to represent man. This is "the novelistic unity of time" which Beach says defies analysis.

The metaphor of descriptive setting, the use of an ancient past to expand the significance of a simple present, is carried on throughout the novel, but is most fully created in the opening chapters. At the end of Chapter 1 two ancient but sub-eternal articles are introduced: a Roman road, and Rainbarrow. The road is "an aged highway," the barrow "still more aged"; and except for these, the only innovations on the heath are "the very finger-touches of the last geological change" (p. 7). Diggory Venn and Thomasin—two unlikely characters—enter this scene in Chapter 2. The reddleman stops his cart to rest, and gazes across the heath:

> The scene before the reddleman's eyes was a gradual series of ascents from the level of the road backward into the heart of the heath. It embraced hillocks, pits, ridges, acclivities, one behind the other, till all was finished by a high hill cutting against the still light sky. (12–13)

This last feature, which so attracts Venn's gaze, is Rainbarrow:

> This bossy projection of earth above its natural level occupied the loftiest ground of the loneliest height that the heath contained. Although from the vale it appeared but as a wart on an Atlantean brow, its actual bulk was great. It formed the pole and axis of this heathery world. (13)

As Venn watches the barrow, a figure advances to the top of it: "The first instinct of an imaginative stranger might have been to suppose it the person of one of the Celts who built the barrow, so far had all modern date withdrawn from the scene" (p. 13). The person is Eustacia Vye, however, the antagonist of the novel, the restless "queen of the solitude" (p. 14) who cannot comprehend the size or the relevance of this world, and thus cannot live up to the demands it makes of her.

Hardy continues to build the metaphoric suggestiveness of the world of the novel, insistently reiterating its timeless immensity. As Eustacia stands down from the barrow, a group of locals appear in her place. In the light of the bonfire which they build, the ancient barrow shows as "the segment of a globe, as perfect as on the day when it was thrown up" (p. 16):

18

It seemed as if the bonfire-makers were standing in some radiant upper storey of the world, detached from and independent of the dark stretches below. The heath down there was a vast abyss, and no longer a continuation of what they stood on. . . .

It was as if these men and boys had suddenly dived into past ages, and fetched therefrom an hour and deed which had before been familiar with this spot. The ashes of the original British pyre which blazed from that summit lay fresh and undisturbed in the barrow beneath their tread. The flames from funeral pyres long ago kindled there had shown down upon the lowlands as these were shining now. (17)

To demonstrate Hardy's intention or even so particular an awareness as I attribute to him here in the creation of Egdon Heath would be hard and dangerous, except that the manuscript of *The Return of The Native*[8] offers considerable evidence of changes and additions to descriptive detail which are significantly relevant to this aspect of his art. The changes and additions which Hardy made to the extant manuscript drafts of the novels fall into two reasonably definable patterns. Frequently he changes or adds to a manuscript (or adds in the printed version) phrases, sentences, and paragraphs not in the original manuscript, which serve to further establish the metaphoric use of setting, either making the focus of the allusion or description more clearly thematic, or simply adding further details to the already established metaphor of expansive timelessness. He also adds lines which help to define his concept of the hero, and sometimes these two kinds of alterations work together. The relative frequency of these changes makes it possible for one to deduce a pattern of significant thematic qualification.[9]

The manuscript paragraph describing the fire atop Rainbarrow ends:

The cheerful blaze streaked the inner surface of the human circle—now increased by other stragglers, male and female—with its own gold livery, and even overlaid the dark turf around with a lively luminousness, which softened off into obscurity where the barrow rounded downwards out of sight. (fol. 14)

Then Hardy adds the section partially quoted above, changing the tone of the scene described, urging the eternal and permanent qualities of the barrow, its immutability as the one stage for all of history, and its

19

microcosmic role as the central and representative stage for this novel.[10] The added section of the paragraph reads:

> It showed the barrow to be the segment of a globe, as perfect as on the day when it was thrown up, even the little ditch remaining from which the earth was dug. Not a plough had ever disturbed a grain of that stubborn soil. In the heath's barrenness to the farmer lay its fertility to the historian. There had been no obliteration, because there had been no tending. (fol. 13v)

Then, two paragraphs later, after the above-quoted sentence, "The flames from funeral pyres long ago kindled there had shown down upon the lowlands as these were shining now," there is a long cancellation, followed by this much-revised and carefully reworked passage:

> Festival fires to Thor and Woden had followed on the same ground and duly had their day. Indeed, it is pretty well known that such blazes as this the heathmen were now enjoying are rather the lineal descendants from jumbled Druidical rites and Saxon ceremonies than the invention of popular feeling about the Gunpowder Plot. (fol. 15)

This section reinforces the existence of an ancient past alive in the world of the present by linking the present age to past ceremonies through history.

The main significance of this time-extending setting is in what it says about the characters who do the principle acting. As the stage grows to represent for Hardy both the world and a larger and more significant time than that of rural nineteenth-century England, one looks to the main characters for an existence large enough for this stage. Immediately following the paragraph just quoted, another paragraph is added in the manuscript suggesting the act of lighting the bonfires as a Promethean gesture, ritualistically indicative of the size of the spirit of man:

> Moreover, to light a fire is the instinctive and resistant act of men when, at the winter ingress, the curfew is sounded throughout Nature. It indicates a spontaneous, Promethean rebelliousness against the fiat that this recurrent season shall bring foul times, cold darkness, misery and death. Black chaos comes, and the fettered gods of the earth say, Let there be light.

20

There is Hardy's hope: man, despite his smallness, is heroic, and over and over in history he must demonstrate this heroism. Only man is capable of heroism, that chance by its nature seeming to belong neither to gods nor demons; indeed, the gods who would be heroes have become man. As Hardy enlarges and intensifies the world of Egdon Heath to include the extremes of both time and space, he suggests the size his characters will assume and the significance of their coming actions—and the measure, in each case, is the hero's. The addition of the Promethean postulate is relevant only generally and generically for the rustic chorus on Hardy's stage at the particular moment of this one scene; they are not Protheans, and for them the myth is meaningless. Its chief significance is for the one hero—the one large character—of the novel, Clym Yeobright, for whom its relevance is particular and clear. Clym's accomplishment is his realizing and living up to the terms of this Promethean ideal.

Hardy is not afraid of exaggeration, if exaggeration is what heroism must be. The opening narrative section of this novel ends, in Chapter 3, with a statement of the dramatic heightening and enlargement Hardy has intended in his description of the place of the action:

> Those whom nature had depicted as merely quaint became grotesque, the grotesque became preternatural; for all was in extremity. (18)

Together with the suggested greatness of the action and of the characters who will act, this exaggeration in nature's pretensions has been a part of *The Return of the Native* from its first page on. In Chapter 1, again, Egdon is described as having "a lonely face, suggesting tragical possibilities" (p. 6). The description forebodes great and significant action; and it is said, then, of Egdon, that "Every night its Titanic form seemed to await something" (p. 4). In the manuscript, Hardy first writes his last sentence:

> Every night its Titanic form seemed thus to await something.
> What it seemed to await it is hard to say.

Then the second sentence is revised, first to "What it seemed to await could hardly have been decided," then to "What it awaited none could say" (fol. 2). Then, in the first printed edition, this is cancelled as well, so that the whole sentence runs without interruption toward its original point. The final version reads:

21

> Every night its Titanic form seemed to await something;
> but it had waited thus, unmoved, during so many centuries,
> through the crises of so many things, that it could only be
> imagined to await one last crisis—the final overthrow. (4)

This last revision seems to indicate Hardy's discovery of what, in symbolic terms, the world of Egdon Heath represents and what, in terms of metaphor of setting, it suggests. He has now "imagined" its function as well as its description. The heath exists now from the ancient past to the end of the future, seeming thus to promise for the action of the novel a great symbolic crisis, the tragical possibilities of which should be so nearly cataclysmic as to symbolize something of the "final overthrow" of man and the world. But the end of *The Return of the Native* is not like the end of the world at all. The heath is still unchanged, unmoved, and Clym has not revised or improved anything of life on it significantly. In the end, life still goes on. The triumph, and it is a carefully limited one, is in Clym's understanding of the value of life, as it goes on. This understanding is his heroism.

Though the description of Egdon's adumbrative timelessness is concentrated for the most part into the opening few chapters, suggestive references to the heath's ancient but still vital history continue throughout the novel, keeping the largeness and inclusiveness of the metaphor constantly in the reader's consciousness. On their way to Mrs. Yeobright's house on Christmas eve, the mummers and Eustacia travel "not over Rainbarrow now, but down a valley which left that ancient elevation a little to the east" (p. 153). The reference to Rainbarrow and its age insists that, despite the flirtatious and bold comedy of Eustacia's participation in the mumming, there is still a large seriousness to the whole drama, the seriousness of "sable features" in a darkling and intense world. Eustacia, who is drawn toward Rainbarrow and herself draws others there, is not just larking in her visit to see Clym. Preparatory to Clym's declaration of his intention to remain in the country and not return to the ephemeral trades of man in Paris, the heath is represented as "a place which had slipped out of its century generations ago, to intrude an uncouth object into this" (p. 205). Here the suggestion of Egdon's long and continuing history is not just a gratuitous reminder of the idea of the past; it works, rather, to assure us of the mythically repetitious continuity of man's troubles and failures in this world, thus suggesting the difficulties necessarily ahead for Clym.

As the story progresses, similar suggestions are made and related to character and action. Because of the heavy insistence upon the metaphoric and mythically representative nature of the setting from the story's very beginning, allusions throughout the novel to historical objects, persons, and events in their relation to the present are received by the reader with a continuing awareness of their relevance to and meaning for that present. The heath is "A tract of country unaltered from that sinister condition which made Caesar anxious every year to get clear of its glooms before the autumnal equinox" (p. 60); Eustacia and Wildeve meet "in the little ditch encircling the tumulus—the original excavation from which it had been thrown up by the ancient British people" (p. 94); Clym rests on Egdon, the scene momentarily seeming "to belong to the ancient world of the carboniferous period, when the forms of plants were few, and of the fern kind" (p. 241)—for "On Egdon there was no absolute hour of the day" (p. 152). The effect of these many allusions is both immediate and cumulative, supporting the claim of the best characters to a universal significance in the history of man. Given this expanded stage, they must act for all of us; and as they free us by their strength and strength of will, they become our heroes.

The dramatic size of the characters, then, is suggested by the condensed and intensified time in which they must act. The justification for the highly coincidental nature of the novel's actions and events is that same metaphor of setting. Yet just as easily as it gives the characters of the novel the opportunity to stand as great figures, representative of the heroic in man, the large, blind, and resisting immutability of Egdon Heath can reduce them to microscopic insignificance, to what we fear is our own real size: "the imperturbable countenance of the heath, . . . having defied the cataclysmal onsets of centuries, reduced to insignificance by its seamed and antique features the wildest turmoil of a single man" (p. 384).

Clym and Eustacia are supposed to act on a stage metaphorically expanded to represent universally the world of man; they are themselves drawn toward Egdon, and they draw everything of time and creation to themselves at the elevated center of this stage. Still, Clym can seem "a brown spot in the midst of olive-green gorse, and nothing more" (p. 298), and "of no more account in life than an insect":

> He appeared as a mere parasite of the heath, fretting its surface in his daily labour as a moth frets a garment, entirely

> engrossed with its products, having no knowledge of anything
> in the world but fern, furze, heath, lichens, and moss. (328)

Not only does Clym appear thus diminished to others, he even sees himself reduced by the heath as "the arena of life" to "a bare equality with, and no superiority to, a single living thing under the sun" (p. 245). And in the company of Wildeve, Eustacia is described as one of "two horns which the sluggish heath had put forth from its crown, like a mollusc, and had drawn in again" (p. 99).

Hardy works more determinedly in *The Return of the Native* than he does in any other novel to reduce his characters to a state of cosmic insignificance. And as they try to rise from this diminution their voices are often shrill, their plans and ambitions melodramatic. In the end, only Clym succeeds in overcoming this reductive mechanism, and the heroic stature he attains is achieved in what is the first full demonstration of Hardy's formula for survival and endurance. Presenting Clym to the reader for the first time, the narrator describes his face as

> one of these faces which convey less the idea of so many years
> as its age than of so much experience as its store. The number
> of their years may have adequately summed up Jared, Ma-
> halaleel, and the rest of the antediluvians, but the age of a
> modern man is to be measured by the intensity of his history.
> (161)

The last line—which appears in slightly different forms in *A Pair of Blue Eyes* (p. 303) and *Tess of the D'Urbervilles* (p. 160)—is the first principle of Hardy's vision and his art. Here it is used argumentatively, first, to justify the use of coincidence: in an intense world, Hardy says, we must accept coincidence as dramatic fact. Second, the line is used to define the nature of Clym's existence in the whole metaphoric and symbolic texture of the novel: he is Hardy's hero, the one character whose life successfully imitates or measures up to the grandeur of the supporting setting, and whose character is strong enough to bear life on such terms.

It is character, of course, and not setting, that Hardy is interested in. He is concerned with man, and committed to finding and demonstrating his potential. In order to test his heroes, to measure their character, he intensifies the world in which they live and act. His problem, in part, is that he has no way of expressing this intensification except through exaggeration. Rather than exaggerate his characters directly, in their description or action, he exaggerates the world in which they live, in space and more importantly in time, and then subtly suggests their relationship to this larger world. Dramatic action takes place primarily in time, and Egdon Heath, the place of this novel, exists primarily as the place of time expanded. At a quiet moment Egdon seems to be a place "where any man could imagine himself to be Adam without the least difficulty" (p. 123). This narrative remark is made at the beginning of the second book of the novel, "The Arrival"; winter is at hand, Christmas and the New Year are coming, and Clym is about to "return" to the heath. He can return as Adam—to an ironical "Eden" (p. 284)—because Egdon does not mark the passing of time, and exists outside time:

> In the course of many days and weeks sunrise had advanced
> its quarters from north-east to south-east, sunset had receded
> from north-west to south-west; but Egdon had hardly heeded
> the change. (113–114)

If Clym returns as Adam, Eustacia is, of course, his Eve. One expects from these allusions a significant existence for the two—an existence if not largely heroic, still concerned with the introduction, at least, of heroism into the world of man.

Hardy measures the significance of his characters by the important intensity of their existence and their bearing up in the face of it. Although Hardy says that "the age of a modern man is to be measured by the intensity of his history" (p. 161) rather than by the number of his years, he usually finds it impossible to represent that intensity by other than an exaggerated and symbolic span of time. Thus Michael Henchard will live his one "moment" of existence, from the time of "The Creation" to the day of the sounding of "the great trumpet," in the double time of ancient and modern Casterbridge; Tess will be sacrificed in the metaphorical context of all history at Stonehenge; and all of Jude Fawley's life will come to its real and symbolic climax on "Remembrance Day." In *The Return of the Native*, however, no character finds such a tragic fate, though the stage of Egdon is set for just such tragedy: "it had waited thus, unmoved, during so many centuries, through the crises of so many things, that it could only be imagined to await one last crisis—the final overthrow" (p. 4). Hardy's problem, thus, is how to satisfy the expectations which the reader is led to entertain.

25

Egdon Heath is not a world which the characters must act against, but a world which they must act in, a stage which they must act on. As we measure the characters in the context of this world and its assertions, assumptions, and demands, so the characters measure themselves and assert themselves in relation to their stage, their setting, their environment. As they act, and as they see and feel themselves and each other in action, they sometimes discover in their world and among its properties the images and metaphors through which they can describe and even interpret their situations. In the end of the novel, Clym has achieved this knowledge, and as he preaches of and from experience on the top of Rainbarrow he can be said to have learned what his novel is about.

Most of the major characters respond to experience as though it were somehow more than simply or singularly human—as though their crisis were something like "the final overthrow." Their generalizations about life become the various philosophical keys to the novel. Thomasin and Diggory Venn are the exceptions to this rule, being scarcely involved in the dramatic or philosophical argument at all. Thomasin accepts things as they happen on the assumption that all situations and occurrences are simple and somehow simply ordained; and though she is involved in the plot-tangles of the novel, Thomasin is not involved in its tension and compression the way Mrs. Yeobright, Eustacia, and Clym are. Diggory, for all his machinations and his altruistic plotting, does not become involved in the stress of the action either; and in the end of the novel, after he has been painlessly transformed from reddleman back to dairy farmer, he marries Thomasin as though the crises of the novel simply had never been. He and Thomasin function like Faulkner's Lena Grove and Byron Bunch in *Light in August*. They live in the decompressed moment of life, and they represent, more or less comically, the normal situation for man.

The two serious female characters, Mrs. Yeobright and Eustacia Vye, are caught in the intensity of Egdon's exaggeration of experience, and they are both destroyed by it. Though Thomasin and Diggory seem to exist unaware of the tragic potential of the indifferent world around them—and such is what Egdon frequently represents, in part—Mrs. Yeobright and Eustacia live in constant awareness of that world and of their place and station in it. Mrs. Yeobright is the less important of the two characters, but hers is the more satisfying and successful part.

Eustacia is an almost purely melodramatic character, whereas Mrs. Yeobright has a true and substantial dignity about her for all of her pettiness. The contrast between the two becomes most clear when one compares their separate responses to the fatal accidents of situation which confront them.

Mrs. Yeobright is not a grand creature. As a character she is what her role requires of her: a compulsive mother, possessive in her attitude toward Clym—and thus an agent in his catastrophe—and pettishly critical in her response to Thomasin. She has one fine scene, with Johnny Nonesuch, which is among the better dramatic scenes one finds in Hardy. But the scene of her destruction has its success in part at least in its preparation. Earlier, in a conversation with Thomasin, Mrs. Yeobright voices her stern and exaggerated self-pity as a complaint against Clym, "Clym must do as he will—he is nothing more to me. And this is maternity— to give one's best years and best love to ensure the fate of being despised" (p. 251), and Thomasin responds with a brief corrective argument. Then, in a finely executed line, Mrs. Yeobright defines what will become part of Hardy's typical point of view toward life—what will become, when concluded as an idea, his measure of man's dignity and his heroism: "Thomasin, don't lecture me—I can't have it. It is the excess above what we expect that makes the force of the blow" (p. 252).[11] Mrs. Yeobright falls, fails, under the blow which weighs in excess of her expectations; the hero, for Hardy, must stand up under it, as in the end Clym does. Still, Mrs. Yeobright measures up better than Eustacia does, and she knows what the problem of living is, even though she can't cope with it. Mrs. Yeobright pleads, wishfully, "Let the past be forgotten" (p. 187). The reference of the line is not just the particular contextual reference to her past difficulties with Damon Wildeve, but a reference to the whole universe of condensing experience. It is because Mrs. Yeobright understands more of existence that her grief in this world is larger, more real, and more meaningful than Eustacia's.

Eustacia is introduced to the novel in the pantomime of the end of Chapter 2. Hers is the figure atop Rainbarrow that "an imaginative stranger might . . . suppose . . . one of the Celts who built the barrow, so far had all modern date withdrawn from the scene" (p. 13). Then she disappears; and when she reappears in Chapter 6, again atop all the history and pre-history of the setting, she carries with her a telescope and an hourglass, the symbolic significance of which would seem to suggest

27

a combination of intensification and measurement. Eustacia looks through the glass into the distance, and calls to the barrow-stage Damon Wildeve, the character who, with her, begins the intrigue of the novel.[12] But the intrigue can only be a melodramatic one, because the characters involved are characters from melodrama. Eustacia herself knows that Wildeve is utterly insignificant: she "feels that nothing is worth while, and fill[s] up the spare hours of her existence by idealizing Wildeve for want of a better object. This was the sole reason of his ascendency: she knew it herself" (p. 81).

Eustacia's feeling "that nothing is worth while" stems from her petulant nature, from her emotional immaturity and irresponsibility. Mrs. Yeobright knows what Elizabeth-Jane learns in *The Mayor of Casterbridge*, "that happiness [is] but an occasional episode in the general drama of pain" (p. 386); and fearing "the force of the blow," she acknowledges its immanence. Eustacia, however, rejects this unkind reality, and refuses to submit to the limits which it seems to set. That this is the reality in which one must find the measure of one's dignity does not interest Eustacia; the eternal and timeless realities of life are less her concern, Hardy says, than the "Boulevards in Paris" (p. 220).

In describing Eustacia's "isolation," the narrator remarks of her:

> To have lost the godlike conceit that we may do what we will, and not to have acquired a homely zest for doing what we can, shows a grandeur of temper which cannot be objected to in the abstract, for it denotes a mind that, though disappointed, forswears compromise. (81)

There is admittedly something partly whimsical about this comment, seen in its full context; still, the serious assertion is clear—Eustacia is not willing to accept the responsibility her situation requires of her. For Hardy, the abstract is irrelevant; the novels generally assert doing over dreaming, and the occasional nature of the poetry as well as its pervading theme both plainly say this. But Eustacia cannot commit herself to life; and from this inability to leave her girlish daydreams and join life come both the accident of her death and the serious failure of her life. Her passions are, for Hardy, the wrong ones, and her existence thus becomes irrelevant. The reader is told of Clym's "abundance of sympathy" (p. 219) and that he "loved his kind" (p. 203) just before Eustacia says to him, "I have not much love for my fellow-creatures. Sometimes I quite hate them" (p. 219). Then follows a conversation between the two about the world in which they live, Clym willingly, Eustacia against her will:

> "You are lonely here."
>
> "I cannot endure the heath, except in its purple season. The heath is a cruel taskmaster to me."
>
> "Can you say so?" he asked. "To my mind it is most exhilarating, and strengthening, and soothing. I would rather live on these hills than anywhere else in the world."
>
> "It is well enough for artists; but I would never learn to draw."
>
> "And there is a very curious Druidical stone just out there." He threw a pebble in the direction signified. "Do you often go to see it?"
>
> "I was not even aware that there existed any such curious Druidical stone. I am aware that there are Boulevards in Paris." (220)

Eustacia is uninterested in what is philosophically given as the life of this novel, the world of Egdon Heath. As a creation in the novel, she is reasonably believable, though Hardy has little sympathy for people no larger than she turns out to be. For as a character, a person in the world of the novel, she is a failure. Despite her seeming power to attract men, despite her involvement in the action and movement of the drama, she is personally insignificant. As the novel progresses one realizes that she cannot be heroic, and that her charm is in the moral or personal sense adolescent and in the aesthetic sense melodramatic. Her supposed size is from the beginning but romantic or rhetorical inflation, and it is only as Clym, "the Native," comes to supersede her, to push her into the role of the outsider, that the novel settles into its proper and successful seriousness.

Eustacia does not live up to the moral requirements of the fiction. As a person, she does not fulfill the premise asserted for the novel in the description of the Egdon stage; she fails to exist as largely, as relevantly, as universally or heroically as the stage and setting demand. Her interest is not in Egdon, which she finds "uncongenial" (p. 416) and her "ruin" (p. 415), but in a small, worthless, ephemeral world of "town bustle" (p. 220). As the Eve who must tempt Clym's Adam in this tightly ironic "Eden" (pp. 123, 284), Eustacia cannot even require of him conscious disobedience. The bored sexuality with which she taunts Clym is nothing more subtle or complex than a child's restlessness at its inability to entertain itself. Much more interesting, in terms of psycho-sexual symbolism, is the impotence-qua-blindness from which Clym suffers in his distressed attempt to deal with Eustacia and her ambitions.

Near the end of Book Five, as Eustacia goes out from Mistover Knap to meet Wildeve, Hardy suggests that what is about to happen will be more than melodrama. She goes toward the Quiet Woman, where she is to meet Wildeve; but she goes, for the sake of Hardy's symbolic narrative method, via Rainbarrow. As she approaches its summit, one is invited

> to dwell on nocturnal scenes of disaster in the chronicles of the world, on all that is terrible and dark in history and legend—the last plague of Egypt, the destruction of Sennacherib's host, the agony in Gethsemane. (421)

Eustacia has not been a sympathetic character (not even for Hardy) and the representation of her perverse and selfish response to life and people has been for the most part crudely melodramatic. But now, following this narrative suggestion of timeless calamity and the adumbrations of a new disaster, we are asked to sympathize with her:

> Any one who had stood by now would have pitied her, not so much on account of her exposure to weather, and isolation from all humanity except the mouldering remains inside the tumulus; but for that other form of misery, which was denoted by the slight rocking movement that her feelings imparted to her person. Extreme unhappiness weighed visibly upon her. (421)

The "queen of the solitude" who stood atop the barrow in Chapter 2 repeats that original pose now, swaying, tottering, about to fall. Yet because the promise of the novel has been disappointed already as regards Eustacia, it is difficult at the end to make her situation fit with the significant tragic events "in the chronicles of the world," with "all that is terrible and dark in history and legend." Her relationship with "the mouldering remains inside the tumulus" is neither strong nor real. Nor is her companion in this final scene significant as a character: once again he is seen by Eustacia as not "a Saul or a Buonapart" (p. 422); indeed, he is but a villain, and his smallness is hardly a secret from anyone. His failure, of course, comes as a part of Eustacia's. The "queen of the solitude" turns out to be nothing more than the queen of spades in an old and worn deck of cards, and one must look elsewhere for a sufficient central character.

The hero of the novel is Clym—and he is, perhaps surprisingly, the most fully representative of Hardy's heroes. He suffers, learns, grows, and endures. He accepts and comprehends the heath, and as he does he finds for himself (and through him the reader finds) the objective correlative of the setting. In his coming to understand his world, Clym fulfills himself as a person. He becomes, in the end, a sort of "itinerant open-air preacher" (p. 485); and the translation for that occupation may well be "artist," thus making Clym a self-projection, perhaps, for Hardy. However Clym fulfills himself, and whatever this means, in doing so he fulfills the promise of the novel to concern itself with serious matter and significant people. Clym's whole existence, from his introduction through his trial to his final resolution, is constantly described in relation to the setting of the heath, through which that promise is made. Egdon is the typical Hardy world, hard, inimical, unchanging, the representative stage for all of man's history; and Clym's measured success on that stage is Hardy's pledge to something other than Fatalism or pessimism or determinism. Clym's resolution is a careful statement of Hardy's hopes, and those hopes neither change nor disappear in the fifty years from the publication of *The Return of the Native* to Hardy's death. Clym is most significant as a hero—but not as a tragic hero, not as a defeated hero; and he is essentially Hardy's *own* hero.

The Return of the Native is Clym's novel. It has been asserted frequently that Eustacia is the central character, and that once she is killed at the end of Book Five the novel is really finished—in five acts, like a play. But that is not what Hardy wrote; for the unity and structure of the whole as he composed it one needs that sixth act, "Aftercourses."[13] Clym is the title character, and it is only in Book Six that he completes his task in the novel and can bring the novel to its proper close. The happy ending which some critics have claimed was added to the novel— using Hardy's own note as supporting evidence for their claim—is but incidental to the major focus of the whole. Its addition does not mar the form of Eustacia's tragedy—both the form and the tragedy are pure critical invention. Furthermore, what Hardy protests to have added because of "certain circumstances of serial publication" (note, p. 473)

31

is not the part of the conclusion which deals with Clym, but simply the marriage of Thomasin and Diggory Venn.[14]

Although Clym is introduced into the action late in the novel—he does not even arrive on the scene until Chapter 6 of Book Two—his entry is prepared for from the beginning; he is "the Native," who "returns." Everything before that moment is, in one sense, but preparation for it. The setting, the supporting characters, the potential incidents are all established. What is to be required of the hero is spelled out, and the lines of his conflict in character and action are drawn.

The first specific description of Clym comes earlier in Book Two, Chapter 3, as Eustacia listens to him converse with Mrs. Yeobright and Thomasin. The quality of the voice is not described, nor are Clym's actual words recorded. Rather, what he says is reported summarily, with the emphasis placed on his relation to Egdon Heath:

> Sometimes this throat uttered Yes, sometimes it uttered No; sometimes it made inquiries about a timeworn denizen of the place. Once it surprised her notions by remarking on the friendliness and geniality written in the faces of the hills around. (136)

In opposition thus to Eustacia, Clym is from the beginning attached sympathetically to the heath; and as soon as he speaks for the first time for himself it is discovered that his ambitions are also directly related to his native place.

The end of Chapter 3 of "The Arrival" describes Eustacia's attempts, after she has heard Clym speak, to meet him face to face. The rhetoric and the dramatics of the narrative statement seem carefully planned to achieve their effect:

> The first occasion passed, and he did not come that way.
> She promenaded a second time, and was again the sole wanderer there.
> The third time there was a dense fog; she looked around, but without much hope. Even if he had been walking within twenty yards of her she could not have seen him.
> At the fourth attempt to encounter him it began to rain in torrents, and she turned back.
> The fifth sally was in the afternoon: it was fine, and she remained out long, walking to the very top of the valley in which Blooms-End lay. She saw the white paling about half

a mile off; but he did not appear. . . . She resolved to look for the man from Paris no more.

But Providence is nothing if not coquettish; and no sooner had Eustacia formed this resolve than the opportunity came which, while sought, had been entirely withholden. (139–140)

Chance is perverse, though not, obviously, foreordained; and in this concentrated world chance happenings do occur. The fated nature of Eustacia's attempts to meet Clym finds its parallel in a statement like "Because I didn't bring my umbrella, it rained." Chance—Hardy's "Hap" —is insistently, grotesquely accidental, though dumbly, blindly ordered by the Immanent Will; and in its most compressed and intensified form such accident becomes dramatically coincidental.

The crisis which is to be Eustacia's first meeting with Clym is introduced in the opening sentence of the new chapter which follows the lines just quoted: "In the evening of this last day of expectation, which was the twenty-third of December, Eustacia was at home alone" (p. 141). The time, again, is symbolically Hardy's favorite time of year: the time when the cycle of the seasons changes, when the days are their shortest, when the Christian mythology is reborn, when the old year ends and the new year begins.[15] It is a time of compression, when what happens must happen most quickly, most intensely—when, thus, the wryest and gravest of coincidences can be expected.

The opening description of Clym takes up this point explicitly. His is "one of those faces which convey less the idea of so many years as its age than of so much experience as its store"; and this "singular" countenance (p. 162) tempts Hardy to the assertion, again, that "the age of a modern man is to be measured by the intensity of history," rather than by its duration (p. 161). The paradox here is that though Clym is a "modern man" he is still the typical, representative hero in the long history of man. His model, for Hardy, is presented in that added paragraph alluding to the Promethean spirit in all men. Late in the novel Clym warns Eustacia that he is capable of rebelling "in high Promethean fashion" (p. 302) should the occasion arise; and earlier, at his first introduction, the narrator remarks concerning his look of "natural cheerfulness striving against depression" that "the deity that lies ignominiously chained within an ephemeral human carcase shone out of him like a ray" (p. 162). The demonstration of this heroic compassion is to be found in Clym's "great plan" for the conversion and enlightenment of

33

the world of the heath. Given the other allusions and suggestions planted in the novel, this ambition matches the Promethean too closely for mere spontaneous accident. Clym describes his choice of a prospective occupation on Egdon as opposed to the occupation he has quit in Paris:

> "But you mistake me," pleaded Clym. "All this was very depressing. But not so depressing as something I next perceived—that my business was the idlest, vainest, most effeminate business that ever a man could be put to. That decided me: I would give it up and try to follow some rational occupation among the people I know best, and to whom I could be of most use. I have come home; and this is how I mean to carry out my plan. I shall keep a school as near to Egdon as possible, so as to be able to walk over here and have a nightschool in my mother's house. But I must study a little at first, to get properly qualified." (202)

The aim here expressed is in the realm of the practical—but it is fully idealistic, nonetheless. As he expresses his ambition elsewhere, its dimensions become more clear: "I want to do some worthy thing before I die," he tells his mother (p. 206); and again, "There is no chance of getting rich. But with my system of education, which is as new as it is true, I shall do a great deal of good for my fellow-creatures" (pp. 238–39). His compassion for his fellows is Hardy's compassion and it is never again expressed so fully or so clearly in any of Hardy's characters. Though Gabriel Oak tends to the bloated sheep out of a similar sympathy, and Tess helps the wounded birds mercifully and humanely, and Jude responds with innocent kindness to the rooks, still Clym is the only one of Hardy's heroes whose compassion is the first essential of his story, to be asserted over and over by word and by deed. The occasions which Hardy reports of Gabriel's, Tess's, or Jude's compassion are but incidents descriptive of the goodness of their characters, whereas Clym's compassion is the focal point, finally, of his novel. "Talk about men who deserve the name," says Clym, again to Mrs. Yeobright,

> "can any man deserving the name waste his time in that effeminate way, when he sees half the world going to ruin for want of somebody to buckle to and teach them how to breast the misery they are born to?" (207)

Clym's question is a paraphrase of Hardy's own typical response to life— and once more it is not pessimistic, but guardedly opposite to that. In speaking as he does, Clym takes on the role set up for him as the hero's: "Yeobright loved his kind. . . . What was more, he was ready at once to be the first unit sacrificed" (p. 203). His determination is that "spontaneous, Promethean rebelliousness against the fiat that this recurrent season shall bring foul times, cold darkness, misery and death. Black chaos comes, and the fettered gods of the earth say, Let there be light" (p. 18).

The representation of Clym's compassion and his heroism, his suffering and his learning, is admittedly sometimes awkward. This may be so partially because the undertaking is so ambitious; one expects to find the hero faced with some situation representative of or of a size with either the first tragedy, in Eden, and Adam's bearing up under it, or the final heroic spasm of Adam's last descendents on this earth. That Clym can neither find nor make such a situation may be due, further, to his being the typically inarticulate Hardy character. For all that the dramatic situation would require of him, Clym cannot communicate verbally. He talks at length and often, but he is always making speeches, not talking to people. His success comes from what the narrator is able to impress upon us of Clym's character and his response to his situation; and what Hardy expresses in this way is essentially his own response to life.

On the level of plot as well as on a scale measuring emotional pitch, *The Return of the Native* builds toward its crisis as the marriage of Clym and Eustacia approaches. As Clym leaves his mother's house for the cottage which is to be his and Eustacia's, a storm strikes on the heath, providing what should be the keynote for the climax. The storm cannot disturb the heath, for "Egdon was made for such times as these" (p. 247); and what is foreboded here is Clym's near-destruction by the mute, dumb intrusion of chance. The marriage takes place the day after Midsummer Day, at the time of the traditional "summer Christmas," another of Hardy's favorite days because of its natural, calendric aspect of crisis. Then follows the production of plot-intrigues and maneuverings which lead to the chance rejection of Mrs. Yeobright at Clym's door and her subsequent, resultant death.

The scenes of Clym's agony following from this crisis—his mad scene (pp. 365–72) after his mother's death, and the scene of his accusation of Eustacia (pp. 385–91)—are failures, dramatically. Hardy cannot make a Lear of his hero, nor an Othello; Clym's ranting is not that of the Moor, nor that of the "traditional King of Wessex" (p. v), but a stilted, broken, speech-making rhetoric that belongs more easily to the theatre of melodrama than to that of tragedy. Yet though these central scenes are failures, the novel does not fail with them. Rather, it rises from these failures with Clym. With what might be called the props of his drama used and disposed of, with Mrs. Yeobright, Eustacia, and Wildeve all dead, Clym alone remains, undestroyed, laboring under an heroic obligation to survive. His desperation—or frustration, rather, for Clym himself rejects the notion that he is ever "desperate" (p. 449)—is redoubled by Eustacia's death: "She is the second woman I have killed this year," he tells Diggory. He continues:

> "It is I who ought to have drowned myself. It would have been a charity to the living had the river overwhelmed me and borne her up. But I cannot die. . . . If it had pleased God to put an end to me it would have been a good thing for all. But I am getting used to the horror of my existence. They say that a time comes when men laugh at misery through long acquaintance with it. Surely that time will soon come to me." (449)

Clym's recovery from such "hopeless" thought—as he calls them—is assisted to a degree by the simple goodness of life which he sees in Thomasin and Venn as they are finally brought together. More importantly, however, Clym's recovery is based in his own serious reflections on the meaning of the intense life which has been his to live and see. In the manuscript of *The Return of the Native* the denouement is first managed without Clym's studied ruminations, and the story runs then straight to the marriage of Diggory and Clym's cousin. The way in which Clym finds first the better relief from his grief and then his mission in life seems to have occurred to Hardy later, and is added overleaf to the manuscript. The added paragraph (the most important one in the first Chapter of the last section of the novel) reads:

> He frequently walked the heath alone, when the past seized upon him with its shadowy hand, and held him there to listen to its tale. His imagination would then people the spot with its ancient inhabitants: forgotten Celtic tribes trod their tracks about him, and he could almost live among them, look in their faces, and see them standing beside the barrows which swelled around, untouched and perfect as at the time of their

erection. Those of the dyed barbarians who had chosen to cultivate tracts were, in comparison with those who had left their marks here, as writers on paper beside writers on parchment. Their records had perished long ago by the plough, while the works of these remained. Yet they had all lived and died unconscious of the different fates awaiting their relics. It reminded him that unconjectured factors operate in the production of immortality. (fol. 403v)

Though this last sentence, with its emphasis on chance—and with later emendations of "unforeseen" for "unconjectured" and "evolution" for "production"—is the point sentence of the paragraph, it does not represent the total meaning and effect of the paragraph. Clym tries to think back to Eustacia, but instead, he goes all the way back. His meditation upon the past and the seeming continuum of history in the lives and fates of men recalls for the reader once more the timeless significance of his experience, and the microcosmically representative nature of Egdon Heath. The recollection of "forgotten Celtic tribes" and their "barrows" recalls specifically Eustacia's figurative appearance atop Rainbarrow at the end of Chapter 2, where her shadowy form was described as like "the person of one of the Celts who built the barrow" (p. 13).

The idea—Clym's, Hardy's—for what happens in the last scene of the novel also comes from this allusion to the unchanging in history. The symbolic recalling of the dead Eustacia does not make her, in her absence, a greater figure, but rather suggests Clym's assumption of the central position in the novel and the important universality of his experience. And it is from this experience and his comprehension of it that Clym preaches, the plan having suggested itself to him "when the past seized upon him with its shadowy hand, and held him there to listen to its tale":

> On the Sunday after [the wedding of Thomasin and Venn] an unusual sight was to be seen on Rainbarrow. From a distance there appeared to be a motionless figure standing on the top of the tumulus, just as Eustacia had stood on that lonely summit some two and a half years before. But now it was fine warm weather, with only a summer breeze blowing, and early afternoon instead of dull twilight. Those who ascended to the immediate neighborhood of the Barrow perceived that the erect form in the centre, piercing the sky, was

> not really alone. Round him upon the slopes of the Barrow a
> number of heathmen and women were reclining or sitting at
> their ease. They listened to the words of the man in their
> midst, who was preaching. . . . This was the first of a series
> of moral lectures or Sermons on the Mount, which were to be
> delivered from the same place every Sunday afternoon as
> long as the fine weather lasted. (483–84)

The figure, of course, is Clym's, and he is preaching, in his "Sermons on
the Mount," Hardy's thesis of "loving-kindness." He preaches discourses
"sometimes secular, and sometimes religious, but never dogmatic." His
texts are "taken from all kinds of books" (p. 484), and their meaning is
found and applied from the experience of the clichéd but intense book
of life. Clym leaves alone "creeds and systems of philosophy, finding
enough and more than enough to occupy his tongue in the opinions and
actions common to all good men" (p. 485). These last lines are added
in the manuscript, for insertion in the final paragraph of the novel.[16]
Clym's sympathetic response to life comes, like Hardy's, from looking at
life; and this addition has Clym, like his creator, refuse to be a "philosopher," preferring to depend on his compassionate response to men and
their situations for his vision:[17]

> Some believed him, and some believed not; some said that
> his words were commonplace, others complained of his want
> of theological doctrine; while others again remarked that it
> was well enough for a man to take to preaching who could
> not see to do anything else. But everywhere he was kindly re-
> ceived, for the story of his life had become generally known.
> (485)

The "story of his life" is the background from which Clym preaches.
His compassion for his fellow-creatures, and the understanding of life
he gains through his experience and his expansive vision of that experience form the basis for his choice and his interpretation of texts.

Hardy's text for the novel is his epigraph from Keats: "To sorrow/
I bade good morrow / . . . / But ah! she is so constant and so kind!" His
meditation on this text is told as the story of Clym's life. Both the moral
lesson and the artistic creation are at times clumsy, weak, and melodramatic. Still, however, there is a moral and artistic strength to the
story. Hardy achieves this by setting the novel on its great symbolic stage,
Egdon Heath, and by developing Clym through the course of the novel

to his conquest of experience, through suffering. In terms of human or artistic significance, the other characters hardly even exist "as flies to wanton boys," and this is the greatest weakness of the novel; but Clym grows to heroism and humanity as he comes to understand life. He finally stands firmly, legitimately, atop the timeless Rainbarrow, at the center of Hardy's created world. Clym is the observer, the learner, and finally the teacher, who works with sympathy and compassion; and perhaps this is also Hardy as well as Clym, urging almost shyly but still heroically, "Let there be light."

NOTES TO CHAPTER II

1. Johnson, *Art of Thomas Hardy*, pp. 43, 46–47.

2. Quotations from Chapter I of *The Return of the Native*, used in the review of the novel in *The Graphic*, 7 December 1878, p. 279.

3. Cf. Edward Wright, in "The Novels of Thomas Hardy," *Quarterly Review* 199 (April 1904) p. 408: "So impressive is [Egdon Heath] that many a reader will forget sooner the conduct of the action itself than the scene of the action."

4. H. C. Duffin, *Thomas Hardy* (Manchester, 1916), pp. 16, 128; review, *The Observer*, 5 January 1879; Joseph Warren Beach, *The Technique of Thomas Hardy* (Chicago, 1922), pp. 97–99, 105, 101; D. H. Lawrence, in *Phoenix* (London, 1936), p. 415; Rutland, *Writings and their Background*, p. 179; Albert Guerard, *Thomas Hardy* (Cambridge, Mass., 1949), p. 6; Evelyn Hardy, *Thomas Hardy: A Critical Biography* (London, 1954), pp. 162–63.

5. *Thomas Hardy* (New York, 1964), p. 91.

6. Ibid., p. 92.

7. Ibid.

8. University College Library, Dublin.

9. Cf. Richard Ohmann, in "Methods in the Study of Victorian Style," *Victorian Newsletter* 27 (Fall 1966): "If stylistic choices operate among alternate formulations of propositional content, then a *pattern* of such choices—a style—implies a characteristic way of conceiving, relating, and presenting content. A habit of mind and feeling. A conceptual world" (p. 2).

10. Cf. John Paterson, *The Making of The Return of the Native* (Berkeley, 1960): "Thus, although Rainbarrow is actually situated on the outskirts of the heath, it appears in the novel, for reasons which have to do with its symbolic meaning and with the focus of its action, at the heath's very center" (p. 122).

11. In the manuscript the last sentence quoted is corrected from beginning "The force of the blow is the difference between . . . " to the reading here given (MS fol. 245).

12. Damon doesn't actually come to the barrow; he comes to Captain Vye's house at Mistover Knap instead. But Mistover is "nearly in the center of the heath" (p. 143), and, surrounded by a "bank or ditch" (p. 214), is linked descriptively to Rainbarrow,

where there is a "little ditch encircling the tumulus—the original excavation from which it had been thrown up by the ancient British people" (p. 94).

13. Dale Kramer, in "Unity of Time in *The Return of the Native*," *Notes and Queries* (August 1965): 304–05, has made an interesting and perceptive observation about the way Hardy thinks of time: "Hardy's ironic, ego-deflating gloss upon time gives a philosophical unity to his depiction of man's place in the universe at the same time that the vaguely defined year of man's time unifies the human plot. The supposedly unsophisticated novelist utilizes the artificial convention of temporal unity as an organic means to subtly clarify and amplify his delineation of man's lonely transience." But "transience" is not all—and Kramer is led into this mistake by ignoring the last part of the novel. In order to make the time of the novel cover "one cosmic day" (i.e., the classical "one day" becomes the year's one day, through its four seasons, since one day in the time of Nature is equal to one year in the time of man) Kramer limits its time to the twelve months of Books One through Five.

14. Their supposedly unwarranted happiness is, in a way, the comic relief which suggests the decompression of the intense world and the reintroduction of "normal" existence. And Hardy's insistence on the place of the normal may be seen in his otherwise irrelevant attachment of Diggory and Thomasin to "an aged highway . . . an old vicenal way" (p. 7) at their introduction, and again to that same "old Roman road" at the end of the novel. The title of Chapter 2 of "Aftercourses"—"Thomasin Walks in a Green Place by a Roman Road"—is an added chapter-title, much reworked, in the manuscript; and the meaning Hardy seems to intend for the matching of Venn and the girl thus is one of the continuity of love in the world, despite its calamities. The declaration he makes in the last stanza of "In Time of 'The Breaking of Nations' " is similar.

15. As I have already mentioned, Hardy uses the time between the twenty-first of December and New Year's Eve Day as the time of significance in almost all of the novels, as well as in some half-dozen short stories and in numerous poems. That he is working carefully in this novel with his symbolic calendar—with the winter solstice and with the summer solstice, with Christmas and with the "summer Christmas," St. John's or Midsummer Day—is easily demonstrated by reference to the timing of events: Clym returns to Egdon on December 23 (p. 141); Wildeve and Thomasin marry a few days after Christmas, between then and New Year's Day (pp. 183–93); Clym and Eustacia marry on June 25, the day after Midsummer Day (pp. 248, 255); Diggory gives up dealing in reddle at Christmas (p. 457); Thomasin and Diggory marry on June 25, "on the twenty-fifth of next month," as Thomasin tells Clym early in May (pp. 458–59, 464, 468, 475); and Clym begins to preach on Rainbarrow on the first Sunday after June 25 (p. 483).

16. Fol. 428v, for insertion on fol. 429.

17. Perhaps the most precise statement of this attitude on Hardy's part is in the poem, "Nature's Questioning," see below, pp. 141–42. For Hardy, one comes to an understanding of the world, not by asking questions or developing systems or sets of doctrines, but by observing life with sympathy and generous feeling; and from these fragments of experience one makes whatever vision one can—and from this vision, so constructed, come such poems as those which project the thinking and assume the voice of God or the Immanent Will.

III

THE MINOR NOVELS:
DISCOVERY OF TECHNIQUE (1871–1876)

> *Reading the* LIFE OF GOETHE, *Schlegel says that*
> *"the deepest want and deficiency of all mod-*
> *ern art lies in the fact that the artists have no*
> *mythology."*
>
> THOMAS HARDY'S NOTEBOOKS
> 16 June 1875

Hardy's first novel, *Desperate Remedies*, was published in 1871. The history of its writing is well
enough known, or at least is quite accessible in any number of standard
works. The novel shows promise for Hardy, but is not itself close to
that promise. It is clumsy, plotty, and romantic, often in a rather melodramatic way. It is of interest here, however, for the trying out of
technique, the basic plot conception, and the previews it affords of
Hardy's later works. The theme of *Desperate Remedies* is, on one level,
that simple one which will become typical in Hardy's works: the problems of matrimonial relations, of establishing a successful and lasting
relationship between husband and wife. But there are, in effect, two
distinct sets of characters here, two generations of lovers; and the structural relationship which Hardy establishes to unite the two makes the
novel much more complexly interesting than it is in its basic thematic
concern with the matrimonial problems.

Desperate Remedies is diagrammed on a scheme of progressive calendar time, and the chapter titles and subdivisions list the days and

41

hours of the action. Onto this easy scheme Hardy grafts a plot, common enough in fiction, based on the intrusions of the past into the present. The principal characters of the present are Owen and Cytherea Graye, Aeneas Manston, and Edward Springrove; the characters out of the past are Manston's mother, Cytherea Aldclyffe, and the Grayes' father, Ambrose Graye. The preparation for the juxtaposition of these two generations and their stories is not sufficient to satisfy one's demand for dramatic plausibility, though Hardy argues the point several times early in the novel. In Chapter 1 Cytherea Graye says to her brother, concerning their late father, "And there was an excuse for his past, though he never would claim it" (p. 12). The whole of the novel grows out of this "excuse," and the father's unknown past complicates his children's future. The elder Graye's first love was the first Cytherea, Miss Aldclyffe, who broke their engagement when she found herself pregnant with another man's child. Her retreat from this love affair is ended a generation later when, by accident, Cytherea Graye becomes known to her. Miss Aldclyffe tries then to recreate and reenact that broken passion and romance from her past by uniting Cytherea Graye and Manston, her illegitimate son.

Cytherea Graye and her brother are in one sense the central characters of this novel of mystery and romance. They are the main actors, acted upon both by circumstances and by other characters. Yet the novel may be something more than just mystery and romance; and because of the spontaneous simultaneity which coincidence seems to effect, the novel belongs perhaps more to Miss Aldclyffe than it does to them. The central coincidence itself—the bizarre juxtaposition of these two sets of characters—demands justification, however, or at least some kind of explanation. In the later novels Hardy will use Wessex to satisfy this requirement, and coincidence will be made legitimate, will almost be normalized, by the metaphoric juxtapositions of past and present which produce intensified time and timelessness. But Hardy does not yet have Wessex (it is introduced in *Far From the Madding Crowd*, in 1874) and he must establish the coincidental recurrence of the past in *Desperate Remedies* argumentatively rather than dramatically. Cytherea and Owen discuss the possibility of coincidence in normal life in Chapter 9. They have just begun to discover the facts of their father's past as it relates to and exists in their present.

"Do you believe in such odd coincidences?" said Cytherea.
"How do you mean, believe in them? They occur sometimes."
"Yes, one will occur often enough—that is, two discon-
nected events will fall strangely together by chance, and
people scarcely notice the fact beyond saying, 'Oddly enough
it happened that so and so were the same,' and so on. But
when three such events coincide without any apparent reason
for the coincidence, it seems as if there must be invisible
means at work." (168–69)

That "seeming" with which Cytherea offers to explain coincidence may
be an interesting philosophical reference for the student of Hardy, but
the more important emphasis of the statement is on the idea of coincidence and its real probability—which establishes, for Hardy's purposes,
its legitimacy as an artistic convention.

Hardy believes in coincidence. In choosing the epigraph for this first
of his novels he states his thesis: coincidence is both necessary and legitimate in dramatic art. The epigraph is from the Introduction to Sir
Walter Scott's *The Monastery*:

Though an unconnected course of adventure is what most
frequently occurs in nature, yet the province of the romance-
writer being artificial, there is more required from him than
a mere compliance with the simplicity of reality.[1]

In its significance, however, as well as in the craft with which it is
managed, Hardy's use of coincidence goes much beyond Scott's. Hardy's
vision of man and his situation suggests to him the unsuspected crossing
of paths; and his historical sense of things suggests to him that such
paths have always crossed and always will. Usually Hardy's coincidences
are not just gratuitous; most often the juxtaposition of events is caused,
in a physical or psychological or moral way, by the past or present actions of the character involved. Past and present wind easily onto the
same pole in Hardy's art; this is the basic plot and the skeleton of the
general theme in every novel except *Under the Greenwood Tree*, *The
Trumpet-Major*, and *The Woodlanders*, and it is at the center of many
of his best poems.

When the past and the present meet—and this is the nature of the
primary coincidence in *Desperate Remedies*—in Hardy's world, an in-

tense dramatic situation is created. The pressure of the time is doubled, and the essence of the moment is revealed. "My art," he wrote in his diary in January of 1886, "is to intensify the expression of things."[2] Then, in August of 1890, he wrote:

> Art is a changing of the actual proportions and order of things, so as to bring out more forcibly than might otherwise be done that feature in them which appeals most strongly to the idiosyncrasy of the artist.[3]

He continues the note later, reiterating:

> Art is a disproportioning—(i.e., distorting, throwing out of proportion)—of realities, to show more clearly the features that matter in those realities. . . .Hence "realism" is not art.[4]

This "idiosyncrasy of the artist," however, must be turned to artistic technique. The foreshortening of existence into the intensity of coincidental time and space relations requires narrative or dramatic preparation and justification. In *The Mayor of Casterbridge* and *Tess of the D'Urbervilles* there is a fault in the past of the central character which justifies the intrusion of that past into the present. And in these and in other novels, Hardy eases the burden of coincidence by establishing descriptive and thematic metaphors to suggest and support the juxtaposition of seemingly discoordinate events.

But in *Desperate Remedies* the past seems to be only artificially related to the present. Miss Aldclyffe intervenes in the present, trying to recreate symbolically her own existence, trying to relive her own life in the lives of the younger characters of the novel. Her past is not Cytherea Graye's responsibility, and thus there is no moral or psychological justification for its recurrence in her life. The coincidence is artificial, and its results seem irrelevant. But this is only true if Cytherea is the central character of the novel. If Miss Aldclyffe is the central character then one has to evaluate things from a different point of view. Miss Aldclyffe is both the motivating force of the novel and—because what she causes to happen is happening, symbolically and vicariously, to her—the central character. The coincidence of her intrusion is still artificial, but at least it is now necessary and it shows "the idiosyncrasy of the artist." She attempts, perversely, to make Cytherea relive her life for her; since she could not marry Ambrose Graye, she tries to make her namesake,

Graye's daughter, marry her son, the son whose illegitimate conception was the cause of her refusal to marry.

The elder Cytherea first met Ambrose Graye at Christmastime in 1835; three weeks after this, in mid January, he asked her to marry him and was refused. We are told these facts in the opening chapter of the novel, as Hardy covers quickly "The Events of Thirty Years," years which remove the elder Graye from life and the first Cytherea seemingly from the story. But she soon reappears, as Cytherea Aldclyffe; and in that still inexplicable and partially unjustifiable coincidence, Miss Aldclyffe accidentally retains Cytherea Graye as her companion.

The situation which develops as Miss Aldclyffe begins to manipulate Cytherea Graye's life toward a corrected reenactment of her own is one which many of Hardy's critics have found both obvious and perplexing. It is almost standard now to point to Miss Aldclyffe's lesbianism, and then to ask why it is there. Chapter 4 is much taken up with the representation of her infatuation with Cytherea, already hinted at in the previous chapter. Beyond this, however, it is only once mentioned, when the narrator comments that Cytherea "was often almost compelled to go [to Miss Aldclyffe's room] against her will" (p. 267).

The introduction of what is supposed to be lesbianism into the novel is almost as useless as it is obtrusive. If one can forget the seemingly sexual reference—and it is this which gets in the way—the real meaning and significance of the relationship between the two women can be seen. Miss Aldclyffe is Cytherea I, and the way she becomes involved in the present of this story is by idealizing her past and wishing to have it re-created correctly in the present through the agency of Cytherea II, Miss Graye. Thus what seems to be irrelevant lesbianism is Hardy's attempt to suggest the basic plot and the thematic structure of the novel. On the level of character and the subconscious, it represents Miss Aldclyffe's symbolic ritual for the imposition of her life upon the younger girl, as though by their very closeness the two should become one.

The marriage which Miss Aldclyffe plans for Cytherea is, of course, the wrong one. Aeneas Manston is the villain of the story. The dramatic climax of the novel comes as their marriage takes place—and again the time is early January, as it was when Miss Aldclyffe refused to marry Ambrose Graye. Specifically, the time is the fifth of January, which is called "Old Christmas Eve" (pp. 262–63). Again, Christmas is a favorite time for Hardy: the time, in the myth of history, of the changing of ages; and annually, at New Year's, the time of change from one year to another, with the seeming momentary compression of past and future into a single moment of pure present. This symbol of intensified time is undefined, however, in this or any other novel; it is only through Hardy's repeated use of Christmas and the end of the year that one discovers it.

Almost as soon as this marriage takes place complications occur, the past is exposed, and time stops. Manston's past (he is discovered to be married already) is introduced, and Edward Springrove, Cytherea's proper lover—the proper lover for her in *her* story—simultaneously and coincidentally returns to the scene after an absence of almost eighteen months. Then, from the end of Chapter 13 to the end of Chapter 21, the progress of the novel is held in a sort of stasis. The lapse of time on Hardy's calendar is eighty-two days, but the confusion of Manston's past adventures holds in extended suspension everything but the attempts made to discover and expose that past. Suddenly the suspension is broken, Manston's crime is revealed, and he hangs himself. The long extended climax which has grown from Cytherea's wedding on is finally ended by Manston's death; and Miss Aldclyffe, the character responsible for this action and its crisis, dies as her symbolic revivification fails.

As the present of Cytherea Graye escapes from the imposition of Miss Aldclyffe's past, the intensity which has been built on coincidence is released. Fifteen months after the deaths of Manston and Miss Aldclyffe, Cytherea marries Springrove. The time is Midsummer, and the present fulfills itself, simply, without the interference of the past.

In his second novel, *Under the Greenwood Tree* (1872), Hardy makes a whole story out of the antics and pleasures of his rustic chorus. The result is a delightful, even beautiful, entertainment. The most serious it ever becomes is in the almost whimsical representation of its social theme of the passing of an age, quietly described by the displacement of the "Mellstock Quire" and the installation, in their stead, of an organ. The problem of the novel is one of choice—of lovers, as usual—and its comic poignance is in this dramatization of simple lives.

A Pair of Blue Eyes (1873) is a more ambitious novel, but not really as successful as its predecessor. It is also a more serious novel in the way it sees the world. And technically, from the point of view of Hardy's artistic technique, it is a much more valuable novel for the study of Hardy's method and his later accomplishments. The plot of the novel is again concerned with lovers' choices: this time, however, there are elements introduced experimentally into the fabric of the fiction which are larger than either the characters or their choices. Unless one is to say that Hardy's interest in history—the use of historical reference which so frequently surrounds his characters—is simply an obtrusive, irrelevant obsession which has nothing to do with his, one must try to find out how he makes history work for him.

When Hardy is at his best, his historical sense is genuinely integral to his work. Evelyn Hardy remarks that "the overlapping of the strata of history increasingly impressed Hardy";[5] and as it did, it grew to be the base, the forming principle, of his mythology. One can see the development of his use of history by comparing the simple speech of one of the rustics in *A Pair of Blue Eyes* with that of Dealer Buzzford, later, in *The Mayor of Casterbridge*. The first remarks only on the historical past in telling a local tale: "But once in ancient times one of 'em, when he was at work, changed clothes with King Charles the Second, and saved the King's life" (p. 6). Buzzford tells his tale of the other Charles, compressing the ancient history of Wessex dramatically as he does so:

> "Casterbridge is a old, hoary place o' wickedness, by all account. 'Tis recorded in history that we rebelled against the King one or two hundred years ago, in the time of the Romans." (59)

The overlapping of historical ages is what is used to attract Henry Knight's attention to the peculiarity of his situation several times in *A Pair of Blue Eyes*. He and Elfride Swancourt and Stephen Smith, Elfride's other suitor and Knight's former pupil, meet once in the vault of the ancient Luxellian family. It is in this vault that Elfride is finally to lie, ironically, as the thrice-bereaved Lady Luxellian. Stephen points out one of the coffins on this occasion as that of Elfride's namesake. "Lady Elfride Kingsmore—born Luxellian" (p. 298). This is Elfride's grandmother; and Elfride, Knight, and Stephen are linked together and tied back into the history of repeating difficulties through Elfride I, who as a young girl ran away with her lover.

The idea of ancestry interests Hardy also. In *Desperate Remedies* Miss Aldclyffe's family is introduced as descended from "an ancient family

47

whose genealogical tree was interlaced with some of the most illustrious and well-known in the kingdom" (p. 2). No use is ever made of this reference; it is just there, strangely. In *Tess of the D'Urbervilles* the theme of the decline of an age is represented in Tess's family's degeneration from landed gentry d'Urbervilles to peasant Durbeyfields; and the interrelation of the generations of history is indicated partially by this and partially by the creation of the new d'Urberville in Alec, who acts irrevocably in Tess's present as well as from her past. The Stancys of *A Laodicean* are another old and fallen family; the idea of family is part of the problem of *Two on a Tower*; the ancestry of Edred Fitzpiers figures in *The Woodlanders*; and families go back centuries, unite, regenerate, and repeat themselves in *The Well-Beloved*. "Anyone," says Evelyn Hardy, "who turns the pages of Hardy's copy of the three great volumes of Hutchin's [sic] *History of Dorset* will see how genealogy held him in thrall."[6] In *A Pair of Blue Eyes*, Mr. Swancourt congratulates Stephen Smith—erroneously—on his ancestry (p. 15), and then notes that his own family is rooted "far back in the mists of antiquity" (p. 16). Later, discovering his error in regard to Stephen's family and his daughter's interest in him, Swancourt comments, "We have been coming to nothing for centuries, and now I believe we have got there" (p. 89).

Desmond Hawkins's complaint, that Hardy "loves to drag in an antiquarian tidbit without much concern for its relevance"[7] may seem appropriate commentary on Hardy's use of such reference here. It is certainly valid criticism on a number of occasions. But in the context of Hardy's whole attitude toward time and history, even seemingly irrelevant references to the historical or prehistorical are partially justifiable; he is trying out this pattern of reference as a means of suggesting a larger scope and meaning for his characters and their actions. That is, he is learning to generalize by using his expansive time metaphor.

Perhaps the best example in *A Pair of Blue Eyes* of Hardy's use of the "overlapping strata of history" is in the famous scene on the Cliff Without a Name, involving Elfride and her appropriately named Knight. Coincidence is underlined in several places, especially as Elfride repeats with Knight scenes from her flirtation with his friend and former student, Stephen. As he points these out in the novel, Hardy insists on the idea of repetition or doubling in its plot. Elfride is saved by Knight from a dangerous venture onto the parapet of an old and crumbling church tower. Elfride mentions her sensation to Knight:

"You are familiar, of course, as everybody is, with those strange sensations we sometimes have, that the moment has been in duplicate, or will be."

"That we have lived through the moment before?"

"Or shall again. Well, I felt on the tower that something similar to that scene is again to be common to us both." (185)

It is not déjà-vu which interests Hardy; it is the inverse of that phenomenon which he introduces here in Elfride's sense that the future will at some time repeat this moment. Using "the idiosyncrasy of the artist" as his license, Hardy creates a psychological phenomenon which is more useful and appropriate thematically than déjà-vu. Three chapters later, on the bluff of the Cliff Without a Name, the scene is repeated and fulfilled, with the roles of the two characters reversed. To indicate the seriousness of the moment Hardy draws up descriptively a moment of timelessness, and uses it to reinforce Knight's actual experience. The strange phenomena which are to serve for the moment of timelessness are described before the accident:

"Over that edge . . . where nothing but vacancy appears, is a moving compact mass. The wind strikes the face of the rock, runs up it, rises like a fountain to a height far above our heads, curls over us in an arch, and disperses behind us." (233)

Knight demonstrates what this strange current is like by throwing a small stone over the edge of the cliff. It is carried back up and behind them, in the arc Knight has predicted. "They themselves," the narrator says, "were in a dead calm" (p. 233).

Then Knight accidentally slips over the verge, and is trapped just a few short yards down the edge. As he clings to the bare face of the rock, the narrator conjures up an obvious man-versus-the-world scene through the metaphor of the timelessness of the particular situation:

He reclined hand in hand with the world in its infancy. Not a blade, not an insect, which spoke of the present, was between him and the past. The inveterate antagonism of those black precipices to all strugglers for life is in no way more forcibly suggested than by the paucity of tufts of grass, lichens, or confervae on their outermost edges. (240)

49

The metaphorical effect of this comes from Knight's consciousness of the relationship between the setting and his situation:

> By one of those familiar conjunctions of things wherewith the inanimate world baits the mind of man when he pauses in moments of suspense, opposite Knight's eyes was an imbedded fossil, standing forth in relief from the rock. . . . Separated by millions of years in their lives, Knight and this underling seemed to have met in their place of death. (241)

Through this impressive—to Knight, at least—metaphor of situation, and through the "compression of . . . experiences" usual under such circumstances, the timeless moment is achieved dramatically. "Time closed up like a fan before him," says the narrator. "He saw himself at one extremity of the years, face to face with the beginning and all the intermediate centuries simultaneously" (p. 242). This is the first instance in Hardy's fiction of a dramatic moment of timelessness effectively supported by its descriptive rendering, and brought off with sufficient fullness as a scene.[8] The scene is in relative isolation in the novel, however, and through its exaggeration distorts the shape of the whole. But the technique here introduced is used and reused in Hardy's later novels, and is essential to their artistic structure.

There are other parallels to the later novels throughout *A Pair of Blue Eyes*: parallels of scene, theme, and technique. The opening paragraph of Chapter 2 stands as a sort of practice in narrative description for the opening set piece of *The Return of the Native*. The effect is not the same, nor does it have the rich symbolic and metaphoric texture of the introduction to Egdon Heath and Rainbarrow; still, the basis for the later description can be seen here. More important than this descriptive introduction, however, are the several narrative comments and germs of scenes which first appear here and are reused later. One such scene might be pointed out specifically: a minor one, in which Elfride is unable to confess to Knight her former infatuation with Stephen (pp. 346–47). The resolution of this attempt at confession is similar to Tess's problem with her hidden past, in her scene with Angel Clare before their marriage (pp. 165–66); and the scene of Elfride's forced confession and its result (pp. 376–84) is parallel to Tess's with Angel on the first night of their marriage (pp. 286–301).

The line repetitions are more specific. As Elfride, Knight, and Stephen part after their strangely premonitory meeting in the Luxellian vault, the narrator comments, "Measurement of life should be proportioned rather to the intensity of the experience than to its actual length" (p. 303). As it is used here, the statement is a commentary specifically and especially on the nature of the scene just completed, and generally on the kind of dramatic existence in which man is constantly involved. The same assertion is made in almost the same words in *The Return of the Native* (p. 161), and again in *Tess of the D'Urbervilles* (p. 160). The next sentence in *A Pair of Blue Eyes* reads, "Their glance, but a moment chronologically, was a season in their history." This statement expands time and, if one accepts with Hardy the dictum immediately preceding it, increases the size and importance of the scene. The line is repeated more legitimately in *The Mayor of Casterbridge* at the climax of Michael Henchard's scene on Mai-Dun. Henchard sees Sailor Newson coming out of the past into his present, enacting a coincidence of repetition that spans and condenses twenty years, and the narrator reports that Henchard "lived a lifetime the moment he saw it" (p. 358).

The first major indication of Hardy's serious vision comes in *Far From the Madding Crowd* (1874). In ambition and accomplishment both, it is the most significant of the ten minor novels. Its heroes are comic romance characters, Gabriel Oak and Bathsheba Everdene; but the world around them has a potential for more serious drama. Not only is Weatherbury inhabited by simple Wessex folk and lovers who will find a happy end; it also shelters—and exposes—Farmer Boldwood and Fanny Robin.

Part of the ambition of *Far From the Madding Crowd* is the introduction of Wessex itself, Hardy's "partly real, partly dream-country" (p. vi). In the Preface of 1895–1902, Hardy comments that the novels he projected for himself at the time of the writing of this one "seemed to require a territorial definition of some sort to lend unity to their scene" (p. v). The unity of scene which he establishes for them in Wessex not only ties them together, but more importantly it gives each novel individually a specific stage for the support of its action. As Hardy exploits this world in setting the novels which follow *Far From the Madding Crowd*, its exhumation from a past no more recent than "the Norman Conquest" or the times of "the Heptarchy" (p. vi) becomes a major part of his art. In this novel, however, though the description of the setting is rich and full, it is limited in its function and supports the action in only the most neutral way. The fabricated intensity which the characters live in or through, whether comic or pathetic or near-tragic, is not really related to the temporally and spatially expansive world which Wessex can so easily represent.

The Preface to *Far From the Madding Crowd* also contains Hardy's description of the changing age in southern England. In the novel itself, however, this theme is hardly taken up. *Far From the Madding Crowd* is not an historical novel, but, as Hardy called it, a novel of "Character and Environment"; and it is primarily a comic novel, with a strain of serious pathos. Fanny Robin's plight, though in its conception somewhat melodramatic, is described with sincere and effective compassion. The destruction of Boldwood is little short of tragic; and the figure he presents, of the good man silenced by his own intensity and destroyed by the failure of his dreams, prefigures strongly Michael Henchard, Hardy's "Man of Character." But these elements are only parts of the whole, and are subordinate to the essential comedy of the whole. The resolution of the novel is a happy one, as goodness and faithfulness, somewhat subdued by experience, prevail.

Hardy's interest in coincidence and the grotesque is turned largely toward this comic effect in *Far From the Madding Crowd*, and his representation of condensed or extended time is directed for the most part toward the comic limitation of his characters. Throughout the novel the comedy of human relations is described, and the pervasive tone of the narrative supports and justifies this point of view. The novel begins with a sketch of Gabriel Oak: "When Farmer Oak smiled, the corners of his mouth spread till they were within an unimportant distance of his ears, his eyes were reduced to chinks, and diverging wrinkles appeared round them, extending upon his countenance like the rays in a rudimentary sketch of the rising sun." (p. 1). The description runs on for several paragraphs, one devoted to Gabriel's watch, which "had a peculiarity of going either too fast or not at all" (p. 10). The perversity of this instrument seems likely to insure Gabriel's being at best at the right place at the wrong time: "The smaller of its hands, too, occasionally slipped round on the pivot, and thus, though the minutes were told with precision, nobody could be quite certain what hour they belonged to" (p. 2). The watch thus doesn't measure time at all—suggesting, perhaps, the impossibility of man's attempt to make existence and history so easily chronological.[9] Though the watch keeps track of immediate things, it has no relation to any world larger than sixty minutes can comprehend—unless, of course, it condenses time, metaphorically, into the chance repetition of a single hour. This latter could be true, if the novel were *The Mayor of Casterbridge* or *Tess of the D'Urbervilles*, if the character were Henchard or Tess, plagued by the past and its repetition. But the character set with this careless marking of time is Gabriel Oak, who will wait through fifty-seven chapters for Bathsheba Everdene before the happy ending can be found.

The novel also seems more serious than comic as Hardy prepares for Bathsheba's introduction at the end of Chapter 2. The description of the place reminds one of the later opening description of Egdon Heath in *The Return of the Native*. The first sentence of the chapter reads, "It was nearly midnight on the eve of St. Thomas's, the shortest day of the year" (p. 8). The time and the time of year seem significant, if not ominous: midnight, the shortest day of the year, and Christmastime all suggest serious arrest and then change.

The place is Norcombe Hill, "covered on its northern side by an ancient and decaying plantation of beeches" (p. 8). The suggestive details are here: the wind is strong, the sky is grandly open, the rapidly turning dome of the universe is exposed to view. But from this description and its implications Hardy quickly returns to an immediate perspective view, and the narrator suggests the difficulty in believing "that the consciousness of such majestic speeding is derived from a tiny human frame" (p. 10). The double effect of this statement—the expression of what is almost a dilemma for the narrator—is typical of Hardy's problem with man's size. Man is infinitesimally small in relation to the universe; yet he is so large as sometimes to comprehend, often to fight against his fate. This difficulty is rather easily resolvable in *Far From the Madding Crowd*. Because the hero is limited in dramatic stature by his comic conception, the contest between man and the comic universe can be resolved at the expense of this character. Oak plays a tune on his flute, in competition with the wind and the sounds of nature. His tones are clearer than the wind's, and his tune is all his own. But Gabriel plays locked up in a tiny shepherd's hut on the hill, "a small Noah's Ark on a small Ararat" (p. 10), and the heroic aspect of the competition is turned to comedy. The dimensions are limited, and there is no option for grand metaphor or microcosm: Gabriel's Ark is of the design and size generally used "by toy-makers" (p. 10).

Throughout this novel cosmic power is kept at a distance, though it does seem on occasion close to intervention; and the condensing, extending time which could suggest tragedy is tied back and through to the present in a series of humorous and deflationary ways. At the sheep-shearing in Bathsheba's barn the narrator comments on the harmony of folk and setting, and the easy, unhurried continuity of time:

> in Weatherbury three or four score years were included in the mere present, and nothing less than a century set a mark on its face or tone. Five decades hardly modified the cut of a gaiter, the embroidery of a smock-frock, by the breadth of a hair. Ten generations failed to alter the turn of a single phrase. In these Wessex nooks the busy outsider's ancient times are only old; his old times are still new; his present is futurity. (166)

This tranquillity is relaxing and reassuring; and because the tranquil past is long here, progress can be viewed with a light irreverence and history can be deprived momentarily of its more somber dramatic character.

Age—the age of a man this time—is treated similarly. By his non-response to the orderly passing of time, Grandfather Smallbury, the "ancient maltster" (p. 60), counts his age to be a dignified and thoroughly wonderful one hundred and seventeen. When this is cut down by reason and mathematics to a mere ninety-one he feels hurt, and in a pet of comic paranoia says, "I suppose ye'll say next I be no age at all to speak of" (pp. 71–72).

There are numerous other similar texts in *Far From the Madding Crowd*. Hardy's use of time and history to deny comically the exaggeration of character and event is generally contradictory to his usual method in the later novels; but it is important that he has the means, now, of defining the size of his characters and their world. The metaphor he uses in this novel is the same metaphor of expanded time that he will use in the dramatic argument of Clym's novel; he has simply reversed its effect here.

Even the passing of the age is viewed as comic in *Far From the Madding Crowd*. One of the rustic critics at Warren's malthouse reports that

an old well is "turned into a solid iron pump with a large stone trough."
Another—it seems to be Grandfather Smallbury again—replies, in a
parody of sententiousness, "Dear, dear—how the face of nations alter,
and what we live to see nowadays" (p. 124). But for all of the comedy
of this kind of incidental abuse of a larger time-consciousness, repetitive
time and intense timelessness do have a part in the novel. The fickleness
of fate or chance and the potential constancy of man's affections play
back and forth across the characters: destroying Fanny, Troy, and Boldwood, saving the still innocent Oak and a finally subdued Bathsheba.
Once again Hardy asks his readers to interpret his characters by watching them repeat their actions over and over again. Disaster, for Hardy,
comes always as the present is interrupted by the intrusion of the past.

The climax of the action comes in Chapter 53, as Troy returns from
his long absence and supposed death to interrupt the engagement of
Boldwood and Bathsheba. Again, the time of the year chosen for the
climax is Christmas. There is a party at Boldwoods on Christmas eve,
and Bathsheba is scheduled to accept his proposal on this occasion.
Except for the time-of-year metaphor—the use of Christmas as intense
time—Hardy offers no preparation for the dramatic interruption of
events which Troy's return effects. The narrator does insist on the irony
of return, however, just at the moment of Troy's intrusion. Boldwood
calls to the unrecognized interloper as he arrives, "Come in, come in!
. . . and drink a cheerful Christmas beaker with us, stranger!"

> Even then Boldwood did not recognize that the impersonator
> of Heaven's persistent irony towards him, who had once be-
> fore broken in upon his bliss, scourged him, and snatched his
> delight away, had come to do these things a second time.
> (433)

As Troy tries to claim his wife, Boldwood rebels. The irony—the frustration—of this return destroys his sanity. His straight and passionate
devotion to Bathsheba leaves him no alternative, and he murders
Troy. Then, his madness and pain combining to form an heroic sense of
duty, Boldwood retreats to Casterbridge jail, and turns himself in:
"the door was closed behind him, and he walked the world no more"
(p. 436).

Oak, however, has remained passive in his fidelity to Bathsheba, and
he is finally rewarded with a sobered bride. Boldwood's love has been

an intense passion, and it is of such stuff that ecstasies and tragedies are made. But since his smiling introduction Oak has lived in a comic world, and intensity of experience has never been the code of his character. Boldwood's attachment to Bathsheba is intense and unrelenting; and each time he approaches her it is like a repetition of the first. Their situation is singular, from Boldwood's point of view, even in time: he buys her wedding presents and writes the dates on the boxes six years hence, in anticipation of the time when they will marry. For Oak, on the other hand, time is continuous and progressive; and he wins Bathsheba in the end simply by waiting. Throughout the novel, from their first separation on, Gabriel keeps returning to Bathsheba; and in the end, his time being fulfilled, he is rewarded for this simple recurrence.

Hardy manages the balance and mixture of comedy and pathos well in *Far From the Madding Crowd*. In Fanny Robin and Boldwood he has the characters of a pathetic, near-tragic story, and in Oak and his chorus of supporters he has the cast for a comedy. The predominance of this comic element is what separates *Far From the Madding Crowd* from *The Return of the Native*, *The Mayor of Casterbridge*, *The Woodlanders*, *Tess of the D'Urbervilles*, and *Jude the Obscure*. The elements of seriousness and stern compassion which characterize these novels are present in this, but it is more essentially akin in its lightness to that first of the "Novels of Character and Environment," *Under the Greenwood Tree*.

The theme, manner, and vision of *The Hand of Ethelberta* (1876) make it a sort of sport among Hardy's works, seemingly a crude attempt at something like a comedy of manners. Yet it is in some ways very much within the Hardy canon, despite its London and society involvement. It can hardly even pretend to be what one calls the comedy of manners because of its typically Hardyean reliance on the grotesques of situation and coincidental event. *The Hand of Ethelberta* is not a great or even a polished novel, but it is reasonably well-written, excites an interest, and even as it slips into somewhat confusing oppositions in single characters it attracts the imagination. But the exaggeration of circumstances is disproportionate to Hardy's thematic ambition and the worth of the occasion, and there is no real strength or serious significance to either character or character involvement. Because of a few basic merits as a story told, however, and for what it demonstrates of

Hardy's discovery and development of a style, a technique, and a particular aesthetic and philosophical vision, *The Hand of Ethelberta* is worth more than a cursory dismissal.

The plot opens typically: out of the past comes Christopher Julian, a former sweetheart, into Ethelberta's present. The meeting of the two occurs in the first chapter, and a few months later, in Chapter 2, Christopher explains the past and the coincidence of its revival in the present. His first love affair with Ethelberta failed, he tells his sister, some years ago. Then on a recent summer visit (that which took place in Chapter 1) to Anglebury, while he "was crossing the heath"—actually the edge of Egdon Heath—he "met this very woman" (p. 20). What reminds him of the meeting now, in the autumn, is the arrival by post of a volume of poems written by Ethelberta. The last poem in the book is called "Cancelled Words," and Julian recognizes that the poem is addressed to him. The meeting on the heath has revived the past, and Ethelberta's poem insists on the continuing vitality of that past; thus the words in print, in fact, have not been "cancelled."

The plot of this "Comedy in Chapters" continues from here, as suitors, including Julian, apply for the favor of Ethelberta. Their suits and the situations in the story which accompany them are not very interesting; the only noteworthy thing about them is their conception—and each of the suitors for Ethelberta's hand tries to take her back into some past. None of this past-reference, however, seems really significant. For the most part, it simply indicates again Hardy's interest in the idea of the past, of the juxtaposition of existences in time or of times in one existence. The visit Ethelberta makes to Corvsgate castle is the most successful and useful of the novel's references to the past, though its introduction is by no means essential to action, theme, or structure. It is a good scene, carefully worked out dramatically, and it is the occasion for the construction of a typically Hardyean metaphor of the relation of man to space, time, and history.

Ethelberta is interested in going to Corvsgate because "what was left in any shape from the past was her constant interest, because it called her to herself and fortified her mind" (p. 256). The suggested perspective view of life is reductive, naturally, rather than expansive: "the hints that perishing remnants afforded her of the attenuating effects of time even upon great struggles corrected the apparent scale of her own." (pp. 256–57). As her view is described, however, it seems to be more than a view just of the area. The terms chosen for its representation are those which would seem to make it a world, in both space and time:

> the country on each side lay beneath her like a map, domains behind domains, parishes by the score, harbours, fir-woods, and little inland seas mixing curiously together. Thence she ambled along through a huge cemetery of barrows, containing human dust from prehistoric times. (258)

The obvious inference from all of this is that of the humility of the individual situation in the historical universe. The cosmic insignificance, or the comic futility, of Ethelberta's struggle to maintain her family, her sham existence in society, and her final sacrifice of herself in marriage to Lord Mountclere are perhaps described in contrast by what she sees as she stands "on the top of a giant's grave in this antique land" (p. 258).

Still, I question the validity of this scene for the novel. The details of history given here are inessential to its thematic focus. At best, the repeated reference is typically Hardyean; and perhaps map, barrow, and castle in this novel are what suggest themselves so successfully in the next that he wrote, *The Return of the Native*. Egdon's profile is already strongly evident in "the everlasting heath, the black hills bulging against the sky, the barrows upon their round summits like warts on a swarthy skin" (p. 396).[10] Eustacia Vye assumes Ethelberta's posture atop the "giant's grave in this antique land" (p. 258) for her role as "queen of the solitude" in Chapter 2 of the later novel. And in recounting the history of Corvsgate castle, the crudely named Dr. Yore traces its development from "a mount with a few earthworks" through Norman and Elizabethan times "and so downward through time to the final overthrow of the stern old pile" (pp. 265–66). This "final overthrow" is what Egdon Heath seems to await, one is told, in the opening of *The Return of the Native*.

One last point might be made here about *The Hand of Ethelberta*. As far as its significance for Hardy's developing art is concerned, the novel shows well how strong was his inclination toward the grotesques of coincidental or recurrent events. Supporting this usage within the novel, indirectly, is a review of criticism which seems almost explicitly to be Hardy's discussion of some of his own ideas about fiction. Ethelberta is a story-teller in London for a season, and the critical essays which Hardy quotes in the novel are reviews of Ethelberta's performances. Her art is not just in reading stories, or even in dramatic readings. What is remarkable about Ethelberta is that she is a "Novel-teller" (p. 125). One of the critics quoted says:

> "When once we get away from the magic influence of the story-teller's eye and tongue, we perceive how improbable, even impossible is the tissue of events to which we have been listening with so great a sense of reality, and we feel almost angry with ourselves at having been the victims of such utter illusion." (125)

Hardy was constantly aware of the problem of artistic illusion, and his vision of life and action dramatically foreshortened made the difficulty of suspending disbelief all the more a problem. Unable to use tongue and eye as his "Novel-teller" could to persuade her hearers of the reality of her "improbable, even impossible," "marvellous" tales, Hardy had to devise some other way to guarantee his illusion. The technique he chose was descriptive—and though it does not work well in this novel, it is still at work in principle. The metaphor of setting, for Hardy, serves to attract the reader just as Ethelberta's personality enchants her listener.[11] The illusion to be defended is Hardy's vision of the world, which is represented in that description of the symbolically vitalized state from which, in a sense, the novel is "told." Stage and setting, then, provide the sense and mood of the work metaphorically, and the dimensions of the dramatic action—the ring, the arena for what Hardy recalled as the "collision between the individual and the general"[12]—are established. The first centrally significant and fully successful use of this technique is in *The Return of the Native*, published next after *The Hand of Ethelberta*, in 1878.

NOTES TO CHAPTER III

1 Hardy might also have been impressed by an earlier passage in this same Introduction of Scott's, in which he discusses his choice of setting for *The Monastery*:

> The localities of Melrose suited well the scenery of the proposed story; the ruins themselves form a splendid theatre for any tragic incident which might be brought forward; joined to the vicinity of the fine river, with so many recollections of former times. . . .

The situation possessed farther recommendations. On the opposite bank of the Tweed might be seen the remains of ancient enclosures, surrounded by sycamores and ash-trees of considerable size. These had once formed the crofts or arable ground of a village, now reduced to a single hut, the abode of a fisherman, who also manages a ferry. The cottages, even the church which once existed there, have sunk into vestiges hardly to be traced without visiting the spot, the inhabitants having gradually withdrawn to the more prosperous town of Galashiels, which has risen into consideration, within two miles of their neighborhood.

2. F. E. Hardy, *Life of Hardy*, p. 177. See p. 24 and p. 118 for the narrative representation of this idea in the novels.

3. Ibid., p. 228.

4. Ibid., p. 229.

5. Ibid., p. 222.

6. Ibid., p. 224.

7. *Thomas Hardy* (London, 1950), p. 87.

8. See Hawkins, *Thomas Hardy*, p. 27.

9. Cf. the clocks in Chapter 4 of *The Mayor of Casterbridge*, which indicate more seriously something very much the same, and the clocks in Chapter 5 of *The Return of the Native*, which prove by their disagreement that "on Egdon Heath there was no absolute hour of the day."

10. In *The Return of the Native*, Rainbarrow is described as "a wart on an Atalantean brow" (p. 13).

11. Cf. Hardy on story-telling in F. E. Hardy, *Life of Hardy*—"A story must be exceptional enough to justify its telling. We tale-tellers are all Ancient Mariners, and none of us is warranted in stopping Wedding Guests . . . unless he has something more unusual to relate than the ordinary experience of every average man and woman" (p. 252).

12. See "Candour in English Fiction," *The New Review*, January 1890: "There is [now] a revival of the artistic instincts toward great dramatic motives—setting forth that 'collision between the individual and the general'—formerly worked out with such force by the Periclean and Elizabethan dramatists, to name no other" (p. 16; reprinted in Harold Orel, *Thomas Hardy's Personal Writings* [Lawrence, Kansas, 1966], p. 114.)

IV

THE MINOR NOVELS:
DEVELOPMENT OF TECHNIQUE (1880–1897)

> *Time shuts up together, and all between then and*
> *now seems not to have been!*
>
> ENTER A DRAGOON
> *December, 1889*

After *The Return of the Native*, the direction of
Hardy's career as a novelist should have been set.
His next novel should have been *The Mayor of Casterbridge*. But as
with most artists, so too with Hardy: it is impossible to diagram a career
so simply. After *The Return of the Native* come *The Trumpet-Major,
A Laodicean*, and *Two on a Tower*; between *The Mayor of Caster-
bridge* and *Tess of the D'Urbervilles* comes *The Woodlanders*; and *The
Well-Beloved*, revised from an earlier story, comes last, after *Jude the
Obscure*.

But though Hardy's work after 1878 cannot be described as a progression from success to success, still even the minor novels which follow
The Return of the Native all contribute in some way to the total
formulation of his vision and his art. *The Trumpet-Major* describes in
part Hardy's starting to think about his grand scheme for the epic-
drama; his notes for what was eventually to become *The Dynasts* begin
in 1875 and run through 1882 with little interruption.[1] *A Laodicean* is
another trying out of the typical Hardyean plot scheme in comedy; and
were it not for the complications of his extreme illness during most of
its composition, it might have turned out much better. According to its
preface, *Two on a Tower* was grandly conceived to measure man against

the universe; that it fails of this ambition may be because Hardy did not yet have either the sure technique or the proper tale for such a work. He seems to have found both, however, in the two years after this novel's publication, during the long writing of *The Mayor of Casterbridge*, which he began in 1884.[2] *The Woodlanders*, Hardy's next novel, is an attempt to strike again the tune of *Far From the Madding Crowd*, but in a grander, more somber, and more pathetic key. *The Well-Beloved*, finally, is Hardy's fantastic attempt to dramatize just the essence of his idea about the intensity of existence; in making this fantasy, he exaggerates the entire setting and its every detail into a singularly insistent metaphor of stilled time to support the plot and the theme.

In 1879 Hardy mentioned to Leslie Stephen a plan for an historical novel. Mrs. Hardy quotes Stephen's reply:

> "I can only tell you what is my own taste, but I rather think that my taste is in this case the common one. I think that a historical character in a novel is almost always a nuisance; but I like to have a bit of history in the background, so to speak; to feel that George III is just around the corner."[3]

Most of Hardy's fiction not only has that "bit of history in the background," it uses that history for more than just background. But in *The Trumpet-Major*, published in 1880, Hardy wrote a straight historical novel, following Stephen's suggestion almost to the letter.

The Trumpet-Major is Hardy's only actual historical novel, though they all have reasonably specific dates in English history for their action.[4] But in *The Trumpet-Major* the actual historical time of the action is important in and of itself—almost as important, in a sense, as the characters who inhabit it. Hardy's many gifts include the ability to isolate human beings and their human significance from the fabric of history as well as the ability to attach a symbolically universal history or myth-history to the particular situation of a character. *The Trumpet-Major* exemplifies the first of these talents. Hardy finds the life of his characters, their vitality and their attractiveness, and he displays his discovery dramatically by placing them within the framework of their documented historical setting. Hardy's primary interest is, as always, with his characters, and his sympathies are with them as people rather than with their time in history. Still it seems that this novel is a romantic attempt to recreate for its own sake, almost, a disappearing and soon to be forgotten time in history. As he says in the 1895 preface, he is concerned in this novel with constructing "a coherent narrative of past times from the fragmentary information furnished by survivors" (p. vi); one of the scenes, the narrator says, "has been described [to him] times out of number by members of the Loveday family and other aged people now passed away" (p. 39).

Neither the time nor the events of this novel have any particular dramatic relation to the present of its telling, nor is the time itself complex or compounded. Rather, the historical past is treated simply as an independent segment of time, unrelated to any scheme of the general fate of man. The time of the novel is just a background. The characters and the situations in which they are involved are simple in their significance, and the justification for the telling of their story is that it is a pleasant story imagined and recreated nostalgically out of a time which merits artistic preservation.

The material Hardy uses in *The Trumpet-Major* is the same material he uses in the Wessex scenes of *The Dynasts*; and there as here these scenes are essentially scenes of comic relief. Hardy's comedy is often brilliantly entertaining; and were it not for the grandeur of his larger, more serious works we would perhaps find a way to remark our appreciation of his comedy more frequently and more fully than we do.

A Laodicean is badly melodramatic, and overall probably the worst of Hardy's novels. We should be interested in the parties to the romance, but they fail to excite our response, and are overshadowed by the formulation of the argument and its execution in the plot itself. The plot is built upon that typically Hardyean argument of several plans to restore the past into the present coupled with several unwanted intrusions of the past into the present. Paula Power, the heroine, wants to restore Stancy castle, a "fossil of feudalism" (p. 22), an "ancient pile" (p. 37) "along whose steps sunburnt Tudor soldiers and other renowned dead men had doubtless walked many times" (p. 25). Captain de Stancy, of the fallen family which once owned the estate, wants to restore the de Stancy line through marriage with Paula. De Stancy's rival is George Somerset, the young architect hired by Paula to direct the actual restoration of her castle. In the end, the castle is not restored, nor is the de Stancy line; de Stancy's own guilty past intrudes into his present in the person of young Will Dare, his illegitimate son, who destroys de Stancy's chances and then destroys the castle itself. Although the past is thus obliterated, Paula still feels the attraction of its romance. She and Somerset, now her husband, agree "that it would be well to make an opportunity of a misfortune, and leaving the edifice in ruins start their married life in a mansion of independent construction hard by the old one, unencumbered with the ghosts of an unfortunate line" (p. 481). As Paula thinks of this, however, her adventure with the past teases her spirit and she sighs to George, to close the novel, "I wish my castle wasn't burnt; and I wish you were a de Stancy!" (p. 481).

This peculiar elaboration of the plot and the argument does not, by itself, save the novel. The characters seem more like tokens than people as they think, speak, act, and exist according to the formula Hardy has prepared. Informational elements introduced supposedly to clarify or describe the characters frequently turn out to be more relevant to Hardy's thesis than they are to the characters. This explains in part why Captain de Stancy and his bastard son are not satisfactorily developed as characters, and why Hardy attempts to establish Paula through the use of such a strange set of interests as he gives her. Dare is hardly even proposed as a character in the novel, and his conspiracy with de Stancy makes it almost equally unnecessary for de Stancy to become a real person. The introduction of Dare as the emblem of the Captain's past is all that is needed to define him in relation to the argument, and a stereotype of tempter, villain, and lover is substituted for what should have been his dramatic credibility. Hardy creates Paula as a young person interested both in things modern and in things antique, and the details which describe these eccentric interests are proposed as the evidences for her character and personality. The modern in her character is represented by her telegraph, which obtrudes throughout the novel as a clever trick and a silly distraction; the past is planted with references to her interests in the castle, and in "hoary mediaeval families with ancestors in alabaster and primogenitive renown" (p. 371).

There are many more details, similarly descriptive of Paula's peculiar situation. She is a modern girl on the one hand; and on the other she is first tempted by the romantic past and then threatened by it. The temptation is that of the castle; the threat is that of de Stancy and Dare—who are, again, attached to that past and to its symbol, the castle. Because of the predominance of the setting of the story, the significance of the characters as characters—as people—is lost. The problem is similar to that which one encounters with Egdon Heath in *The Return of the Native*, though Stancy Castle is hardly so interesting as that "great inviolable place." Yet so much of what happens in this novel happens to the castle or in relation to it that the first English edition of the novel bore as its full title *A Laodicean; or, The Castle of the De Stancys*—which might indicate either Hardy's indecision as to the central focus of his novel or perhaps simply his awareness of the duality of that focus.

The formula Hardy uses for the plot of *A Laodicean* produces, finally, a comedy; and though the comedy is not an artistic success, it is an interesting experiment for Hardy. By inverting the results of each of Paula Power's confrontations with the past, by turning them from comic to tragic, one comes up with several of the central scenes in the story of Tess Durbeyfield. Paula is enamored of a past which is not her own and which, because of this, she can escape when it threatens her. Tess, however, is pushed into exploring her own family history. Paula is threatened by a new de Stancy, Tess by a new d'Urberville; and whereas de Stancy's past is revealed in time for Paula to reject him and it, Tess is seduced by Alec, and thereafter is unable to escape from either that one sin in her own past or her metaphorically relevant past as a d'Urberville, until finally she reenacts in an ironically altered way an old d'Urberville legend and murders her seducer.

In *Tess of the D'Urbervilles* the formulaic involvement of the past is used metaphorically and symbolically as support for the dramatic situation, and the fate of the central character predominates over all the other considerations in the novel. But that novel is one of the "Novels of Character and Environment"; and *A Laodicean* is one of what Hardy called his "Novels of Ingenuity."

Hardy listed his next novel, *Two on a Tower* (1882), among his "Romances and Fantasies." It is the third novel in as many years, and though significant in its ambition, it is little more than entertaining in its execution, except as it demonstrates again Hardy's typical way of composing a story. In the Preface of 1895 he explains what had been his aim in writing the novel:

> This slightly-built romance was the outcome of a wish to set the emotional history of two infinitesimal lives against the stupendous background of the stellar universe, and to

> impart to readers the sentiment that of these contrasting
> magnitudes the smaller might be the greater to them as
> men. (v)

The ambition is typically Hardyean, both in its concern to establish the importance of human activity and in its attempt to involve the cosmic world with such activity. In execution, however, *Two on a Tower* fails on both counts. The "stupendous background" is never successfully brought into relation with the action, and the "emotional history" of the characters involved is not significant enough, dramatically, to bear comparison with any such grand scheme.

The universe of the novel is set in the usual way both in space and in time, with reference to an ancient past glossing the description of an isolated place. The novel opens on "the old Melchester Road" in Wessex, and the "central feature" of the landscape is "a circular isolated hill" atop which stands the tower (p. 1). The hill is initially described in the manuscript[5] as "an isolated hill" (fol. 1), but then its mythologically suggestive circularity is added interlinearly and it becomes

were
an old Roman camp—if it <s>was</s> not an old

castle, or an old Saxon field of Witenagemote
British <s>one</s>—

<s>an</s> remains of an   an
with   outer and inner vallum.

(fol. 3)

Supposedly "Many ancient Britons lie buried" around the tower (p. 65), and there are "palaeolithic dead men feeding [the] roots" of the forest surrounding it (p. 122). The narrator tries to attach his hero and the main action of the romance to the reputation of this long past. But the ancient has no emotional relevance to the situation here as it does, say, in *The Return of the Native*; and the situation of the present does not match the situation from the past dramatically as it does in *The Mayor of Casterbridge* and *Tess of the D'Urbervilles*. Hardy asserts a connection between the present circumstances of Swithin St. Cleeve and Lady Constantine and their setting:

> What events had been enacted in that earthen camp since
> it was first thrown up, nobody could say; but the primitive

simplicity of the young man's preparations accorded well with the prehistoric spot on which they were made. Embedded under his feet were possibly even now rude trinkets that had been worn at bridal ceremonies of the early inhabitants. Little signified those ceremonies to-day, or the happiness or otherwise of the contracting parties. That his own rite, nevertheless, signified much, was the inconsequent reasoning of Swithin, as it is of many another bridegroom besides; and he, like the rest, went on with his preparations in that mood which sees in his stale repetition the wondrous possibilities of an untried move. (133)

But the connection doesn't convince us—or, if it does, not in the way Hardy wanted. Rather than enhancing the action of the romance metaphorically, the significance of this gloss is to diminish the story's importance. By making Swithin's preparations for his marriage—and this marriage is the central issue of the whole plot—"inconsequent" though "unconventional," Hardy reduces him to the cast of an ordinary young man doing, unconvincingly, extraordinary melodramatic things.

Swithin is said to be aware of a connection between actions and their setting, as the "vivid circumstances of his life" cause him "ever to remember the external scenes in which they were set" (p. 265), and at the climax of the action Lady Constantine finds the historically oriented setting of the tower "an appropriate background" for what is happening (p. 122). But the setting has no essential connection with the action; its historical character is completely irrelevant.[6] Hardy expresses his theory about the unchanging, ironically "indifferent" nature of times in this world, but in doing so he destroys the "infinitesimal" creatures for whom he wants our sympathy. In *The Return of the Native* he diminishes Clym in relation to the universe, and gives him the most ordinary of careers, initially; but he can build Clym back up again, because of what he is and what he will choose to do. Though Clym may be relatively small physically, he can still be as large as Prometheus through his courage; and though the action that takes place on Egdon Heath is not actually that "final overthrow" which the heath awaits, in terms of Clym's intense and painful experience and his moral courage in the face of it, the action is grandly significant. In *Two on a Tower* Hardy cuts Swithin down, but because neither his moral character nor his dramatic situation is important enough, he cannot be reconstructed; and no amount of suggestive reference about his fitting the dimensions of a larger world than that which he inhabits will help. The metaphor of history, which Hardy employs half-heartedly in this novel, can only support a character; it cannot make one.

Swithin and Lady Constantine have to become significant characters because, as Hardy planned the novel, they must act out their drama—their "emotional history" is all it is to be—in relation to one which they sometimes watch in the stellar world, and they are not supposed to suffer by the comparison. On the occasion of their first and accidental meeting at the tower, Swithin describes the "catastrophe" of the "cyclone in the sun" which he is watching through his telescope (p. 7). Lady Constantine pauses, "as if to consider the weight of that event in the scale of terrene life," then asks, "Will it make any difference to us here?" Hardy does not allow the young astronomer to answer the question, thus leaving unstated the proposed relevance of this cosmic maelstrom to the lives of his characters. The sun suffers such catastrophes "often enough," says Swithin—which could suggest that calamity should be viewed as a common occurrence in this life, if solar phenomena were a reflection of earthly events. But the connection is not made, nor could it be made, since the drama of Swithin St. Cleeve's romance with Vivette Constantine is not one of even everyday cosmic significance.

Hardy gives Swithin a telescope much in the same way that he assigns Paula Power a telegraph; and the adolescent intellectualism which Swithin's telescope represents hardly qualifies him for a principal's role in man's struggle against the universe. His partner has as little claim, perhaps less. She complains unheroically that Swithin should not study the stars: "It makes you feel human insignificance too plainly," she says (p. 32). Thinking of such things, she continues, "overpowers me! . . . It makes me feel that it is not worth while to live; it quite annihilates me" (p. 32). Swithin's response to this admission of the "infinitesimal" measure of human existence "against the stupendous background of the stellar universe" is that he simply loses himself in the larger world of the stars: "think how it must annihilate me to be, as it were, in constant suspension amid them night after night" (p. 32).

Swithin's "suspension" is important for Hardy.[7] Swithin's knowledge of the workings of the larger world is supposed to prepare him to comprehend and thus to bear the intense crisis to come in his own world. And though Hardy does not achieve an effective correlation of the human world and the cosmic, there is still the frequent assertion of the figurative parallel, which is fulfilled when the cyclone, the "circular hurricane" (p. 120), strikes the tower. The "resulting catastrophe" is that "the dome that had covered the tower has been whirled off bodily" (p. 120), and St. Cleeve and Vivette are left exposed to "Nature's crushing mechanics" (p. 119) and their plans for elopement are upset. The storm is referred to as having an "apocalyptic effect" (p. 122), as though enacted from "a chapter in Revelation."[8] But this cyclone and its "catastrophe," though mimicking those of the sun which Swithin has watched in his state of "constant suspension," do not correspond dramatically, and are not worthy of such exaggeration. The characters involved are still the characters of a small romance, and the phenomenal situation is melodramatic.

Again, the technique Hardy wants to use and the theme he wants to use it for are bigger than his subject matter. The great plan, reminiscent in its ambition of *The Return of the Native*, is not realized in the execution. *Two on a Tower* was written between early December of 1881 and 19 September 1882 at the outside; Hardy himself said that "though the plan of the story was carefully thought out, the actual writing was lamentably hurried."[9] By the end of February 1883 Hardy had completed *The Romantic Adventures of a Milkmaid*, which he described as "a short hastily written novel."[10] Then he began work in earnest on his next novel, which occupied him "for at least a year," through 17 April 1885.[11] It is in this novel, *The Mayor of Casterbridge*, that Hardy accomplishes something like what he planned for *Two on a Tower*. Michael Henchard meets his fate with the dignity of a hero, and his character is in itself significant enough to let him fit a metaphor which measures and includes, not the cosmic space which is presented in *Two on a Tower*, but universal time. In *The Mayor of Casterbridge* Hardy finds a proper hero and a suitable story; and turning his personal interests and his dramatic vision to the service of his art, he makes skillful, sophisticated use of the techniques which he tried and developed in his first nine novels.

Although *The Woodlanders* (1888), the novel which Hardy wrote following *The Mayor of Casterbridge*, is not a major novel, it still deserves much fuller treatment on its own terms and merits than I can give it here.[12] It is a rich novel, eloquent, beautiful, and sad. Perhaps there is too much, however, of "melancholy romanticism" (a phrase Hardy uses in the novel with reference to one of the characters) for *The Woodlanders* to impress one very much, or for the impression to last. The novel and some of the characters in it are strong and vital: Giles Winterborne and Marty South are two of Hardy's finest and fullest creations. Giles is an early Jude, without Jude's ambition and thus without his tragedy, and Marty is both a model for Tess in her simplicity and sensitivity and an untutored Elizabeth-Jane in her passive acceptance of the way life works. These two characters are supported by other finely created people, like the Melburys and their daughter Grace, Suke Damson, old Mr. South, and various minor rustic types. These are all people who belong to the countryside around Little Hintock. At the beginning of the novel Grace, who has been away to school in the more sophisticated world outside, returns home to fight the battle of reconciling her old and new values and sensibilities. Since Hardy wants the plot of the novel to run on this line, he introduces two other outside elements in the persons of Edred Fitzpiers and Felice Charmond, their purpose being to tempt Grace away from her simple heritage. But then the plot itself becomes crudely simplistic, partly because the characters representing the outside world are so badly done.[13]

But even this plot is woven with other complexities, and Fitzpiers and Mrs. Charmond are given situational supplements to their characters. First Grace Melbury has been promised as a bride for Giles, because Grace's father considers himself indebted to Giles's father from the days of their own marriages. By having Grace marry Giles, Melbury will right the wrong he did to the elder Winterborne in a previous generation (p. 273). When Fitzpiers is introduced as a rival to Giles, he is given ancient family connections around Little Hintock to establish his presence and his suit in some way comparable to Giles's. Then when Felice Charmond is introduced as living at Hintock House, she is given not an historic attachment to a place but a previous acquaintance with Fitzpiers. She asks, "How many years have passed since first we met?" and he answers, "How the time comes back to me" (pp. 226–27). The past, as it is made to register in the novel, adds to its romantic tone and texture, not to its dramatic life. This pattern of past reference is typical of Hardy's method of construction, and typical of his idea of a dramatic situation; but the past acts more to reinforce a romantic, even melodramatic, mood in this novel than to affect its essence.

Fitzpier's connection with "the oldest, ancientest family in the country" (p. 54) is alluded to throughout the novel. "He represents a very old family" (p. 69), a "venerable old family" (p. 185), a "romantical family" who were "lords of the manor for I don't know how many hundred years" (p. 191). Not content with having Edred a descendant of the ancient Fitzpiers family, Hardy gives him the equally historical Baxbys as maternal ancestors, whose family relics are the nearby "ruins of Sherton Castle" (p. 192).

The first use that Hardy makes of this connection with the past is a purely romantic one: Grace feels in marrying Fitzpiers "as if [she has] stepped into history" (p. 192), and speculates on the idea "of so modern a man in science and aesthetics . . . springing out of relics so ancient" (p. 193). This somber past is also used ironically once, to underline Fitzpiers's idle alienation from Grace and his involvement with Mrs. Charmond, his boyhood dream-creature. Fitzpiers is looking out meditatively over a gate from the top of a hill as Grace approaches him:

> "What are you looking at?" she asked.
> "O! I was contemplating my mother's people's old place of Sherton Abbas, in my idle way," he said.
> It had seemed to her that he was looking much to the right of that cradle and tomb of his ancestral dignity. . . . She did not know that [the place where Mrs. Charmond was staying] lay in the direction of his gaze. (242)

Later in the novel, when Fitzpiers has left Grace, she meets Giles at Sherton, and looking at "a high marble tomb to the last representative of an extinct Earldom, without a thought that it was the family with which Fitzpiers was maternally connected," she remembers only that the last time she was at Sherton with Giles she was just returning from school and was prepared to be his wife (p. 337).

This use of historical reference does help to establish the very romantic tone of the novel (though perhaps it would be better without that tone) and as a kind of Hardyean plot-metaphor it serves to tie the figures of the intrigue together. There are other references to time and history, however, which seem to be but the product of an habitual frame of mind and not in any way useful. As Grace watches the ancient Midsummer eve mating ritual she feels "as if she had receded a couple of centuries in the world's history" (p. 173). Again, when she first visits

Fitzpier's house and sees him sleeping, he appears as "a recumbent figure within some canopied mural tomb of the fifteenth century" (p. 149). And early in the novel Robert Creedle answers a boy's question about the length of his memory by an exaggerated collapsing of time in the style of Dealer Buzzford in *The Mayor of Casterbridge*: "O yes. Ancient days, when there was battles, and famines, and hang-fairs, and other pomps, seem to me as yesterday" (p. 86).

More to the point in *The Woodlanders* are the simple assertions of the opening paragraphs that the story to be told, though typical and simple, is still significant. Along the road through the quiet rural district where the novel is to be set one can indulge oneself legitimately in romantic recall:

> The spot is lonely, and when the days are darkening the many
> gay charioteers now perished who have rolled along the way,
> the blistered soles that have trodden it, and the tears that
> have wetted it, return upon the mind of the loiterer. (1)

This is a world, the narrator claims, "where from time to time, dramas of a grandeur and unity truly Sophoclean are enacted in the real, by virtue of the concentrated passions and close-knit interdependence of the lives therein" (pp. 4–5). The remark would be a proper one for the introduction of *The Return of the Native, The Mayor of Casterbridge, Tess of the D'Urbervilles,* or *Jude the Obscure;* but *The Woodlanders* is not so Sophoclean in its theme or in the dramatization of that theme, and one does not find either the "concentrated passions" or the "close-knit interdependence of lives" here that one finds in those other novels. Hardy also asserts the fact of coincidence and the idea of intense relationships in various references to "the Unfulfilled Intuition" (p. 59), the "intangible Cause which has shaped the situation" (p. 95), "Fate" (p. 130), the "design" of "Nature" (p. 154), and the "powerless" state of "the human will against predestination" (p. 227)—this last remark being Mrs. Charmond's, not Hardy's. But *The Woodlanders* does not support these theses of intensity, and they stand, like most of the references to time and history, more as signs of Hardy's ideas and interests than as functional, integral parts of the novel.

The central character in *The Well-Beloved* (1897) is Jocelyn Pierston, described in the novel's three parts as "A Young Man of Twenty," "A

Young Man of Forty," and "A Young Man of Sixty." This novel is Hardy's last formal experiment in fiction, one in which the protagonist is ageless for forty years and experiences the dramatic reentry of his past twice, in the forms of his beloved's daughter and granddaughter. This is a modification of the usual Hardy theme of recurrence. The present, for Pierston, is constant and static for forty years, and in the world outside himself the progression of time twice allows a reincarnation from what should be measured as his past.

In 1889 Hardy noted in his diary, "The story of a face which goes through three generations or more, would make a fine novel or poem of the passage of time."[14] The first version of the novel was begun the next year, and issued serially in 1892 as "The Pursuit of the Well-Beloved." Hardy revised it the year after the publication of *Jude the Obscure*, and it was published then in 1897. The novel is openly and insistently co-incidental, as its germinal note would suggest; but this is not to say that chance and coincidence are bare or gratuitous. In the expanded version of the novel Hardy not only pays "particular attention to the solution of the plot," as Purdy indicates;[15] he also fills out the background with many additional details which suggest and support the basic fantasy of coincidence and recurrence.[16] The theme which emerges from Pierston's repetitive romances with the three generations of Avice Caros is the simplicity of man and the complexity of his search for happiness. In the odd, happy irony which concludes *The Well-Beloved* this happiness is to be found only in the destruction of dreams. And these dreams, which are enacted as the "reality" of the novel, are what Beach calls the awkwardly fictionalized "poetic fantasy" of Hardy's creation.[17]

Pierston's refusal to submit to the normal process of time is Hardy's basic material for both the plot and the theme of the novel; further, it is at the center, dramatically, of the myth which must be established in order for the plot and the theme to seem credible. What enables the reader to accept Pierston's living for forty years without changing, without aging, without having any experience other than the successive re-enactments of an earlier experience, is the metaphor of setting which supports the action of the novel and its central character's amazing career. The Isle of Slingers and Jocelyn Pierston could each be said to have "A Face Upon Which Time Makes but Little Impression."[18]

The Isle of Slingers, so named after its ancient inhabitants, is described in the Preface of 1912 as a "peninsula carved by Time out of a single stone" (p. v). In the opening chapter of the novel, as Jocelyn comes out onto the Isle, returning from London to the place of his birth, the narrator describes his thoughts: "More than ever the spot seemed what it was said once to have been, the ancient Vindilia Island, and the Home of the Slingers" (p. 3).[19] Forty years later, in Chapter 1 of Part III, Pierston is introduced in Rome, where "the quarries of ruins in the Eternal City" lend their air of timeless, "Eternal' antiquity to support the Wessex setting of his own unchanging, timeless existence, and he is "reminded . . . of the quarries of maiden rock at home" (p. 146). That home, "the hoary peninsula called an island," still "looked just the same as before" (p. 145).

Hardy develops and reiterates this setting throughout the novel. In comparing the past of his characters to the age of the setting, he remarks: "The reader is asked to remember that the date, though recent in the history of the Isle of Slingers, was more than forty years ago" (p. 19).[20] Later, in justification of the repetition of Avice through three generations and as a suggestion of the link between history on the island and history in the lives of the characters, Hardy notes:

> Like [Jocelyn's] own, [Avice Caro's] family had been island-
> ers for centuries—from Norman, Anglian, Roman, Balearic-
> British times. . . . The Caros, like some other local families,
> suggested a Roman lineage, more or less grafted on the stock
> of the Slingers. (76)[21]

This suggestion of historical identity and descent is used to tie Avice, as Jocelyn's recurring "Well-Beloved," into that long past which makes the history of a single life seem so momentary and yet, through its repetition, almost eternal. As Jocelyn goes to make inevitable love to his own almost mythological beloved, the scene is described: "Tradition urged that a temple to Venus once stood at the top of the Roman road leading up into the isle; and possibly one to the love-goddess of the Slingers antedated this" (p. 76).[22] Such suggestions of antiquity and historic continuity through ages recur throughout the novel. They establish the base metaphor for the timelessness of the experience and the coincidence of its repetition which is the whole action of the story. Only toward the end of the novel, when a different past from that involving his three Avices has returned upon him, does Jocelyn realize "that the conjunction of old things and new was no accident" (p. 204).[23]

74

There is no reason here for reading this as an intimation of a fatal control of Jocelyn's life and free will; rather, one is asked to put together his temperament and his historical environment to find the proper mood and occasion for such coincidence and accident as he meets.

The metaphoric and mythological establishment of the setting and the suggestive association of that setting and its mood with the current occasion are what make this story coherent and comprehensible. As Jocelyn walks the cliffs of the island, under the combined influence of the place and his own thoughts, he seems "to hear on the upper wind the stones of the slingers whizzing past, and the voices of the invaders who annihilated them, and married their wives and daughters, and produced Avice as the ultimate flower of their combined stocks" (p. 104).[24] Later, as he meets Avice III at "Henry the Eighth's Castle," an ancient ruin on the peninsular arm of the island, the antiquity of the site supports his consciousness of his own past:

> Like the Red King's Castle on the island, the interior was open to the sky, and when they entered and the full moon streamed down upon them over the edge of the enclosing masonry, the whole present reality faded from Jocelyn's mind under the press of memories. Neither of his companions guessed what Pierston was thinking of. It was in this very spot that he was to have met the grandmother of the girl at his side, and in which he would have met her had she chosen to keep the appointment, a meeting which might—nay, must—have changed the whole current of his life. (166)

One of Pierston's London friends speaks to him of Avice I as "a woman you last saw a hundred years ago" (p. 77). The exaggeration is used for effect—like the furmity-woman's narration of Michael Henchard's wife-selling in *The Mayor of Casterbridge*. Late in the novel, when the whole repetition has closed its last circle, when Jocelyn has finally given up his fantasy and married the woman for whom he jilted the first Avice, and Avice III (whose family name is now coincidentally Pierston) is about to marry that same woman's son, Jocelyn sighs, saying he has "lived a day too long" (p. 206).[25] It seems as though his life, or a part of it, is finally completed. He actually has, now, a past which is separate from his present. The life he has lived "too long" has been, in effect, but a single day, the first day; and it is now closed. Only after forty years of repeating the same single experience does Pierston finally finish living that experience. Most of his life—and most of this novel—is included in that one long "moment."

There are more explicit statements of the idea of recurrence in *The Well-Beloved*: Chapter 6 of Part II is entitled "The Past Shines in the Present," and Chapter 9 of Part II is called "Juxtapositions." Chapter 8 of Part II, "His Own Soul Confronts Him," begins with Pierston looking from his window at the second Avice, at "her who was the rejuvenated Spirit of the Past to him" (p. 103). But as the novel ends, Jocelyn, whose "inability to ossify with the rest of his generation threw him out of proportion with the time" (p. 150), is busy destroying the setting of the past and introducing a current and contemporary world to the Isle:

> His business was, among kindred undertakings which followed the extinction of the Well-Beloved and other ideals, to advance a scheme for the closing of the old natural fountains... and supplying the townlet with water from pipes.... He was also engaged in acquiring some old moss-grown, mullioned Elizabethan cottages, for the purpose of pulling them down because they were damp; which he afterwards did, and built new ones with hollow walls, and full of ventilators. (217–18)[26]

It is as though, once the intense center of his life, that long moment of enchantment, has passed, Jocelyn determines to eradicate the unchanging past which surrounds him—as indeed he should, since that ancient, unchanging setting has supported his own agelessness throughout the novel.

Jocelyn's romance with the three Avices has been, in part, a romance with the island. He is an artist, a sculptor; and his material as an artist has been both imaginatively and substantially of and from the Isle. His attempt to create the beautiful in carvings of local stone and his pursuit of the "Well-Beloved," of his "bird of the heart," have been connected in the suggestive setting of the fantasy. As his dreams fail, Jocelyn determines for a normal, decompressed reality, and as he does so he retires from his work as well. W. R. Rutland remarks that "the best part of [*The Well-Beloved*] is the manner in which the rocky Isle of Portland provides a changeless background to the insubstantial dreams of Pierston."[27] This is true, except for the allegation that Pierston's dreams are "insubstantial." They are substantial both mythologically and in the given "reality" of the fiction. But in the conclusion of the novel the dreams are destroyed, and Portland, Hardy's Isle of Slingers, and Jocelyn Pierston's metaphor for his own story, is changed.

Often in Hardy's work the only safety seems to be in having no past, and the only possible comedy in living a totally simple existence. Of his thirty-seven tales collected in four volumes of short stories, a number illustrate this point. Although the catastrophic intrusion of the past into the present is frequently the dramatic plan of these stories, because of the limitations of the form Hardy usually spends less time establishing the metaphoric effect which would justify that intrusion. The metaphor is still there, however, and the technique, though limited, is still the same. An intense world demands intense action.[28]

In the chronology which Hardy indicates for the composition of the tales the first instance of this kind is found in "The Waiting Supper," written in the autumn of 1887 and published in *A Changed Man* in 1913. In the story, Christine Everard is secretly betrothed to young Nicholas Long, but does not marry him. She marries instead James Bellston, who misuses her and disappears. Finally, years after Bellston's disappearance, Long persuades Christine to marry him. The marriage is to take place on Christmas eve, and on the evening before Long is to come to supper. This is the supper that is kept "waiting," out of all proportion with normal time. Indeed, time—in the person of an old clock—actually stops just before Nicholas is due to arrive, and just before the announcement that Bellston is at that moment on his way to Christine's house, ironically timing his return from her past to coincide with her formal rejection of that past. Bellston does not arrive, though the supper is kept waiting for him all night, and the wedding is cancelled. Later, we discover that Bellston was accidentally killed on his way to Christine's that night, and Long could have eaten his supper after all. The intensity of that moment of Bellston's promised intrusion, however, does not die easily or quickly away:

> For a curious unconsciousness of the long lapse of time since his revelation of himself seemed to affect the pair. There had been no passing events to serve as chronological milestones,

and the evening on which she had kept supper waiting for him still loomed out with startling nearness in their retrospects. (80–81)

Only when Bellston's death has been proved by the discovery of his remains seventeen years later can Christine say, "The weight is gone from our lives; the shadow no longer divides us: then let us be joyful together as we are, dearest Nic" (p. 83). The treacherous, persistent past is finally destroyed, and only now can the present and the possibility of a future be faced with hope and joy. Christine quotes a line of verse to close the story, suggesting to Long that they can now "With mirth and joy let old wrinkles come" (p. 83).

In "The Grave by the Handpost," a story written at Christmas time in 1897 and eventually reprinted in *A Changed Man*, Hardy again uses Christmas as his seasonal setting and a crossroads for the central physical scene. The story opens with a description reminiscent of that in "The Three Strangers."

> I never pass through Chalk-Newton without turning to regard the neighboring upland, at a point where a lane crosses the lone straight highway dividing this from the next parish; a sight which does not fail to recall the event that once happened there; and though it may seem superfluous, at this date, to disinter more memories of village history, the whispers of that spot may claim to be preserved. (125)

The high point at which the roads cross attracts our attention, and we look up to see what is happening or about to happen there. The highway crosses the lesser road at just its middle point, and the bisecting highway is described as "the lonely monotonous old highway known as Long Ash Lane, which runs, straight as a surveyor's line, many miles north and south of this spot, on the foundation of a Roman road" (p. 130). Long Ash Lane, the narrator says, "has often been mentioned in these narratives" (p. 130)—and the idea of situating the action of a story at a crossroads has been used before, too. Ideas, interests, and hopes are at cross purposes throughout "The Grave by the Handpost," and its final irony is in the failure of an attempted duplication of events.

The tale is about old Sergeant Holway, who commits suicide because his son accuses him of having ruined his life by making him a soldier. The Sergeant is being buried at the crossroads as the story opens. The son returns at this moment, and makes arrangements for the removal of his father's body to a decent burial place in the church yard. Then the son leaves, and the proposed reinterment is never carried out. Years later, the son comes back a Sergeant-Major, and discovers the unaltered fate of his father's corpse. One Christmas eve—a time chosen here, perhaps, for the irony of joyous regeneration celebrations—Sergeant-Major Holway kills himself, after leaving a note requesting his burial beside his father at the crossroads. "But the paper was accidentally swept to the floor," the story concludes, "and overlooked till after the funeral, which took place in the ordinary way in the churchyard" (p. 141).

Not burial, but exhumation is the story of "A Tryst at an Ancient Earthwork," published first in 1885 and then included in *A Changed Man*. Between these times it was published once under the title "Ancient Earthworks at Casterbridge." The earthwork Hardy is referring to is Maiden Castle, or " 'Mai Dun,' 'The Castle of the Great Hill,' said to be the Dunium of Ptolemy, the capital of the Durotriges, which eventually came into Roman occupation, and was finally deserted on their withdrawal from this island" (p. 172). In discussing the impressiveness of Mai Dun Hardy uses the same technique of suggestion that he uses in setting up Maumbury Ring in *The Mayor of Casterbridge*. The tryst is a midnight one, and the narrator reports his impression of Mai Dun at that hour:

> Impressive by day as this largest Ancient-British work in the kingdom undoubtedly is, its impressiveness is increased now. After standing still and spending a few minutes in adding its age to its size, and its size to its solitude, it becomes appallingly mournful in its growing closeness. (173)

Despite the sentence structure the description is effective in establishing the mood and the metaphor of timelessness-through-history which Hardy wants. He wants it here purely for its own effect; indeed, the matter of the story is terribly slight if the descriptive elements are removed. Yet one is interested in the story, because its experience is like that of a time-machine. The drama is not fantasy, however; it is a legitimate experience in a real present time and in a real place. But the place has an aura of its own which seems to impel the imagination beyond its own time and beyond the simple act:

> I am startled by a voice pronouncing my name. Past and present have become so confusedly mingled under the association of the spot that for a time it has escaped my memory that this mound was the place agreed on for the aforesaid appointment. (179)

The narrator and his archaeologist friend begin their work, and "by merely peeling off a wrapper of modern accumulations we have lowered ourselves into an ancient world" (p. 181). Until called back by the fury of a storm, the narrator does not notice "what is going on in the present world," and his "companion digs on unconcernedly; he is living two thousand years ago, and despises things of the moment as dreams" (p. 182).

Whatever dramatic intensity this story has is generated by means of narrative description. The ruin is set up romantically, and we are urged to respond to its immensity in space and in time. Hardy must be very much aware of what he can do with descriptive setting and the creation of timeless moments for the centers of dramatic action; and as he tells the story as an anecdote from his own experience, it would seem to indicate that he felt strongly the common reality of such influential and suggestive correspondences of past and present.

The novel Hardy was busy writing in 1885, when this story was first published, was *The Mayor of Casterbridge*, in which he utilizes this technique of suggestive setting to substantiate his claims for Michael Henchard's dramatic size. And Mai-Dun and Dorchester's other major ancient relic, Maumbury Ring, are the two most significant stages on which Henchard plays.

NOTES TO CHAPTER IV

1. F. E. Hardy, *Life of Hardy*, pp. 106, 114, 152.
2. Ibid., p. 168.
3. Ibid., p. 127.
4. See Carl J. Weber, *Hardy of Wessex* (New York, 1940), p. 162, for a figuring of the dates of the action in the novels.

5. Houghton Memorial Library, Harvard University, Cambridge, Mass.

6. Even the Bishop of Melchester relates the present to the past through the setting. While playing at bowls he recalls the time of Shakespeare's Richard II, and says to Lady Constantine, "it is an interesting old game, and might have been played at that very date on this very green" (p. 196). It is almost as though Hardy is writing out of habit.

7. In the manuscript the actual metaphor of his suspension is added interlinearly. The sentence originally reads "think how it must annihilate me to be in the constant presence of the circumstance," and is altered then to "think how it must annihilate me to be *as it were* in constant *suspension* amid them" (fol. 36; italics mine).

8. The Wessex Edition of the novel, the first edition, and the manuscript all have "a chapter in Revelation"; the Macmillan Library Edition, following the 1919 Mellstock edition, has "like Sodom and Gomorrah" (p. 121).

9. Richard L. Purdy, *Thomas Hardy: a Bibliographical Study* (London, 1954), p. 44.

10. Ibid., p. 48.

11. F. E. Hardy, *Life of Hardy*, p. 171.

12. The best full treatment of *The Woodlanders* is to be found in Douglas Brown, *Thomas Hardy* (London, 1961), pp. 70–89; see also Rutland, *Writings and Background*, pp. 211–17.

13. So many of Hardy's outsiders are badly done, among them Eustacia and Farfrae, perhaps because Hardy could not sympathize with the values which his plans require them to stand for.

14. F. E. Hardy, *Life of Hardy*, p. 217.

15. Purdy, *Bibliographical Study*, p. 95.

16. Though no manuscript of *The Well-Beloved* survives, a number of interesting comparisons can be made between the serial publication of the story in 1892 and the expanded version published in 1897. The most significant details of the additions to the 1897 version will be noted below. "The Pursuit of the Well-Beloved" ran in *The Illustrated London News* from 1 October through 17 December 1892.

17. *Technique of Hardy*, p. 128.

18. The title of the first chapter of *The Return of the Native*.

19. Not in "The Pursuit of the Well-Beloved," this sentence is added in *The Well-Beloved*.

20. Added by Hardy in revision.

21. Two long descriptive paragraphs containing these and other references linking the Pierstons and the Caros to the Isle of Slingers are added here in Hardy's revision.

22. Added by Hardy in revision.

23. Added by Hardy as a part of the new conclusion of *The Well-Beloved*.

24. Not in "The Pursuit of the Well-Beloved." The sentence there reads "He walked the summit till his legs ached, and still she did not come." In the revised version of the novel this reads "He walked the wild summit till his legs ached, and his heart ached—till he seemed to hear," etc.

25. Added in *The Well-Beloved*.

26. Added by Hardy as a part of the new conclusion of *The Well-Beloved*.

27. Rutland, *Writings and their Background*, p. 218.

28. Recurrence and return are the basis for plot, form, dramatic content, and meaning in many of Hardy's stories. I will not discuss all of them here, though I would refer any interested reader to three stories from *Life's Little Ironies*: "A Tragedy of Two Ambitions," "For Conscience' Sake," and "To Please His Wife."

V

THE MAYOR OF CASTERBRIDGE

> *"Casterbridge is a old, hoary place o' wickedness,*
> *by all account. 'Tis recorded in history that we*
> *rebelled against the King one or two hundred*
> *years ago, in the time of the Romans."*

THE MAYOR OF CASTERBRIDGE
1886

Hardy's 1895–1912 preface to *The Mayor of Casterbridge* notes that, "The incidents narrated arise
mainly out of three events, which chanced to range themselves in the
order and at or about the intervals of time here given, in the real history
of the town called Casterbridge and in the neighbouring country. They
were the sale of a wife by her husband, the uncertain harvests which
immediately preceded the repeal of the Corn Laws, and the visit of a
Royal personage to the aforesaid part of England" (p. v). There are but
five characters drawn in detail for the acting out of this seemingly simple
story, and four of them serve primarily to involve and entangle the
fifth. Hardy called the novel "more particularly a study of one man's
deeds and character than, perhaps, any other of those included in my
Exhibition of Wessex life" (p. vi). Michael Henchard, the one "Man of
Character," is supported and crossed at every turn by Susan, Elizabeth-
Jane, Farfrae, and Lucetta. And he is interfered with by the furmity-
woman, by the local chorus of rustics, and by his own private Fedullah,
Joshua Jopp.[1] His career, thus involved and complicated, is the plot of

the novel. He sells his wife, loses all he has misguessing the harvest, and is publicly disgraced at the visit of the Royal personage.

Hardy's problem is how to make Michael Henchard larger than he is as the mayor of a small country town. The novel belongs strictly and almost entirely to Henchard: its full title is *The Life and Death of The Mayor of Casterbridge: A Story of a Man of Character*. Though his term as mayor is over in Chapter 27 and his title is taken soon thereafter by Donald Farfrae, still he remains mayor—as Lear remains King. But being mayor—or King—is not enough. Nor is it enough for Hardy that Henchard stands as symbol for the passing of an age in England's history, for this makes him neither Oedipan nor of a kind and size with Lear. Hardy's plot for Henchard stresses his tragic fault, as his one mistake keeps returning to haunt him throughout his life; but this alone does not make the story of his fall great drama, or tragedy, even if we call him always "a Man of Character." Henchard's existence is not an intellectual one, either, for the sensitive critical vision is given to Elizabeth-Jane. Henchard's awareness is limited to himself and that immediate world in which he strives, not only for survival, but for the dignity of a man free to meet his fate. It is in achieving this freedom that he becomes, legitimately, "a Man of Character," that he makes himself significantly "The Mayor," that he becomes the novel's hero.

Henchard grows always toward this size throughout the novel. In *The Return of the Native* a stage for universally representative action is constructed overtly at the beginning of the novel, and the stage almost outsizes the characters who are asked to live up to its demands. In *The Mayor of Casterbridge* Hardy is much more subtle, and takes his time about building both the stage and the character to fit it. He exercises what Albert Guerard would call his "tact" in the use of his material, and he controls his own imaginative response to it with patient care. It is only toward the end of the novel that we realize for sure the immensity of Henchard's pain and the intensity of his tragedy, and we can accept it there, because of the narrative and dramatic preparation Hardy has made earlier. He has constructed a world which expands in time, metaphorically, to accommodate first Henchard's specific past and then Henchard himself, as representative man. His fate is made slowly, cumulatively, though it is foreshadowed from the very beginning. Ironies accumulate, as events recur one after another from the past to buffet Henchard for his mistake. At each turn he is defeated, but he never surrenders. He blots out his dignity, but each time he returns to the struggle with a new determination. We are sure, finally, of his stature and its legitimacy as we see his resolution in the face of his fate, as that fate is fulfilled. He has left Elizabeth-Jane, knowing the physical return of Sailor Newson to be imminent, and he walks out on the road across the heath:

> He went on till he came to the first milestone, which stood in the bank, half way up a steep hill. He rested his basket on the top of the stone, placed his elbows on it, and gave way to a convulsive twitch, which was worse than a sob, because it was so hard and dry.
>
> "If I had only got her with me—If I only had! Hard work would mean nothing to me then! But that was not to be. I —Cain—go alone as I deserve—an outcast and a vagabond. But my punishment is *not* greater than I can bear!" (361)[2]

This is Henchard, trying for once to articulate his pain, trying to express his determination against despair. In the awkward, stumbling lines that he utters his tragedy becomes obvious; with the whole action of the novel behind them, these stilted and stifled words of Henchard's describe in him the strength of man's soul. And as Cain, the firstborn son of Adam, he achieves that awful dignity which characterizes tragic—and heroic—man.

The novel opens as Henchard, Susan, and Elizabeth-Jane approach Weydon Priors. For six paragraphs not a word is spoken as character and adumbrations of the fate of man, setting and the metaphoric extension of setting in time are described. Henchard is a young man of twenty, a haytrusser, taciturn and phlegmatic in his attitude. (The detail of his walk given here will be repeated in amended form as he leaves Casterbridge almost twenty-five years later, and walks to that milestone on the heath.) Susan is represented as having "the hard, half-apathetic expression of one who deems anything possible at the hands of Time and Chance, except, perhaps, fair play" (p. 2). And though there are two bad editorial intrusions—almost a rarity in this novel—immediately after the lines quoted, these lines are legitimately descriptive of Susan's attitude. What this pantomine or moving tableau shows us of Henchard and Susan is so precise in its meaning that we can readily accept such a generalization about her character.

Hardy insists on a close and minute awareness of physical objects, of motions, of sounds; it is from this attention to details that he forms his vision as a novelist and as a poet. And from this kind of scrutiny he suggests the intensity of existence which, without such attention, would be missed. Just before Michael and Susan meet a man from Weydon Priors and begin to speak with him—just, that is, at the end of this opening dumb show—Hardy introduces the sound of a pathetic bird-song in the background, and suggests through this the unchanging and timeless fate of man:

> For a long time there was none [i.e., no sound], beyond the voice of a weak bird singing a trite old evening song that might doubtless have been heard on the hill at the same hour, and with the self-same trills, quavers, and breves, at any sunset of that season for centuries untold. (3)

The fair at Weydon Priors is introduced through the turnip-hoer they meet, and Henchard and his family proceed there, to the introduction of the furmity-woman, a "haggish creature of about fifty" (p. 4) who provides for Henchard's downfall with her rum. She is the carrier, in a sense, of the guilt of the novel: of Michael Henchard's guilt, in which she has such a large part, as trafficker in illegitimate and evil things. She is set here as the embassy of evil, the character opposed to Susan and to whom Henchard is attracted. The furmity-woman appears four times in the novel: here, as witness and accessory to Henchard's mistake; in Chapter 3, when Susan returns to Weydon fair-field to find the way to Henchard's present; in Chapter 28, to expose Henchard's past at Weydon Priors in his present; and finally in Chapter 36, to urge one more discovering of the past, this time of Henchard's past with Lucetta. The furmity-woman gives Henchard drink, and he proposes the sale of his wife: "She shall take the girl if she wants to, and go her ways. I'll take my tools, and go my ways. 'Tis simple as Scripture history" (pp. 9–10). The simplicity which characterizes Henchard's speech here stands for the blocked, seemingly spare lines of the whole novel; and such terrible compressed simplicity actually does suggest "Scripture history."[3] This is Henchard, blindly describing his own future, in which he becomes a Cain who begs not to be removed from existence but to be removed from memory: to have his existence forgotten, because of the burden of his past.

But what seems to be Biblical spareness and straightness, and what seems to be Henchard's simple and straight fate, cannot be so; time is already set up with a complexity that denies the possibility of a simple present. It is the past that will occur in the dramatic and ironic unfolding of chronology. As Susan, sold by her husband for five guineas, leaves the furmity-tent with Sailor Newson, one of the women cries out, "I'd go, and 'a might call, and call, till his keacorn was raw; but I'd never come back—no, not till the great trumpet, would I!" (p. 14). This "Scripture history" of Michael Henchard's life expands, eventually, through such suggestions as this, so that his "moment" of existence in the long history of the world begins "at the beginning," at "the Creation" (p. 231)—as he commits his sin of wife-selling at Weydon fair-field —and ends only when things have come full circle, when his past has been fulfilled as his present or future, when the Apocalyptic days of Revelations are lived out (p. 215) and the "great trumpet" mentioned in this opening chapter has sounded him out of existence. Through its artistically planned recurrence in various ways throughout the novel, this opening scene at Weydon Priors becomes the emblem of the fatal transcendence of time in *The Mayor of Casterbridge*. This transcendence is not simply the return of the past or the central character's past, however; Hardy uses his setting metaphorically, bringing all of history and prehistory into the present existence of the novel, to emphasize actual recurrence and to justify such, symbolically, as natural phenomena in a dramatically intense world. As the intensity of the physical situation and its largeness in time are being established, the hero's simple story attaches simultaneously to this larger scheme so that he becomes, through the narrative presentation of his tragedy on this stage, a man representative of all men in all of time. The immensity of this symbolic identity is compressed for Henchard into a single moment of existence which is as timeless as eternity. As his existence transcends time it transcends individual existence, and he assumes the size and spiritual stature Hardy has set out to give him as "a Man of Character."

Beach says that "Hardy's greatness lies . . . in the association of events with the setting in which they occur."[4] Earlier he makes a more perceptive comment about Hardy and his use of setting. He speaks of Hardy's "time-vision which is one of the richest resources of the poet" as this is used in depicting character. This vision he describes as the "faculty of setting the plainest figures of today in a perspective of ages, in a shadowy synthesis that, while it dwarfs the present scene, yet lends it a grandeur, too, a dignity and a noble pathos borrowed from those of time itself."[5] Harold Child reaches a similar conclusion in trying to explain Hardy's use of history and historical references: "The insignificance of man, the briefness of his days, are always present in Hardy's mind; he nevel fails to see them from the point of view of the indifferent power, and the enormous past is always with him as a moment of time."[6] The emphasis on man's "insignificance" is an oversimplification which distorts Hardy's artistic as well as his philosophical vision; but the awareness of the influence of time and historical setting in time expressed by both Beach and Child is significant.

Julian Moynahan, in an article on *The Mayor of Casterbridge*, finds in it a "remarkable sense of continuity of the past with present times which is expressed through the archaeological features of the setting."[7] And J. H. Fowler, after quoting some lines from the opening chapters of *The Return of the Native*, says of Hardy's use of time and history for plot and setting:

> Nothing is more characteristic of Hardy than the deep sense, to which these passages bear eloquent testimony, of the antiquity of man and the still greater antiquity of the earth. "The thing that hath been is the thing that shall be, and there is no new thing under the sun." That sentiment is as old as Ecclesiastes, but the feeling expressed by Hardy is more complex and is the direct result of modern discoveries. Ecclesiastes, in other words, merely thinks of human existence as the purposeless repetition of the same monotonous acts. Hardy's thought is rather of the continuity of existence —each act that we do, each sight that we look on, reaching back into an incredibly remote past, with no break in the links that bind us to the beginning of time.[8]

Representing the continuity of man's existence in the long history of the world, however, is not in itself worth much. And if the grandeur of the universe is set up to diminish man, then the artist loses his hero. Although at times Hardy does stress the comparative finitude of man's stature, his technique is most essentially directed toward the exaggeration of man's size, and he describes this heroic size for man through the metaphoric reference of time and history. Man's life—at any rate, Michael Henchard's life—is so short in terms of universal or cosmic history that his existence becomes momentary and, through the intensity of that moment, so long as to measure in its experience all of time.

Late in *The Mayor of Casterbridge*, after Henchard's past has been exposed by the furmity-woman, Sailor Newson returns to Casterbridge. Henchard's discovery of this (a preview, since Newson on this occasion does not actually come into the town) is one of the dramatic climaxes of the novel. The setting is given, linking the time of the scene in the chronology of the novel to prehistory:

> Two miles out, a quarter of a mile from the highway, was the prehistoric fort called Mai Dun, of huge dimensions and many ramparts, within or upon whose enclosures a human being, as seen from the road, was but an insignificant speck. Hitherward Henchard often resorted, glass in hand, and scanned the hedgeless *Via*—for it was the original track laid out by the legions of the Empire. (357)

The stage for the action is thus built, and our attention is attracted to it and to the relatively small figure occupying it. I would say about this stage what Guerard says about Maumbury Ring, as he remembers it from a schoolboy reading: that the grand image of "Hadrian's soldiery mysteriously reappearing in broad daylight" is called up "in one rather pedestrian sentence." Guerard continues:

> The point I want to make is simple enough. Not subtlety or elaboration of art but the imagined material itself gives the best scenes of the novel their strength. And Hardy had the instinct or the art to let this material speak for itself. He becomes diffuse or flabbily abstract only when the material is inadequate, or when he is not himself convinced of its truth.[9]

The scene at the Ring is carefully set, so that Hadrian's soldiers may come quickly alive at the moment of their mention. Similarly, the scene at Mai Dun is set, not with "subtlety or elaboration of art," but through reference to the effect already achieved in "the imagined material itself," through the introduction of another of those ancient and time-transcending places which provide the basic supportive mood of the whole novel.

Once the stage is ready, and Henchard is placed upon it, Hardy creates what amounts to an immediate vacuum in time, a briefly spotted eternity for the action of the scene. Henchard happens to be on this spot, happens to look with his telescope in the right direction, and sees on the horizon the sailor who bought his wife twenty years ago. Henchard's past is imposed on his present, on the authority of the metaphoric juxtaposition of prehistory and the present in the setting. Henchard, paralyzed on the spot by the recognition of Newson's face, "lived a lifetime the moment he saw it" (p. 358).

For the important scenes of the novel, Hardy forces chronological time out and replaces it with the still, simple, static and intense moments of timelessness. What is achieved is the creation of something like tragic "spots of time." Around and on scenes so spotted Hardy builds *The Mayor of Casterbridge*. The scenes are almost invariably coincidental, in the large sense of the term: each scene is the dramatization of a fatal juxtaposition of events, and the intensity of the lives involved makes the grotesque juxtaposition legitimate.

The Mai Dun scene is a good example of what can be proposed as Hardy's awareness of the effect he was creating through the use of this technique. In the manuscript of *The Mayor of Casterbridge*[10] its original casting is very different, and its effect is much less.

At the close of chapter 42 Henchard eavesdrops on Elizabeth-Jane and Farfrae and discovers the seriousness of their courtship. In the manuscript, Henchard first listens from his hiding place as Farfrae calls her "Dear Elizabeth-Jane" (fol. 442). He knows where they often meet, and in the next paragraph he goes out along the Budmouth road to observe them:

> The absorbing interest which the courtship—as it evidently now was—had for Henchard, led him to a further step. A quarter of a mile from the highway was a prehistoric earthen fort of huge dimensions and many ramparts, within or upon whose enclosure a human being, as seen from the road, was but an insignificant speck. Hither Henchard resorted, glass in hand, and scanned the hedgeless *Via*—for it was the original track laid out by the legions of the Empire—to a distance of two or three miles. His step-daughter had passed by on her walk some time before; and she presently emerged from a cutting in the hill, bound homeward.

90

> Then a figure came from behind the Ring at the other edge of the landscape, and advanced to meet her half-way. Applying his spyglass, Farfrae was discovered. They met, joined hands, and—Donald kissed her, Elizabeth-Jane looking quickly round to assure herself that nobody was near. (fols. 442–43)

There are numerous things wrong with these paragraphs. The introduction of Mai Dun and the mention of the Ring are purposeless, since they are not used. Mai Dun is wasted under Henchard because the scene doesn't measure up to what the setting suggests. The Ring, set with its long and still vital past, means nothing for Farfrae or Elizabeth-Jane, so it is useless to have Farfrae emerge from behind its slopes. The telescope is not symbolic but an appendage, as it is used neither to contract distance nor to focus. Rather, it is used awkwardly to pan from one side to the other, swinging from Elizabeth-Jane walking up from the south to Farfrae walking out from the north. And Elizabeth-Jane, one is told, is coming from one of her meetings with Newson, whom she is supposed to see "two or three times a week" (fols. 450–51).

In the revision of this scene, Elizabeth-Jane's walks are innocent if coy exercises in meeting Farfrae; she does not know anything about Newson. When Henchard goes out onto Mai Dun "to read the progress of affairs between Farfrae and his charmer" (p. 357), he already knows that Farfrae calls her "Dearest Elizabeth-Jane" and that he has kissed her (p. 353), since these two minor discoveries are pulled together into the one brief scene which Henchard observes from hiding in the Ring. What happens—what Henchard sees—in the revision of the Mai Dun scene, however, is of major importance. Henchard puts his telescope to his eye as he stands on the outer ring of the prehistoric fort, looking to find Elizabeth-Jane and Farfrae meeting again. Elizabeth-Jane represents his past, standing for the daughter he sold. As he scans the old Roman road through his glass, he sees the man from that past walking into his present. The telescope now serves as a useful symbol: it reminds the reader that space, events, and time can be compressed, and that the distant can be brought close. The useless reference to the Ring has been eliminated, the distraction of looking all up and down the landscape is removed, and only Henchard, Newson, the telescope, and Mai Dun are left. There was no significance to the historical aspect of the castle when Henchard used it as a stage from which to observe Elizabeth-Jane and Farfrae kissing. But now it serves to set up the intrusion of the past, and the irony of Henchard's standing upon the ruins of a prehistoric past still extant in the present is inherent in the scene: the Michael Henchard of 1850 calls up his own past from 1830, through the symbolic agency of a telescope.

The change in the meaning of the scene is immense. From this scene, as revised, comes the climax of the novel. Newson appears, his face is recognized, and time stops: "Henchard lived a lifetime the moment he saw it."[11] He can't move, and in the violence of this timeless, motionless situation, Henchard's whole life is spent. His past has imposed itself finally, physically, upon his present: and his future, too, is spent. When he is dead, his last will is read: "& that no man remember me" (p. 384). The tormented soul, on its way to eternal timelessness, asks to have this timeless, intense moment which has been its human existence isolated from the more normal and less tragic history of man.

Maumbury Ring is Hardy's other important symbolic stage in *The Mayor of Casterbridge*, and its very richly detailed representation sets much of the emphasis for the later descriptions of Mai Dun, several minor stages, and, at the end, Egdon Heath. The Ring is, for Hardy, "merely the local name of one of the finest Roman Amphitheatres, if not the very finest, remaining in Britain." It occupies a prominent spot at the edge of Casterbridge, which

> announced old Rome in every street, alley, and precinct. It looked Roman, bespoke the art of Rome, concealed dead men of Rome. It was impossible to dig more than a foot or two deep about the town fields and gardens without coming up-on some tall soldier or other of the Empire, who had lain there in his silent unobtrusive rest for a space of fifteen hundred years. (80)

This historical aspect of the setting, however, seems remote from Michael Henchard's drama, and little more than a dead past which has buried its dead: "They had lived so long ago, their time was so unlike the present, their hopes and motives were so widely removed from ours, that between them and the living there seemed to stretch a gulf too wide for even a spirit to pass" (p. 80).

But despite the fact of time, despite the remoteness of the Roman past, which he admits, Hardy insists on mood and impression: the Ring is to ancient-rooted Casterbridge "what the ruined Coliseum is to modern Rome," and "the dusk of evening . . . the proper hour at which a true impression of this suggestive place could be received" (p. 81). According to this "impression," the arena is "still smooth and circular, as if used for its original purpose not so very long ago" (p. 82). It is mysteriously "suggestive" too, and has established itself in local tradition:

> for some old people said that at certain moments in the summer time, in broad daylight, persons sitting with a book or dozing in the arena had, on lifting their eyes beheld the slopes lined with a gazing legion of Hadrian's soldiery as if watching the gladiatorial combat; and had heard the roar of their excited voices; that the scene would last but a moment, like a lightning flash, and then disappear. (82)

The result of this description, the best and most elaborate metaphoric use of setting in all of Hardy's works, is the firm establishment of a past still existing, still living in the present. This is the spot Henchard chooses, then, "as being the safest from observation which he could think of for meeting his long-lost wife" (p. 82). Their meeting, "in the middle of the arena" (p. 83), is parallel to and even suggested by the recurrence of Rome and Romans: for Susan brings the past, alive, into the present. The thematic result of their meeting, of course, is their decision to remarry: again, to bring an event out of the past to its conscious, ritualistic re-creation and reenactment in the present.

Susan is known, ironically, as "the Ghost" to the boys of Casterbridge (p. 95)—as the ghost from the past, haunting the present into which she has come to make her claim. When she dies, she is buried with a past more antique than hers, in

> the still-used burial ground of the old Roman-British city, whose curious feature was this, its continuity as a place of sepulture. Mrs. Henchard's dust mingled with the dust of women who lay ornamented with glass hairpins and amber necklaces, and men who held in their mouths coins of Hadrian, Posthumus, and the Constantines. (153)

It is perhaps awkward and hard to accept Susan's consorting, even in death, with historical figures. But we are reminded of her arrival in Casterbridge and that first meeting with Henchard by the historical reference of this scene. And the spot is used immediately to begin another stylized part of the novel, with the introduction of Lucetta.

Evidently Hardy originally did not plan to juxtapose Elizabeth-Jane's visit to Susan's grave with the introduction of Lucetta. The narrative section quoted above does not appear in the manuscript at all, and when she meets Lucetta, Elizabeth-Jane is said to be out for a walk in the woods rather than on a visit to her mother's grave. But in the first conceived scene, Hardy was working in a similar direction, and Elizabeth-Jane was already thinking of Romans and the Ring and Mai Dun:

> So Elizabeth-Jane walked and read, or looked about and thought of the shadowy beings she mentally designated as "Romans" who had laid out these square angles and banks, and that earthen theatre hard by, and that stupendous fort which rose against the sky behind. (fols. 193–94)

Still, it is of no significance that Elizabeth-Jane thinks of Romans, or notices ancient earthworks. But if Hardy makes the association more specific, as he does in the revision for the published text of the novel, he can make a dramatic connection through the historical reference, and thus make the coincidence of the meeting of Elizabeth-Jane and Lucetta aesthetically acceptable, through the effect of the metaphorical setting. Two people whose meeting will be seen as appropriate as soon as it occurs, meet in a place which will reinforce that appropriateness. Elizabeth-Jane visits her mother's grave, and the description of this spot reminds one of the Ring, where Susan met Michael when she first arose out of his dead past into his present. Also visiting Susan's grave in this "churchyard old as civilization" (p. 123) is Lucetta, another figure out of Henchard's past.

Lucetta's function in the novel will have to be discussed again later in this chapter. I might point out here, however, that she is associated with Henchard's past, and has a past herself, and like Henchard is destroyed by her past, by that part she shared illegitimately with him. Still, Lucetta is only a small type, at best, of Henchard. She determines to be free, saying, "I won't be a slave to the past—I'll love where I choose!" (p. 204)—and upon Henchard's exposure she runs away to marry Farfrae.

The stage which was set for Susan and Henchard to meet on is used by Lucetta and Henchard (p. 216), and seems ready to accept Lucetta and Farfrae. In the manuscript Hardy's temporary, perhaps momentary intention was to have them meet there:

During the day she went out to the Ring, and by chance or design a figure met her there. As soon as she saw Elizabeth-Jane after her return indoors she told her she had decided to go away from home to the seaside—to Port Bredy for a few days. Casterbridge was so gloomy. (fol. 289)

But the opening lines of the paragraph are cancelled, and the sentence is revised to read, "During the day she went out to the Ring, and to other places, not coming in till nearly dusk." It seems as though Hardy's original intention was to have Farfrae and Lucetta meet and decide to marry at the same spot that Henchard chose for his first meeting with Susan and his sort of second Susan, Lucetta. Since the sentence is made ambiguous now, and since they do in fact marry at Port Bredy within the next three days, perhaps they still do meet at the Ring: whatever the case may be, Hardy has removed the emphasis on what would have been an irrelevant coincidence, and the reference to the Ring is now just a passing allusion to a prominent landmark in the city. For the metaphoric unity of the novel it is hardly legitimate for Farfrae, the outsider who has no past at all, to use the Ring to meet Lucetta, whose only past is with Henchard on the Isle of Jersey. The Ring, like Mai Dun, is reserved for more purposeful symbolic uses than this.

If this restriction on the use of the Ring eliminates one of the parallels of the novel, it does not change the effect of the extreme stylization of the entire work. In some sense, only one thing happens in the novel: Michael Henchard sells his wife. As he awakes the morning after this he wonders, "Did I tell my name to anybody last night, or didn't I tell my name?" (p. 17) and, at the end of the novel, when his guilt has grown from name through soul, he asks "that no man remember me" (p. 384). The wife-selling recurs in reminders throughout the story: both Henchard and the reader are kept continually aware of it. When Susan returns to Weydon Priors in Chapter 3 to try to find Michael, she asks the furmity-woman, "Can you call to mind . . . the sale of a wife by her husband in your tent eighteen years ago today?" (p. 24), and Chapter 4 begins with a reference to that "tragical crisis . . . the transaction at Weydon Fair" (p. 26). Henchard is described in Casterbridge, in Chapter 17, as being made of "the same unruly volcanic stuff . . . as when he had sold his wife at Weydon Fair" (p. 129). And Michael, begging Elizabeth-

Jane to accept him as her father after Susan's death, reminds himself of his past crime as he says to her, "Don't take against me—though I was a drunken man once, and used your mother roughly—I'll be kinder to you than *he* was" (p. 141).

Not only do these allusions keep us aware of what specific mistake committed at what specific time and place is Henchard's tragic fault, his *hamartia*; they also insist that that past is not dead, that it still exists in the present. Susan brings it in herself; Henchard is still made of the same stuff now as then; and his confession of what he once was, which he wants to atone for now, is the expression of his own conviction first that that past is still vital and can be reworked and remolded in his present, and second that whatever punishment or pain comes to him now is but "what he had deserved" (p. 144).

From the beginning Henchard recognizes his fault in selling Susan, and his responsibility for his act. When he awakens from his drunkenness the morning after he has sold her, he reflects that his grief, his guilt "was of his own making, and he ought to bear it" (p. 17). He wants to believe that he can make "a start in a new direction" (p. 18) after this. But "Character is Fate" (p. 131) in Hardy's world of causal relationships, and twenty years after this act and his attempt at reform, Henchard will feel again that pain is "what he had deserved" (p. 144). His only triumph is in the heroic determination which closes his career, as he accepts this fate, finally and irrevocably, in his loneliness: "I—Cain—go alone as I deserve—an outcast and a vagabond. But my punishment is *not* greater than I can bear" (p. 361).

The recurrence of Weydon Priors as one of the important places of the novel also reminds us of what happened there. Susan, sold and gone from there, must return there with Elizabeth-Jane to find her way back to Henchard. And Henchard himself finally returns there, too, in Chapter 44. The first two visits are set up very carefully as parallels, and part of the effect of this is to bridge the gap of nearly twenty years between Chapter 2 and Chapter 3. The last visit is set up as a dramatic, symbolic, almost ritualistic repetition of that first trip, too, only this time Henchard is alone. He has been walking away from Casterbridge for five days. "It now became apparent that the direction of his journey was Weydon Priors, which he reached on the afternoon of the sixth day" (p. 367). His pilgrimage is a return to the beginning of it all: he is returning to the scene of the crime. Symbolically, he is turning things full circle, preparing for the end.[12]

Henchard is from the beginning a man of forms and symbols. In preparing to swear his oath "to avoid all strong liquors for the space of twenty years" he requires "a fit place and imagery; for there was something fetichistic in this man's beliefs" (pp. 17–18). He requires the choir at the Three Mariners—who are sitting by "like the monolithic circle at Stonehenge in its pristine days" (p. 266)—to sing a formal curse for Donald Farfrae. He insists on the form of his previous dignity as mayor, wearing "the fretted and weather-beaten garments of bygone years" (p. 306), "the very clothes which he had used to wear in the primal days" of his mayoralty (p. 303), and he meets the Royal personage this way, waving a flag in his hand. Finally, in writing his last will and tacking it above his head he makes his last gesture toward ordering and dignifying his existence—which is what all form and ritual are for.

Perhaps because of Henchard's ritualistic awareness, his "fetichistic" psychological makeup, the suggestiveness of the repetitions throughout the novel is never lost on him. As he makes the choir at the tavern sing the psalm to curse Farfrae, he explains his irony to them: "As for him, it was partly by his songs that he got me over, and heaved me out" (p. 270). Later, as Henchard sits in the loft of the granary waiting to challenge Farfrae to physical combat, Farfrae unwittingly turns the irony back on him, by humming

> a song he had sung when he arrived years before at the Three Mariners, a poor young man, adventuring for life and fortune, and scarcely knowing whitherwards:—
>> "And here's a hand, my trusty fiere,
>> And gie's a hand o' thine."
> Nothing moved Henchard like an old melody. He sank back. "No; I can't do it!" he gasped. (312)

Finally, in his last will, Henchard unravels all his mistakes, and untwists the curse he had sung for Farfrae to apply it to himself. Those verses from the psalm, "And the next age his hated name/Shall utterly deface" (p. 268), are repeated in Michael's final and summary request, "that no man remember me."

There are other examples of repetition, which need not be explicated in depth here. Henchard's dependence on the weather twice ruins him:

in Chapter 16, when his planned holiday entertainments at Poundbury Ring are ruined by rain, and he loses face to Farfrae; and in Chapter 27, at the harvest, when it is "more like living in Revelations . . . than in England," when the end of the world does come, financially, for Henchard, as he misguesses the weather. And there are striking parallels as well as serious artistic achievements in the death scenes of Susan, in Chapter 18, and Lucetta, in Chapter 40.

Lucetta's whole existence in the novel is interesting in its formal artistic conception. She is a continuation of Susan, a second character coming up out of Henchard's past. At the same time, however, she is a partial Gloucester to Henchard's Lear, running through the same or similar griefs with him, suffering for and destroyed by the past she shares with him. She tries to break from the bonds of her past, and this destroys her. The past cannot be forgotten because it cannot be made to die. Henchard reads her old love letters to himself aloud for her husband, Farfrae, and "her own words greeted her in Henchard's voice, like spirits from the grave" (p. 285). In reading the letters, Henchard is tempting himself to what he thinks will destroy Farfrae—the exposure of the past. But Farfrae's happiness and success are tied best to the future, only momentarily to the present, and not at all to the past. The letters represent Lucetta's past, and her happiness is dependent on keeping that past hidden. When it is exposed—economically, through the agency of Henchard's own destroyers, the furmity-woman and Jopp—Lucetta is destroyed. The town revives an old custom, and has a skimmity-ride, depicting Lucetta's past with Henchard. The shock is so great for her that she has a miscarriage, thus losing the future she has planned with Farfrae, and dies.

Henchard's fault in relation to Lucetta is similar to his fault in relation to Susan, so that Lucetta's role in the novel becomes in part a reworking of Susan's to heighten the effect. Repetition and the suggestion of repetition through the stylization of material represent the intensity of existence that Hardy wants. This intensity is suggested by the structure of the novel; it is supported, metaphorically, by the setting and by numerous descriptive and dramatic references; and it is actual in the real, literal, and specific juxtaposition of past and present, in the intrusion of certain past events into the present. This intrusion is dramatized as coincidence, and its dramatic effect—the past repeating itself, displacing the present—is the creation of that timelessness which allows the expansion of character and incident to a universal significance.

The two major stages in *The Mayor of Casterbridge* have been examined at some length. The whole of Casterbridge is a "stage" (p. 355), and there are several other, smaller ones which are constructed on principles at least similar to those employed in the construction of the Ring and Mai Dun. High Place Hall, the house Lucetta takes in Casterbridge, represents metaphorically the past and the unhappy reconstruction of it, at the same time that it stands as a sort of gray *memento mori,* representative of the humility of human accomplishments. Ten Hatches Hole, where Henchard goes to commit suicide, is described briefly as "a circular pool formed by the wash of centuries" (p. 257). This seemingly insignificant detail, despite its brevity, operates in the metaphoric context of the whole novel. It is at Ten Hatches Hole that Henchard prepares to take his life, but he is saved by the most grotesque of coincidences: he sees himself floating in the water beneath him. The ironic and exactly timed intrusion of the effigy from the skimmity-ride becomes all the more a dramatic, symbolic interference if one accepts that Ten Hatches Hole exists in an expanded time that runs for "centuries." As both irony and coincidence grow larger, they make Henchard more important, so that it is not just his own life he contemplates taking, but that of the hero in us all. Smaller lives—Lucetta's, the effigy's—have been sacrificed to save him, because, Hardy insists, Henchard is worth more and can bear more.

The last stage Hardy describes is his general Wessex stage, Egdon Heath. Egdon is the world—or like it—and Henchard walks out into it to die. It is "that ancient country whose surface never had been stirred to a finger's depth, save by the scratching of rabbits, since brushed by the feet of the earliest tribes" (p. 286). And if all Michael Henchard has done in the face of his fate is scratch at the surface of this timeless immensity, still he has risen as man in the dignity of his effort, and his scratching is etched along with the brushing of the feet of those earliest tribes on the history of man and his world.

There are a number of statements of compression or expansion of time in *The Mayor of Casterbridge*. Dealer Buzzford casually introduces this technique in the remark which serves as the epigraph for this chapter: "Casterbridge is a old, hoary place o' wickedness, by all account. 'Tis recorded in history that we rebelled against the King one or two hundred years ago, in the time of the Romans" (p. 59). Hardy worked carefully with this humorous and cleverly effective bit of historical inaccuracy. The original form the statement takes in the manuscript is straight, simple, and accurate:

> hoary
> "Casterbridge is a old ~~ancient~~ place o'wickedness, by all ac-
> rebelled against
> count. 'Tis recorded in history that we ~~helped kill~~ the King
> one or
> ~~about~~ two hundred years ago; and for my part, I can well
> believe it." (fol. 73)

Then, by means of an interlinear addition, Hardy pushes the "one or two hundred years ago" past back into "the time of the Romans," and all of history is foreshortened.

Something similar happens in the furmity-woman's scene at court. She is described, first, as

> an old woman of mottled countenance, attired in a shawl of
> that nameless tertiary hue which comes, but cannot be made
> —a hue neither tawny, russet, hazel, nor ash; a sticky black
> bonnet that seemed to have been worn in the country of the
> Psalmist where the clouds drop fatness; and in an apron that
> had been white in times so comparatively recent as to con-
> trast visibly with the rest of her clothes. The steeped aspect
> of the woman as a whole showed her to be no native of the
> country-side or even of a country-town. (229)

This description seems deliberately calculated to elude time. The furmity-woman is said to belong to no local place, though we know her only from Weydon Priors to Casterbridge. When she first appeared in the novel, in its opening chapter, her apron was white—and now the time of that whiteness, twenty years ago, is suggested as "comparatively recent" in her history, and is pushed thus into proximity with the present. Then she begins to tell the story of that earlier time:

> "Twenty years ago or thereabout I was a selling of furmity
> in a tent at Weydon Fair—"
> " 'Twenty years ago'—well, that's beginning at the begin
> ning; suppose you go back to the Creation!" said the clerk,
> not without satire.

100

But Henchard stared, and quite forgot what was evidence
and what was not. (231)

The end is the same as that of the other example given, to make the
present representatively larger. The technique, however, is slightly different. The past—of twenty years and of all of time—is condensed so
that the present can encompass more of it, and the scene in the present
is expanded and taken back through time to cover all the past. To effect
this expansion, Hardy again revised carefully. The descriptive paragraph
quoted above is written into the manuscript in almost final form. But
the dialogue that follows has one important interlinear addition, which
seems to be evidence of Hardy's awareness of what he was doing. After
the clerk says, "well, that's beginning at the beginning," Hardy inserts
a new line for him, "suppose you go back to the Creation!" (fol. 287)
which emphasizes the ironically suggested expansion.

A third quotable example of the seemingly deliberate creation of
metaphors of timelessness through dialogue occurs in Chapter 26, as
Henchard goes to see Mr. Fall, the weather-prophet. Henchard asks him
how he is sure of his prediction of "tempest" for the harvest time.

"You are not certain, of course?"
"As one can be in a world where all's unsure. 'Twill be
more like living in Revelations this autumn than in England.
Shall I sketch it out for 'ee in a scheme?" (214–15)

This adumbration of Henchard's fall is done in apocalyptic terms, and
through the suggestion of a larger world and a universal time for him
to act in, his destruction becomes, symbolically, the end of the world.
Again, Hardy works out the line in the manuscript. The first legible
draft seems to make no sense at all: " 'Twill be as much like living in
Revelations this autumn as living elsewhere can be" (fol. 268). The
main idea is already there, perhaps having somehow suggested itself.
But the term and the idea have yet to be turned from expletive reference to thematic and dramatic metaphor, which is what Hardy does,
finally. The manuscript looks like this:

more
" 'Twill be ~~as much [?]~~ like living in Revelations this autumn
than   in England
~~as~~ living ~~elsewhere can be.~~"

This kind of atmosphere legitimizes the action of *The Mayor of*

Casterbridge. After the exposure of Henchard's Weydon Priors past in the present of Casterbridge, Hardy explains its importance in terms of this atmosphere:

> Had the incident been well known of old and always, it might by this time have grown to be lightly regarded as the rather tall wild oat . . . of a young man, with whom the steady and mature (if somewhat headstrong) burgher of to-day had scarcely a point in common. But the act having lain as dead and buried ever since, the interspace of years was unperceived; and the black spot of his youth wore the aspect of a recent crime. (251)

It is because of the characteristic mood of the novel, too, that Newson can pop in and out, dramatically, as he does. And though this mood would suggest that his entrance needs little preparation, still Hardy sets each appearance he makes. The first time he visits Henchard, the corn-factor is living in Jopp's house, which is set with the casual apostrophe of "trees which seemed old enough to have been planted by the friars" (p. 254) of the old Franciscan Priory, in ruins close by (p. 145). "The cottage itself," the narrator continues, "was built of old stones from the long dismantled Priory," and stands near the spot of the original mill where the water has "raised its roar for centuries" (p. 255).

This setting detail, small as it may seem, still serves to maintain the mood of the novel, and thus helps to justify the coincidence of Newson's return. In presenting Newson's return, Hardy chooses, as he often does, to emphasize the coincidence. Newson has stopped by once, while Henchard is out attending the death of Lucetta. When he returns, Jopp describes the visitor, who "gave no name, and no message." Henchard replies to this, "Nor do I gi'e him any attention" (p. 331). Newson returns in the next chapter, and confronts Henchard:[13] "So here I am. Now—that transaction between us some twenty years agone—'tis that I've called about" (pp. 335–36). The intrusion is so sudden—and then, equally quickly, it is over, and he is gone. Henchard tells him that both Susan and Elizabeth-Jane are dead, and he departs: "Henchard heard the retreating footsteps upon the sanded floor, the mechanical lifting of the latch. . . . Newson's shadow passed the window. He was gone" (p. 338). Henchard's lie "had been the impulse of a moment"—and the next time Newson returns, Henchard lives his whole "lifetime" in that "moment."

One of the major objections to *The Mayor of Casterbridge* is Albert Guerard's complaint that the novel is too long, that Chapters 28–30 and 36–40 are grossly overplotted.[14] The chapters he cites are, for the most part, weak, though the finely done court scene of Chapter 28 is essential, and the end of Chapter 40 contains those few, beautiful lines that make up the representation of Lucetta's death. But Guerard appreciates the power of *The Mayor of Casterbridge,* and it seems to be this appreciation that makes him call attention to what he sees as its flaws. (One wonders if he means to include Chapter 28 in his blacklist, since he says that the furmity-woman's return is unforgettable for him, and central to that stylized formality which makes the novel.)[15] Similarly, I am tempted to call attention to the instances of editorial interference in the novel, simply because they are so few. Hardy rarely—never, in the rest of his fiction—had or exercised the patience and control which is so obvious in his handling of *The Mayor of Casterbridge. Tess of the D'Urbervilles,* perhaps the next best of his novels, is marred by his editorializing and by his frequent perversion of the narrative character and point of view. He solves the problem in part in this novel by his conception of Elizabeth-Jane. She views the world much as Tess does; but she is not the central character, and she is set up to assume, logically and reasonably, the point of view assigned her. Elizabeth-Jane inherits from her mother —"one who deems anything possible at the hands of Time or Chance except, perhaps, fair play" (p. 2)—her vision of life. She sees early that life is "a tragical rather than a comical thing; that though one could be gay on occasion, moments of gaiety were interludes, and no part of the actual drama" (p. 63). As Elizabeth-Jane develops (too quickly, in Chapter 24 and 25) the narrator rephrases her philosophy for her:

> Yet her experience had consisted less of pure disappointments than in a series of substitutions. Continually it had happened that what she had desired had not been granted her, and that what had been granted her she had not desired.
> (205)

Finally, in the conclusion of the novel, we are told for the last time what Elizabeth-Jane's vision is, and it is effectively Hardy's own vision, justified by the "experience" of the novel. Elizabeth-Jane serves as interpreter of the experience of Henchard's intense and tragic existence for the normal world. Her awareness keeps the novel in the world of actual people and actual England in a specific midnineteenth-century time.

The story Elizabeth-Jane interprets is the story of "Faust" (p. 131)—who sold something of his, too, for some twenty-odd years of happiness; of a Job-like creature, for a moment (p. 143); of "Cain" (p. 361), our brother. Henchard has been the "great tree in a wind" (p. 141), "a vehement gloomy being" (p. 131), "a dark ruin" (p. 376) in the course of the novel. And in the end he is the great silent creature who faces his fate and is overcome.

I said at the beginning of this study of Hardy's technique that one of the curious things about his art was his inability to make his characters speak. This generalization has been qualified several times for the minor novels. However, in *The Mayor of Casterbridge* it is too exactly true, and still the novel is a great dramatic success. Characters don't talk things out; they stand mutely facing each other while the narrator explains. Elizabeth-Jane doesn't tell anyone how she feels about life; rather, the narrator explains her vision to the reader. And Henchard's last will is not only written rather than spoken, it is delivered to Elizabeth-Jane by an intermediate character who cannot even read. Perhaps this device—or trick—is really very effective for the dramatization of Henchard's character, for since Whittle can't read, the original power of the statement is saved for the moment of its disclosure, though Henchard himself has been dead for half an hour.

Henchard's silence is total: his only speech is that grand, turgid, wrenched Cain speech. Silence finally pervades his whole existence—past, present, and the future that never comes to be. His will is:

"That Elizabeth-Jane Farfrae not to be told of my death,
or made to grieve on account of me.
"& that I be not bury'd in consecrated ground.
"& that no sexton be asked to toll the bell.
"& that nobody is wished to see my dead body.
"& that no murners walk behind me at my funeral.
"& that no flours be planted on my grave.
"& that no man remember me.
"To this I put my name.
Michael Henchard."
(384)

In the chapter of *Sartor Resartus* entitled "Symbols," Teufelsdrockh says, "Speech is of Time, Silence is of Eternity." And in response to Henchard's last silence, Elizabeth-Jane says, "But, there's no altering—so it must be" (p. 384). An intensified, imperative "Amen" is all one can say to the career, the fate, the will of Michael Henchard: "so it must be."

Then the world is relaxed, diminished, and returned to its more usual self and size. As this happens, Hardy reiterates Elizabeth-Jane's vision, her understanding through experience—as a reminder, perhaps, of that intense repetition which has been the core of the novel: "Her experience had been of a kind to teach her, rightly or wrongly, that the doubtful honor of a brief transit through a sorry world hardly called for effusiveness." (p. 385) But she is now fortunate, and a new horizon has appeared for her. Still, Henchard's tragedy has been an experience, a lesson in life, not just a catharsis. And as the novel concludes,

> she did not cease to wonder at the persistence of the unforeseen, when the one to whom such unbroken tranquility had been accorded in the adult stage was she whose youth had seemed to teach that happiness was but the occasional episode in a general drama of pain. (386)

The quiet and tenuous hope expressed here is what we need—and nothing more would fit. I think of lines like Albany's, at the close of *King Lear*:

> The weight of this sad time we must obey;
> Speak what we feel, not what we ought to say.
> The oldest hath borne most; we that are young
> Shall never see so much nor live so long.

And that longevity of Lear's, of which Edgar speaks, is measured not just by his years, but by "the intensity of his existence."

The chorus's last lines in *Oedipus Rex* come to my mind also:

> Make way for Oedipus. All people said,
> 'That is a fortunate man';
> And now what storms are beating on his head!
> Call no man fortunate that is not dead.
> The dead are free from pain.

105

Michael Henchard, "a Man of Character" whose "Character" makes his "Fate" (p. 131), belongs on that same list which includes Oedipus and Lear, both of whom remain, in spite of their crimes, great men, grand heroic figures who represent the size of the soul of man. It has been pointed out that "Character is Fate" was not said by Novalis, literally, but by George Eliot purporting to quote Novalis.[16] In *Heinrich von Ofterdingen* Novalis says "Ich einsehe, dass Schicksal und Gemüt Namen eines Begriffes sind"; and in *The Mill on the Floss* George Eliot says " 'Character,' says Novalis, in one of his questionable aphorisms—'character is destiny.' " George Eliot disagrees with her adapted Novalis; circumstance, she insists, plays a part in the determination of one's fate. Hardy agrees with Novalis; and though circumstance, even the doubling circumstance of coincidence, intrudes on his characters more frequently than it does on George Eliot's, it does so only to dramatize their fates. The seeming interference of circumstance with the mind's, the soul's, the character's self-determination is in the scheme of Hardy's dramatic art but the product, symbolically, of that self-determination. This is what establishes the tragic inevitability characteristic of Hardy's finest work in prose and in poetry. Here Michael Henchard, like Faust, creates his own fate, and cannot escape from it.[17]

The Mayor of Casterbridge is the finest of Hardy's achievements. It is tightly structured in its form, magnificent and true in its creation and presentation of character, and brilliant in its use of a whole metaphoric atmosphere to suggest and support its dramatic and thematic ambitions. More than any other of Hardy's works *The Mayor of Casterbridge* belongs on that short list of masterpieces in the history of English literature.

NOTES TO CHAPTER V

1. I am indebted for this last point, which seems to me quite relevant, to Mr. John Lee Marlow, a former student of mine at the University of Notre Dame. That Jopp is to Henchard as Fedullah is to Ahab helps explain Jopp's function in the novel and makes it easier to see him as more than the usual villain, which he would otherwise seem to be.

2. William Rutland (*Writings and their Background*, p. 39) has noted that Hardy was greatly impressed by these lines from the *Prometheus* of Aeschylus: "The fate which is ordained must be borne as best it may, knowing that the might of Necessity

may not be contended with." The obvious parallel in the novels is this speech of Henchard's; and it seems reasonable to speculate from Hardy's use of the first part of the sentence and then his rejection of the second part that Aeschylean Necessity is not central to Hardy's concept of man's fate.

3. Guerard remarks that watching Henchard is like watching "a figure of Old Testament strength and courage." "Like the Old Testament chroniclers," he says, "Hardy rarely elaborates his big scenes, and there are times when the very phrasing has a Biblical simplicity." He concludes that the first six chapters of *The Mayor of Casterbridge* "offer one of the simplest (and one of the greatest) openings in all fiction" (Introduction to *The Mayor of Casterbridge* [New York, 1956], p. vi). W. R. Rutland notes that "Hardy's favorite reading in the Bible were the narratives. . . . After Genesis, his favorite single books were Job, the Psalms and Ecclesiastes" (*Writings and their Background*, p. 4). And Rutland points out Hardy's interesting note, written on Easter Sunday in 1885, less than two weeks before he finished the manuscript of *The Mayor of Casterbridge*: "Evidences of Art in Biblical narratives. They are written with a watchful attention (though disguised) as to their effect on the reader. Their so-called simplicity is, in fact, the simplicity of the highest cunning" (F. E. Hardy, *Life of Hardy*, p. 170).

4. *The Twentieth Century Novel* (Chicago, 1941), p. 141.

5. *Technique of Hardy*, p. 211.

6. *Thomas Hardy*, p. 21.

7. "*The Mayor of Casterbridge* and the Old Testament's First Book of Samuel," *PMLA* 71 (1956): 118–30.

8. "The Novels of Thomas Hardy," English Association Pamphlet 71 (London, 1928), p. 7.

9. Introduction to *The Mayor of Casterbridge*, p. viii.

10. Dorset County Museum, Dorchester.

11. This line is used originally in the manuscript in Chapter 44, as Henchard arrives at the wedding feast and discovers Newson dancing with Elizabeth-Jane: "That face—Henchard lived a lifetime the moment he saw it—that face was Newson's" (fol. 467). Cf. the revised text: "That happy face—Henchard's complete discomfiture lay in it. It was Newson's, who had indeed come and supplanted him" (p. 376).

12. There is a possibility, too, of an ironic twist on Genesis here. Michael Henchard returns, on the last day of his activity, the "sixth," to review creation, to review the world from its beginning in an attempt to understand what has been. On his seventh day of timelessly compressed existence, he dies.

13. In attempting to justify Newson's intrusion on Henchard, Hardy creates some problems for himself. Perhaps he would have been better off depending on the mood he has created for the novel through his relentlessly symbolic setting and his metaphors of timelessness, compression, and the intensity that suggests the coincidental. The meeting of Henchard and Newson is prepared for twice: when the unidentified stranger appears at Peter's Finger in Chapter 36 (pp. 299–300), and at the end of Chapter 40, when Jopp says that "a traveller, or sea-captain of some sort" has been by (p. 331). However, when the two meet, either Newson lies to Henchard about his arrival—for no reason at all—in saying that he "got here by coach, ten minutes ago"

(p. 335); or this is a slip on Hardy's part; or both the preparatory bits are wrong. The first of these, the arrival at Peter's Finger—and Newson is "the man who asked the way" there (p. 335)—could have been two weeks before the skimmity-ride, and thus two weeks before the meeting at Jopp's cottage; but the stranger at the Mixon Lane pub says that he "shall be in Casterbridge for two or three weeks to come" (p. 300), and he later tells Henchard that he "went to Casterbridge on my way to Falmouth" (p. 335). And the second brief preparatory scene is completely impossible, unless Newson is lying, since Jopp reports his visit to the cottage as Henchard returns late in the evening, and the sailor doesn't pay his second call until the next morning is "fully broke" (p. 251), which interval is longer than the "ten minutes" since his arrival.

14. *Thomas Hardy*, p. 36; Introduction to *The Mayor of Casterbridge*, p. vii.

15. *Thomas Hardy*, p. 13.

16. Gordon S. Haight in his note in the Riverside edition of *The Mill on the Floss* (Cambridge, Mass., 1961), p. 351, and W. E. Yuill in " 'Character is Fate': a Note on Thomas Hardy, George Eliot, and Novalis," *Modern Language Review* 57 (1962): 401–02.

17. Cf. Benjamin Sankey, "Henchard and Faust," *English Language Notes* 3 (December 1965): 123–24. Sankey identifies Hardy's description of Faust as from Carlyle's "Goethe's Helena."

VI

TESS OF THE D'URBERVILLES

*Experience is as to intensity, and not as to
duration.*

TESS OF THE D'URBERVILLES
1891

The thesis of dramatic intensity upon which
Hardy builds his fiction is not as poignant in
Tess of the D'Urbervilles as it is in *The Mayor of Casterbridge*. Though
the idea is as insistently present as a philosophical and even aesthetic
bias, the focus of this novel is not so powerfully singular or so free from
editorial remarks and argumentative intrusions as it is in Michael
Henchard's story. Hardy seems to be trying to do two things: present
the representative tragedy of *Tess of the D'Urbervilles* on the one hand,
and argue the case of "A Pure Woman Faithfully Represented" on the
other. The two, however, do not easily come together in a complementary way. The argument about society and its rules is not proved or
demonstrated by Tess's fate; rather, she seems almost to work and act
against Hardy's tentative assertion about the nature of morality. She
has a mind of her own: a conscience and a consciousness. And despite
Hardy's seeming attempt to make her the victim of a ruthless, relentless
society, or societal code, she becomes a tragic heroine. She develops a
vision of herself and the world which is separate from Hardy's anti-
convention propaganda and social criticism.

The significant hero cannot live or act in isolation from the world,
nor can he be a hero if his situation is solely within society. Hardy places

109

Tess very much in the local world of Wessex in space and in time. She acts within this world and, in one sense, according to its rules. Her consciousness, however, grows larger than that of the society in which she lives. As she is a descendent of the ancient d'Urbervilles, her heroic consciousness—and the point is that heroism is so much a matter of consciousness—fulfills not only the now in which she lives but the history which she represents as well.

The significant hero has to make his own fate in the world, and then by the exercise of his consciousness he has to meet that fate. Neither public opinion nor the law of God will suffice to judge the hero. His experience must be personally conceived and comprehended, and its consequences absolutely associated with it in his understanding. The tragic denouement is inevitable, thus, not because of the intervention of some external force, but because the hero, in his consciousness of justice and the nature of things, insists that it be so. The hero then becomes larger than his world, larger than the normal world in which he performs his actions. Not only is the hero responsible for his fate; he defines the terms of his fate as well. Thus Michael Henchard identifies himself in the Cain speech, and writes the awful sentence of his last will. Thus Jude Fawley chants his own anathema on "Remembrance Day" at the end of his story. Tess's death at Wintoncester is much more, of course, than the hanging of a murderer, and more too than the death of a girl victimized by an oppressive social morality. Tess knows what her death means. When she says almost mystically at Stonehenge, "I am ready" (p. 505), she is speaking her comprehension of what must come. In order for us to understand what this is and why it is so impressive we must go back to the beginning. If we are to know this novel, we must read it all as a preparation for that statement, and we must determine how each element of the fiction fits the precise and specific focus of the statement.

Tess of the D'Urbervilles has been represented by several critics as an epic novel, in contradistinction to *The Mayor of Casterbridge* as a dramatic novel. I have suggested at the beginning of this chapter that the total focus of this novel is not as close, generally, as the focus of *The Mayor of Casterbridge*. If we read *Tess of the D'Urbervilles* as a novel of social criticism or, even more simply, as but a story, this is probably quite true. What does the d'Urberville business have to do with Tess's seduction? What is the essential link between Tess's story and the description of the passing of an age in English history? Which is primary, the story or the history? If we read the novel carefully as Tess's tragedy these questions are answerable. Everything fits—except for the editorial criticism of the way we live now. And everything fits in the way it usually fits in Hardy's fiction—through the translation of the d'Urberville material into supportive metaphor, through the mythic correlation of details suggesting the single but representative act in the microcosm of time and space.

The descriptive elements and Hardy's choice of details not only support and emphasize Tess's tragedy, they also carry the burden of that minor social and historical theme of the changing of an age. In *The Mayor of Casterbridge* Henchard stands both as the independent hero and as the singular representative of the decline of the age; and his fall fulfills the parallel but secondary historical theme more than that theme serves to support and reinforce his tragedy. In this sense *Tess of the D'Urbervilles* is the more closely focused of the two novels: the secondary theme seems joined to the primary one of Tess's tragic destruction almost necessarily. The theme of the passing of an age is represented in the fall of Tess's family from landed gentry d'Urbervilles to peasant Durbeyfields; the interrelation of the generations of man is indicated partly by this and partly by the creation of a new d'Urberville in Alec, who acts irrevocably in Tess's present as well as from her past to bring about her tragedy. It is ironically the agony of Tess Durbeyfield—not d'Urberville—that makes her the figure she is and allows her to stand, for us and for Hardy, as representative of the heroic fate of man.

Tess's novel is written with a strong purpose, it seems: one which can only be called didactic. As Hardy insisted on Michael Henchard's being "A Man of Character," so he insists on Tess's being pure. His purpose turns to the arguments of the social critic and, more importantly, urges on the ineluctable tragedy of Tess's drama. The full title of the novel is *Tess of the D'Urbervilles: A Pure Woman Faithfully Represented.* In its richest sense her purity is, like Henchard's character, paradoxical. Like Henchard, she commits one great sin against her virtue, and the redemption of this sin seems always to be frustrated.

Tess's tragic fault is her seduction by Alec d'Urberville. This mistake intrudes throughout the novel to insist upon her destruction. As she leaves her seducer to return home, she meets the mad religious sign painter who warns her of the unforgetful and essentially unforgiving nature of man and the world, and exposes to us the intensity of her guilty self-consciousness. In his manuscript Hardy first had the painter write "THE, WAGES, OF, SIN, IS, DEATH";[1] the fulfillment of this red prophecy comes, dramatically, in the death of Sorrow, in the murder of Alec, and in Tess's hanging. But then Hardy changed the legend to read, as it now does, in "staring vermillion": "THY, DAMNATION, SLUMBERETH, NOT." These words are to Tess much more immediately and personally "accusatory." The significance of the first sign is one of future thematic fulfillment, the kind of adumbration we find so easily, for example, in George Eliot. The second rendering, however, describes the whole philosophical and argumentative thesis of the novel —that the past is never dead—and at the same time creates a significant dramatic moment out of this oracular confrontation between Tess and the voice of her fate. Editorially, Hardy criticizes society for holding Tess responsible for her one sin, and for making her feel guilty for her submission to Alec; yet at the same time he creates in Tess a character whose substance is the very convincing honesty with which she feels that guilt. As she acts out the novel, and as Hardy forms the whole more and more about her, Tess moves constantly in relation to those red words: "THY, DAMNATION, SLUMBERETH, NOT." Tess's self-consciousness makes it seem to her "as if this man had known her recent history; yet he was a total stranger" (p. 101). The next sign he paints— "One," he says, "that it will be good for dangerous young females like yerself to heed"—reads, "THOU, SHALT, NOT, COMMIT—" (p. 102). It is as though the commandment were written especially for her.

Her seduction haunts Tess both physically and psychically. She is ritualistically conscious of it, keeping track of it and reminding herself of it, much as Henchard would:

> She philosophically noted dates as they came past in the revolution of the year; the disastrous night of her undoing at Trantridge with its dark background of The Chase; also the dates of the baby's birth and death; also her own birthday; and every other day individualized by incidents in which she had taken some share. (124–25)

This reflective consciousness is broken by a sudden impulsive determination to try for a future, to free herself: "To escape the past and all that appertained thereto was to annihilate it, and to do that she would have to get away" (pp. 125–26). The place she chooses is Talbothays, in the valley of the Great Dairies and their luxuriant sensuousness. As she sets out "now in a direction almost opposite to that of her first adventuring" (p. 127), she thinks that "she might be happy in some nook that had no memories" (p. 125). She walks out across Egdon Heath to begin life anew, going, she supposes, to a new world. The narrator seems to agree with her conception, commenting that "To persons of limited spheres, miles are as geographical degrees, parishes as counties, counties as provinces and kingdoms" (p. 126). The world condenses, thus, in its physical size, and Tess becomes a larger member of it as a consequence.

One of the reasons for Tess's choice of Talbothays is that is stands "not remotely from some of the former estates of the d'Urbervilles, near the great family vaults of her granddames and their powerful husbands" (pp. 126–27). The fall of the d'Urbervilles is completed, in one sense, in Tess's life; and their fall through the time of history serves as a metaphoric reminder for Tess of her own fall: "She would be able to look at them, and think not only that d'Urberville, like Babylon, had fallen, but that the individual innocence of a humble descendent could lapse as silently" (p. 127). At the same time, however, Tess participates in the past of the d'Urbervilles, repeats a legendary part of their history, and is destroyed by her association with them. Her family, she senses, "was so unusually old as almost to have gone round the circle and become a new one" (p. 164); and in the repetition which Tess's life describes the "Fulfillment"—Phase the Seventh is so entitled—is both ironic and redemptive.

Tess's migration from Blackmore Vale to "her ancestral land" (p. 127) suggests to the reader that she cannot escape her past, as she has hoped, that she cannot "annihilate" it, that she can never find, in this small, tight world, a "nook that [has] no memories." This suggestion is underlined, and perhaps proved by a parallel example, almost immediately upon her arrival at Talbothays. In the opening words of Chapter 18, "Angel Clare rises up out of the past" (p. 147). He sees Tess: "then he seemed to discern something that was familiar, something which carried him back into a joyous and unforeseeing past, before the necessity of taking thought had made the heavens gray. He concluded that he had beheld her before; where, he could not tell" (p. 155). Their past together is from the time of innocence, from the time of the May-walk at Marlott on the day that John Durbeyfield discovered that his family indeed had a history. Tess's historic relation with Alec is the crime of her past which could have been prohibited, she thinks, if only Angel had danced with her on that day. His return into her life is too late, as it will be again at the end of the novel.

Angel's love for Tess reminds her in the legitimacy of its request of the illegitimacy of her affair with Alec. When Angel proposes to her, Tess rejects him "with grave hopelessness, as one who had heard anew the turmoil of her own past" (p. 222). Tess's mother "did not see life as Tess saw it," however; "That haunting episode of bygone days was to her mother but a passing accident" (p. 246). For Tess, her liaison with Alec is the primary fact and fault of her life. Part of her agony is that she is not given, until the end of the novel, the chance or the circumstances for confronting it, for living up to it and perhaps conquering it.

But at Talbothays, in a seemingly new and different world, Tess hopes to find another and simpler resolution to the problem. There she "appeared to feel that she had really laid a new foundation for her future" (p. 140). Under the mood of the place—and Talbothays, as it is described, is the embodied symbol of the sensuousness of innocent physical love—Tess determines to be free of Alec: "She dismissed her past—trod upon it and put it out, as one treads on a coal that is smouldering and dangerous" (p. 246). Eden thus recovered, as it were, Tess agrees to marry Angel. Seven days before their wedding, they drive off together into town. It is Christmas eve, and on such an auspicious occasion, in Hardy's time symbology, the smouldering past bursts into flame. Tess is confronted with the tale of her fall and is saved from its destructive impact only by Angel's refusal to believe the story. In her naiveté, then, Tess assures herself: "We shall go away, a very long distance, hundreds of miles from these parts, and such as this can never happen again, and no ghost of the past reach there" (p. 266). Escape, as Tess sees it, is a matter of space; but in Hardy's world it is time—the undying moments of an oppressive and retributively demanding past—that must be reckoned with.

Finally, on New Year's eve, Tess tells Angel of her past, and she pays for her honesty. After Angel has left her, she meets the man who identified her before her wedding and runs from him as he presents her again with her fault. She flees to Flintcomb Ash and there meets one of the other dairy maids from Talbothays. Marian suggests to her that they talk of the past in order to revive it, that they "talk of he, and of what nice times we had there, and o' the old things we used to know, and make it all come back again a'most, in seeming" (p. 366). Through Marian and what she says, and through the general progress of events in the novel, the past is consciously and intentionally carried forward alive in and existent with the present. Izzy, another Talbothays maid, two of the women from the d'Urberville estate at Trantridge, and the man Tess has run from all come to Flintcomb Ash, trapping Tess amid suggestions of her past. Then, as though the occurrence of so many coincidental meetings justifies another and greater coincidental meeting, Alec d'Urberville himself intrudes upon Tess's present, at the end of Phase the Sixth. The metaphoric justification for these accidental meetings—through setting and the allusions to larger repetitions, history, and the condensation of time—will be discussed later. The point now is to conclude quickly the long catalog of the various intrusions of Tess's past into her present until, at the climax of the novel, the past is resolved and the present destroyed. Alec returns to Tess at Marlott, and later finds her at Kingsbere, amid her d'Urberville ancestors, at "the spot of all spots in the world which could be considered the d'Urberville home" (p. 461). Then Angel comes back, by way of the cross where Alec and Tess have met, and through the place of Tess's birth where he first saw her at the dance. He goes to Sandbourne, and creates at his arrival the thematic climax of the novel. Both lines of Tess's past meet her at once; she is living with Alec when Angel finally comes to claim her as his wife.

The dramatic climax of the novel comes at Stonehenge, after Tess has made her heroic choice and has killed Alec. Her first fault catches her here. She has freed herself, cleansed herself—she is confident that Angel will "forgive" her now she has "done that" (p. 492)—but still she must pay for this "annihilation" of her past. The dilemma is the dilemma of tragedy; and in her almost trancelike state, Tess rises to heroism in accepting her fate. Her waking response to the presence of the deputies is almost mystical in its comprehension: "It is as it should be," she says; "I have had enough. . . . I am ready" (p. 505). What we understand here is the complementary meeting of Tess's story with the greater history of man. And in this symbolic place, to which it seems that Tess responds almost as much as we do, something of man's noble, heroic, and paradoxical guilt is expiated by her sacrifice on the ancient altar stone.

115

Hardy's interest in history is frequently shown in his interest in ancestry. At the beginning of this novel, Parson Tringham tells John Durbeyfield that he is "the lineal representative of the ancient and knightly family of d'Urbervilles" (p. 4). Sir John, then, as declined or degenerate "representative" of the past, says, " 'Tis recorded in history all about me" (p. 7), and links himself back to "King Norman's day" (p. 28). Part of the effect of this reference to the past is to expand the world of the present, much as Dealer Buzzford's description of Casterbridge was used in that novel. The other part of the effect, related to this, is to suggest the repetitious continuum of history. Tess complains that the only use to learning "that I am one of a long row" is in "finding out that there is set down in some old book somebody just like me, and to know that I shall only act her part" (p. 162). "The best," she says, "is not to remember that your nature and your past doings have been just like thousands' and thousands', and that your coming life and doings 'll be like thousands' and thousands' " (p. 162). We are all related, through the family of history—Adam's, d'Urberville's, man's. And what this signifies is not the fatal impossibility of man's success or freedom in this life, but the universality of Tess's experience. We cannot afford to be thrown off entirely by Tess's petulance, which is not so much Hardy's view of life has his challenge to himself to find the significant measure of a human creature, which will come in Tess's transcendence of that continuum in her "Fulfillment."

Tess's family is used to tie her story and its coincidences to each of the places of the novel, to each of the stages on which she acts out her life. The idea of d'Urberville is the motivation for her trip to Trantridge: to visit her rich and supposedly undeclined relative, Alec. Her choice of residence at Talbothays places her near her ancestral home at Kingsbere, on the edge of Edgon Heath. Edgon is described toward the end of the novel in its usual timeless character: "every irregularity of the soil was prehistoric, every channel an undisturbed British trackway; not a sod having been turned there since the days of the Caesars" (p. 480). Kingsbere itself is the resting place of "the bones of [Tess's] ancestors" (p. 132), "the spot of all spots in the world which could be considered the d'Urberville home, since they had rested there for full five hundred years" (p. 461). It is this spot, then, that Alec chooses for his next to last intrusion into Tess's life. Lying atop a d'Urberville altar-tomb, Alec comes to life from Tess's own past as well as from her ancient, ancestral past.[2]

Ironically, Angel Clare is also interested in the d'Urbervilles and feels "attached" to them (p. 213) by this interest. He shows Tess the various places of her past, beginning with "the fragment of an old manor house of Caroline date" (p. 238):

> "That," he observed, to entertain her, "is an interesting old place—one of the several seats which belonged to an ancient Norman family formerly of great influence in this country, the d'Urbervilles. I never pass one of their residences without thinking of them." (239)

He chooses another of Tess's ancestral properties as their first married residence, a house "which, before its mutilation, had been the mansion of a branch of the d'Urbervilles" (p. 261). He introduces Tess there, saying, "Welcome to one of your ancestral mansions" (p. 276). And he begins to tell her of the d'Urberville legend: "A certain d'Urberville of the sixteenth or seventeenth century committed a dreadful crime in his family coach; and since that time members of his family see or hear the old coach whenever—" (p. 272). The day on which Angel tells Tess this is New Year's eve, their wedding day. Tess, asking the chance to begin a new life, is refused by the continuing existence of her past, as this scene points up so precisely. Her fault, the sin with Alec, is represented in the intrusion of the "ghostly" (p. 213) past of her family on the eve of the New Year.

Alec finally finishes telling Tess the tale of the legendary d'Urberville coach. "It has to do," he says, "with a murder committed by one of the family, centuries ago" (p. 452).

> "One of the family is said to have abducted some beautiful woman, who tried to escape from the coach in which he was carrying her off, and in the struggle he killed her—or she killed him—I forgot which." (452)

This ancient murder is then repeated—and fulfilled—in the present, as Tess kills Alec.

The repetition of an ancient past in the present and the continuing existence of that past as a generally and mythically relevant force serve as supportive metaphors for the relentless pursuit of Tess by her own particular dramatic past, the tragic fault of her submission to Alec, which finally destroys her. Hardy paraphrases the line he used in *A Pair of Blue Eyes* and *The Return of the Native* to express the significance of all of this: "experience is as to intensity, and not as to duration" (p. 160). Intensity is central even to the way Tess looks at her own life. She sees herself as

> a woman living her precious life—a life which, to herself who endured or enjoyed it, possessed as great a dimension as the life of the mightiest to himself. Upon her sensations the whole world depended to Tess; through her existence all her fellow-creatures existed, to her. The universe itself only came into being for Tess on the particular day in the particular year in which she was born. (198–99)

The universe which Tess creates out of her existence is tragic, and as it unfolds it becomes more and more evident that the seed of the tragedy is planted in the very beginning.[3] The actual place of her temptation and submission, The Chase, is a sort of ominously preserved Eden. It is "the oldest wood in England" (p. 87) "—a truly venerable tract of forest land, one of the few remaining woodlands in England of undoubted primaeval date" (p. 42). Her expulsion from this Eden sends Tess out upon the earth, to the small and withering existence of her home at Marlott, and then, for escape, to the rich and seemingly second Eden of Talbothays, "the Valley of the Great Dairies . . . in which milk and butter grew to rankness . . . the verdant plain so well washed by the river Var or Froom" (p. 132–33). At Talbothays the "waters were clear as the pure River of Life shown to the Evangelist," and Tess's "hopes mingled with the sunshine in an ideal photosphere" (p. 133–34). When Tess is with Angel here in the mornings "they seemed to themselves the first person up of all the world," and it "impressed them with a feeling of isolation, as if they were Adam and Eve" (p. 167).

From Talbothays Tess flees to the hellishly postlapsarian world of Flintcomb Ash, where with Marian she remembers "that happy green tract of land where summer had been liberal in her gifts . . . . green, sunny, romantic Talbothays" (p. 365). They try together to recall that Eden for their peace of mind, "to make it all come back again a'most, in seeming" (p. 366). But Tess cannot remain even at Flintcomb Ash.

118

She is hounded there, too, by Alec, who greets her saying: "A jester might say this is just like Paradise. You are Eve, and I am the old Other One come to tempt you in the disguise of an inferior animal" (p. 445). Tess retreats once more, eventually to Kingsbere, where Alec follows her again; and when he appears this time "the old Other One" is in the guise of one of Tess's ancestors, "the oldest of them all" (p. 464). Finally, in flight after she has killed Alec, she comes to Stonehenge, the place of her sacrificial and salvific fulfillment.

The scene at Stonehenge is the most important in the novel. Hardy concentrates his whole effort here to insist on the size of his heroine and the greatness of her tragedy. As the same time this scene is the final and climactic representation of Hardy's own nondramatic point of view, and the voice of the critic speaks, proclaiming Tess the "victim."

There are two major sets of metaphors at work in this scene which finally come together as one in the murder of Alec. The first is the metaphor of blood, suggesting both Tess's loss of her virginity and her final destruction. Tess wears a red ribbon at the traditional May-walk —and she is "the only one of the white company who could boast of such a pronounced adornment" (p. 12). She is splashed with the blood of the dying Prince, after he is speared by the shaft of the mail cart (p. 35). As a result of this misfortunate loss of the horse, Tess allows herself to be persuaded to visit her "relatives" at Trantridge. There she is fed the ripe, red strawberries from Alec's garden, and is decked in a spectacle of red roses (p. 47), and pricks her chin on the thorns (p. 50). After her seduction, she meets the sign painter who accuses her in "staring vermillion words" (p. 101). She returns to Marlott, and while working in the field her arm is bruised and abraided by the stubble, and bleeds (p. 112). Then, life and convention having pursued her like fates or furies, and her crime having become so complex as to allow no easy retribution or resolution, Tess kills Alec, and his blood stains—crudely— through the ceiling as an ace of hearts (p. 488). Though Tess's blood is not actually shed in the end, she is sacrificed symbolically at the place which supposedly would have required, in its own time, the spilling of blood.

The second pattern of symbolic reference used to prepare for the Stonehenge scene is a series of three white coffins or altars. The first is the "empty stone coffin" in the churchyard of the old d'Urberville man-

119

sion, in which Angel places Tess on the night of their marriage and mutual confession (p. 318). Her past forces her, symbolically and in actuality, toward her future at Stonehenge, and disallows any free and satisfactory existence between those times. Tess has only three experiences in life: her seduction, and the twin acts of her revenge or expiation and her sacrifice. Her other experience, falling in love with Angel and marrying him, is denied to her in the meaning of his sleepwalk to the open coffin with her in his arms, and in her second burial on the altar at Stonehenge. The second of the stone symbols appears in Chapter 52, as the Durbeyfields arrive at Kingsbere and Tess enters the church of her ancestors. She passes "near an altar-tomb, the oldest of them all, on which was a recumbent figure" (p. 464). The figure is not an effigy, however; it is Alec. The stone slab on which he lies prefigures, ironically, the bed in which he is murdered. That bed, its white sheets stained with his blood, is the last of the stone symbols and the one in which the altar-coffin and blood metaphors are united. It is the altar of Tess's act of expiation for her fault. Although she finally does "annihilate" her past by destroying Alec, she does not really escape it, nor does she gain a future, except in her brief, wild honeymoon with Angel and in the lives of Angel and 'Liza-Lu beyond the end of the novel.

Tess's existence is governed by the law of tragedy relentlessly imposed and enforced. Hardy's insistence on his theme insures this. Though Tess is seduced, she is still—or finally—a pure woman. Her purity is redeemed throughout the novel in her heroism, and she is fulfilled in the end. The fulfillment is tragic, however, and thus in some sense it is sacrifice as well. It would be easy to say that Tess is sacrificed to the conventions of man's limitations, which is what Hardy wants to say, in part. More significant, however, is Tess's sacrifice of herself for the sake of her honesty and dignity; and in this Tess redeems man from his limitations, and achieves her freedom.

Though the scene at Stonehenge is not the best accomplishment of Hardy's art, it is his most ambitious attempt at rendering the world of the action in metaphoric and symbolic terms. With Stonehenge, he suddenly expands the dimensions and significance of Tess's tragedy to the extremes of suggestive reference. Tess is made to belong to Stonehenge, to its immensity in time and its incomprehensible towering aspect. The scene, however, may be too large for the rest of the novel, despite the preparation for it in the suggestions of sacrifice discussed above. Tess's tragic size is to be discovered primarily in the representative aspect of her life, as this is suggested by the history of the ancient line of d'Urbervilles, and the intensity of her existence is represented in the coincidental intrusions and recurrences of the past in the present. But nothing quite like Stonehenge can be anticipated from this. Stonehenge could have fit in *The Return of the Native* easily enough, and perhaps the texture of *The Mayor of Casterbridge* would have been enriched by the addition of another stage to go with Maumbury Ring and Mai-Dun. But in a novel not set physically on timeless, eternal Egdon Heath or amid Roman and prehistoric ruins, Stonehenge seems perhaps too expansive and too much a symbolic place.

But these are aesthetic considerations. And though it may be argued that the Stonehenge scene is symbolically awkward or aesthetically outsized, this does not diminish its thematic and philosophic significance. Angel tells Tess that Stonehenge is "older than the centuries; older than the d'Urbervilles" (p. 502). And that it is so is just the point. Tess's tragedy has been suggested as the general tragedy of man, heightened and intensified by the conventional intrusion of the past—and its fault—into the present. This recurrence of the past has been supported, metaphorically, through the use of Tess's ancestry. Suddenly, now, the d'Urberville history is not enough; Tess's life and fate are greater and more significant that the d'Urberville history can indicate. As Tess becomes conscious of her relation to Stonehenge, we are asked to accept on the strength of this new metaphor of setting a greater symbolic dimension for the whole novel. Stonehenge is the old "heathen temple" (p. 502) where sacrifices were made to the sun in primal days, before the worship of any modern God (p. 503). Tess is placed on the altar stone of that ancient worship, and Hardy remarks at the close that "the President of the Immortals, in Aeschylean phrase, had ended his sport with Tess" (p. 508). This would make it seem that Tess is sacrificed to the gods, to Fate, to the unsympathetic manipulator of man's destiny. Yet Tess's fault is her own volitional tragic fault, not an imposition of a necessary fate upon her from the beginning. Her fate is determined, in the tradition of tragedy, by her own act—by the act that initiates the action of the rest of the tragedy. And though her final destruction at Wintoncester is accomplished at the hands of men acting from the straight, cruel standards of society, it is done with Tess's full and understanding submission.

The Stonehenge scene is exemplary of Hardy's characteristic strength and weakness as an artist as well as of his dramatic vision. Hardy's art is best in its narrative, and his descriptive technique is usually superb. But for some reason he does not just describe Stonehenge, and the scene is flawed because of this. The narrator reports the arrival of Tess and Angel:

> He listened. The wind, playing upon the edifice, produced a booming tune, like the note of some gigantic one-stringed harp. No other sound came from it, and lifting his hand and advancing a step or two, Clare felt the vertical surface of the structure. (501)

What is wrong here is not just the sentence structure, but more importantly the violation of the description by the intrusion of Angel. Hardy vitiates the force of the description with Angel's feeling the stone and, later in the same paragraph, "carrying his fingers forward" to discover "the collosal rectangular pillar," and "stretching out his left hand" to feel another. The presence of Angel denies Hardy the distance he needs for the representation of descriptive detail.

Tess manages to speak her lines in the dialogue of the scene well enough, though Angel's remarks (like Farfrae's at the end of *The Mayor of Casterbridge*) are clumsy, crude, or inane. Together Tess and Angel identify the place as "Stonehenge," the "heathen temple." Then Clare says: "Yes. Older than the centuries; older than the d'Urbervilles! Well, what shall we do, darling?" (p. 502). The same mistake appears again a few paragraphs later, as he says to Tess: "Sleepy are you, dear? I think you are lying on an altar" (p. 502). And he explains the object and timing of the ancient sacrificial rites at Stonehenge just as grotesquely:

> "Did they sacrifice to God here?" asked she.
> "No," said he.
> "Who to?"
> "I believe to the sun. That lofty stone set away by itself is in the direction of the sun, which will presently rise behind it." (503)

Tess speaks her lines with simplicity and dignity. What she says brings up her association with the scene: "One of my mother's people was a shepherd hereabouts, now I think of it. And you used to say at Talbothays that I was a heathen. So now I am at home" (p. 502). And she

122

humbly suggests the largeness of her existence in her symbolic isolation in the great, timeless temple of sacrifice:

> "I like very much to be here," she murmured. "It is so solemn and lonely—after my great happiness—with nothing but the sky above my face. It seems as if there were no folk in the world but we two; and I wish there were not—except 'Liza-Lu." (502)

Hardy's best method, however, is demonstrated a few paragraphs later, in strict narrative description:

> In a minute or two her breathing became more regular, her clasp on his hand relaxed, and she fell asleep. The band of silver paleness along the east horizon made even distant parts of the Great Plain appear dark and near; and the whole enormous landscape bore that impress of reserve, taciturnity, and hesitation which is usual just before day. The eastward pillars and their architraves stood up blackly against the light, and the great flame-shaped Sun-stone beyond them; and the Stone of Sacrifice midway. Presently the night wind died out, and the quivering little pools in the cup-like hollows of the stones lay still. (504)

The long descriptive paragraphs of the final chapter of the novel are equally effective. The distance of the narrator from the spot is such that no sound need be represented to the reader. Angel and 'Liza-Lu climb the hill out of Wintoncester "impelled by a force that seemed to overrule their will," and stand still "in paralyzed suspense" beside the first milestone (p. 507). Tess's end is declared in the silent gesture of the raised black flag, and again the world returns to a more normal, more peaceful, less intense existence:

> And the d'Urberville knights and dames slept on in their tombs unknowing. The two speechless gazers bent themselves down to the earth, as if in prayer, and remained thus a long time, absolutely motionless: the flag continued to wave silently. As soon as they had strength they arose, joined hands again, and went on. (508)

Angel and 'Liza-Lu carry away the experience of the tragedy, much as Elizabeth-Jane does in the end of *The Mayor of Casterbridge*.

The final effect of *Tess of the D'Urbervilles* is perhaps as great as that

123

of *The Mayor of Casterbridge*, due largely to the boldness of Hardy's vision in the use of Stonehenge, and to his careful artistry in the representation of Tess's death. As a whole, however, the novel is not as well executed as *The Mayor of Casterbridge*, and it does not always have the dramatic force that Michael Henchard's novel has. *Tess of the D'Urbervilles* is marred most by Hardy's frequent impatience and the resultant intrusiveness of his narrator. The novel is sometimes clumsy in its manner, mistaken in its diction, especially in dialogue, and insensitive or unsubtle in its choice and dramatization of scenes. Still, despite all of this, Hardy's great creative instinct substantiates the tragedy of a young country girl who becomes as large as the largest heroine through the intensity of her existence and her significant consciousness of that intensity, played in the metaphoric context of the descriptive and narrative references of the novel. The simple but impressive plot structure is based upon the coincidental recurrence of events and the characters involved in them. Coincidence is justified, as usual in Hardy's fiction, through the actual and dramatic relation of the past to the present and through large metaphors of association; and Hardy's convention, that "experience is as to intensity, and not as to duration" (p. 160), is described in the expansion of the time context of the story through the reference to history.

Thus, in the end, Hardy makes Tess Durbeyfield significantly one of the d'Urbervilles. Her being so places her in a more general and inclusive context than that in which country girls are usually found. It is our world, finally, in which she lives, and our fates which in some heightened sense she lives. Through her we know something more about the general, historical, and continuing plight of our race; and we know something more about the heroic acceptance of that plight. Though Hardy cries out in the end that "the President of the Immortals . . . had ended his sport with Tess"—and though we may want to agree with him —we know, surely, from our experience in the novel that it has been more real, more meaningful, and much more moving than that.

NOTES TO CHAPTER VI

1. MS fol. 108. Dorset County Museum, Dorchester, England.
2. Hardy's determination to make use of the idea of d'Urberville in the texture

and the sense of the novel can be seen in certain emendations made in the manuscript and later revisions to the printed text. Dairyman Crick's remark to Tess immediately upon her arrival at Talbothays—that he has heard "that a family of some such name as yours in Blackmore Vale came originally from these parts, and that 'twere a old ancient race that had all but perished off the earth—though the new generations didn't know it" (p. 139)—is inserted in the manuscript (*verso*, fol. 150). Tess's later scene with Alec at Kingsbere in Chapter 52 is expanded from one brief paragraph in the manuscript, and this revision is entered after the serial version was published. In the manuscript and serial versions, Tess visits the family vaults on her way to Talbothays, in Chapter 16; missing altogether are the description of Kingsbere as the place "where lay those ancestors of whom her father had spoken and sung to painfullness: Kingsbere, the spot of all spots in the world which could be considered the d'Urberville home" and Tess's dramatic confrontation with Alec. See also Mary Ellen Chase, *Thomas Hardy from Serial to Novel* (Minneapolis, 1927), pp. 84–85 and 92–94, for a detailed discussion of this change from serial publication to the first edition.

3. And the confession of her fault to Angel on the New Year's eve that is their wedding day seems like the heroic act of the "Last Day" of this universe (p. 287).

VII

JUDE THE OBSCURE

As you got older, and felt yourself to be at the centre of your time, and not at a point in its circumference . . . you were seized with a sort of shuddering, he perceived.

JUDE THE OBSCURE
1895

Late in *Jude the Obscure* the hero says, "I was, perhaps after all, a paltry victim to the spirit of mental and social restlessness, that makes so many unhappy in these days" (pp. 393–94). We can be distracted from the focus of the novel if we take this curiously self-pitying statement seriously as the truth of the matter. Jude makes several such comments as mouth-piece for Hardy's critical argument which, if read as crucial statements for the novel, reduce it to a clumsily didactic and propagandistic period piece with some sort of quasi-historical relevance. But this is not what *Jude the Obscure* is. *Jude the Obscure* is concerned with the experience of another large representative man, like Henchard, or Tess, or even Clym Yeobright, caught in a world of tragic possibilities and fated to come to terms with himself in that world. Hardy, like Faulkner, kept "telling the same story over and over to [him]self and to the world."[1]

Just three paragraphs before Jude complains about being a "paltry victim" he has been capable of seeing things as they really are, for him. He is conscious of his flaw: "my impulses—affections—vices perhaps they should be called—were too strong not to hamper a man without advantages" (p. 393). He recognizes also the conflict of his ambitions with

126

his situation: "it was my poverty and not my will that consented to be beaten." The novel is built from these two elements of character and environment, and is intensified in action by Jude's impatience: "It takes two or three generations," he says, "to do what I tried to do in one" (p. 393). In the end, Jude's triumph—his only and heroic triumph—is that of his will; in every other way he is destroyed.

More than any of the other novels, *Jude the Obscure* is sparely and rigorously constructed. The model seems more than ever to come from Aeschylus or Sophocles, Hardy's favorite dramatists. A fatal choice—or perhaps not even a choice, but rather a kind of essential and inevitable reflex action—is made, several unsuccessful attempts are made to correct that mistake, and then at the conclusion the hero reconciles himself to the fate he has created for himself by that first act, and it collapses on his shoulders, destroying him. Jude is seduced by Arabella and marries her, and Sue Bridehead marries Phillotson; then, throughout the long middle sections of the novel, after both couples have separated, Jude and Sue try to make a life together—try to revise what has gone before. But what happens in this part of the novel doesn't happen at all, in a sense; what Jude and Sue try to make happen cannot happen. And Sue remarries Phillotson, and Jude returns to Arabella.

Jude's one real physical act—that choice or reflex action—is his marriage to Arabella, and this, or the circumstance which leads him to it, is his mistake. It is his tragic fault, and it exposes to us early those "impulses—affections—vices perhaps they should be called" that he later identifies as the flaw in his character. He realizes almost immediately that marriage to Arabella is a mistake, even before he knows that Arabella has tricked him. Still, it is not just the marriage that makes and marks Jude's downfall; his physical, sensual self and its "impulses—affections—vices perhaps" make him Arabella's easy victim. The marriage becomes, then, the dramatic symbol for the weakness in Jude's character. It is because Arabella can have a claim on Jude through his weakness that this first marriage is so important. The argument of the novel is not really about marriage and divorce as institutions, conventions, conveniences, or inconveniences; the focus is on character, as it usually is in Hardy's work. *Jude the Obscure* is the intense and penetrating representation of the complex and significant character of Jude himself, and everything in the novel contributes to this.

The other side of Jude's drama is his dream of Christminster: and this, too, is a fault for him, another of his "impulses—affections—vices perhaps." As a character, Jude is caught between his dream of vague Christminster as the "heavenly Jerusalem" and the reality which limits his life. Sue, Phillotson, and Arabella are all three involved in this tension, the end of which is the identification of Jude. His dream is absurdly idealistic, not because he cannot be admitted to Christminster, but because the Christminster he wants to enter does not exist. Similarly, his marriage to Arabella is a fault, not because Arabella is evil, but because it is antithetical to even his legitimate ambitions, and because he has thus tricked himself again in loving her and in marrying her.

Jude Fawley is the fourth of the large central characters for whom Hardy envisions heroism and perhaps tragedy. Clym Yeobright grows slowly in *The Return of the Native*, comes through frustration to understand the proper dimensions for his ambitions, and seems almost by a process of elimination to assume his heroism and stand atop Rainbarrow. In *The Mayor of Casterbridge* Henchard is the only center throughout the novel; every character and every situation are used in his creation as a hero and in the dramatic exposition of his tragedy. Tess's character and situation are constructed similarly to Henchard's, but with a less rigorous singularity of focus. Jude, however, has a different relation to the rest of the inhabitants of his novel, and even to their circumstances and situations. Everything in the novel is his in the sense that he is created as much through the characters who support him as he is established in and by himself. Arabella, Sue, and Phillotson serve not to involve and entangle Jude in a plot so much as to mirror certain aspects of his character. They have an almost Lawrentian coexistence through and in Jude. Of the four characters, one is Jude, and the other three are to a significant degree aspects of Jude. Sue is his alter-ego, assimilating and exchanging ideas and attitudes with him throughout the novel; Phillotson is Jude in his impotence, in his intellectual dream and its failures; and Arabella is the force of physical human passion in him. As we see this interrelationship of characters, and as we see the structure of the novel linked with it, what is otherwise a grotesque plot of repetition becomes both meaningful and aesthetically acceptable.

Phillotson is initially Jude's ideal for himself. As the young schoolmaster leaves Marygreen at the beginning of the novel, he goes to fulfill the ambitions he leaves with Jude. The next time we see Phillotson he is indeed at Christminster, but in a position very much short of the goal to which he aspired. Then he marries Sue—almost, I think, because Jude can't. Later, when he relinquishes her to Jude, he insists that he will not be inconvenienced because he plans to write " 'The Roman Antiquities of Wessex,' which will occupy all my spare hours" (p. 281). This plan is parallel as a dilettante's hobby to Jude's later interest in lectures "on ancient history" (p. 315); and it becomes more and more obvious that success and satisfaction for the present or the future cannot be found in such excursions into what in this novel is but an irrelevant past. Phillotson is always presented in some adumbrative, parallel, or complementary relation to Jude, and except when he is needed for one of these occasions, he does not appear in the novel.

In Sue Hardy represents so much that is or becomes Jude himself that the statements of their essential oneness are easy summaries or stipulations, finally, not argumentative propositions. They are "one person split in two" (p. 276), "such companions that they could hardly do anything of importance except in each other's company" (p. 338), and they are possessed of such a "complete understanding, in which every glance and movement was as effective as speech for conveying intelligence between them" that they seem "almost two parts of a single whole" (p. 352). They are "counterparts" (p. 172), both interested in books (p. 9), and even both born in the same room (pp. 9, 130). Yet Sue exists always in violent opposition to Jude. She meets his hope for a domestic future by refusing to marry him, and she greets his spiritual and intellectual understandings and beliefs with heretical contradictions. What she represents in this is Jude's frustration, which is hers as well. As Jude and Sue talk—and they are Hardy's first articulate major characters—they introduce the various ideas of the novel. But the ideas are not themselves important, finally; what is important is that Jude and Sue are exposed to each other and to themselves in the abrasive context of life. Through the assimilation and change that takes place in their ideas and opinions, their dialogue becomes, because of its focus, almost a dramatic representation of Jude's singular conflict with himself.

Jude's self includes, necessarily and essentially, an element which Sue denies: sexuality. Although her frigidity is interesting and valid for her own character (like Clym Yeobright's blindness in *The Return of the Native*) it is more important as it is related to Jude's character. Sue can deny passion because passion is what Jude must overcome in himself.

Arabella represents as well as meets and takes advantage of Jude's animal instincts; she is the weakness which humiliates and destroys him. He is drawn to this girl who strikes him in the face with a pig's pizzle; he is drawn by "something in her quite antipathetic to that side of him which had been occupied with literary study and the magnificent Christminster dream" (pp. 45–46).

Jude's marriage to Arabella makes it impossible for him to attain the future of his dreams. Again, as in so many of Hardy's novels, the hero's fate is determined inexorably by one significant act. He cannot escape from his past, or, to state it more precisely, for this novel, he cannot achieve a future. Hardy has revised the pattern slightly. Philosophically the assertion is the same: one cannot escape from what one has done. Thematically the idea is the same: that which one has done will keep recurring, keep intruding, demanding its expiation or fulfillment. But aesthetically the representation has changed slightly. No longer is the present action of the novel set in conflict with a past kept alive by the suggestions of history and prehistory. The time of the novel is both literally and metaphorically the time of Jude's ambitions, not the time of their fulfillment. Jude doesn't achieve some success and then get destroyed by the intervention of some past he had hoped was dead behind him—and in this the novel is slightly different from *The Mayor of Casterbridge* and *Tess of the D'Urbervilles*, slightly different from everything Hardy has done before.

Jude is stuck in a particular time with Arabella, and with his unrealized dreams; and in the metaphor of space or place which typically supports the marking of time in Hardy's world, Jude is stuck at Marygreen, the primary setting of the novel, where Jude first dreamed his dream, and where he first met and then married Arabella. This time and this place remain and recur, refusing to allow the future. There is no expansion of time in the mythic dimensions of historical reference to suggest the significance or the intensity of life in this novel. Rather, the dramatic intensity of Jude's career is found in the collapse of time into the brief, unrelenting moment of his ambition and frustration. The moment is as intense as that "stillness of infinite motion" (p. 133) which he imagines is the great life of the university. In this novel Egdon Heath, Roman ruins, and ancient families are not meaningful, even metaphorically or symbolically; Marygreen, and the time from Jude's innocence to his experience, are all that count.

To suggest Jude's—and with him, Sue's—isolation in the present Hardy often describes the general setting with reference to the destruction of the past and its influence. These descriptions may seem at first glance to be of a kind with set piece descriptions of the ancient past in other novels. Unlike those descriptions, however, these represent a past that is dead, overgrown, and irrelevant. They point up Jude's isolation in a new and different world. In the opening chapter of the novel, Marygreen is described as

> as old-fashioned as it was small. . . . Old as it was, however, the well-shaft was probably the only relic of the local history that remained absolutely unchanged. Many of the thatched and dormered dwelling-houses had been pulled down of late years, and many trees felled on the green. Above all, the original church, hump-backed, wood-turreted, and quaintly hipped, had been taken down, and either cracked up into heaps of road-metal in the lane, or utilized as pig-sty walls, garden seats, guard-stones to fences, and rockeries in the flower-beds of the neighbourhood. (6)

In place of this relic, a new and modern church is built, "by a certain obliterator of historic records" (p. 6), and the past is forgotten.

The field in which the boy Jude works at the beginning of the novel is crossed by an old path, "trodden now by he hardly knew whom, though once by many of his own dead family" (p. 10). Perhaps the most important word in this sentence is "dead," added interlinearly in the manuscript,[2] since the past seems so absolutely unimportant in the present:

> The fresh harrow-lines seemed to stretch like the channelings in a new piece of corduroy, lending a meanly utilitarian air to the expanse, taking away its gradations, and depriving it of all history beyond that of a few recent months, though to every clod and stone there really attached associations enough and to spare—echoes of songs from ancient harvest-days, of spoken words and sturdy deeds. Every inch of ground has been the site, first or last, of energy, gaiety, horse-play, bickerings, weariness. Groups of gleaners had squatted in

> the sun on every square yard. Love-matches that had pop-
> ulated the adjoining hamlet had been made up there between
> reaping and carrying. . . . But this neither Jude nor the rooks
> around him considered. (10)

Hardy takes care to set up a past which could influence the present,
and which could offer a means of expansion for the significance of the
acts of the present. But he denies the possibility each time he introduces it:

> Not a soul was visible on the hedgeless highway, or on
> either side of it, and the white road seemed to ascend and
> diminish till it joined the sky. At the very top it was crossed
> at right angles by a green "ridgeway"—the Icknield Street
> and original Roman road through the district. This ancient
> track ran east and west for many miles, and down almost to
> within living memory had been used for driving flocks and
> herds to fairs and markets. But it was now neglected and
> over-grown. (17)

For all that the past is dead and overgrown, still Jude does not recognize it. He finds "mediaeval art in any material . . . a trade for which he
had rather a fancy" and he works "restoring the dilapidated masonries
of several village churches" (p. 37) before going to Christminster to
become enchanted by the "ancient mediaeval" colleges there (p. 91) and
the future he thinks they promise him. He does not know "that mediaevalism was as dead as a fig-leaf in a lump of coal; that other developments were shaping the world around him, in which Gothic architecture
and its associations had no place" (p. 99). He studies Greek and Latin,
attends lectures on "ancient history" (p. 315), and wanders around some
"circular British earthbank . . . thinking of the great age of the trackway,
and of the drovers who had frequented it, probably before the Romans
knew the country" (p. 61). Vainly and ironically, he uses his works and
studies and musings among the decaying relics of the past "as stimulants
when his faith in the future was dim" (p. 101).

The ironic significance of Jude's interest in this ancient past is made
clear in the history Hardy establishes for him and for Sue. Hardy does
not stop with the simple negation of a vital relationship between the
historical past and the present. The decay of the larger past of the novel's
setting and its fundamental disconnection from the present serve as re-
inforcement for the essential isolation of Jude himself. In the opening

of Chapter 2, Jude's brief history is summarized by his aunt, who explains that his father and mother are both dead, and that Jude has been sent to live with her; that, in effect, he has no past, no roots, nothing in this world that goes back beyond himself. On one occasion, as Jude and Sue prepare to attempt marriage, Jude reaches out in search of his past:

> Meanwhile Jude decided to link his present with his past
> in some slight degree by inviting to the wedding the only
> person remaining on earth who was associated with his early
> life at Marygreen—the aged widow, Mrs. Edlin, who had been
> his great-aunt's friend and nurse in her last illness. (339)

The irony is in Jude's seeming to have a choice in the matter of relating his past and his present, and in his misdefinition of both terms. As he prepares to marry Sue there are two people—neither of them Mrs. Edlin —who belong to his early life at Marygreen, and who could recognize and testify to the hold which that life has on this marital endeavor. Arabella and Phillotson are the link, and the past they inhabit is at one with the present. The only real influence any more than immediate past has is a negative one, which occurs in reference to Jude's and Sue's unsuitability for marriage. By means of an almost naturalistic use of the influence of heredity, Hardy establishes their inability to secure a happy future together. Both Jude's and Sue's parents—and Sue's mother was a Fawley— were unsuccessful in marriage, and this is represented as characteristic of the family. The influence of the past would insure the failure of the future.

At times Hardy slips, perhaps from habit, into the use of the past to extend his characters and the weight of their actions. Early in the novel, in response to Jude's calling her "modern," Sue says: "So would you be if you had lived so much in the Middle Ages as I have done these last few years! The Cathedral was a very good place four or five centuries ago; but it is played out now" (p. 160). This would be legitimate, since Sue is busy breaking away from the conventions and traditions of the past at this point, and since the past is consistently represented as moribund. But she continues: "I am not modern, either. I am more ancient than mediaevalism, if you only knew" (p. 160). This is nothing but Hardy's sententiousness imposed upon Sue. Later on Hardy makes another and similar reference to the past, and is again mistaken in his allusion. While Sue is being her most modern and unconventional Jude says to her:

133

> "Sue, you seem when you are like this to be one of the women of some grand old civilization. . . . I almost expect you to say at these times that you have just been talking to some friend whom you met in the Via Sacra, about the latest news of Octavia or Livia; or to have been listening to Aspasia's eloquence, or have been watching Praxiteles chiselling away at his latest Venus, while Phryne made complaint that she was tired of posing." (327)

Not only is this association wrong for Sue and for the novel, it is badly executed as well. The manner is loose, the tone unsure, and the repetitiousness of its examples ambiguously mixed. Much more to the point and much more impressive is Jude's reverie at "The Fourways," in the middle of Christminster, after his rejection by the Master of Biblioll College:

> He . . . thought on what struggling people like himself had stood at that Crossway, whom nobody ever thought of now. It had more history than the oldest college in the city. It was literally teeming, stratified, with the shades of human groups, who had met there for tragedy, comedy, farce; real enactments of the intensest kind. At Fourways men had stood and talked of Napoleon, the loss of America, the execution of King Charles, the burning of the Martyrs, the Crusades, the Norman Conquest, possibly of the arrival of Caesar. (139)

Jude finds his relationship to history here, and Hardy argues through his musings for the dramatic intensity of common, everyday experience in seemingly ordinary lives. The suggestive power of the historical association is to make Jude less "Obscure" and, almost in the earlier Hardy manner of metaphorical expansion or connection, to make him more a representative figure.

Still, this connection does not expand either the real or the metaphorical time of the novel, as that is done in *The Return of the Native*, *The Mayor of Casterbridge*, *Tess of the D'Urbervilles*, and momentarily in various of the other novels. The important time in *Jude the Obscure* is the present; and the essential place is that which belongs to that basic present, Marygreen. Christminster is the place of Jude's dreams only; and though he visits there, takes up residence there, and dies just outside its walls on its "Remembrance Day," he never really belongs there or lives there.

Jude first sees Christminster—as a boy, formulating his dream—in a sort of vision. One of the workers on the roof of Brown House describes seeing it "when the sun is going down in a blaze of flame, and it looks like—I don't know what." Jude suggests that it may look like "The heavenly Jerusalem" (p. 18)—and then, with the coming of sunset, prepares to see it. As the "vague city" shows itself he sees "points of light like the topaz," then "vanes, windows, wet roof slates, and other shining spots upon the spires, domes, freestone work, and varied outlines that were faintly revealed" (pp. 19, 20). Jude feels and maintains in his imagination this "gigantic" dream of the "gorgeous city—the fancied place he had likened to the new Jerusalem," and it "acquired a tangibility, a permanence, a hold on his life" (p. 20). But Jude never achieves this dream. He keeps remembering it, and returning to Christminster in search of it; but he is always turned back, frustrated and humiliated, to the place before Christminster, to the place where the dream was made. Marygreen and Arabella and the time of his first marriage are the real limits of Jude's world, and it costs him his life, finally, to defy them.

Because Jude can have no future, because his dreams cannot be fulfilled, his attempt to marry Sue legally never works, and their life together becomes a kind of painful static nonexistence. Ironically, Hardy calls their first kiss "a turning point in Jude's career" (p. 261)—ironically, since it leads him simply to more nothing. Together they are incapable of action, and even of life as things turn out. As they turn away from one attempt at marriage, the narrator reports: "They thought it over, or postponed thinking. Certainly they postponed action, and seemed to live on in a dreamy paradise" (p. 328). Their paradise, however, is a false one—like Christminster, a dream—and the product of their liaison is but a fitfully momentary happiness. They are like the lovers in a tragic version of the scene on Keats's famous urn, in which even the immediate moment of bliss is frustrated and finally denied. When Little Father Time has killed their children and himself, Sue tells Phillotson that she is glad: "It blots out all that life of mine" (p. 479). She burns her best embroidery that she had worn with Jude, "to blot [him] out entirely" (p. 451); "it reminds me," she says, "of what I want to forget" (p. 441).

The result of this negation of their lives together, this blotting out of

135

their pretentions to get beyond their earlier lives, leaves only one course open to Jude and Sue—and they go back, Jude to Arabella and Sue to Phillotson. Phillotson, acting as Gloucester to Jude's Lear in a structural sense again, explains what this means. His return to the small school at Marygreen, where he began, is "a small thing to return to after my move upwards, and my long indulged hopes—a returning to zero with all its humiliations" (pp. 382–83). It is this "zero" that Jude returns to, that he finally acknowledges at "The Remembrance games" (p. 488), his "Humiliation Day" (p. 390), as he chants *"Let the day perish wherein I was born, and the night in which it was said, There is a man child conceived"* (p. 488). This is the tragic, ironic fulfillment of Jude's existence. But he understands it now, and can accept it. He commits "suicide" in order to escape—or defeat—destruction. He tells Arabella, on the night he returns from his last visit to Marygreen, and on the eve of his last "Remembrance Day":

> "You think you are stronger; and so you are, in a physical sense, now. . . . But I am not so weak in another way as you think. I made up my mind that a man confined to his room by inflammation of the lungs, a fellow who had only two wishes left in the world, to see a particular woman, and then to die, could neatly accomplish those two wishes at one stroke by taking this journey in the rain. That I've done. I have seen her for the last time, and I've finished myself—put an end to a feverish life which ought never to have been begun!" (473)

Seen this way, Jude's death is an act of choice, accomplished through the exercise of his consciousness and will. With this comes the triumph of his heroic strength. By recognizing and accepting his fate—but so ordering it as he does by his last act—Jude wins the dignity he has lost in his fight with himself and this world.

Jude the Obscure is the bleakest of Hardy's novels. Though the novel begins with Jude only a boy, we recall nothing before his young manhood except the fact of his orphanage and isolation, his sensitive response to cruelty, his dream of Christminster, and a few remarks foreshadowing what is to come. Jude, the narrator says, "was the sort of man who was born to ache a good deal before the fall of the curtain on his unnecessary life should signify that all was well with him again" (p. 13). The boy feels this of himself: "As you got older, and felt yourself to be at the centre of your time, and not at a point in its circumference, as you had felt when you were little, you were seized with a sort of shuddering, he perceived" (p. 15). What we remember is Jude "at the centre" of his time:[3] from his idealization of Phillotson to his meeting with Arabella to his discovery of Sue, through the central alliances, and then to the final resolution.

As a boy Jude carves an inscription on the back of a milestone on the road to Christminster:

Thither

J. F.

(85)

At the end of Part I, after his first marriage with Arabella is broken up, Jude returns to this spot to remind himself of his aspirations and renew his determination. Years have passed and he is still at that same milestone. Then, throughout the middle of the novel, Jude struggles to get ahead, fights with himself and with his ambitions and with the world. A version of himself is killed in Little Father Time's suicide,[4] and his life with Sue is erased in Time's murder of their children. Sue then returns to Phillotson, and Jude is seduced once again by Arabella. The beginning of the story is being reenacted, and Jude is taken back to the occasion of his fall. The physical locations are reversed, however; Jude and Arabella are now at Christminster instead of Marygreen, and Sue (whom he met at Christminster) and Phillotson (who went there as Jude's precursor and ironic surrogate) are at Marygreen. This reversal may be indicative of the perversity of fate, or it may be simply an added ironic measure of the futility of dreams.

Jude and Arabella go to her father's house, to repeat their original union: "The circumstances were not altogether unlike those of their entry into the the cottage at Cresscombe, such a long time before. Nor were perhaps Arabella's motives. But Jude did not think of that, though she did" (p. 455). Once in the house, Jude makes the next association:

> "But,—are we out in our old house by Marygreen?" asked
> the stupefied Jude. "I haven't been inside it for years till
> now! Hey? And where are my books? That's what I want to
> know?" (455)

At Marygreen, in the meantime, Sue and Phillotson have been reunited:

> It was like a re-enactment by the ghosts of their former selves of a similar scene which had taken place at Melchester years before. (446)

Jude goes to see Sue, then, for the last time, to fulfill his last two wishes: to see her, and to die. On his return from this final visit to Marygreen he stops at the milestone again, to recall his frustrated expectations:

> He came to the milestone, and, raining as it was, spread his blanket and lay down there to rest. Before moving on he went and felt at the back of the stone for his own carving. It was still there; but nearly obliterated by moss. (472)

The end comes, and Jude is destroyed: not by his fate, or by perversity, or by God, but by himself. In his final consciousness of why it must be, and in the act of his will which controls it, he makes of that destruction his triumph. Jude's character, like every hero's, has been his fate, and has been the making of his destiny.

Jude is not so much a different kind of hero from Clym Yeobright or Michael Henchard or Tess as he is a hero differently represented. In the best of his ambition Jude is much like Clym; in his suffering and his strength and his bitterness he is like Henchard; and as the tragic victim of frustration and the ironies of perverse circumstance he is like Tess. He is unlike them, however, in that the scope of his life is much smaller, the breathing space much tighter, the time much shorter—or so it seems. By comparison with Jude's, Tess's and Henchard's tragedies seem almost leisurely. The expansive worlds of their novels make awesome the vital recurrences of the past in the present, but the effect is not the same as that produced by the terrible repetition of one set of events and the eradication or denial of any other activity in Jude's novel. When Jude lies down in the rain outside Marygreen, and feels that "nearly obliterated" inscription of his dream or vow—"Thither, J.F."—everything collapses; he has caught his death at the one milestone of his life.

NOTES TO CHAPTER VII

1. William Faulkner, letter to Malcolm Cowley, 1944 in *The Faulkner-Cowley File* (New York, 1966), pp. 14–15.
2. MS fol. 7. Fitzwilliam Museum, Cambridge University.

3. Hardy originally had Jude consider the possibility of being at "the centre of space" (MS fol. 13). In substituting "time" for "space" he brings the allusion more into the pattern of the novel's method.

4. Cf. Jude as "an ancient man in some phases of thought, much younger than his years in others" (p. 26), who "wished . . . he had never been born" (p. 31) and "continued to wish himself out of the world" (p. 32), and Little Father Time as "Age masquerading as Juvenility" (p. 332), who expresses "the beginning of the coming universal wish not to live" (p. 406). And Jude surmises, ironically, that someday Little Father Time may cry out, "Let the day perish wherein I was born, and the night in which it was said, There is a man child conceived" (p. 330).

VIII

THE POETRY AND THE DYNASTS: A CONCLUSION

We'll close up Time, as a bird its van,
We'll traverse Space, as spirits can,
Link pulses severed by leagues and years,
Bring cradles into touch with biers;
So that the far-off Consequence appears
Prompt at the heels of foregone Cause.

THE DYNASTS

(1903)

In the Fore Scene of *The Dynasts* the Spirit of the Pities engages the Spirit Ironic over whether what takes place on this earth, among humans, is tragedy or comedy. Their brief exchange is important because it gives us a key to the proper identification throughout Hardy's works of the critical perspective from which he views the world, and the predominant tone of his writings. If one keep's one's distance, as the Spirit Ironic would have, and looks down from on high at a world seemingly inhabited by busy, confused mites, what is called life may well seem comic. But if one looks closely at what goes on here, as the Spirit of the Pities urges, from such a distance that human beings seem to be men, not indiscriminate specks, what they do, because it is significant to them, becomes worthy of one's concern and sympathy. This latter perspective makes confusion and frustration in the world of men seem tragic; and the Spirit of the Pities urges the rest of the Phantoms of the Overworld to view the "spectacle" which is the subject of the play "closelier than your custom is" (p. 4).

140

Although Hardy presents both views regularly, in his fiction as well as in the mass of his poetry, the view he urges upon us as the better one is the close and compassionate one. By applying this pressure of close observation to the lives of simple and otherwise historically obscure people like Clym, Henchard, Tess, and Jude, Hardy finds and dramatizes their significance and heroism. His poetry follows this same line in two ways: by representing a variety of simple people and understated human situations, and by generalized arguments about the primary importance of these people and their lives. As a poet Hardy is above all else a sensitive, compassionate observer—and as such he is at his best as a teacher. "In Time of 'The Breaking of Nations,'" written in 1915, is perhaps his most eloquent general observation on this point, concluding:

> Yonder a maid and her wight
> Come whispering by:
> War's annals will cloud into night
> Ere their story die. (511)

In "Nature's Questioning," published in *Wessex Poems and Other Verses* (1898), the first of his eight volumes of poetry, Hardy sets up the inclination to speculate on causes and definitions of things around us; and after reciting the various questions and postulations made to explain the nature of life on this earth, he responds in his own voice in the last stanza:

> Thus things around. No answerer I . . .
> Meanwhile the winds, and rains,
> And earth's old glooms and pains
> Are still the same, and Life and Death are neighbours nigh.
> (59)

All the questioning is, to Hardy's sense, a distraction from the act of living—the sympathetic, communicative act of living; for not only does the questioning and the surmising fail to change the nature of mortality, it wastes this mortal life by neglecting it. But Hardy always seems to feel the temptation to philosophical questioning. Samuel Hynes attributes this questioning to his Victorian heritage and its cultural environment. There are numbers of poems—several dozen at least —that are argumentative in this way, and a large part of *The Dynasts* is the same. The conflict in Hardy's poetry runs, in a general sense, between these thesis verses—dramatized, mythologized, or argued directly as statements—and his lyrical poems. By the time of *The Dynasts*, which is still early in Hardy's long career, the questioning is over, as such. The philosophical matter becomes more one of assertion and description than one of questioning. The idea of Immanent Will is as far as Hardy will go in attempting to define the primary force which motivates existence, and with his Spirit of the Pities he hopes that through the influence of man, through either his goodness or his suffering, the Will can be brought from its neutral sleep of indifferent energy toward some more benign involvement in the world and in our lives.

In 1907 Edward Wright wrote to Hardy about *The Dynasts*, and in his reply Hardy discusses the Will and Its meaning. Wright argued that the term "unconscious impulse" would be more appropriate than "unconscious Will" to describe this force. Hardy answers:

> I quite agree with you in holding that the word "Will" does not perfectly fit the idea to be conveyed—a vague thrusting or urging internal force in no predetermined direction. But it has become accepted in philosophy for want of a better. . . . The word that you suggest—Impulse—seems to me to imply a driving power behind it; also a spasmodic movement unlike that of, say, the tendency of an ape to become a man and other such processes.
>
> In a dramatic epic—which I may perhaps assume *The Dynasts* to be—some philosophy of life was necessary, and I went on using that which I had denoted in my previous volumes of verse (and to some extent prose) as being a generalized form of what the thinking world had gradually come to adopt, myself included. That the Unconscious Will of the Universe is growing aware of Itself I believe I may claim as my own idea solely—at which I arrived by reflecting that what has already taken place in a fraction of the whole (*i.e.*, so much of the world as has become conscious) is likely to take place in the mass; and there being no Will outside the mass—that is, the Universe—the whole Will becomes conscious thereby: and ultimately, it is to be hoped, sympathetic. . . .
>
> This theory, too, seems to me to settle the question of Free-will v. Necessity. The will of a man is, according to [this theory], neither wholly free nor wholly unfree. When swayed by the Universal Will (which he mostly must be as a subservient part of it) he is not individually free; but whenever

142

it happens that all the rest of the Great Will is in equilibrium
the minute portion called one person's will is free. . . .[1]

The Will is the total, potentially conscious "force" of the Universe.
It is evolutionary, and has no existence separate from its parts. It is
itself unknowable, except as Its influences can be identified in the
recognition of causal relations among Its parts as they move. It is a
natural force, a force "that stirs and urges everything" as he calls It in
"The Convergence of the Twain."

In his essay on Wincklemann, Walter Pater describes the world in
relation to man living in it and aware of it in terms much like Hardy's,
later. Speaking of "the universality of natural law, even in the moral
order," Pater says:

> For us, necessity is not, as of old, a sort of mythological per-
> sonage without us, with whom we can do warfare. It is rather
> a magic web woven through and through us, like that mag-
> netic system of which modern science speaks, penetrating us
> with a network, subtler than our subtlest nerves, yet bearing
> in it the central forces of the world.[2]

This weblike force is at once real and imaginary, for Pater and for
Hardy. It is real as a natural force; it is imaginary as a representation of
that natural force. "Natural laws we shall never modify," Pater says,
"embarrass us as they may; but there is still something in the nobler
or less noble attitude with which we watch their fatal combinations."[3]
The "something" is that which will free us. It is the artist's vision,
which must "rearrange the details of modern life, so . . . that it may
satisfy the spirit" by giving the spirit "a sense of freedom."[4]

Hardy's concern with the natural reality of the Immanent Will is a
simple one. By the Immanent Will he means an inherently limited,
causally-oriented universe, all of whose parts are mutually involved.
The imaginary or imaginative existence of the Will is derived from his
sense of this natural order, and exists by name only as a metaphoric
representation of the sum of the Universe. All of the parts in their
interrelated coexistence create the Will—and this is the sense in which
Hardy talks about It in his poems and in *The Dynasts*.[5] If the Will
ever "becomes conscious," as Hardy asserts It may—both in his letter
to Wright and in the last lines of *The Dynasts*, unwritten at the time
of that letter[6]—It will do so primarily and most significantly in man.

143

The force that governs us is not from a God, but in nature, and thus also in ourselves. The relevant God for Hardy is the potential God within us—who may never be omnipotent or fully wise.

Had Hardy's concern really been with the alleged malevolence or culpable indifference of a God—had he indulged himself in that argument and allowed himself to become a questioner—he would probably have acceded to pessimism, to fatalism, to the frustration of a deterministic point of view. But he kept his attention on man, and by concentrating on the observation of men he not only avoided, legitimately, the possibility of philosophical desperation, he found through his observations that best faith of "evolutionary meliorism." Ironically even this attitude was called pessimism by his critics. He described his philosophy as "really a series of fugitive impressions" garnered from his "exploration of reality . . . with an eye toward the best consummation possible: briefly evolutionary meliorism" (pp. 526–27).

The argument over Hardy's philosophical point of view shouldn't arise—but it does, and always has. What we are told always is that Hardy is a pessimist, a determinist, a fatalist. Fate is a familiar concept, of course; it is a commonplace of our speech and our literature. Basically what we are wont to call fate is the psychologically derived substitute for acceptance of our natural lot and our own responsibilities: as Arnold's Empedocles says, we "Make Gods to whom to impute/The ills we ought to bear." What we call fate is the simple factual presence of the external world as it impinges upon our living and our lives. The interaction of the self with the external world is, again, an example of that motion or natural motivating force which Hardy calls the "Immanent Will." Seen in this way, fate "determines" not what we do but the result of what we do. When Hardy says in *The Mayor of Casterbridge* that "Character is Fate," he is not saying that Michael Henchard is governed by a predetermined and unalterably foreordained fate; rather, he says that Henchard must make his fate by what he does, his character acting in coordination with his circumstances. Fate, in Hardy's world, is no more a deterministic moral, immoral, or amoral force than that which one encounters by sticking one's finger in the fire: in this analogical instance, one's fate, predetermined only by the nature of fire and the physical susceptibility of man, is simply to burn.

Fate is, of course, necessarily dramatic. We do not call fate the occasion of being missed by a train at an unguarded railroad crossing when there is no train there as we cross. The accident of timing—what Faulkner calls the "mischancing of human affairs"[7]—is what we call fate. One need not deny that this force is a living one just because it is an accidental one, in part; one can deny, however, even for that circumstantial part, the assertion of its malevolence. Hardy never calls it malevolent; it is for him almost an existential force, "dumb," "indifferent," "blind," "unconscious," "incompetent," even perverse, from our point of view sometimes, but not malevolent. The only consciousness in Hardy's fate is that which comes after the fact of action, on the part of the character involved. And when Hardy dreams and hopes that the Immanent Will may someday awaken to moral competence, he is speaking of that better future when men will act collectively in concert with the natural world to achieve the harmony of a peaceful life.

So what we call fate is the operation of the vital natural world as seen from man's involved point of view, as "characterized" by man. It is thus a term which we use to describe on the one hand chance situations, and on the other cause and effect relationships involving us with the larger world of other people and natural facts.[8] What we want we do not always get—and this has been our commonest experience throughout all of history, the experience most central to our art, and the experience without which we would have had neither any dramatic art nor, perhaps, any history worth our studying. We are frequently the victims of "Crass Casualty," of that "mischancing of human affairs," of the accidental juxtaposition of contraries; and we are required, too, to suffer the consequences of our own acts. Of these two kinds of fate, that which is the result of man's actions, the consequence which follows necessarily upon the moving cause, is the most important for Hardy. The fate of simple coincidence, of that accidental juxtaposition of falling safe and pedestrian, is not really very interesting, except as it occasions an expression of sympathy or compassion for the victim. But as man is responsible in some way for ironic coincidence, for the destructive collision of events, the situation assumes a vital poignance, and some general aspect of the human condition is once again opened up to analysis.

The assumption that man is responsible for his fate identifies Hardy as a moralist. His morality is not much different from Sophocles' or Shakespeare's—and they were his mentors. This kind of morality goes beyond that initial idea of immediate responsibility, too. It is involved in that large acceptance of life which insists on understanding and eschews judgment; it is that belief in life which lets him find the significant in the small, the meaningful in the mean and quotidian; and it is that compassionate response to life which makes him see in the problem of man's responsibility to and for himself the potential tragedy of the human predicament. Hardy's morality pushes him to find in common, simple people and their situations significant representations of all of us and our history, and to make of such generalizations the only real judgements he ever makes on the world he sees.

Hardy's antideterminist ideas are too obvious for critics to have ignored them for so long—as they have. They can be seen in poems from "Hap" (written in 1866, though published only in 1898) and its acknowledgement of "Crass Casualty" and "dicing Time" (p. 7), through the complaint of "The Bedridden Peasant" against "Time and Chance" and the "Unknowing God" (p. 113), and the assertion by the Lord in "By the Earth's Corpse" that "all the wrongs endured" by man have been "undesigned" (p. 115), and many other similar statements through the other volumes of verse, down to the Immanent Will's argument in "A Philosophical Fantasy" (written in 1926, and published in *Winter Words* in 1928) that it acts by *"purposeless propension"* rather than "intention" or "so-called scheming" (p. 856).

Hardy is so much aware of sadness and pain that he seems sometimes surprised, like Elizabeth-Jane, at the intervention of happiness in this life; yet he is not a fatalist, not even a pessimist. He believes in love and fellow-feeling, in "loving-kindness" (p. 306) and "life-loyalties" (p. 57), and dreams of the day when some Voice will announce "The Great Adjustment is taking place/ . . . . /And Right shall disestablish Wrong" (p. 688). Though he recognizes—eloquently—in "To an Unborn Pauper Child" that

> laughters fail, and greetings die;
> Hopes dwindle; yea,
> Faiths waste away,
> Affections and enthusiasms numb; (116)

and that "skies spout fire and blood and nations quake," that "No man can change the common lot to rare"; still, at the conclusion of the poem he insists with all the sober irrationality of necessary belief,

And such are we—
Unreasoning, sanguine, visionary—
That I can hope
Health, love, friends, scope
In full for thee; can dream thou'lt find
Joys seldom yet attained by humankind! (117)

This faith in the validity of past and present existence and the possibility of a better future sustains Hardy and is the basis for his compassionate response to mankind—for what was earlier called his large morality. Only from such a persistent belief could he build tragedy that would not reduce itself to absurdity and heroes who would not lose their dignity in suffering such tragedy. Hardy's belief is not the infatuated romantic optimism of a moment, but a careful, realistically-oriented philosophical and moral consideration. Belief may seem a strange word to use in talking about Hardy. But Hardy believes in man very strongly, and this belief legitimizes his ideas of fate as men make it and of history as men have lived it. He believes in the potential of man to live intensely and heroically, and this belief makes possible his use of coincidence as an aesthetic and philosophical convention. And as Hardy believes in man and his potential, he also believes in art, holding to "a forlorn hope, a mere dream. . . of an alliance between religion, which must be retained unless the world is to perish, and complete rationality, which must come, unless also the world is to perish, by means of the interfusing effect of poetry" (p. 531). Poetry will not keep the world from perishing; but by putting together myth or dream and fact, the ideal and the real, poetry can make man free.

Northrop Frye has claimed as the basic qualification of man's existence his "being in time," and the sense of this limitation he calls "the ironic vision."[9] Hardy's vision is most consistently ironic, to be sure, but it is also something more than ironic in its faith in man and its commitment to his freedom. Frye's comment may help to clarify this. It has often been assumed that Hardy's ironic vision is at one with his alleged pessimism, and the one attitude has been offered as proof of the other.

Frye says that "nineteenth-century pessimism . . . produced the philosophy of Schopenhauer and the novels of Thomas Hardy," and he calls them "ironic rather than tragic."[10] He continues:

147

> What makes tragedy tragic, and not simply ironic, is the presence in it of a counter-movement of being that we call the heroic, a capacity for action or passion, for doing or suffering, which is above ordinary human experience.[11]

It has been part of the work of this book to argue and demonstrate the tragedy in *The Mayor of Casterbridge, Tess of the D'Urbervilles, Jude the Obscure*, and to a degree in *The Return of the Native*, through an analysis of the heroic character of the protagonists in just those terms. Hardy's insistence on the size of his heroes—on their "capacity for action or passion, for doing or suffering, which is above ordinary human experience"—has been the main focus of this discussion. What I have tried to demonstrate is that Hardy knows the same thing about tragedy that Frye knows, and that he has exerted himself through his elaborate metaphorical use of time and the related motifs of coincidence and repetition to intensify the lives of his heroes and thus represent their extraordinary capacities for experience.

Hardy's metaphoric use of time—foreshortened to create the intensity of timelessness, expanded to include all of history in the momentary, cumulative, and universal density of the present—is more complex than Frye's introductory definitions of irony and tragedy can handle. Hardy is not concerned with "being in time" as the basic, ironic limitation of life, though he is terribly conscious of mortality. Frye would have it that mortality is the final and ineluctable determinant of the ironic vision. But Hardy accepts the fact of death—accepts it so profoundly, often, that when his subject or his theme leads him to death's interference with life his vision is not one of ironic frustration, but reconciliation. True, Tess's "fulfillment" is ironic in that she must die—and the Hardy who reports that "the President of the Immortals . . . had ended his sport with Tess" is reporting frustration, not reconciliation. And Hardy's suffering in the Poems of 1912–13 is that of the man who says too late what can never be heard. And in a poem like "During Wind and Rain" the speaker's visions of life are crossed by the rhyming refrain of death. Death is everywhere present in Hardy, in the novels and in the poetry; but his response to it is consistently more than just a lament that it marks, however poignantly, the end of mortal life.

Tess has fulfilled herself at the end of the novel in a way that is not just ironic, but heroic; and this fulfillment is not tagged onto the work, but is born out of its dramatic essence. In her murder of Alec and that almost transcendent, mystical honeymoon with Angel which follows— it takes her out of life, beyond life—Tess completes her life and achieves the heroism that sets us free at her death. The poems of 1912–13 are love poems, remarkable not for their recognition of death but for their re-creation of a sense of life. To find Hardy the ironist in these poems, or in "During Wind and Rain," we must either read them very simplistically or overread them with an abstracting, philosophizing sophistication; and either way we end up reading what they are about rather than what they are. What these poems are is an expression of the mystery of life—which includes death, in a sense: "Life and Death," he says in "Nature's Questioning," "are neighbours nigh" (p. 59).

Hardy recognizes mortality as a qualification of man's existence, but he refuses to accept that that existence can be justly measured by such a qualification. He meditates on this point in "The Clasped Skeletons," as he views remains found "In an Ancient British barrow near the writer's house." He thinks first of the relative brevity of individual lives in the long span of time, and then this thought turns, typically for Hardy, to a quiet denial that duration, the measure of time, is to the point of life at all.

> Ere Paris lay with Helena—
> The poets' dearest dear—
> Ere David bedded Bathsheba
> You two were bedded here. . . .
>
> So long, beyond chronology,
> Lovers in death as 'twere,
> So long in placid dignity
> Have you lain here!

> Yet what is length of time? But dream! (834)

Earlier, in "The Absolute Explains," one of those several poems in which philosophical speculations are presented through the voice of a supernatural character, Hardy describes time as even less than an awesome dream; it is "toothless" (p. 716), "a mock" (p. 718). Time does not exist, he says; it is merely the name we have given to the limitation of our cramped, mortal perspective. Things do not cease to be in what we call the past, or come into being in what we call the future; they

149

just are—in another dimension beyond our usual comprehension and experience: "So thus doth Being's length transcend/ Time's ancient regal claim/ To see all lengths begin and end." "So, Time," he concludes, "You are nought/But a thought/Without reality" (pp. 718–19).

"Such a dream is Time" (p. 404) that it is not important; and yet it is useful to Hardy, in his poetry much the same as in his novels. It is useful not as a concept, but as a metaphor. Hardy is not concerned with time as an abstract principle or as a mechanical device for some kind of linear measurement. He is aware that years pass, things age, and people die; but the only interest he has in time as a denominator of this aspect of life is aesthetic, rather than philosophical or scientific. Occasionally he uses time to diminish individual existence, relative to the general history of man and the world; more importantly, he uses time condensed and time expanded as metaphors for the intensity of experience which transcends normal temporal measure. And what Hardy says, then, is that within the continuum of history, the limiting circle of time, man can accomplish something at least of importance through the exercise of his moral courage. Man's heroism, if he can achieve it, can redeem for him his dignity.

In its simplest form, this metaphor of time is used to add historic resonance to a present act. The sonnet "Zermatt" recalls the first conquest of the Matterhorn in its octave, and then, in the sestet, dignifies the event—curiously, perhaps even irrelevantly—through the calling up of a distant, more important past.

> Yet ages ere men topped thee, late and soon
> Thou didst behold the planets lift and lower;
> Saw'st, maybe, Joshua's pausing sun and moon,
> And the betokening sky when Caesar's power
> Approached its bloody end; yea, even that Noon
> When darkness filled the earth till the ninth hour.
>
> (97)

A similar use of the past occurs in "By the Barrows," another sonnet. This time the octave is devoted to a brief description of an ancient battle on the heath; in the sestet another, smaller battle is recounted from "our modern age," and Hardy claims as a heroine comparable to those of history the woman who "Fought singlehandedly to shield a child—/One not her own—from a man's senseless rage" (p. 246).

150

In "At Castle Boterel" the speaker recalls for himself and his lover a single, beautiful moment, and reinforces its unique grandeur paradoxically by reference to history:

> It filled but a minute, but was there ever
>   A time of such quality, since or before,
> In that hill's story? To one mind never,
>   Though it has been climbed, foot-swift, foot-sore,
>   By thousands more.
> Primaeval rocks form the road's steep border,
>   And much have they faced there, first and last,
> Of the transitory in Earth's long order;
>   But what they record in colour and cast
>   Is—that we two passed. (331)

History is background, like the fossils in the face of Beeny Cliff in *A Pair of Blue Eyes*, like Egdon Heath in the opening of *The Return of the Native*.

The burden of "The Roman Road" has, similarly, nothing to do with Rome or Roman history directly, though the poem begins and ends invoking that past by repeating the words of the title. The road is the setting for the poem:

> The Roman Road runs straight and bare
> As the pale parting-line in hair
> Across the heath. (248)

The road has survived the passing of time, and excites an interest in famous ancient times and people.

>   And thoughtful men
>   Contrast its days of Now and Then,
>   And delve, and measure, and compare.

They envision

>   Helmed legionaires, who proudly rear
>   The Eagle, as they pace again
>   The Roman Road.

But the speaker's experience in this situation is different. Re-experiencing his own past, he sees his mother,

> Guiding my infant steps, as when
> We walked that ancient thoroughfare,
> The Roman Road.

By juxtaposing and re-experiencing this in the context of the larger past of history, Hardy achieves a greater, stronger, and more affective recall. Rome is not diminished by the comparison, nor is any direct claim made for a general historical recognition of his mother; but somehow—aesthetically, perhaps paradoxically—a significant and respected stature is quietly established for her.

There are numerous other poems in which allusions to the past enrich the experience of the present, and the continuum of history is freed from the measure of time so that the past can even coexist with the present. The seventh song of the series "At Casterbridge Fair" is such a poem. It is "After the Fair,"

> And midnight clears High Street of all but the ghosts
> Of its buried burghees,
> From the latest far back to those old Roman hosts
> Whose remains one yet sees,
> Who loved, laughed, and fought, hailed their friends,
> drank their toasts
> At their meeting-times here, just as these! (226)

Elsewhere Hardy uses the familiar patterns of history to underscore and emphasize the events of the present. In "Embarcation," a poem from *Poems of the Past and the Present*, he recalls the wars of Vespasian, of Cerdic and the Saxons, of Henry with France, to demonstrate the repetition of events. Now, from the same place as those earlier armies landed or embarked,

> Vaster battalions press for further strands,
> To argue in the selfsame bloody mode
> Which this late age of thought, and pact, and code,
> Still fails to mend. (78)

Similarly, in "Channel Firing," as another war is prepared for, one of the speakers refers to "our indifferent century," and God's reassuring voice says that "The world is as it used to be." The strength of this poem, however, is not in these assertions, but in the larger imaging of the argument in historical terms in the final stanza:

152

> Again the guns disturb the hour,
> Roaring their readiness to avenge,
> As far inland as Stourton Tower,
> And Camelot, and starlit Stonehenge. (288)

The lighter tone of irony has been replaced suddenly by heavy, somber rhetoric; the opening "Again the guns" is suggestive, in its sound and in its sense, of the continuum—much as with one of Arnold's favorite word combinations, "again begin," to suggest the same kind of repetition. The image with which the poem concludes is at first reading seemingly spatial; but Stourton Tower, Camelot, and Stonehenge measure together no great spatial expanse, so that if this is the reference it is significant only rhetorically. One must quickly see, however, that the measure which the reference takes is not spatial, but temporal: and Stourton Tower, Camelot, and Stonehenge together span all of recorded history and beyond.

In April of 1887 Hardy wrote a series of poems while on a trip in Italy. They are mood pieces, meditations for the most part on the double world of antiquity and modernity, or historic death and contemporary life, that he saw. In each of the three sonnets in the group—"In the Old Theatre, Fiesole," "Rome: On the Palatine," and "Rome: Building a New Street in the Ancient Quarter"—he engages the past through its mythical immediacy in the present. The doubling—and the conjunction of past and present is both effective and affective—is what gives these poems their theme and their experience. Hardy stands in Rome, "Time's central city," and feels his own life "blended . . . with lives long done,/ Till Time seemed fiction, Past and Present one" (p. 93).

Hardy combines this kind of mood or meditation response to the past with a dramatic situation in a number of poems, achieving in them more nearly the same kind of effect that he works for so often in the novels. But the use of time in these poems is generally mythic alone, rather than mythic and metaphorical. That is, elements of history or historical reference are introduced simply for their expansive suggestiveness, rather than as suggestive and effective aspects of the past in dramatic juxtaposition with the present. "The Well-Beloved" is a good example of this. As the lover walks toward Kingsbere to wed his beloved, he

> edged the ancient hill and wood
> Beside the Ikling Way,

> Nigh where the Pagan temple stood
> In the world's earlier day. (121)

He sees a figure, seemingly drawn

> Out from the ancient leaze,
> Where once were pile and peristyle
> For men's idolatries.

She identifies herself as his "dream" of love and beauty, and then disappears:

> Thereat she vanished by the lane
> Adjoining Kingsbere town,
> Near where, men say, once stood the Fane
> To Venus, on the Down. (123)

Hardy is manipulating the present, teasing the idea of a singular, isolable immediate now with the vaster world of ideals and ideal forms out of the history of man—the history of love.

In "The Revisitation" both the mythic aspect and the metaphorical effect of the past are more fully presented, and are more closely relevant. The speaker remarks at the outset on his being situated "In an ancient country barrack known to ancient cannoneers." The time, accidentally, is the same as that when, twenty years before, he and his lover had parted near this spot. The coincidence surfaces in his consciousness:

> And a lapsing twenty years had ruled that—as it were to
> grieve me—
> I should near the once-loved ground. (177)

He goes, then, under the spell of the occasion, to their former trysting place:

> Round about me bulged the barrows
> As before, in antique silence—immemorial funeral piles—
> Where the sleek herds trampled daily the remains of flint-
> tipt arrows
> Mid the thyme and chamomiles;
> And the Sarsen stone there, dateless,
> On whose breast we had sat and told the zephyrs many a
> tender vow,
> Held the heat of yester sun, as sank thereon one fated mateless
> From those far fond hours till now. (178)

154

The unchanging antiquity of the place first suggests the universal typicality of such an affair. Then the speaker reflects on the passing of time—of twenty years, a generation—in their lives, but notes that nothing has changed at the scene of their parting. The long, historic past of the place is related both to the present moment of his reverie and to the past time of that affair, and the double relevance of that long, unchanging history prepares us for the dramatic reintroduction and reenactment of their parting.

> And so, living long and longer
> In a past that lived no more, my eyes discerned there, suddenly,
> That a figure broke the skyline—first in vague contour, then stronger,
> And was crossing near to me.

The figure, of course, is hers. Their meeting is justified metaphorically by its setting, and they act accordingly. He takes her to "the ancient people's stone whereon I had sat," and she says, "It is *just* as ere we parted" (p. 179). They talk, then, and fall asleep against each other until dawn. In the beginning light of the new day they are parted again—on the one hand because time has passed and she is old, on the other because nothing has really changed and they are reenacting their past parting even as they meet. Both of these explanations are contained in the paradox of his statement as she appears the night before. The past of their love, he says, is "a past that lived no more"; yet in his reverie and out of its strength he is "living long and longer" in that dead time. The suggestive quality of the setting provides the metaphorical support and justification for the dramatic action of the poem, and simultaneously it insists as mythic fact that there be no change, that the past action be repeated—pathetically, not heroically; ironically, not tragically—and that this be, indeed, a "Revisitation."

The whole of Hardy's art—his vision and his technique—is described again in his poetry. There is finally no essential difference between his prose and his verse. The novels are written by a poet who knows that the link between art and life is experiential, not didactic; and the novelist who is concerned to find the dignity and heroism of simple people living simple lives goes on to write his poetry with that same concern forming his themes and ideas. None of the novels fails completely as art or experience—even *The Well-Beloved*, which, with *Jude the Obscure*, comes closest to being an argument about a theme rather than its dramatic expression. But many of the poems fail as poems because they are just eloquent, abstract arguments and elaborate, visionary statements, formed poetically.

Most of them fail because Hardy is trying to answer the questions which experience must always raise. In "Nature's Questioning," which ends with Hardy's rejecting the attitude of questioner or answerer, it takes him six stanzas of indulging the temptation to cosmic speculation before he can make his resolve. And although the resolve is emphatic and impressive, its weight is modified considerably by Hardy's masked indulgence in the speculation preceding it. When he wants to speculate thus philosophically, Hardy frequently assumes the mask of an hypothetical God, as in poems like "God-Forgotten" (p. 112), "God's Education" (p. 261), "The Blow" (p. 449), "The Absolute Explains" (p. 716), and others. The speakers of these poems talk about Hardy's best themes and ideas; but they are curiously cerebral voices, not characters, and their musings remain detached from life and from poetry. From behind his mask, often ironically, Hardy talks about the need for compassion in this unfriendly world; but as long as he is behind that mask he cannot himself exercise compassion. He loses the intimacy of the poem and its situation, and falls back to theorizing in verse form. In his preface to *Poems of the Past and the Present* (1901) he wrote:

> Unadjusted impressions have their value, and the road to a true philosophy of life seems to lie in humbly recording diverse readings of its phenomena as they are forced upon us by chance and change. (75)

At his best, in his fiction and in his poetry, Hardy works according to this plan. As I have argued earlier, however, the humility he avows here is matched with faith in man and pride in his potential; and from these he elaborates a world in which to do his "recording."

Hardy's best impressions are of the details of ordinary life as individual men live it, and he records them with rich compassion. He wants to find men's dignity and their heroism, as these are the qualities which alter, however slightly, the ironic repetitions of history. His better poems and his fiction make us feel the truth and the relevance of character or situation. The art which accomplishes this is the art of lyrical and dramatic action and its description. In the lesser poems, those of a more theoretical nature, the narrative voice, masked or unmasked, seems often to be musing, meditating in abstraction on the basic thematic problem. The sometimes heavy destructive ironies of these poems—as in the conclusion of "God-Forgotten," for example, or the bad joke in the middle of "Channel Firing"—are disguises for the sentimentalism that Hardy is susceptible to when he moves away from particular people and particular situations.

At his best, Hardy looks constantly at the small, immediate world, and insists as he writes about it that it is the largest world we can ever know, and the world that we must know. For its moment it is all, and everything; and in that moment everything stops. What makes the poignance of such a moment is most frequently the influence of causal morality, the intervention of some antecedent qualification which must modify the present. To support this assertion of the dramatic relationship of past and present, in terms of history as well as individual life, Hardy most frequently uses the techniques of arrest and distortion of time, of coincidence and the temporal coincidence of repetition supported by the time metaphor. Our focus is not taken away from the small world and its drama by all of this, however; rather, it forces our more intense concentration on what is before us, emphasizing it and its significance, enabling us to see it better and larger. In order to get as much as possible before our eyes without distracting us from our particular focus, Hardy expands his simple people and simple, lyrical appreciations of life by stopping the time that would slight them with its passing. In time stopped, the usual dimensions of history are voided, and the commonest moment can become large enough to command our highest respect. Hardy's own typically quiet way of explaining this he wrote as the concluding stanza to "The House of Silence," in which he describes the "quiet place" which is his home:

> "It is a poet's bower,
> Through which there pass, in fleet arrays,
> Long teams of all the years and days,
> Of joys and sorrows, of earth and heaven,
> That meet mankind in its ages seven,
> An aion in an hour." (445)

In 1888—some thirteen years after his earliest notes adumbrative of *The Dynasts*, but still nearly fifteen years before the first part would be published—Hardy wrote concerning the state and nature of fiction:

> Good fiction may be defined here as that kind of imaginative writing which lies nearest to the epic, dramatic, or narrative masterpieces of the past. One fact is certain: in fiction there can be no intrinsically new thing at this stage of the world's history. New methods and plans may arise and come into fashion, as we see them do; but the general theme can neither be changed, nor (what is less obvious) can the relative importance of its various particulars be greatly interfered with.[12]

Two years later he wrote:

> There is [now] a revival of the artistic instincts toward great dramatic motives—setting forth that "collision between the individual and the general"—formerly worked out with such force by the Periclean and Elizabethan dramatists, to name no other.[13]

These statements show Hardy's ideas about fiction, and where these ideas come from. He seems to value least the narrative voice as such, willing to depend almost entirely on the "stronger irradiation" of the dramatic situation[14] for effect. It is as though he envisions as the novel of the future—that is, of the twentieth century—a play with expanded narrative stage directions, like Shaw's, perhaps, or Tennessee Williams's. But this dramatic-novel which Hardy has in mind is much larger in its scope and in its commitment to those "great dramatic motives" than anything of Shaw's or Williams's—larger, finally, than almost anything else we know in modern literature. *The Dynasts* is not only Hardy's great play,[15] as an "Epic-Drama" and according to his theory about the future of the art of fiction, it is his new novel as well. And it is also his great major poem.

Because it is all three things—play, novel, poem—*The Dynasts* is difficult to deal with. We can say that Hardy's fiction is dramatic and poetic, and mean that its action is "emotional and dramatic—the highest province of fiction"[16] and that its sense and density can be penetrated only through an understanding and appreciation of its poetry. But we must read *The Dynasts* at every moment with the consciousness that it is a dramatic and poetic narrative, a poetic epic-drama, elaborately constructed out of all the conventions from chorus to mummers to dumb show, from panorama and spectacle to lyric poetry. Because of this difficulty, the most profitable and useful approach to *The Dynasts* may be through an analysis, not of its form, but of its ideas and themes, and of the aesthetic and philosophical formulae explored in their dramatization.

It is not my purpose, again, to explain Hardy's ideas in terms of their relation to Spencer or Schopenhauer or von Hartmann or Mill. I have indicated in the introductory chapter where readers may go to find such matters written about at length. I propose to continue looking for Hardy's ideas in his own work, where their complexity is rich and immediate, and where the dramatic modulations and qualifications of their supposed contradictions can be found and understood. My concern in this chapter is not to place Hardy and his ideas in their proper place in the derivation of philosophical history; my purpose is rather to examine the work at hand, looking both for the patterns that emerge from the "series of fugitive impressions" and for their validation in the lives of the play. In approaching *The Dynasts* in this way we will find both its form and its real relation to the rest of Hardy's work.

The Dynasts opens with the philosophical question, "What of the Immanent Will and Its designs?" The answer, given by the neutral Spirit of the Years, is an extremely complex one:

> It works unconsciously, as heretofore,
> Eternal artistries in Circumstance,
> Whose patterns, wrought by rapt aesthetic rote,
> Seem in themselves Its single listless aim,
> And not their consequence.

In "New Year's Eve," a poem written at the time of Part II of *The Dynasts*, Hardy uses the same terms to make the same point. God has "finished another year," and when questioned by man—"And what's the good of it?"—he replies:

> "My labours—logicless—
> You may explain; not I:
> Sense-sealed I have wrought, without a guess
> That I evolved a Consciousness
> To ask for reasons why.

159

"Strange that ephemeral creatures who
By my own ordering are,
Should see the shortness of my view,
Use ethic tests I never knew,
Or made provision for!"

The "ethic" consciousness, or conscience, is man's, for Hardy, and it is on the basis of this theory that he proclaims himself a meliorist. At the end of the poem the God, another mythological personality of the Immanent Will, recedes to his natural unconsciousness:

He sank to raptness as of yore,
And opening New Year's Day
Wove it by rote as theretofore,
And went on working evermore
In his unweeting way. (261)

In the passage from *The Dynasts* the Will is unconscious and "listless"; and yet It seems to have an aim. That aim is the working of "patterns," of "artistries in Circumstance." The patterns, however, are woven by "rote," by some kind of reflexive memory, in part. The Will operates on "rapt aesthetic rote," unconscious art united with simple reflex action.

What Hardy is arguing is, first, that the Will has no "designs," in the sense of plans and determinations, except as we invent them in our mythologies and assign them to it; second, that the Will represents in a metaphorical way the totality of life, of the vitality of existence; third, that because life is naturally passionate and not isolationist, meetings will occur and patterns will develop in the necessary—*i.e.*, natural—interrelations of phenomena; fourth, that there is something beautiful in these patterns, even in the pattern of the whole, if only we could see it—that there is a "design" to things, in an aesthetic sense, though this design often contradicts our ethical, moral sense of justice. Again, the tension is between unconscious planning on the part of the Will and the consciousness that is conscience in man.

The spirits of the Overworld discuss these points throughout the play —and the dialectic is sometimes as abstract and undramatic as the summary above. But the Chorus of Intelligences is not conceived of by Hardy as having a dramatic part in the play, really. They are not people, but Intelligences; their role is to view the actions of men within the scheme of things. At the end of the play, the Spirit of the Years looks at the world one last time and says:

> Thus doth the Great Foresightless mechanize
> In blank entrancement now as evermore
> Its ceaseless artistries in Circumstance. (521)

The terms are still the same; nothing has changed, for all of Europe's wars. And the only words left to be said beyond these are the prophetic, hopeful hymnings of the Chorus of the Pities, who dream of the perfection of the world through the coming to consciousness of the Immanent Will.

What happens between the beginning and this end can be variously described. The one hundred and thirty scenes contain Hardy's argument about the Will, and the evidence to support that argument. They present the drama of Napoleon, too, and the history of his era. And they present numerous people—little people, simple people, real people—as a part of the evidence, caught up in that history, engaged in living in those times. The first of these three aspects of *The Dynasts* is what is usually discussed by critics. The second is what earns the play its title and provides its hero. The third is perhaps what is most natural for Hardy to write about, and what he does best.

Napoleon is the chief dynast, and as such is Hardy's hero. Samuel Hynes thinks he "must have seemed to Hardy . . . the last figure in Western European history to whom epic stature could be ascribed."[17] Perhaps this is true. But at the same time that he stands Napoleon up so high as a hero, Hardy is using the drama of the smaller people as a counterbalance, playing their simple dignity against the emperor's power, their suffering against his ambition. As the play draws toward its conclusion Napoleon seems more and more to be at one with those simple people, and the sense of the play changes. Napoleon is thwarted by circumstances, frustrated in his ambition to inhabit "the topmost niche/In human fame" (p. 520), and is brought down to the common human size. The theme of the play is not that of "In Time of 'The Breaking of Nations,' " that simple lives "go onward the same/Though Dynasties pass." But as the end nears, Napoleon becomes more human, it seems; we see him more as a man than an emperor, and our sympathy for him grows.

And this is as it should be. Hardy's interest, again, is in the close par-

161

ticulars and senses of human existence, not in significant abstractions. Napoleon is another representative man for Hardy, though the dramatization of his career is done in reverse fashion from that of the heroes of the novels. Napoleon begins with history on his side, as an established figure rather than an obscure nobody. The course of the drama represents his decline in power, ending with his final defeat at Waterloo. But Napoleon, defeated as emperor, triumphs as a hero. He cannot win his wars—ever—because he cannot end them; he has "Empery's insatiate lust of power," as Hardy calls it elsewhere, in speaking of World War I.[18] Napoleon has done what Napoleon had to do, which is what it means to have "obeyed" the Immanent Will (p. 519). He has fulfilled his destiny as a character—fulfilled it as his character and the circumstances determined it.[19] He is still a proud man in his last speech, but more conscious of what he has been, what he has done, what he has tried to do.

> O hideous hour,
> Why am I stung by spectral questionings? . . .
> Why did the death-drops fail to bite me close
> I took at Fontainebleau? Had I then ceased,
> This deep had been unplumbed. . . .
> If but a Kremlin cannon-shot had met me
> My greatness would have stood: I should have scored
> A vast repute, scarce paralleled in time.
> As it did not, the fates had served me best
> If in the thick and thunder of today,
> Like Nelson, Harold, Hector, Cyrus, Saul,
> I had been shifted from this jail of flesh,
> To wander as a greatened ghost elsewhere.
> —Yes, a good death, to have died on yonder field;
> But never a ball came passing down my way!
> So, as it is a miss-mark they will dub me;
> And yet—I found the crown of France in the mire,
> And with the point of my prevailing sword
> I picked it up! But for all this and this
> I shall be nothing. . . .
> To shoulder Christ from out the topmost niche
> In human fame, as I once fondly felt,
> Was not for me. I came too late in time
> To assume the prophet or the demi-god,
> A part past playing now. My only course

> To make good showance to posterity
> Was to implant my line upon the throne.
> And how shape that, if now extinction nears?
> Great men are meteors that consume themselves
> To light the earth. This is my burnt-out hour. (519–20)

There is nothing here, perhaps, that we can sympathize with directly, except the awareness of the changing, perhaps humanizing, aspect of history that no longer allows of great men as prophets or demigods. Napoleon still speaks as a dynast, albeit a vanquished one. The speech with which the Spirit of the Years answers this is what finally makes Napoleon just a man, and evokes our sympathetic response:

> Worthless these kneadings of thy narrow thought,
> Napoleon; gone thy opportunity!
> Such men as thou, who wade across the world
> To make an epoch, bless, confuse, appal,
> Are in the elemental ages' chart
> Like meanest insects on obscurest leaves
> But incidents and grooves of Earth's unfolding;
> Or as the brazen rod that stirs the fire
> Because it must. (521)

This speech is often quoted as typical of Hardy's dramatic and philosophical point of view—Hynes says, for example, that it "points the moral" of the play.[20] It has been the burden of this whole book to argue against such reductive assertions, and to demonstrate instead how Hardy uses such diminution of man and his achievements to set up the contrast that will underscore man's dignity and his heroism. Napoleon may be a peculiar Hardy hero—his faults are more culpable than Henchard's or Tess's or Jude's, certainly—but he is still a hero, Hardy's representative man, and "one of us." The pessimistic perspective from which the Spirit of the Years speaks at the end simply does not satisfy the dramatic situation and its affect. It is one side of the argument, going all the way back to the question of whether this whole spectacle of human existence is comedy or tragedy. What the Spirit of the Years says contradicts our emotions and our sense of values, our sympathetic allegiances and our beliefs—and in Hardy's world we must believe finally in man. The problem is one of point of view. However much Hardy may have assumed at times the role of a neutral observer of life, he was never comfortable in the kind of unresponsive neutrality from which the Spirit of the Years speaks and views the world. The Spirit of the Years speaks without understanding what people are and what they feel; it speaks from the Overworld, and it has an overview of life which makes it impossible for it to sense what individual life is. The Spirit of the Years cannot appreciate or comprehend what has actually happened in this play, because it doesn't understand suffering, heroism, human dignity. "Nay," Hardy wrote in *The Woodlanders*,[21] "from the highest point of view, to precisely describe a human being, the focus of a universe, how impossible!" (p. 42).

The Spirit of the Years concludes not only that man is insignificant in what he does because of the necessary aspect of life in the Will, but also that any man is insignificant in the long spectacle of history. Hardy's answer to the first is to affirm the idea of heroic freedom within or along side that necessity, the idea of character and environment. And his answer to the second—not given directly in this play except in the Fore Scene—is again that time is irrelevant as a measure of human action and its importance. Time is impressive dramatically, and Hardy's typical interest in time is dramatic rather than historic, as it is manipulated to foreshorten, condense, and intensify life, not as a measure of some interval. At the end of the Fore Scene the General Chorus of Intelligences chants together:

> We'll close up Time, as a bird its van,
> We'll traverse Space, as spirits can,
> Link pulses severed by leagues and years,
> Bring cradles into touch with biers;
> So that the far-off Consequence appears
> Prompt at the heels of foregone Cause. (7)

These lines explain the aesthetic and philosophical form of the play, in effect. It is to be built on the principle of dramatic foreshortening, or stylized proportioning, and will operate on the assumption of a general or universal causal relationship among phenomena. The impressive cosmic apparatus of the play presents the overview of things, and adjusts time and space so as to call attention to ironies of chance and coincidence as well as to causes and consequences. Time does not exist as such in the Overworld; time is a dimension of the mortal world of men. Once again, then—to compare Hardy's technique here with that of the novels

164

and poems—the present of the action is enlarged by association with a timeless perspective. The Spirits and Intelligences have chosen the ten years of the Napoleonic wars as a representative period in the history of man. Collapsing it and intensifying it, dramatically, to point up the constant causal relationships among phenomena, they use what goes on as evidence and example in their argument about the nature and definition of cause and consequence.

But in the larger sense, finally, of Hardy's play, the main argument is not that among the Spirits of the Overworld, but rather that between the Overworld and the world of men. The principle argument of the play is the same one which occurs directly or indirectly in so many of Hardy's poems and is concerned with the determination of the proper viewpoint and focus, the proper way of seeing things. The play is set first in the large timeless scene of the Overworld which gives it its mythic dimension and makes the action more than just history. Then the scene changes, and the cosmic perspective becomes but the larger background against which the important dramatic action is played.

The primary focus of the play is the world of men. This, after all, is what the Spirits of the Overworld are arguing about. Our concern with this real world, however, and this we must share with Hardy, is not an argumentative one or a philosophical one, but an immediately and sympathetically involved one. We have been asked to look at life, not from a cosmic or celestial distance, but "closelier than [our] custom is" (p. 4). At the end of the After Scene, the Chorus of the Pities speaks last words of all, about the world of men, the world with which they sympathize. They dream and prophesy the coming of a state of universal "loving-kindness" in some future time. It is the time of history, now, that is needed for the slow progressive evolution of life towards the better, for the coming to "consciousness" of the natural and metaphorical Immanent Will. And what this progress amounts to along the way is the coming of individual men to consciousness, both of themselves and of their world.

The Dynasts contains a review and a synthesis of Hardy's speculations about the nature of human existence, made relevant in art—as opposed to philosophy—through their dialectical integration with the drama played out in the lives of men. At its best *The Dynasts* is a moving and effective work of art, whether we call it a play, a poem, or a new novel, an "Epic-Drama." As a whole it is flawed, to be sure: the ambition and the form were not quite manageable. But even as it is flawed, Hardy's motivating spirit, his aesthetic and philosophical bias, is impressively present. The vision is the same large and compassionate one we have seen from the beginning, and the techniques used in the dramatic representation of that vision are the same. Hardy described both his vision and his technique when he wrote in 1888 of "dramas of a grandeur and unity truly Sophoclean . . . enacted in the real, by virtue of the concentrated passions and closely-knit interdependence of the lives therein."[22] He saw life that way, and he made his art to correspond.

NOTES TO CHAPTER VIII

1. F. E. Hardy, *Life of Hardy*, pp. 334–35.

2. *The Renaissance* (New York, 1961), p. 218. *The Renaissance* was originally published in 1873.

3. Ibid.

4. Ibid.

5. The Buddhist explanation of the principle of causation in the phenomenal universe is presented, traditionally, in an image almost identical to Hardy's: "A net is made up of a series of ties, so everything in this world is connected by a series of ties. . . . It is called a net because it is made up of a series of connected meshes, and each mesh has its place and responsibilities in relation to other meshes." *The Teaching of Buddha* (Tokyo, 1966), p. 39.

6. F. E. Hardy, *Life of Hardy*, p. 336. In February of 1908 Hardy wrote to Edward Clodd concerning the originality of "The idea of the Unconscious Will becoming conscious with flux of time" (Ibid., p. 454).

7. *Absalom, Absalom!* (New York, 1936), p. 101.

8. "Faith" is our term for belief in that which we do not know; "fate" is our term for the acknowledgment of happened or happening real events.

9. *Fools of Time* (Toronto, 1967), pp. 3–4.

10. Ibid., p. 4.

11. Ibid., pp. 4–5. Cf. Byron's Manfred: "Think'st thou existence doth depend on time? / It doth; but actions are our epochs" (II, i, 51–2).

12. "The Profitable Reading of Fiction," *Forum* (March 1888), pp. 60–61; reprinted in Orel, *Personal Writings*, p. 114.

13. "Candour in English Fiction," p. 16; reprinted in Orel, *Personal Writings*, p. 126.

14. "The Profitable Reading of Fiction," p. 61; reprinted in Orel, *Personal Writings*, p. 115.

15. His only other play, "The Famous Tragedy of the Queen of Cornwall," was an utter failure.

16. "The Profitable Reading of Fiction," p. 69; reprinted in Orel, *Personal Writings*, p. 124.

17. *The Pattern of Hardy's Poetry* (Chapel Hill, 1961), p. 155.

18. "In Time of Wars and Tumults," *Collected Poems*, p. 510.

19. *The Dynasts* is in this sense another of the "Novels of Character and Environment," along with *The Return of the Native*, etc.

20. Hynes, *Hardy's Poetry*, p. 156.

21. Hardy was writing *The Woodlanders* when he began to think of "Abstract realisms to be in the form of Spirits, Spectral figures, etc.," for *The Dynasts*; see F. E. Hardy, *Life of Hardy*, pp. 176–77.

22. *The Woodlanders*, pp. 4–5.

167

Bibliography
Index

Bibliography

The standard editions of Hardy's fiction are the Wessex Edition (London: Macmillan and Company, 1912–31) and the Harper and Brothers American editions (New York, 1915 and 1920), printed for the most part from the plates of the Wessex Edition, and the Macmillan Library Edition (London, 1958–62) which uses the text of the Mellstock Edition (London: Macmillan and Company, 1919–20), a deluxe edition for which Hardy made several last alterations and corrections. *The Collected Poems of Thomas Hardy* was first published in complete form by Macmillan and Company in 1930. *The Dynasts* was originally published by them in three parts in 1903, 1906, and 1908; in 1931 it was published together with *The Famous History of the Queen of Cornwall* in one volume. Hardy's various essays, prefaces, and other minor writings have been collected by Harold Orel in *Thomas Hardy's Personal Writings* (Lawrence, Kansas: University of Kansas Press, 1966). Other material is available in *Thomas Hardy's Notebooks*, edited by Evelyn Hardy (New York: St. Martin's Press, 1955). No comprehensive publication of Hardy's letters has yet been attempted. Carl J. Weber has edited two small volumes of letters, *Letters of Thomas Hardy* (Waterville, Maine: Colby College Press, 1954) and *'Dearest Emmie': Thomas Hardy's Letters to His First Wife* (New York: St. Martin's Press, 1963). *Thomas Hardy's Correspondence at Max Gate* (Waterville, Maine: Colby College Press, 1968) is a catalogue compiled by Carl J. and Clara C. Weber, describing the five thousand letters on file in the Dorset County Museum. (Most of these letters are to Hardy, rather than from him.)

Most of the manuscripts of Hardy's novels are still extant and available for study. *Tess of the D'Urbervilles* is at the British Museum; *Jude the Obscure* is at the Fitzwilliam Museum, Cambridge University; *The Return of the Native* is in the library of University College, Dublin. The Dorset County Museum holds *The Mayor of Casterbridge, The Woodlanders, Under the Greenwood Tree,* part of *Far From the Madding Crowd,* and part of *The Dynasts* as well as a typescript of Harley Granville-Baker's 1914 production of *Scenes from 'The Dynasts'* in London.[1]

In 1928 and 1930 Macmillan and Company published a two volume biography, *The Early Life of Thomas Hardy, 1840–1891,* and *The Later Years of Thomas Hardy, 1892–1928.* Although attributed to Florence Emily Hardy, this biography is generally recognized to be Hardy's own work. It was reissued in 1962 in one volume as *The Life of Thomas Hardy.* Other biographies of interest are Carl J. Weber's *Hardy of Wessex* (New York: Columbia University Press, 1940; revised 1962) and Irving Howe's *Thomas Hardy* (Macmillan and Company, 1967). *Providence and Mr. Hardy* (London: Hutchinson and Company, 1966) is a somewhat silly and overblown biographical reading of Hardy's poetry by Lois Deacon and Terry Coleman.

The standard bibliography of Hardy's works is Richard L. Purdy's *Thomas Hardy: A Bibliographical Study* (New York: Oxford University Press, 1954).

Among the critical studies of Hardy's works, a few stand out from the hundred and more published. The best was also the first: Lionel Johnson's *The Art of Thomas Hardy* (London: John Lane, the Bodley Head, 1894). Among the more useful books written during Hardy's lifetime are Lascelles Abercrombie's *Thomas Hardy: A Critical Study* (New York: Mitchell Kennerley, 1912), Harold Child's *Thomas Hardy* (New York: Henry Holt and Company, 1916), Samuel C. Chew's *Thomas Hardy, Poet and Novelist* (New York: Longmans, Green and Company, 1921), and Joseph Warren Beach's *The Technique of Thomas Hardy* (Chicago: University of Chicago Press, 1922). Ernest Brennecke's study of Hardy's philosophy, *Thomas Hardy's Universe* (London: T. Fisher Unwin, 1924), also belongs to this period.

In 1938 William R. Rutland published *Thomas Hardy: A Study of his Writings and their Background* (New York: Oxford University Press; reissued New York: Russell and Russell, 1962), an excellent critical exploration of the particular and general influences of Hardy's reading on

172

his writings. In 1947 Harvey C. Webster's *On A Darkling Plain* (Chicago: University of Chicago Press) appeared; it is long, and its argument is heavily weighted toward fatalism. Albert J. Guerard's *Thomas Hardy* (Cambridge: Harvard University Press) was published in 1949, and was reissued in 1964 (by New Directions) with an additional essay on Hardy's poetry. Guerard's essays on the novels establish him as perhaps the best of Hardy's critics since Lionel Johnson. J. Hillis Miller's *Thomas Hardy: Distance and Desire* (Cambridge: Harvard University Press, 1970) is an interesting, challenging, but not always convincing psycho-biographical reading of Hardy's works.

Among the books on Hardy's poetry the two best are James G. Southworth's *The Poetry of Thomas Hardy* (New York: Columbia University Press, 1947; reissued Russell and Russell, 1966) and Samuel Hynes' *The Pattern of Hardy's Poetry* (Chapel Hill: University of North Carolina Press, 1961). Two special books of interest are Mary Ellen Chase's *Thomas Hardy: From Serial to Novel* (Minneapolis: University of Minnesota Press, 1927; reissued Russell and Russell, 1964), a study of Hardy's elaborate and extensive revisions from serial to book publication, and John Patterson's *The Making of The Return of the Native* (Berkeley: University of California Press, 1960), an analysis of the composition of that novel. F. B. Pinion's *A Hardy Companion* (New York: St. Martin's Press, 1968) is the best of several Hardy dictionaries.

There are many excellent articles on Hardy. The best collection is the Thomas Hardy Centennial Issue of *The Southern Review*, Volume VI (Summer, 1940), which contains more than a dozen outstanding essays. Four of these are reprinted, along with nine others, in the Twentieth Century Views volume *Hardy: A Collection of Critical Essays*, edited by Albert J. Guerard (Englewood Cliffs, N. J.: Prentice-Hall, Inc., 1963). Among the many other significant essays I would recommend particularly Frank Chapman's "Hardy the Novelist," in *Scrutiny*, Volume III (1934), pp. 22–38, as one of the finest of that journal's "revaluations"; Robert B. Heilman's introduction to the Riverside edition of *The Mayor of Casterbridge* (Cambridge: Houghton-Mifflin Company, 1962), as a model of fine criticism; and Havelock Ellis's "Concerning *Jude the Obscure*," in *The Savoy*, Number 6 (October, 1896), as an interesting period piece in our cultural history.

NOTES TO BIBLIOGRAPHY

1. Granville-Baker's production ran for seventy-two performances at the Kingsway Theatre in London. There have been three other productions of scenes from the play: by the Dorchester Debating and Dramatic Society in 1908, by "The Hardy Players" in Dorchester in 1916, and by the Oxford University Dramatic Society in 1920. A production script for *Scenes from 'The Dynasts'*, selected and edited by Bert G. Hornback, was published in 1968 by the Department of English of the University of Michigan.

Index